Propaganda
and the
German Cinema
1933-1945

Propaganda and the German Cinema 1933-1945

DAVID WELCH

CLARENDON PRESS · OXFORD
1983

Oxford University Press, Walton Street, Oxford OX2 6DP

London Glasgow New York Toronto
Delhi Bombay Calcutta Madras Karachi
Kuala Lumpur Singapore Hong Kong Tokyo
Nairobi Dar es Salaam Cape Town
Melbourne Auckland

and associates in
Beirut Berlin Ibadan Mexico City Nicosia

Published in the United States by
Oxford University Press, New York

British Library Cataloguing in Publication Data

Welch, David
Propaganda and the German Cinema 1933–1945.
1. Propaganda, German—History   2. Moving-
pictures in propaganda—History—20th century
3. Moving-pictures—Germany—History—20th century
I. Title
303.3'75   DD256.5

ISBN 0-19-822598-9

Typeset by Graphic Services, Oxford
Printed in Great Britain at the
University Press, Oxford
by Eric Buckley
Printer to the University

ACKNOWLEDGEMENTS

I should like to acknowledge my debt to the staff of the institutions where my doctoral research was undertaken for making relevant material available. I would also like to express my gratitude to Friedrich Kahlenberg, Eberhard Spiess, Erwin Leiser, Lutz Becker, and Marcus Phillips for their valuable assistance in drawing my attention to material which I might otherwise have overlooked. I owe a special word of thanks to Richard Taylor for his criticism and stimulation. I am also indebted to the staff of the British Film Institute and the Institut für Filmkunde for their help in the location of stills. My doctoral thesis on the Nazi cinema was completed at the London School of Economics and this book is published with the help of a grant from the Isobel Thornley Bequest to the University of London.

Over the years I have incurred debts to many individuals in the preparation of this work and none more so than to my supervisor James Joll, whose kindness, forbearance, and scholarly integrity encouraged my research during the inordinately long period which it took for my ideas to develop. My great debt, however, is to my wife Anne to whom this book is dedicated. It could not have been completed without her continual support and encouragement.

David Welch

London
December 1981

CONTENTS

ILLUSTRATIONS

between pp. 192-3

Comradeship, Heroism, and the Party
1 *Hitlerjunge Quex* (*Hitler Youth Quex*, 1933): the film based on the life of Herbert Norkus, the hero and martyr of the Hitler Youth.
2 Emil Lohkamp in the title role in *Hans Westmar* (1933) which dramatized the life and death of one of the earliest Nazi martyrs, Horst Wessel.

Blood and Soil and Strength through Joy
3 *Olympiade*: the prototype Aryan warrior-sportsman.
4 The death scene in *Ich klage an* (*I Accuse*, 1941) which attempted to justify the Nazis' euthanasia campaign.

The Principle of Leadership
5 *Triumph des Willens* (*Triumph of the Will*, 1935): Hitler alone, juxtaposed against the sky at Nuremberg.
6 *Friedrich Schiller* (1940): the triumph of untutored genius. Horst Casper as the poet Schiller.
7 *Der grosse König* (*The Great King*, 1942): Otto Gebühr as Frederick the Great.

War and the Military Image
8 *Stukas* (1941): comradeship and self-sacrifice in war.
9 *Kolberg* (1945): the heroism of death in combat as Napoleon's invading troops are driven back by the citizens of Kolberg.

The Image of the Enemy
10 The Bolshevik: drunken Red Army soldiers in *Friesennot* (*Frisians in Peril*, 1935).
11 Andrews Engelman as the murderous Bolshevik Commissar in *GPU* (1942).

STATISTICAL TABLES

ABBREVIATIONS

BA	Bundesarchiv, Koblenz
Bavaria FK	Bavaria Filmkunst GmbH
	(founded 11 November 1930)
BDC	Berlin Document Centre
BdM	Bund deutscher Mädchen
DACHO	Dachorganisation der Filmschaffenden
	Deutschlands
DAF	Deutsche Arbeitsfront
DFG	Deutsche Filmherstellungs- und Verwertungs
	GmbH (founded 1937)
DFV	Deutsche Filmvertriebs GmbH
DIF	Deutsches Institut für Filmkunde, Wiesbaden
DNVP	Deutschnationale Volkspartei
DVP	Deutsche Volkspartei
FiFi	Film Finanz GmbH (founded 10 August 1937)
HJ	Hitler Jugend
IFK	*Illustrierter Film-kurier*
IfZ	Institut für Zeitgeschichte, Munich
JCH	*Journal of Contemporary History*
KdF	Kraft durch Freude
KfdK	Kampfbund für deutsche Kultur
KPD	Kommunistische Partei Deutschlands
LBB	*Licht-Bild-Bühne*
LFS	Landesfilmstellen
NSBO	Nationalsozialistische Betriebszellen
	Organisation
NSDAP	Nationalsozialistische Deutsche Arbeiter Partei
OKW	Oberkommando der Wehrmacht
PK	Propaganda Kompanie
RFI	Reischsfilmintendant
RFD	Reichsfilmdramaturg
RFK	Reichsfilmkammer
RFS	Reichsfilmstelle

RGBl	Reichsgesetzblatt
RKK	Reichskulturkammer
RLG	Reichslichtspielgesetz
RM	Reichsmark
RMVP	Reichsministerium für Volksaufklärung und Propaganda
SA	Sturmabteilung der NSDAP
SD	Sicherheitsdienst der SS
SHAEF	Supreme Headquarters Allied Expeditionary Force
Terra FK	Terra Filmkunst GmbH (founded 17 January
Tobis AG	Tobis-Tonbild-Syhdikat AG (founded 1929)
Tobis FK	Tobis Filmkunst GmbH (founded 1938)
Ufa	Universum Film AG (founded 1917)
Ufa FK	Ufa Filmkunst GmbH (founded 17 January 1942)
Ufi	Ufa-Film GmbH (founded 28 November 1942)
VB	Völkischer Beobachter
ZD	Zeitschriftendienst

Domination itself is servile when beholden to opinion: for you depend upon the prejudices of those you govern by means of their prejudices.

Rousseau: Émile

INTRODUCTION

No doubt the effects of history are always easier to seize than the causes. But one thing makes another clearer; these effects fully brought to light by the cinema, will provide clear insights into causes which heretofore have remained in semi-obscurity. And to lay hands not on everything that exists but on everything that can be grasped is already an excellent achievement for any source of information, scientific or historic.

Boleslas Matuszewski, *Une Nouvelle Source de l'Histoire*
(Paris, 1898)

THE aim of this book is to examine Nazi film propaganda as a reflection of National Socialist ideology. Although Nazism is often thought of as a temporary aberration in the history of a nation, it was in fact based on a body of intellectual doctrine that goes back for at least a century. This was the *Völkisch* tradition, which was essentially a product of late eighteenth-century romanticism. I have attempted to trace various components of the ideology which recur in the cinema of the Third Reich, in order to discover what this reveals about the nature of propaganda in general and the ideology of National Socialism in particular.

Totalitarian states aspire to absolute control of all media of mass communication in an attempt to control the opinions of the masses.[1] And of all the means of exerting such covert and psychological influences, none was as highly esteemed by the Government of the Third Reich as the cinema. In one of his first speeches as Minister for Popular Enlightenment and

---

[1] For example, the very need of the Bolsheviks in the 1920s to create for themselves a new historical legitimacy led them to utilize the cinema as a propaganda weapon. Cf. Lenin's famous remark: 'The cinema is for us the most important instrument of all the arts.' Quoted in V. I. Pudovkin, *Film Technique and Film Acting* (New York, 1958), vol. II, p. 44.

Propaganda, Joseph Goebbels declared that the German cinema had the mission of conquering the world as the vanguard of the Nazi troops.[2] As Minister for the dissemination of state propaganda, Dr Goebbels believed in the 'power' of the cinema to influence people's thoughts and beliefs, if not their actions. Although his *Filmpolitik* would eventually assume an important role in the implementation of the Nazis' New Order (*Neuordnung*) in Europe, I have confined myself to films produced in Germany for German audiences. Neither is it my specific intention to quantify the effect of these films. The precise way in which the mass media influence society is still not clearly understood. In a totalitarian police state such as Nazi Germany there was even less interest in public opinion, although the Ministry for Popular Enlightenment and Propaganda did attempt to evaluate the feedback of their more prestigious films by means of the weekly SD (*Sicherheitsdienst der SS*) Reports which appeared for the first time in 1940. There is some disagreement over the value of these reports as a scientific indicator of public opinion.[3] Initially Goebbels appears to have welcomed the reports as a more objective source of intelligence than the Party's local agencies. After Stalingrad, however, they ceased to make such agreeable reading and he took steps to limit their circulation and ultimately to have them suppressed as defeatist.[4] However, they remain the best source of public opinion within the Third Reich and I have included their assessment of audience reaction to films wherever they have been available.

The vast majority of these SD Reports was concerned with the so-called *Staatsauftragsfilme*, films commissioned by the State and generally given a disproportionate amount of time, financial assistance, and publicity. These films were not always overtly political but were invariably classified at the time as *Tendenzfilme*. This was a term employed during the Third Reich

---

[2] *Völkischer Beobachter*, 20 May 1933. Goebbels repeated the claim a year later, *Völkischer Beobachter*, 9 February 1934.

[3] Dr Hans Boberach of the Bundesarchiv, Koblenz, argues that they were excellent for this purpose. See *Meldungen aus dem Reich: Auswahl aus den geheimen Lageberichten des Sicherheitsdienstes der SS 1939–44* (Berlin, 1965).

[4] On 17 April 1943, Goebbels wrote in his diary: 'The SD report is full of mischief. Its recent issues displease me deeply. It is entirely unpolitical and is sent to the various offices unsifted. . . . The nature of the SD report must be quickly changed.' L. Lochner (ed.), *The Goebbels Diaries* (London, 1948), p. 258.

to describe a certain type of film that exhibited 'strong National Socialist tendencies'.[5] In other words, without necessarily mentioning National Socialism, these films advocated various principles and themes identifiable with Nazism which the Propaganda Ministry wished to disseminate at intermittent periods. However the following seven chapters include not only these *Staatsauftragsfilme* but a wide range of film propaganda from short cultural films to full-length documentaries and the famous *Deutsche Wochenschauen* (German newsreels). I have analysed certain films which are representative of a particular theme of *Völkisch* thought rather than simply providing a list of film titles. As almost every film discussed is easily available for hire, readers have the opportunity of seeing them for themselves.

If such a policy of ideological indoctrination was to work effectively, it obviously required careful direction and co-ordination. I have therefore included a chapter on the history and organization of the Nazi film industry, for our understanding of the films cannot be divorced from the wider economic and social framework in which they were produced. But I must stress that this investigation still excludes the majority of 'escapist' films that were produced during the Third Reich principally for entertainment purposes.

In 1970 Professor Grenville Pointed out in his inaugural lecture on 'Film as History':

It might appear curious that serious attention of historians has been drawn so late to a medium which after all has been around for more than half a century, for a length of time in fact that coincides with some definitions of contemporary history. . . .[6]

Grenville concluded his lecture by declaring that 'film evidence is important . . . and if properly handled will illuminate and enrich the study of the twentieth century.'[7] Professor Grenville's main contention was that historians had repeatedly failed to recognize the richness of film as a source of evidence. It would seem unnecessary to argue that film is an overwhelming

[5] An excellent account of *Tendenzfilm* can be found in G. Eckert, 'Filmintendenz und Tendenzfilm', *Wille und Macht, Führerorgan der Nationalsozialistischen Jugend*, Jahrgang 6, vol. 4 (15 November 1938), pp. 19–25.

[6] J. A. S. Grenville, *Film as History: The Nature of Film Evidence* (Birmingham, 1971), p. 3.

[7] Ibid., p. 22.

cultural influence today, and has been since the 1920s at least, however it is only in recent years that historians have come to accept that film can be regarded as a reputable source in just the same way as the more traditional written documents.[8]

One of the many problems confronting the historian is to consider the ways in which films make their impact, and whether or not that influence is substantial enough to warrant serious consideration by the student of that period. Taking an example that is related to this work, one could ask whether films made during the Weimar Republic reveal anything of interest about the nature of that period. Siegfried Kracauer in his *From Caligari to Hitler*, argues that German films of the 1920s foreshadowed the Nazi period and laid bare the psyche of the German nation.[9] His premiss is that films, whether fictional or documentary, can reveal the inner life of a people. By looking at the plots, characters, and style of films, Kracauer believes that one can discover the inner consciousness of the people who made the film and a particular mode of thought and life that govern the inner soul of a nation. Kracauer's method of 'hidden history' is open to abuse and his conclusions are occasionally pursued to absurdity, but even conceding some conceptual weaknesses, his research has proved a seminal work for both students of history and film and remains unsuperseded in its attempt to relate film and the society which created it.

Despite a few similar attempts in more recent years, much of the work that exists today in this field is undertaken by film critics, media sociologists, and journalists. Historians as a profession have been slow to utilize the new source material. There is considerable need for qualified historians to grapple with the still unsolved problems of methodology and conceptualization before film archives yield their resources. The historian of the twentieth century has in his grasp a primary source material, which historians of other periods could not hope to possess but which is only now being understood and

---

[8] For an interesting collection of articles on this subject see P. Smith (ed.), *The Historian and Film* (Cambridge, 1976). In 1981 *The Historical Journal of Film, Radio and Television* was established as a forum for current research in these fields.

[9] S. Kracauer, *From Caligari to Hitler: A Psychological History of the German Film* (Princeton, 1947).

utilized. Only if historians are prepared to broaden the scope of their professional dialogue can they hope to discover ways of dealing with the problem of film as evidence. This work is offered as a contribution to that dialogue.

I

THE HISTORY AND ORGANIZATION OF THE NAZI CINEMA

Let the world learn to look upon our films as a herald of the
German way of life and a messenger of our ideology. There can
be no art but that which has firm roots in our ideology.

Hans Steinbach (Press Chief in RFK) 19 March 1937

1. THE ORGANIZATION OF THE NATIONAL SOCIALIST FILM BEFORE THE TAKEOVER OF POWER

THE film activities of the Nazi Party before 1933 can be described quite briefly. They were of little relevance to the film
industry of the time, but they illustrate the Party's growing
awareness of the importance of a well co-ordinated organization, and an opportunism for learning and adapting new
propaganda techniques.

The first official film produced by the NSDAP (*Nationalsozialistische Deutsche Arbeiter Partei*) was a reportage of
the 1927 Nuremberg Party Rally and it was financed by the
Party leadership from Munich.[1] This film consisted of a few
amateurish shots of the rally together with a number of SA
(*Sturmabteilung der NSDAP*) parades, and from this year
onwards every Party rally was filmed. Films produced at this
time were not made for commercial distribution but were to
be shown at closed Party gatherings. The knowledge that film
was an important propaganda medium was present from the

---

[1] For discussions of the historical background concerning the organization of
the Nazi cinema see W. Becker, *Film und Herrschaft* (Berlin, 1973); J. Spiker,
Film und Kapital (Berlin, 1975); H. Barkhausen, 'Die NSDAP als Filmproduzentin.
Mit Kurzübersicht: Filme der NSDAP 1927–45', in G. Moltmann and K. F. Reimers
(eds.), *Zeitgeschichte im Film- und Tondokument* (Göttingen, 1970), pp. 145–76.
For the most comprehensive account in English, see M. S. Phillips, 'The German
Film Industry and the Third Reich', unpublished doctoral dissertation (University
of East Anglia, 1974).

early beginnings of the Party. But at this stage they had little finance and even less experience in their propaganda department of the complexities of film. From 1927 this situation began to change. Alfred Hugenberg, press baron and leader of the Nationalist Conservative Party, DNVP, had bought the largest and most prestigious German film company, Ufa (*Universum-Film-Aktiengesellschaft*). From now on the political and social activities of the NSDAP were captured by Ufa newsreels (*Ufa-Tonwochen*) and shown to the German public on the large network of Ufa cinemas. Until this time National Socialist propaganda had been characterized by the skilful use of rhetoric and controlled manipulation of meetings which depended for its success on the reliability of local organizations.

Towards the end of 1930, Joseph Goebbels, who had been steadily building up the Party following in Berlin since 1926, decided to establish the *NSDAP-Reichsfilmstelle* (RFS) in the capital for the purpose of distributing films throughout Germany.[2] However the project proved to be optimistically premature as the Nazi leadership was not convinced of its necessity and refused to supply the necessary capital. Instead *Gauleiters* (Regional Party leaders) were encouraged to make their own films of Party rallies, parades, and so on and distribute them through their own local organizations. Eventually in 1932, ten NSDAP *Landesfilmstellen* (LFS) were created. The LFS were responsible for the distribution of Party films while the NSDAP Film Service (*Filmamt*) which had its headquarters in Munich, was put in charge of film production. Goebbels was therefore still sharing Nazi film-making with his rival Gregor Strasser. In the Autumn of 1932, when Strasser's position in the party became an issue, Goebbels seized the opportunity to undermine his opponent and strengthen his own position by centralizing propaganda even further. Thus by October 1932 all NSDAP film activities were finally transferred to Berlin under Goebbels's control.[3]

During this period the film industry in general was still

---

[2] It was to be headed by Georg Stark who was *Gaupropagandaleiter* in Greater Berlin. See Barkhausen, p. 148.

[3] *Völkischer Beobachter* (hereafter *VB*), 11 October 1932.

recoiling from the continuing effects of the recession in world
trade and the advent of sound films, which involved considerable expenditure at a time when total receipts were falling, companies were going bankrupt, and cinemas were changing hands
at an alarming rate.[4] The German film industry responded
with the so-called *SPIO Plan* of 1932. SPIO (*Spitzenorganis-
ation der Deutschen Filmindustrie e.V.*) was the industry's
main professional representative body and its principle concern
was to strike a satisfactory relationship between the production, distribution, and exhibition sectors while at the same
time retaining the traditional structure of the industry.[5] Significantly SPIO was dominated by the large combines (particularly Ufa) and it was no surprise that they should produce
a plan that discriminated so blatantly against the German Cinema Owners' Association (*Reichsverband Deutscher Lichtspiel-
theater e.V.*) whom they accused of flooding the market with
too many cinemas, price cutting, and retaining a disproportionate share of total receipts. SPIO did not discount the possibility
of securing state aid in order to protect sections of the industry
by maintaining stable entrance prices and controlling programme planning. The Cinema Owners' Association retorted
by complaining, quite justifiably, that they were expected to
exhibit films they were given regardless of their suitability or
box-office appeal.

This conflict within the film industry placed the NSDAP in
a rather delicate position. On the one hand the Nazis did not
have to worry about making their own propaganda films at this
stage as Hugenberg had acquired Ufa to 'preserve it for the
national outlook', which in practice meant producing overt
nationalist films; but on the other hand, they had believed for
some time that the cinema owners were an important element
in their future operations. Indeed, the first success of the Nazi
Weltanschauung in the film industry was the founding of the
Nazi Film Theatre Cells (*NSDAP-Lichtspieltheaterzellen*). This
professional organization with National Socialist aims was
under the supervision of the RFS of the NSDAP in Berlin.

---

[4] The number of cinemas had fallen from just over 5,000 in 1929 to 2,196 in
1932. *Film-Kurier*, 24 June 1933.

[5] Spiker, pp. 60–72. The proposed plan was eventually published in *Film-
Kurier*, 18 February 1933.

Their greatest success was registered in Thuringia under the patronage of Wilhelm Frick, the Thuringian Minister of Education. Within a few months of the Nazi seizure of power this group of cinema owners would undermine the German Cinema Owners' Association by getting their own leader, Adolf Engl, elected as head of the Association, thus immediately securing the Party's influence in all sectors of the industry.

There were also at this stage divisions within the NSDAP itself over the nature of the German film industry. The more radical elements called for immediate nationalization while other sections were committed to reorganization within the traditional capitalist structure. The most radical suggestion was a manifesto published by the Berlin Nazis before the Prussian elections of 24 April 1932. What was required, they argued, was the production of genuine *Völkisch* films reflecting the true aspirations of the German people. In order to encourage such films, production needed to be centralized to control rising costs, and by no longer pandering to the 'decadent' tastes of the international market, such films would be expected to break even solely on returns from the domestic market. The manifesto reflected both an antipathy towards 'modern art' and a degree of ignorance that would have found little favour in the *Filmwelt* except perhaps by the owners of the small independent cinemas, who might have been attracted by this document.[6]

In their desire to show solidarity with the small cinema owners the Nazis felt compelled to show a token hostility to the two major film companies Ufa and Tobis (*Tobis-Tonbild-Syndikat AG*). But towards the end of 1932 the LFS were unable to supply enough films. Moreover even at this stage Goebbels realized that enthusiasm could not be maintained purely on a diet of Party propaganda and so he arranged to supplement their film shows with Ufa *Kulturfilme*.[7] These presented aspects of German cultural activity, often in a highly nationalistic manner. But this did not prevent the NSDAP and the small cinema owners from launching a vitriolic assault on

[6] The manifesto is published in C. Neumann, C. Belling, and H. Betz, *Film-Kunst, Film-Kohn, Film-Korruption. Ein Streifzug durch vier Jahrzehnte* (Berlin, 1937), pp. 144–8.

[7] Weiner Library, NSDAP 'Hauptarchiv', roll 58, folder 1396, 'Dienstvorschrift für die Landesfilmstellen der NSDAP', 2 September 1932. See also Phillips, p. 49.

the proposed *SPIO-Plan* in the Party's own newspaper, the *Völkischer Beobachter*.[8] They declared that it was an attempt to create an Ufa–Tobis monopoly which would eventually eliminate the small independent film-makers. The struggle between these elements both within the industry and the NSDAP and the questions they posed for the future of the German film industry would be answered by the new Nazi government in less than a year after assuming power.

2. 'GLEICHSCHALTUNG' AND THE GERMAN FILM INDUSTRY

As early as the 1920s the National Socialists had infiltrated their members into many spheres of public life.[9] The entire organization of the Party, the division into administrative sectors, and the structure of leadership were built up as a state within a state. The Nazis were therefore well placed to take control of a film industry which had to a large extent prepared itself to be controlled.[10] The *Gleichschaltung*[11] (co-ordination) of the German cinema was affected behind the scenes by a process of which the ordinary citizen was largely unaware. To achieve this end, a plethora of complex laws, decrees, and intricate state machinery was instigated to prevent any form of nonconformity. Pursuing a policy that was to become traditional in the Third Reich, the Party organization was kept separate from state administration at both national and regional levels, while at the same time remaining closely linked.[12]

In the months following Hitler's appointment to Chancellor in January 1933 the divisions within the Party which had flared up in 1932 became an issue again. Certain organizations such as the Nazi 'Trade Union' the *Nationalsozialistische Betriebszellen Organisation* (NSBO) and the Fighting League for German Culture (*Kampfbund für deutsche Kultur*–KfdK) put forward radical solutions to the film industry's problems,

[8] *VB*, 5 January 1933.

[9] The process is described in D. Orlow, *The History of the Nazi Party 1919–33* (London, 1971).

[10] Compare S. Kracauer, *From Caligari to Hitler* (Princeton, 1947), pp. 15–39, 203–72.

[11] *Gleichschaltung* was the term employed by the Nazis which loosely referred to the obligatory assimilation within the state of all political, economic, and cultural activities.

[12] R. Manvell and H. Fraenkel, *The German Cinema* (London, 1971), p. 69.

demanding centralization and the banning of all films which offended the *Völkische Weltanschauung*. Goebbels on the other hand was more realistic and appreciated that the *Filmwelt* did not welcome these forces of Nazi extremism. He was unwilling to undertake an immediate nationalization of the industry not only on ideological grounds but for the pragmatic reasons that Hugenberg, who owned Ufa, was in the new cabinet as Minister of Economics and that the Party in general depended on big business for its finances.

However, on 9 February 1933 at the German Cinema Owners' annual conference the Nazi elements demanded that their leader Engl should be elected to the Association's board. Their argument that the small cinema owners faced bankruptcy in the face of unfair competition from the large combines seemed to be confirmed when the *SPIO-Plan* was published nine days later.[13] On 18 March the entire board of the Cinema Owners' Association resigned thus giving Engl and the NSDAP complete control. They responded by demanding that all cinema owners express unconditional loyalty to Engl's leadership within two weeks.[14]

Cinema owners were not the only sector of the industry to be effectively 'co-ordinated' in this manner; throughout March and April the NSBO had been active in all spheres of film production—from cameramen to film actors and composers. When the Nazis banned all trade unions in early May, the industry's 'official' trade union DACHO (*Dach-Organisation der Filmschaffenden Deutschlands e.V.*) was dissolved and absorbed initially into the NSBO[15] which was itself transferred automatically to the German Labour Front (*Deutsche Arbeitsfront*), the only permissible trade union. DACHO therefore had little chance to prevent its own dissolution, though there is no evidence of any united stand being organized.

It was during these months that Goebbels was making final plans for a Propaganda Ministry that would assume control over all aspects of mass communication. However, because Goebbels was working on NSDAP propaganda for the forthcoming

[13] *Film-Kurier*, 18 February 1933.
[14] *Film-Kurier*, 18 March 1933. Reproduced in J. Wulf, *Theater und Film im Dritten Reich. Eine Dokumentation* (Gütersloh, 1964), p. 266.
[15] The NSBO had to share DACHO with Alfred Rosenberg's KfdK.

election on 5 March, it was decided to delay announcing the creation of this new Ministry until after the Nazis' success was guaranteed.[16] Eventually Goebbels was appointed Reich Minister for Popular Enlightenment and Propaganda (*Reichsministerium für Volksaufklärung und Propaganda*—RMVP) by Presidential decree on 13 March.[17] In June Hitler was to define the scope of the RMVP according to which the new Minister would be responsible for 'all tasks of spiritual direction of the nation'.[18] Not only did this vague directive give Goebbels room to manœuvre against the more radical elements within the Party, it also gave the mark of legality to what was soon to be the Ministry's complete control of all that mattered most in the functioning of the mass media in the Third Reich.

The film industry presented a number of structural, economic, and artistic problems for the builders of the new German society. Corresponding to its importance as a medium of propaganda, film was immediately reorganized after the take-over of power. The Propaganda Ministry was already established when a provisional Reich Film Chamber (*Reichsfilmkammer* —RFK) was set up on 14 July 1933.[19]

Shortly afterwards, on 22 September 1933, Goebbels decided to extend the idea to the whole of German life and form the Reich Chamber of Culture (*Reichskulturkammer*—RKK).[20] The RFK became one of the seven Chambers (*Kammern*) which made up the RKK, the others being literature, theatre, music, fine arts, press, and radio.

3. THE STRUCTURE AND FUNCTION OF THE REICHSFILMKAMMER

The creation of the *Reichsfilmkammer* is an excellent example of the process of co-ordination in that it allowed the RMVP

---

[16] For an interesting insight into this period see J. Goebbels, *Vom Kaiserhof zur Reichskanzlei. Eine historische Darstellung in Tagebuchblättern. Vom 1 Januar 1932 bis zum 1 Mai 1933* (Munich, 1934). English translation by K. Fiedler, *My Part in Germany's Fight* (London, 1935).

[17] The decree is reproduced in J. Wulf, *Die Bildenden Künste im Dritten Reich. Eine Dokumentation* (Gütersloh, 1963), p. 94.

[18] Ibid., p. 94. See also, BA R43II/1149 on the establishment of the RMVP.

[19] H. H. Wollenberg, *Fifty Years of German Film* (London, 1948), p. 36. Significant of the high estimation of the cinema is the fact that the RFK was founded by Goebbels some months before the RKK, of which it became a part.

[20] The document is reproduced in W. Hofer, *Der Nationalsozialismus. Dokumente 1933–45* (Frankfurt am Main, 1957), p. 95.

to exert *its* control over both film-makers and the film industry as a whole. As Propaganda Minister, Goebbels acted as President of the seven Chambers, and through him their jurisdiction spread down to both the nation's regional administrations (*Länder*) and the Party's own specifically political areas (*Gaue*). This not only facilitated the RMVP's control over individual Chambers but, equally importantly, it allowed the Ministry to co-ordinate its propaganda campaigns.

The structure of the RFK was scarcely changed after it had been incorporated into the Reich Chamber of Culture (RKK). Its head and all-responsible President was subordinate only to the President of the RKK, that is, the Propaganda Minister. The first President of the RFK was Dr Fritz Scheuermann, a financial expert who had been involved in secret plans to implement the recommendations of the *SPIO-Plan* which had been merged with the RFK in July. Scheuermann was assisted by a Vice-President, Arnold Räther, who was also head of the Film Office of the NSDAP Propaganda Office. There was an Advisory Council (*Präsidialrat*) consisting of financial experts from the RMVP and the banks; and specialist advisory councils taken from the individual *Fachgruppen*, as the former SPIO elements were now called.[21] The various sections of the industry were grouped together into ten departments.

These ten departments controlled all film activities in Germany. The centralization, however, did not lead to what the Propaganda Minister claimed—the harmonization of all branches of the industry—but it did harm the substance of the German film by limiting personal and economic initiative and artistic freedom.

It must also be remembered that the *Filmwelt* greeted the Nazis with some misgivings. The industry was not entirely convinced that it could expect much constructive assistance from the new regime. To offset these fears and also to gain control over film finance, a *Filmkreditbank* (FKB) was established. It was announced on 1 June 1933 as a provider of credit and help for a crisis-ridden film economy. In his address to film-makers on 19 May Goebbels had already hinted that the Nazis were about to propose a new means of finance for

[21] For a detailed discussion of this extremely complex transition see Phillips, pp. 74–84; Becker, pp. 102–6.

the industry.[22] The idea of a *Filmkreditbank* had originally been proposed in the *SPIO-Plan* with the aim of encouraging independent production by lending money to approve film-makers at highly competitive rates. In practice the FKB was to create the beginnings of the National Socialists' disastrous film policy and to result in the dependence of the private film producers on the Nazi state. However at the time, the FKB was greeted with great enthusiasm from all sides of the film industry. The Nazis' popularity was further enhanced a week later when they reduced the entertainment tax on the average earnings of films from 11½ per cent to 8 per cent.[23]

The *Filmkreditbank* took the form of a private limited liability company formed out of the *Reichskreditgesellschaft*, SPIO (acting as a cover for the RFK), the Commerzbank, Deutsche Bank (with substantial interests in Ufa) and the Dresdner Bank (with interests in Tobis). However, within a year the banks transferred their shares to the RFK and on Goebbels's personal initiative the President of the latter became the *Filmkreditbank*'s chairman.[24]

The FKB functioned to all intents and purposes as a normal commercial undertaking (as envisaged in the original *SPIO-Plan*) except that it was not expected to make large profits. By 1936 the *Filmkreditbank* had actually made a profit of just over RM 9,000,[25] which appeared to substantiate this claim. The procedure for securing finance from the Bank was that a producer had to show that he could raise 30 per cent of the production costs as well as convincing the FKB that the film stood a good chance of making a profit. The film then became the property of the Bank until the loan was repaid. Thus, private finance was excluded from all freedom of credit and opportunities for profit. Within a short time this financial body would also become an important means of securing both

[22] *VB*, 20 June 1933. The full speech is published in G. Albrecht, *National-sozialistische Filmpolitik. Eine soziologische Untersuchung über die Spielfilme des Dritten Reiches* (Stuttgart, 1969), pp. 442-7.

[23] H. Tackmann, *Filmhandbuch als ergänzbare Sammlung herausgegeben von der Reichsfilmkammer* (Berlin, 1938), 'Bestimmung über die Vernugnugungssteuer', 7 June 1933.

[24] See W. Plugge, 'Wesen und Aufgaben des Films und der Reichsfilmkammer', in E. A. Dreyer (ed.), *Deutsche Kultur im neuen Reich* (Berlin, 1934), pp. 125-32.

[25] K. Wolf, *Entwicklung und Neugestaltung der deutschen Filmwirtschaft seit 1933* (Heidelberg, 1938), pp. 19-22.

economic and political conformity. The Bank, acting on behalf of the government, could refuse all credit at the pre-production stage until a film reflected the wishes of the new regime. Significantly, there is no evidence to suggest that the film industry was unwilling to accept this form of self-censorship.

Originally the FKB was inaugurated to assist the small independent producer, however by 1936 it was financing over 73 per cent of all German feature films dealing almost exclusively with distributors who could guarantee that a film would be shown nationwide.[26] The result was that the smaller companies' share of the market continued to decline as the process of concentration was relentlessly increased. This was a further step towards creating dependence and establishing a state monopoly in order to destroy any form of independent initiative.

Apart from regulating the financing of films, one of the main purposes of establishing the *Reichsfilmkammer* was the removal of Jews and other *entartete Künstler* (degenerate artists) from German cultural life, since only racially 'pure' Germans could become members. Whoever wished to participate in any aspect of film production was forced to become a member of the RFK. Goebbels was, however, given the power to issue exemptions to these conditions (*Sondergenehmigungen*) should he require to do so.[27] By 1936, the *Kulturpolitische Abteilung* of the NSDAP film department had published its new illustrated magazine, *Der deutsche Film*. Its main aim was to spread the Party policy relating to the film industry through consciously anti-Semitic film propaganda. Statistics were published in film magazines and books which purported to expose an overwhelming Jewish influence in film production. Curt Belling, a virulent Nazi sympathizer, purported to show the situation on the eve of the Nazi seizure of power; 70 per cent of all scripts were written by Jews, almost 50 per cent of directors working in Germany were Jewish, and 70 per cent of all production companies were owned by Jews.[28] Although the German film industry had been heavily

[26] Bundesarchiv Koblenz (hereafter BA), *Akten des Reichsministeriums für Volksaufklärung und Propaganda, R55/484, Filmkreditbankbilanz,* 1943.

[27] Albrecht, pp. 208-9. In fact a number of 'half Jews' and 'quarter Jews' did remain in the RFK.

[28] C. Belling, *Der Film in Staat und Partei* (Berlin, 1936), pp. 15-16.

dependent on Jewish artists and executives, these figures were a gross exaggeration. However, because Nazi propaganda identified Jewish influence with the downfall of German culture, it was only to be expected that they would use the struggle in the film industry to stir up racial hatred. The man entrusted by Goebbels for the *Entjudung* (removal of Jews) was Hans Hinkel, who in May 1935 was given overall responsibility for all matters relating to RKK personnel policy. Hinkel brought about a radicalization of the RKK policy. Eventually, by arranging for the Jews to have their own separate cultural organization, Hinkel justified the total elimination of Jews from German cultural life.[29] Not surprisingly the result of such policies was the emigration of all those who either could not or would not submit to these conditions. The loss of talent was naturally severe but the Nazis were able to retain the services of many highly qualified technical and artistic staff, and a veritable reservoir of talented actors.

On 28 March 1933, only two months after Hitler became Chancellor, Goebbels introduced himself to the *Filmwelt* at a SPIO-DACHO function at the Kaiserhof. Goebbels presented himself as an inveterate film addict (which he was), and showed considerable ingenuity in mitigating many of the industry's fears caused by the already extensive exodus. He spoke about the attitude of the government to films and the industry which produced them. Films, he said, were to have an important place in the culture of the new Germany.[30]

Goebbels went on to mention four films that had made a lasting impression on him. They were *Battleship Potemkin*, *Anna Karenina*, *Die Nibelungen*, and *Der Rebell*. All films, Goebbels argued, had a potential power to influence people's beliefs and hence their behaviour. However, the German cinema was in a state of spiritual crisis which 'will continue until we are courageous enough to radically reform German films'. He assured his audience that having gained power 'we shall

---

[29] Hans Hinkel was an extremely interesting and important figure in Goebbels's Ministry. As far as I am aware there is no published biography but Phillips, pp. 58–90, contains information of his career taken from the Document Centre, Berlin (Personalakten: SS Officers).

[30] The full text of the speech is reproduced in D. Welch, 'Propaganda and the German Cinema, 1933–45' (Doctoral thesis, University of London, 1979), pp. 45–52.

not leave. . . . the film industry therefore has every reason to feel secure'. Of *Battleship Potemkin*, Goebbels remarked:

This is a marvellous film without equal in the cinema. The reason is its power of conviction. Anyone who had no firm political conviction could become a Bolshevik after seeing the film. It shows very clearly that a work of art can be tendentious, and even the worst kind of ideas can be propagated, if this is done through the medium of an outstanding work of art.

Goebbels's speech presumably explains why the Nazis had continued throughout the 1920s and 1930s to disrupt screenings of the film in German cinemas. However, Goebbels warned film-makers that if they wished to produce National Socialist films 'they must capture the spirit of the time'. What was not required in these films was 'parade-ground marching and the blowing of trumpets'. In calling for the industry's co-operation in this new venture Goebbels concluded by stating that with this new conviction 'a new moral ethos will arise', allowing it to 'be said of German films, as in other fields, "Germany leads the world!"'

The full text of the speech was not published until 1936 although a shortened, carefully censored version was published in the *Völkischer Beobachter*.[31] By omitting his promises to retain artistic freedom and his strictures against merely showing parades and trumpets, the published version reported a speech calculated to appeal to the rank and file Party member. Nothing illustrates more vividly the cynical opportunism with which Goebbels exercised his authority: on the one hand the published speech would appease the more radical elements in the Party who were calling for wholesale changes in the film industry; and yet at the same time he had managed to comfort the film industry and lure them into a false sense of security by confidentially imparting his 'true' intentions which he could not afford to make public.

4. FILM LEGISLATION: THE REICH CINEMA LAW 1934

To consolidate his position Goebbels still desired more power than he had hitherto secured through the RKK legislation. He also needed some form of legal confirmation to be able to supervise films in the early stages of production. Goebbels

[31] *VB*, 30 March 1933.

settled both these issues by creating a revised version of the
Reich Cinema Law (*Reichslichtspielgesetz*), which became law
on 16 February 1934 after long and careful preparation. This
decree attempted to create a new 'positive' censorship by
which the State undertook to encourage 'good' films instead
of merely discouraging 'bad' ones. The *Völkischer Beobachter*
commented:

Hitherto film censorship has been negative. Hereafter, the State will
assume complete responsibility for the creation of films. Only by intensive advice and supervision can films running contrary to the spirit
of the times be kept off the screen.[32]

The new Cinema Law saw three ways of achieving this positive
censorship: a compulsory script censorship, an increase in the
number of provisions under which the Censorship Office (*Filmprüfstelle*) might ban a film, and a greatly enlarged system of
distinction marks (*Prädikate*).

The most significant innovation of the new Cinema Law
was the institution of a pre-censor (*Vorzensor*) undertaken by
an RMVP official called the Reich Film Director (*Reichsfilmdramaturg*). The duties of the *Dramaturg*, who was appointed
directly by the Propaganda Minister, were laid down in para-
graphs 1-3 of the film law.[33] The first *Reichsfilmdramaturg*
was a critic, Willi Krause, a former journalist for Goebbels's
newspaper *Der Angriff* and a reliable member of the NSDAP.
If a producer wished to make a film he had first to submit a
'treatment' (synopsis) to the *Dramaturg*. If this was passed
the full scenario could be written, and this would have to
be approved before shooting could begin. In most cases the
Dramaturg could supervise every stage of production. The
orders issued and the changes suggested by him were binding.
As the representative of the RMVP, he could even interfere
with the censorship exercised by the Censorship Office (*Prüfstelle*) in Berlin.

After the 1934 Cinema Law had been in operation for just
ten months, the law was changed to make the submission of
scripts optional instead of compulsory.[34] The day after the new

[32] *VB*, 17 February 1934. (Translations from German sources are by the author.)
[33] For the full text of the Cinema Law, 1934 and subsequent amendments, see
Welch, pp. 53–66.
[34] This amendment was dated 13 December 1934. See Welch, p. 65.

law was announced, however, the President of the RKK explained that this applied only to scripts, and that 'treatments' still had to be submitted to the Reich Film Director. If he considered the film 'worthy of encouragement' the script could then be submitted to him and he would then arrange for the film to be financed by the *Filmkreditbank*.

The new film legislation greatly extended the powers of censorship which it prescribed in some detail. It replaced the original Law of 12 May 1920 which had regulated films during the Weimar Republic.[35] Although Weimar censorship was initially a democratic one—'films may not be withheld out of political, social, religious, ethical, or ideological tendencies'— the intervention of the censor was permitted when 'a film endangers public order and safety . . . or endangers the German image or the country's relationship with foreign states'. The examination of films was delegated to two Censorship Offices (*Prüfstellen*) in Berlin and Munich. Each officer had two chairmen who examined films with the aid of four assessors drawn from the teaching and legal professions and the film industry itself. However, the 1934 Law joined the two *Prüfstellen* together and incorporated them as a subsidiary office of the RMVP. The procedure by which the Censorship Office reached its decisions was also revised. Under the 1920 Law decisions were arrived at by means of a majority vote and if a film was banned its producer could appeal to the Supreme Censorship Office (*Oberprüfstelle*). After 1934 the power to decide whether or not a film should be exhibited rested entirely with the chairman.

According to Paragraph 4 of the 1934 Cinema Law, all kinds of films were to be submitted to the censor. Public and private screenings were made equal in law. Even film advertising in the cinemas was censored. For each print of a film a censorship card had to be issued which contained the official report on the film together with an embossed stamp of the German Eagle. All film stills had to be embossed in a similar way before they could be released for publicity purposes. In all matters concerning censorship, the Propaganda Minister had the right of

---

[35] For a discussion of film censorship during the Weimar Republic, see D. Welch, 'The Proletarian Cinema and the Weimar Republic', in *Historical Journal of Film, Radio and Television*, vol. 1, no. I, 1981, pp. 3–18.

intervention. He could either appeal to the *Oberprüfstelle* or, by circumventing the *Prüfstelle*, he could forbid the release of various films directly. In the Second Amendment to the Cinema Law of 28 June 1935 Goebbels was given extra powers to ban any film without reference to the *Prüfstelle* if he felt it was in the public's interest. Not only was the entire censorship apparatus centralized in Berlin but the previous rights of local governments to request a re-examination of films was now the exclusive prerogative of the RMVP.

In addition to direct censorship the film industry depended on a system of distinction marks (*Prädikate*), which was really a form of negative taxation. As film allegedly improved, the range of the *Prädikat* system was extended. Previously, the awarding of these distinction marks had been the responsibility of the Chamber for Film Evaluation (*Kammer für Filmwertung*) which, although attached to the Central Institute of Education (*Zentralinstitut für Erziehung und Unterricht*), was independent of the Censorship Office. However, the new legislation gave complete responsibility for awarding these *Prädikate* to the RMVP *Prüfstelle*. Before 1933 the distribution of *Prädikate* was an honour and an opportunity to gain, according to the degree of the distinction mark, tax reductions, but now every film had to obtain a *Prädikat* not only to benefit from tax reductions but to be allowed to be exhibited at all. Films without these distinction marks needed special permission to be shown. A further incentive was that producers with a *Prädikat* now received an extra share of the film's profits. By 1939 the law provided for the following distinction marks:[36]

(a) Politically and artistically especially valuable (awarded from 1933) (*Staatspolitisch wertvoll und künstlerisch besonders wertvoll*)
(b) Politically especially valuable, 1933 (*Staatspolitisch besonders wertvoll*)
(c) Artistically especially valuable, 1933 (*Künstlerisch besonders wertvoll*)
(d) Politically valuable, 1933 (*Staatspolitisch wertvoll*)
(e) Artistically valuable, 1933 (*Künstlerisch wertvoll*)

[36] The dates refer to the year when the *Prädikate* were first awarded.

(f) Culturally valuable, 1933 (*Kulturell wertvoll*)
(g) Valuable for Youth, 1938 (*Jugendwert*)
(h) Nationally valuable, 1939 (*Volkstümlich wertvoll*)
(i) Film of the Nation, 1939 (*Film der Nation*)
(j) Instructional, 1920 (*Lehrfilm*)
(k) National education, 1924 (*Volksbildend*)

The highest distinction mark (a) meant that the entire programme would be exempt from entertainment tax while the lower *Prädikate* reduced the tax proportionate to their value. Film of the Nation (*Film der Nation*) and Valuable for Youth (*Jugendwert*) differed from the others in that they carried no tax relief. However, these were special awards which greatly enhanced a film's status. Furthermore, they were decisive for selection in schools and Nazi youth organizations. After 1938 no cinema owner was allowed to refuse to exhibit a film with a political distinction mark if a distributor offered one.[37]

The *Prädikate* system not only produced certain financial advantages but also helped to establish the appropriate expectations and responses on the part of cinema audiences. These *Prädikate* were naturally a key to the political and propaganda content in the description of films. 'Politically valuable' was clearly a film which completely reflected the aims of the NSDAP. This title was not only given to documentaries like *Triumph des Willens* (Triumph of the Will) but also to feature films with a political message such as *Ich klage an* (I Accuse). The combination of 'politically and artistically especially valuable' signified a special quality and credibility. The distinction marks 'artistically valuable' were understood in the sense of cultural propaganda and were given only to prestige films and those reserved for export.

Under the pretence of discarding all the old hypocrisies surrounding the film industry, the Cinema Law assumed powers which in fact only served to create the formation of a film monopoly controlled by the Party and the State. The result was the adjusting of cinema terminology to fit the ideas of National Socialism, both in terms of the language used in Nazi films and the phrasing of the film law which was kept

[37] Tackmann, 'Dritte AO zur Änderung . . . der AO zur Sicherung angemessener Filmerträgnisse', 21 July 1938, paragraph 7.

as ambiguous as possible so that it could be applied according to the wishes of the moment and the official viewpoint.[38] The producer was informed of the current aims of the government by having his particular film project checked by both the *Filmkreditbank* and the *Reichsfilmdramaturg*. It will be seen during the course of this book that a film was often passed by the Censorship Office only one or two days before its première. This suggests that within a short period of time legal censorship became a mere formality, the real censorship being done elsewhere at an earlier stage in the process of the film's production.

When discussing the implementation of the Nazi Cinema Law it is important to consider the attempts to control film criticism at this time. It is surprising to discover that Goebbels's Ministry did not start to formulate a specific policy regarding film critics until the end of 1935 when Dr Hans Schmidt-Leonhardt, chief of the RMVP's Legal Division, reminded film critics at the anniversary celebrations of the RKK that their first responsibility was to the National Socialist State and not to themselves.[39] Eventually, on 13 May 1936 Goebbels issued a proclamation that banned the writing of critical reviews on the same evening as the performance (*Nachtkritik*). The *Film-Kurier* quoted the Propaganda Minister's reasons for this drastic measure:

Artistic criticism no longer exists for its own sake. In future one ought not to degrade or criticize a well-meaning or quite respectable artistic achievement for the sake of a witty turn of phrase.[40]

Such measures were clearly intended as a warning to critics not to question by means of hostile reviews of officially approved artistic works. However, in November 1936 Goebbels decided to ban all art criticism by confining critics to writing merely 'descriptive' reviews (*Kunstbetrachtungen*).[41] In future all critics would need a special licence from the RKK and these would only be given to critics over thirty. The day following

[38] For an interesting examination of Nazi terminology in general the best account is still, V. Klemperer, *Lingua Tertii Imperii. Die unbewältige Sprache* (Munich, 1949).
[39] Phillips, p. 187.
[40] *Film-Kurier*, 13 May 1940.
[41] *VB*, 28 November 1936. The decree was issued on 27 November and is reproduced in Wulf, *Theater und Film*, pp. 119–20.

Goebbels's famous order his Press Chief at the RMVP, Alfred Ingemar Berndt, informed the Culture Chamber:

Judgement of the art work in the National Socialist State can be made only on the basis of the National Socialist viewpoint of culture. Only the Party and the State are in a position to determine artistic values. . . . If judgement has been issued by those who are appointed to pass judgement on art, the reporter, may, of course, employ the values thereby established. This situation will arise only rarely, however.[42]

This ban on art criticism met with considerable hostility and incredulity from abroad. So much so that within a few months the RFK felt compelled to issue a statement to the foreign press giving the following remarkably candid explanation:

The film of present day Germany must carry in it the ideology of contemporary Germany, only this ideology must never be allowed to become obtrusive bias. Bias which is detected always fails in its purpose.[43]

By this time they had already modified their original ban on the thirty years' minimum age provided a critic could show a record of National Socialist service.[44] He would still require, however, his 'reporter's licence'.

It can be seen then that film criticism was never an aesthetic but always a political question. In practice film criticism came more and more to resemble publicity material associated with any film company attempting to promote a new product. A film deemed important by the RMVP would be introduced to the film public before its première by progress reports on its production. The first performance would be accompanied by an extravagant illustrated report and then, perhaps one or two days later, a favourable analysis which would place the film within its political context. Thus with slogans following the propaganda principle of repetition, the press introduced the public to the films, explained them, and fitted the events of the film into the topical context. Even for a patently bad film a positive review had to be found and 'politically valuable' films were praised on principle. The press were guided in the formation of definitions and the use of language by directives from the RMVP, enabling it to present a common approach

---

[42] *VB*, 29 November 1936. Also quoted in D. S. Hull, *Film in the Third Reich* (Berkeley and Los Angeles, 1969), p. 96. Hull uses the *New York Times* as his source.

[43] *Motion Picture Herald*, vol. 127, no. I, 3 April 1937, p. 16.

[44] The thirty years minimum age for critics was revoked on 24 February 1937.

in its film reviews. Moreover because National Socialism, in order to maintain itself, had to prevent external influences, the few foreign films that were imported were discussed by the press derogatively or simply ignored. By exhibiting only National Socialist films Goebbels was able to maintain conformity and prevent an increasingly isolated German film audience from making comparisons with other political and social systems.

5. EDUCATIONAL FILM PROPAGANDA

The overriding tenet of the Nazi educational philosophy was the political indoctrination of the young. From the beginning its propaganda was directed towards this generation, for which it offered well-defined tasks and aims, and a 'pioneer role'. After all, it was to be this generation that would instil the Nazi *Weltanschauung* in their compatriots and perpetuate the creation of the New Order (*Neuordnung*) in Europe. Accordingly, the initial enthusiasm of German youth was carefully directed and exploited through the concerted co-ordination of mass media—the press, radio, theatre, and film. In particular, the Nazis chose to use the cinema to instil their cultural and political outlook in the masses of German youth. Taking advantage of young people's love for the 'movies' they realized that the cinema was unexcelled in its ability to play upon the emotions; furthermore, it was the perfect medium for combining both entertainment and propaganda.

Three organizations were used to disseminate Nazi thought and practice among German youth: the RMVP, the Ministry of Education (*Erziehungsministerium*), and the Hitler Youth (*Hitler Jugend*). The RMVP wished to create a new politically and artistically conscious audience that would visit the cinema more often than their parents and reject popular sensationalism for a truly revolutionary National Socialist cinema. In 1941 Goebbels told a Hitler Youth audience:

Our state has given film a very important assignment, and is therefore one of the most valuable far-reaching factors in the education of our nation. . . . Its successes, which have led to a real breakthrough for German film art, are an example and incentive for all the peoples of Europe. . . . We do not want to ignore the fact that film must primarily entertain, but at a time when the nation is so burdened, entertainment and politics cannot be divorced and certainly cannot be separated from the tasks of political leadership.[45]

This however came later. At the beginning the Nazis had to establish a complex organization for the use of these films in the classrooms. The films shown were usually propaganda and culture films. Feature films were shown rarely as they would have undercut the ordinary exhibitor. The setting-up of regional and urban picture centres (*Landesbildstellen, Stadtbildstellen*) and the use of films in schools had, in fact, been encouraged by the Reich Minister for Culture during the last years of the Weimar Republic. The aims and methods of such an exercise had therefore already been proved and clearly formulated. Thus, when the National Socialists started their reorganization in 1933 they had the support of the teaching profession, who had for some years participated with complete enthusiasm in the use of film as a visual aid to conventional teaching methods.[46]

On 16 June 1934 the Reich Office for Educational Films was founded to organize the production and distribution of instructional films for the various film centres and for the schools. The activities of the *Landesbildstellen* were coordinated according to the demands of the new regime and by the end of the 1930s their range had been extended from school work to incorporate film activities in high schools and universities.[47] In 1940 this office was replaced by the Reich Institute for Film and Pictures in Science and Education (*Reichsanstalt für Film und Bild in Wissenschaft und Unterricht*). It was a semi-private, limited company, functioning virtually as a department of the Ministry of Education. The Institute specialized not only in film but also in slides and gramophones. By 1943 its organization was divided into 37 regional centres (*Landesbildstellen*) which were further subdivided into urban and rural districts numbering 1,242.[48]

[45] J. Goebbels, 'Der Film als Erzieher. Rede zur Eröffnung der Filmarbeit der HJ, Berlin, 12 Oktober 1941', in *Das eherne Herz, Reden und Aufsätze aus den Jahren 1941/42* (Munich, 1943), pp. 37–46. Also reproduced in Albrecht, pp. 480–83.

[46] Information taken from BA, *Material zur Filmpolitik der Weimarer Zeit (Reichskunstwart), R 32/201–203, 322.*

[47] 'Die Neue Reichstelle für den Unterrichtsfilm', in *Deutsche Filmzeitung*, 25 November 1934.

[48] BA, *Reichsministerium für Wissenschaft, Erziehung und Volksbildung,*

Although the RMVP had a representative on the board of the Institute, Goebbels clearly felt that the possibilities for indoctrinating German youth were too great to be left in the hands of the local educational authorities. As early as 1934, the Minister of Education, Dr Bernhard Rust, had ordered the showing of political propaganda films in all schools. He explained the Party's policy thus:

The leadership of Germany increasingly comes to the conclusion that schools have to be more receptive to the dissemination of our ideology. To undertake this task we know of no better medium than film. The film is necessary, above all, for the youngest of our citizens—the school children. The film must clarify political problems of today, knowledge about Germany's heroic past, and a profound understanding of the future development of the Third Reich.[49]

Consequently Goebbels found it necessary to establish an entirely separate system of *Gaufilmstellen* (Regional Party Film Centres) for the sole purpose of exhibiting political films in conjunction with the work of the Institute. The RMVP was not entirely successful in achieving this objective, for in dividing responsibility with the Ministry of Education unmistakable tensions emerged as conflicts of interest remained unresolved. Thus although the possibilities for film propaganda during school lessons were not as great as might be expected it must be remembered that much of the propaganda value of these largely silent films depended on the spoken commentary given by teachers. Indeed the teaching notes provided with films are much more tendentious than the films themselves. This was only to be expected as the teaching profession represented one of the most politically reliable sections of the population. Ninety-seven per cent of all teachers were enrolled in the Nazi Teachers' Association (NSLB), and as early as 1936 32 per cent of all NSLB members belonged to the Nazi Party, a figure explained partly because the teachers were regarded by the NSDAP as a vanguard for propaganda.[50]

However, schools were merely one part of the Nazi effort to

R21/710, 'Unterlegen über die Reichsanstalt für Film und Bild in Wissenschaft und Unterricht, 1938–45'.

[49] *VB*, 22 June 1934.

[50] This incidence of Party membership was nearly twice as high as that found among the Nazi Civil Servants' Association, R. Eilers, *Die nationalsozialistische Schulpolitik* (Köln, 1963), p. 63.

manipulate youth; the NSDAP were able to enter the schools through the Hitler Youth organization. Education was not confined to the schools; a child's leisure time was also to be organized. The Hitler Youth was central here.[51] The principal emotional attack was the 'Film Hour for the Young' (*Jugend-filmstunde*) arranged by the *Hitler Jugend* for its members. The first *Jugendfilmstunde* began on a monthly basis on 20 April 1934 in Cologne. As a result of their effectiveness, by 1936 they were being organized once a week on a Sunday and on a national basis by the joint efforts of the RMVP and the Hitler Youth.[52] The films were not necessarily confined to political topics but were supposed to represent the finest achievements of the National Socialist cinema. Although the films were made the focal point, they were accompanied by guest speakers who outlined the relevant points and led the discussions which followed the screenings. These lectures, together with small political dramas and community singing and flag hoisting, directed German youth towards the central propaganda themes, emphasized the effect, and glorified the film itself. It was considered so important that Goebbels intervened personally in the Second World War when the Wehrmacht had taken over some clubhouses of Berlin's *Hitler Jugend* and deprived it of its facilities for exhibiting films.[53]

Despite minor problems associated with distribution, the *Jugendfilmstunden* were usually extremely successful, especially when they were arranged on a regular basis. The Secret Police reports (SD Reports) noted that they were much appreciated in the rural areas and small towns where they were often the only means of entertainment, information, and indoctrination available. Reports suggested that these screenings tended to offset the influence of the Church and the revival in religious interest which had been observed in the rural areas that did not have regular *Jugendfilmstunden*.[54]

[51] For the most comprehensive account of the Hilter Youth in English see H. W. Koch, *The Hitler Youth: Origins and Development 1922–45* (London, 1975).

[52] See C. Belling and A. Schütze, *Der Film in der Hitlerjugend* (Berlin, 1937), pp. 30–45.

[53] J. Altmann, 'Movies' Role in Hitler's Conquest of German Youth', in *Hollywood Quarterly*, vol. 111, no. 4, p. 382.

[54] BA, *Akten des Reichssicherheitshauptamtes, R58/159*, 3 April 1941. Also, *R58/155*, 17 October 1940.

Table 1 indicates the high attendance figures at the performances and also the possibilities for indoctrination. It
should be noted that from 1936 failure to attend a Film Hour
resulted in some form of punishment, although there is little
evidence that this threat was ever carried out.

Table 1   *Film Attendance and Performances of the Youth
Film Hours, 1934–43*

Year	Performances	Attendance
1934/5		300,000
1935/6	905	425,176
1936/7	1,725	897,839
1937/8	3,563	1,771,236
1938/9	4,886	2,561,489
1939/40	8,244	3,538,224
1940/1	12,560	4,800,000
1941/2	15,800	5,600,000
1942/3	over 45,290	11,215,000

Source: A. V. Sander, *Jugend und Film* (Berlin, 1944), p. 72; also W. Häcker, 'Der
Aufstieg der Jugend filmarbeit', in *Das Junge Deutschland*, vol. 10 (Berlin,
1943).

The sharp increase in both the number of performances and
visits from 1938 onwards can be explained not only by the
onset of war and the need for entertainment but also by the
RMVP's desire to use film as a means of instilling a war-like
mentality in the minds of the young (see Chapter VI). Great
attention was also given to those areas without cinemas as
the following figures for the period 1942/43 show:

Areas with cinemas	=	24,100 performances with 8,355,000 cinema visits
Areas without cinemas	=	18,240 performances with 2,465,000 visits
Screenings shown in Hitler Youth Camps	=	2,950 performances with 395,000 visits

In order to ensure that as many rural areas as possible received
a regular film service the RMVP established a network of 1,500
mobile film units which travelled the country extensively.
With these screenings German youth was not only assimilated
into the Nazi *Weltanschauung*, but they were also used to
encourage the young generation to enter the movement. The

Jugendfilmstunden thus supplemented the initial work carried out in the schools and provided the second tier of a comprehensive system for the organization and indoctrination of every individual. Moreover, encouraged by the success of the Youth Film Hour the Nazi regime soon decided that the Hitler Youth should make their own films, provided they did not impinge upon the work of the commercial film producers.[55] Only from their own ranks, it was argued, could their experiences, their fight, and their present-day community be shaped. 'Artists will grow out of our movement who will give the German film the face of our young, who will make our experience and our community live.'[56]

The importance of educational film propaganda together with the film-making activities of the Hitler Youth cannot be underestimated. The cinema was undoubtedly one of the most important vehicles for the Nazi indoctrination of German youth. Film propaganda in the schools carefully perpetuated the educational system and directed the young towards those ideological themes which the Party wished to promote. The National Socialists appreciated that the best way of achieving such results was to appeal to the emotions rather than to reason. Furthermore, they realized that the medium of film was unexcelled in its ability to play upon such emotions, for it could be manipulated to combine entertainment with indoctrination according to the wishes of the regime. By disguising its intent, such film propaganda was able to ensure complete interdependence between the propagandizers and propagandized, so that consequently a uniformity of opinion and action developed with few opportunities for resistance. Moreover, the Hitler Youth film productions promoted in a positive light the manner in which German youth were being organized, by stressing the multifarious activities of the youth movement and the ideological commitment of its members. In this sense they also served to give a lead to the rest of the nation. After all it was to be this generation of German youth who were intended to perpetuate the creation of the New Order in Europe. If they were to be successful they had to embody the Nazi *Weltanschauung*, liberated from the outdated fallacies of

---

[55] Goebbels, 'Der Film als Erzeiher', p. 41. See also C. Reinhardt, *Der Jugendfunk* (Würzburg, 1938).   [56] Belling and Schütze, p. 69.

bourgeois liberalism or the Marxist class war. The intentions of educational film propaganda was to create this 'new man' of heroic will. The task of film propaganda in schools and the youth organizations was summed up in 1937 by the official spokesmen of German youth, Belling and Schütze:

Thanks to the National Socialist film educational work, youth is directed towards the heroic and is therefore psychologically prepared and entirely capable of withstanding all pressures.[57]

6. THE NATIONALIZED FILM INDUSTRY, 1937-42

Secure in the knowledge that both film criticism and film education had been reorganized according to the principles of the NSDAP, Goebbels could now start on his next major project, the complete nationalization of the German film industry. Goebbels had good reasons for not nationalizing the industry before the outbreak of war. German politics were still operating within the dictates of foreign policy. Time had to be gained for total rearmament before the war, and to carry out such a programme the State required large quantities of raw materials from abroad, for which in turn it needed foreign currency.

In this context Germany's film exports were an important factor. In 1929, for example, one-third of the cost of approximately 200 feature films produced in German studios was offset by the income from film exports.[58] Table 2 indicates that in the first few years of the Third Reich, the film industry made a reasonable recovery.[59] However, the fact that more films were produced in this period, and that audiences increased must be seen in the light of the decline in export figures, which in 1934-5 became critically obvious in the export value of the film industry's products. It seemed advisable therefore to proceed warily with the nationalization of the cinema industry and not to alarm the outside world unnecessarily until the market at home and in the neighbouring countries under the immediate influence of Germany had been

[57] Belling and Schütze, p. 36.
[58] Wollenberg, pp. 36-7; Spiker, pp. 54-5.
[59] A similar table with slight variations can also be found in M. S. Phillips, 'The Nazi Control of the German Film Industry', in *Journal of European Studies* (1971), vol. I, p. 53.

Table 2 *Cinema Attendance, Receipts, and Taxation, 1932-8*

Year	Tickets sold (in millions)	Gross receipts (in million RM)	Entertainment tax	Average number of visits p.a.
1932/3	238.4	176.4	18.5	4.0
1933/4	244.9	176.3	16.0	4.7
1934/5	259.4	194.6	15.6	5.0
1935/6	303.9	230.9	17.6	5.8
1936/7	361.6	282.1	21.1	6.8
1937/8	396.4	309.2	23.5	7.6

Source: *Jahrbuch der Reichsfilmkammer* (Berlin, 1939).

systematically strengthened to a point where the increased film output of the Third Reich allowed them to be independent of either German exports or the import of American films.

In 1934 an NSDAP handbook claimed that German films should continue to sell extremely well in international markets. It calculated that foreign sales would take an upward turn and that the industry should be striving to achieve 40 per cent of its total income from the sale of German films abroad.[60] But in 1934-5, instead of rising, German film exports went into an alarming decline, accounting for only 8 per cent of the industries' income and in 1938-9 this figure dropped to 7 per cent.[61]

A number of reasons accounted for this catastrophic state, the most important being the growing political hostility towards Germany. The film industry found itself in a difficult position; on the one hand the government wanted to reduce film imports, but because of foreign countries' quota systems, this made exporting difficult. Moreover, many foreign Jewish distributors simply refused to accept German films. The situation was further complicated by the Censorship Office which tended to object to foreign films on ideological and racial grounds. The result was that within a short time foreign distributors gave up trying to exhibit their films in Germany. This led German artists with an international reputation to leave

[60] Plugge, p. 123.

[61] BA, *Akten des Reichsfinanzministeriums, R2/4799*. See also, *Jahrbuch der Reichsfilmkammer* (Berlin, 1937), p. 124.

the country and German films became even more parochial and nationalistic.

The decline in exports would not have been so alarming had it not been accompanied by a sharp increase in production costs in 1935-6. In the same year the President of the Reich Film Chamber (Scheuermann) warned Goebbels that production expenditure had increased by 50 per cent since 1933. Two years later the *Jahrbuch der Reichsfilmkammer* (Film Chamber Yearbook) was gloomily reporting that costs had risen by 35 per cent since the previous year (Table 3).

Table 3 *Production Costs of German Feature Films, 1933-7*

Year	Number of films produced	Total cost (in million RM)	Average in RM
1933	114	28.5	250,000
1934	129	32.2	249,000
1935	92	36.3	394,000
1936	112	50.7	452,000
1937	94	50.5	537,000

Source: BA, *Akten der Ufa-Film GmbH in Liquidation*, *R1091/431*.

As far as the RMVP were concerned this situation called for state intervention. There were a number of options open to Goebbels; he could either support the independent filmmakers, or he could increase the government's hold over the large production companies. In choosing the latter, the gradual nationalization of the film industry, the concentration of film as a propaganda medium was carried out with great care. The task of clearing up the economic problems of the nationalization and disguising them was given to a private company. Goebbels's agent in these transactions and later Reich Delegate to the German film industry was Dr Max Winkler, who had been active as a trustee on behalf of successive German governments since 1919. By disguising the real nature of the transactions, Goebbels was able to claim that the government take-over had been motivated by purely artistic and not commercial reasons. Winkler, in fact, had convinced Goebbels that the best way of achieving the ideologically committed films that he had been demanding was not to force the film industry to become National Socialists but instead to guarantee them financial stability. In this way both production and distribution sectors would be drawn into the Nazi *Weltanschauung* without realizing that they were becoming increasingly the political instruments of the Propaganda Ministry.

In 1936 the shaky financial position of the two major film companies, Ufa and Tobis, gave the RMVP the opportunity they had been seeking. Winkler's method of control was to establish a trust company, Kautio Treuhand GmbH, which would act as a majority shareholder and would administer the assets of the various film companies. The preparations for a state monopoly took place in almost complete secrecy. The take-over of these firms was achieved by the purchase of the majority of shares and the transactions were always carried out as separate dealings. The film press scarcely commented on them, or, if so, only briefly. Thus the process of nationalization went completely unnoticed. Kautio simply bought out ailing companies and administered them for the State as a trustee. Interestingly enough, they were referred to as *staatsmittelbar* (indirectly state controlled), rather than state owned.

Ufa was the first company to be acquired (together with the Scherl empire) in March 1937. Two months later Winkler decided that the Tobis Tonbild Syndikat should be broken up. In August of that year Terra Film AG (a Ufa subsidiary) was amalgamated with one of Tobis's distribution companies (Tobis Rota) to form a new production company, Terra Filmkunst GmbH. Four months later, in December, the original Tobis was transformed and given the new title, Tobis Filmkunst GmbH.[62]

The most pressing problem at this stage, however, was how to finance these *staatsmittelbar* companies. If nationalization was to be effective, Winkler appreciated that a radical reorganization of film finance was needed. This came in the form of a new company called the Film Finanz GmbH (FiFi). Film credit was determined by a supervisory board consisting of representatives from the RMVP, the Reich Finance Ministry (*Reichsfinanzministerium*), the Reich Credit Company *Reichskreditgesellschaft*), Kautio, and the *staatsmittelbar* film companies. The first meeting was held in November 1937 and

[62] Details taken from BA, *R1091/431*.

RM 22 million was allocated (RM 10 million to Tobis and RM 6 million each to Ufa and Terra).[63]

Shortly afterwards Kautio purchased the holding of Bavaria Film AG and on 11 February 1938 it became known as Bavaria Filmkunst GmbH. It was during this time that Goebbels announced that a National Film School, the *Deutsche Filmakademie*, would be entrusted with the task of training new technicians and artists in the service of the National Socialist State.[64] There were twenty-three different courses, including scenario writing, direction, set and costume design, photography, sound recording, acting, even distribution, house management, and laboratory work. The new German cinema, it was claimed, now rivalled Hollywood both in terms of scope and resources. While this was an exaggeration, it is true that when war came in 1939, the German cinema had attained an expertise and technical mastery that was unequalled in Europe.

Winkler, meanwhile, had not finished the process of state intervention. In 1938 the *Anschluss* provided further opportunities. Because of a common language and culture the Austrian film industry had always had close ties with Germany. On 16 December 1938, the whole industry amalgamated to form a new *staatsmittelbar* company, Wien Film GmbH, which immediately came under the jurisdiction of Winkler's Kautio. Later a similar reorganization was carried out in Czechoslovakia with the formation of the Prag Film AG.

By 1939 all the major film companies were *staatsmittelbar*. Not surprisingly they quickly dominated film output. In 1939 they accounted for 60 per cent of all feature film production; in 1941 this figure had risen to 70 per cent. The aim behind this reorganization was to rationalize film-making so that it could respond quickly and efficiently to the demands of the RMVP; in practice this meant simplifying the financing of films and maintaining a strict control over the content of feature films. *Staatsmittelbar* film companies were not intended to compete with each other but to co-operate in producing quality films that would represent the intrinsic values of National Socialism both at home and abroad.

[63] BA, *R2/4807*.
[64] The decree is dated 18 March 1938. It is reproduced in Wulf, *Theater und Film*, p. 302.

The outbreak of war in September created initial problems for the film industry in that shortages of labour and raw materials tended to increase production costs. Another factor which increased costs still further was the disruptive effect of tighter censorship during the making of films. However there emerged as a result of the war two important developments that more than offset these difficulties. Firstly, the military conquests of 1939/40 had created a German dominated film monopoly in Europe; at the end of 1939 German distributors were in the fortunate position of having 8,300 cinemas at their disposal.[65] Secondly, as Table 4 demonstrates, audience receipts increased dramatically as Germans over the age of fifteen began to visit the cinema more regularly.

Table 4 *Cinema Attendance and Receipts in Germany, 1938-44*

Year	Tickets sold (in millions)	Gross receipts (in million RM)	Average cinema visits p.a. (over the age of 15)
1938	441.6	353.3	8.4
1939	623.7	476.9	10.5
1940	834.1	650.0	13.3
1941	892.3	725.7	14.3
1942	1,062.1	894.2	14.3
1943	1,116.5	958.6	14.4
1944	1,101.7	951.3	14.4

Source: P. Pleyer, *Deutsche Nachkriegsfilm, 1946-8* (Münster, 1965), p. 462; G. von Pestalozza, *Film – Statistisches Material* (Weisbaden, 1952), p. 13.

The major problem facing the German film industry at this stage was the supply of films. Winkler was particularly concerned that if Germany was to exploit her position in Europe the industry should be producing at least 100 feature films per year. However during 1941 it became increasingly clear that the target of 100 films was not going to be reached. The only solution lay in a complete take-over by the State. To this end, Winkler compiled a report in September 1941 which would be used a few months later as a justification for nationalization. The report revealed that production had declined by 29 per

[65] BA, *R2/4799*.

cent in 1940/1 compared to 1939/40; production costs had risen by 68 per cent and the combined gross profit of the *staatsmittelbar* companies had fallen by 12 per cent, although average gross profits per film had in fact increased by 25 per cent.[66] The report complained that films were taking too long to make. This was partly due to shortages of workers and raw materials caused by the war, but the report also attached considerable blame to the RMVP. They were commissioning too many expensive large-scale film projects and, more importantly, there was far too much intervention at every stage of film-making, resulting in a failure to keep up with demand for new films. The report concluded by warning that the number of films produced were likely to fall even further and that unless companies became more profitable they would have to be supported by government subsidies.

On 10 January 1942 a giant holding company, Ufa-Film GmbH (called Ufi to distinguish it from its predecessors), assumed control of the entire German film industry and its foreign subsidiaries[67] (see Diagram 1). Such an umbrella organization would not only facilitate a much closer supervision of the industry's economic and political development but from Goebbels's point of view it would also protect the film industry from the financial demands of the Finance Ministry who were causing him considerable anxiety. Discussing Winkler's report in his diary, Goebbels observed:

Winkler gave me a report on the film industry. A number of personnel questions must be discussed. The Finance Ministry is trying to soak us so hard with new taxes that it will hardly be possible to build up any capital reserves for post-war operations. But Winkler is a pretty shrewd financier himself, and knows more about these things than the bureaucrats in the Finance Ministry. He had already found an extraordinarily clever and original way out which will no doubt work successfully.[68]

Ufi had a capital of RM 65 million which was initially held by Kautio and represented the entire assets of the *staatsmittelbar* firms. Although they remained largely unchanged they were

[66] This statistical information is taken from *R2/4791* and *R2/4792*. The latter summarizes the earlier report; it is reproduced in full in Welch, 'Propaganda', pp. 67–70.

[67] K. N. Scheffler, 'Die Verstaatlichung der deutschen Filmwirtschaft 1937 bis 1942 und die Bildung der "Ufa-Film GmbH" ("Ufi")', *Deutsche Filmkunst* (Berlin, GDR, 1961), vol. 9, no. 1, pp. 19–23.

[68] L. P. Lochner (ed.), *The Goebbels Diaries* (London, 1948), p. 111.

now referred to as 'state-owned' (*staatseigne*). To facilitate the purchasing of film theatres throughout Greater Germany a single company, the Deutsche Filmtheater GmbH (DFT), was set up with the intention of regulating the profits from exhibition. Similarly, in order to keep distribution costs to a minimum, the Deutsche Filmvertriebs-GmbH (DFV) was formed; although a centralized, non-profit-making distribution organization, it is significant that all films were still distributed under their old production companies' names. This served to retain a link with the past and also to disguise the State's monopoly.

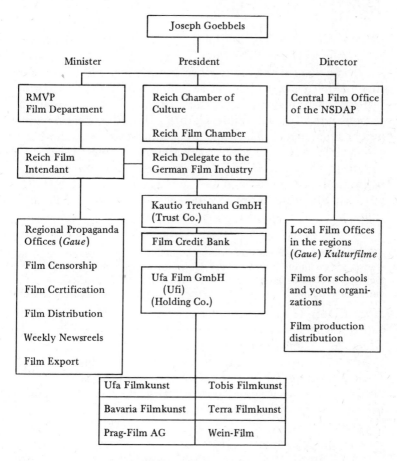

Diagram 1. The Structure of the German Film Industry 1942

Finally on 29 February 1942 Goebbels announced to an audience of film-makers a new body within the Ufi called the *Reichsfilmintendanz*. It would be headed by Dr Fritz Hippler who was already in charge of the Film Section of the RMVP and was the director of the virulent anti-Semitic film *Der ewige Jude* (The Eternal Jew).[69] The *Reichsfilmintendanz* was to concentrate on matters of film 'art' allowing the RMVP to dictate the political affairs of the industry. In practice there was no duplication of labour in that Goebbels was overlord of both bodies and therefore the *Reichsfilmintendant* was directly subordinate to him.

The Propaganda Minister's weaponry was now complete. Ufi had taken over the responsibilities of the Kautio with Winkler once again in charge. The Nazi film industry would remain virtually unchanged for the rest of its existence. Every aspect of film-making, from the selection of subject-matter to production distribution and eventually exhibition was now the immediate responsibility of Ufa-Film GmbH. The *Reichsfilmkammer* had become merely a bureaucratic administrative machine and Ufi, thanks to its vertical organization was a mere receiver of orders from the RMVP. This represented an enormous concentration of a mass medium in the hands of the National Socialist State and more specifically, the Minister for Popular Enlightenment and Propaganda. With his task completed Goebbels could sit back and reflect on the wisdom of his actions:

Film production is flourishing almost unbelievably despite the war. What a good idea of mine it was to take possession of the films on behalf of the Reich several years ago! It would be terrible if the high profits now being earned by the motion-picture industry were to flow into private hands.[70]

A year later at the Ufa jubilee celebration in March 1943, Dr Ludwig Klitzsch (managing director of Ufa) made a speech in which he claimed that competition would be an overriding factor in film production.[71] In view of the measures of organization and control outlined above, it would appear that the Nazi cinema was very much in a strait-jacket with few opportunities for either individual artistic expression or commercial expertise.

[69] Albrecht, p. 32.   [70] Lochner, p. 5.
[71] *VB*, 6 March 1943. Both Klitzsch and Winkler were presented with the Goethe Medal at this ceremony, Lochner, p. 207.

II

GOEBBELS THE PROPAGANDIST

Propaganda does not have anything to do with truth. We serve
truth by serving a Germany victory.

Joseph Goebbels[1]

FROM its inception the NSDAP had always rejected the kind
of liberal democracy that had evolved in most Western European countries by the beginning of the twentieth century. They
fervently believed that the only salvation from the 'degeneracy'
inherent in Weimar Germany was the *Völkischer Staat* which
would emerge through a National Socialist revolution. This
largely explains why all individuals and organizations needed
to be *gleichgeschaltet* (co-ordinated) in the sense of making
them subject to Party control: for the Party was the guardian
of the German world view and through the power and will of
its leader, the Führer, the 'good' society would be brought
into being.

As the custodian of a unique *Weltanschauung* that would
maintain the purity of the Aryan race and allow them to find
genuine expression, the National Socialist State would be responsible not only for the material welfare of its citizens but
their moral and spiritual welfare as well. It would seek to restore a true consciousness to a people so corrupted by non-
Aryans that they were no longer aware of what traditional
German values were. In one of his first declarations of government policy in 1933 Hitler declared:

In relation to the political decontamination of our public life, the government will embark upon a systematic campaign to restore the nation's
moral and material health. The whole educational system, theatre, film,
literature, the press, and broadcasting—all these will be used as a means

[1] W. von Oven, *Mit Goebbels bis zum Ende* (2 vols., Buenos Aires, 1949/50),
vol. 1, p. 32.

to this end. They will be harnessed to help preserve the eternal values which are part of the integral nature of our people.[2]

As the Nazi revolution was to bring about a new consciousness, which would transcend the political structure, it followed that artists too had a revolutionary role to play. When at the height of his power, Hitler gave a succinct summary of his concept of culture and the role of artists in a speech delivered at the opening of the House of German Art in Munich in 1937:

During the long years in which I planned the formation of a new Reich I gave much thought to the tasks which would await us in the cultural cleansing of the people's life; there was to be a cultural renaissance as well as a political and economic reform. . . . As in politics, so in German art-life: we are determined to make a clean sweep of phrases.[3]

Goebbels also shared this view of the future role of German art. In one of his first speeches as Propaganda Minister he declared:

Modern German art's task is not to dramatize the Party programme, but to give poetic and artistic shape to the huge spiritual impulses within us. . . . The political renaissance must definitely have spiritual and cultural foundations. Therefore it is important to create a new basis for the life of German art.[4]

However, after the take-over of power there was some difference of opinion between Goebbels and Hitler as to the exact role of propaganda in the Third Reich, particularly film propaganda. Hitler devoted several sections of *Mein Kampf* to an analysis of propaganda. In a chapter entitled 'War Propaganda' he assessed his audience in this fashion:

The receptive powers of the masses are very restricted, and their understanding is feeble. On the other hand, they quickly forget. Such being the case, all effective propaganda must be confined to a few bare essentials and those must be expressed as far as possible in stereotyped formulae.[5]

According to Hitler, propaganda for the masses had to be simple, it had to aim at the lowest level of intelligence, it had

---

[2] *VB*, 23 March 1933.

[3] N. H. Baynes (ed.), *The Speeches of Adolf Hitler* (2 vols., Oxford, 1942), vol. 1, pp. 584-92. The opening of the House of German Art took place on 18 July 1937.

[4] Quoted in O. Kalbus, *Vom Werden deutscher Filmkunst. Teil 2: Der Tonfilm* (Altona-Bahrenfeld, 1935), pp. 101-10.

[5] A. Hitler, *Mein Kampf* (London, 1939), p. 159. All references to *Mein Kampf* are taken from this edition.

to be reduced to easily learned slogans which then had to be repeated many times, concentrating on such emotional elements as love and hatred.

Goebbels agreed with these sentiments and the RMVP supplied propaganda of this kind both before and after the outbreak of war. In a revealing passage from his wartime diary he noted:

Again I learned a lot; especially that the rank and file are usually much more primitive than we imagine. Propaganda must therefore always be essentially simple and repetitive. In the long run basic results in influencing public opinion will be achieved only by the man who is able to reduce problems to the simplest terms and who has the courage to keep forever repeating them in this simplified form, despite the objections of the intellectuals.[6]

However, Hitler felt that the importance of propaganda would decline once the Party had gained political power. In this respect organization would eventually replace propaganda. For Hitler propaganda was important when organized membership was small; but once the Party had acquired the instruments of state power, its significance would decline and organization would assume a more important role. In *Mein Kampf* he expressed these thoughts as follows:

Propaganda should go well ahead of organisation and gather together the human material for the latter to work up.... When the propaganda work has converted a whole people to believe in a doctrine, the organisation can turn the results of this into practical effect through the work of a mere handful of men. Propaganda and organisation, therefore follower and member, then stand towards one another in a definite mutual relationship. The better the propaganda has worked, the smaller will the organisation be. The greater the number of followers, so much the smaller can be the number of members. And conversely. If the propaganda be bad, the organisation must be large. And if there be only a small number of followers, the membership must be all the larger—if the movement really counts on being successful.[7]

Not surprisingly, given Goebbels's success in master-minding the Party's victory in 1933, he disagreed with Hitler's distinction between propaganda and organization. Goebbels believed that propaganda would be necessary after the take-over of power not only to mobilize mass support for the *Völkischer*

[6] L. P. Lochner (ed.), *The Goebbels Diaries* (London, 1948), p. 22.
[7] Hitler, pp. 473, 475-6.

Staat but more importantly to maintain a level of enthusiasm and commitment for its ideological foundations. Addressing the 1934 NSDAP Rally in Nuremberg Goebbels reaffirmed the importance of successful propaganda:

> May the bright flame of our enthusiasm never be extinguished. It alone gives light and warmth to the creative art of modern political propaganda. It arose from the very heart of the people in order to derive more strength and power. It may be a good thing to possess power that rests on arms. But it is better and more gratifying to win and hold the heart of the people.[8]

With regard to film propaganda it is clear that the concept on which Goebbels based his *Filmpolitik* also differed from Hitler's ideas on the subject. Hitler steadfastly maintained the irreconcilability of art and propaganda, yet a random survey of feature films made during this period reveals that film-makers were attempting to combine both art and propaganda. The German newsreel would spearhead the more overt, aggressive kind of propaganda where news could be manipulated more easily. As we have seen, Goebbels was considerably influenced by the Soviet example; he demanded that film-makers should strive to produce a German *Battleship Potemkin* and, like Lenin, he realized the necessity of mixing entertainment with propaganda so that the propaganda content was disguised.

An analysis of the different types of film produced while Goebbels was head of the RMVP reveals a good deal about Goebbels's policy towards films. During his term of office a relatively low number of overtly propagandist films were produced with a directly political content. Of the 1,097 feature films produced between 1933 and 1945 only about one-sixth were of this kind. The majority of these films were commissioned by 'Order of the German Reich' and entirely financed by the Film Section of the RMVP. The so-called *Staatsauftragsfilme* (films commissioned by the State), however, comprise only 96 titles out of the entire production output.[9] The comparatively small number of political films was

---

[8] *Der Kongress zu Nürnberg vom 5. bis 10. September 1934. Offizieller Bericht* (Munich, 1934), pp. 140-1.

[9] These figures are taken from the *Catalogue of Forbidden German Feature and Short Film Production held in the Zonal Film Archives of the Film Section, Information Services Division, Control Commission for Germany (BE)* (Hamburg, 1951).

supplemented by documentary films and newsreels which became increasingly important in this respect. These will be discussed later. Of the entire production of feature films, virtually
half were either love stories or comedies, and a quarter dramatic films like crime thrillers or musicals; all these were
naturally connected with the National Socialist ideology in
that they were produced and performed in accordance with
the propagandist aims of the period. Table 5, showing the percentage of the types of films shown, gives some insight into
the annual film programme and illustrates Goebbels's intentions of mixing entertainment with propaganda.[10]

Table 5 *The Percentage of Films Exhibited, 1934-44*

Year	Comedies	Dramatic	Political
1934	55	21	24
1935	50	27	23
1936	46	31	23
1937	38	34	28
1938	49	41	10
1939	42	40	18
1940	52	28	20
1941	40	20	40
1942	36	37	27
1943	62	30	8
1944	53	39	8

It can be seen from these figures that there was no clearly
formulated policy regarding the percentage of films that were
to be allocated to each particular category. However it is discernible that as the war dragged on, particularly after Stalingrad, when disillusionment set in, the number of political films
declined and the Nazi cinema served to facilitate escapism or
Wirklichkeitsflucht. The importance Goebbels attached to this
can be illustrated by the fact that he created administrative
machinery to reopen cinemas as quickly as possible after heavy
air raids—with the obvious intention of diverting people's
minds from the present political and human reality of war and
building up their morale.[11] Also by providing relaxation for

[10] The compilation is taken from the RMVP's directives on how films should
be reviewed plus the *Prädikate* that were awarded to each film as this also gives a
clear indication of the type of category that the individual film would be placed
under.
[11] L. Doob, 'Goebbels' Principles of Propaganda', in *Public Opinion Quarterly*

German workers in the form of 'escapist' entertainment Goebbels was performing the political function of strengthening the German war effort.

These figures reflect both the diversification of the Nazi cinema and its inherent escapism, although they can be misleading and should not be misinterpreted. As we have seen, Hitler wanted to exploit film entirely for propaganda purposes. This attitude might be termed the 'lie direct', and was outlined by Hitler in conversation with the actress Tony van Eyck:

Certainly, on the one hand I want to exploit the film fully as an instrument of propaganda, but in such a way that every viewer knows that today he's going to see a political film. Just as in the Sportpalast he doesn't expect to hear politics mixed with art. It makes me sick when I see political propaganda hiding under the guise of art. Let it be either art or politics.[12]

Hitler maintained that one of the key functions of propaganda was to bring certain subjects within the field of vision of the masses. This meant that the population had to be orientated towards specific 'information'. To this end, there can be little doubt that the state-commissioned films were designed to promote various themes of the Nazi *Weltanschauung* in a kind of dramatic, fictionalized form. These *Staatsauftragsfilme*, which figure prominently in my analysis, invariably had a disproportionate amount of finance, artistry, and official publicity expended on them. Although not always overtly 'political', they were produced with the intention of presenting certain themes, such as the Leadership Principle, the People, Blood and Soil, and anti-Semitism (all of which will be discussed), and they set the standards for the film industry in general.

We should at this stage make a general distinction between the political intention of a film and its actual content (a point Hitler never appeared to grasp). In a highly politicized society, even the apolitical becomes significant in that so-called 'entertainment films' tend to promote the official 'world view' of

(1950), vol. 14, pp. 419-42. This point was also substantiated by Albert Speer in correspondence with the author. Speer commented that Goebbels was particularly concerned with uplifting civilian morale after heavy air raids and used every opportunity to convince his colleagues of the importance of the cinema in this respect. Correspondence with author, 20 September 1976.

[12] H. Traub, *Der Film als politisches Machtmittel* (Munich, 1933), p. 27.

things and reinforce the existing social and economic order. Goebbels was well aware of this and believed that 'Entertainment can occasionally have the purpose of supporting a nation in its struggle for existence, providing it with the edification, diversion and relaxation needed to see it through the drama of everyday life.'[13] In the course of the Third Reich Goebbels was frequently called upon by the older Party members to justify his *Filmpolitik* and its apparent failure to explicitly glorify the Nazi movement in films. Alfred Rosenberg was Goebbels's most hostile critic and the Propaganda Minister obviously resented this intrusion into his domain and the fact that he was obliged to defend his policies. In a typical outburst in his diary, Goebbels complained:

Rosenberg is once again criticizing our film production in a recent letter to me. I could answer him with a 'barbed' criticism of the situation in the East: but I am not going to, because the matter seems too trifling to me. In any case, one would have thought that Rosenberg would have other matters to bother about, rather than one or other film that has flopped![14]

However, Goebbels did feel compelled to justify his position and in an earlier entry in his diary he wrote:

Even entertainment can be politically of special value, because the moment a person is conscious of propaganda, propaganda becomes ineffective. However, as soon as propaganda as a tendency, as a characteristic, as an attitude, remains in the background and becomes apparent through human beings, then propaganda becomes effective in every respect.[15]

As opposed to Hilter's concept of propaganda, this aspect of the Nazi cinema might be termed the 'lie indirect'. It is evident from the quotation above that Goebbels believed that successful propaganda should reinforce opinions and feelings that people already hold. Therefore, only a small percentage of feature films should concern themselves with the 'direct lie' as newsreels and documentaries could ensure the regular dose of indoctrination. For this reason cheerful musicals and historical

[13] Speech to the RFK, 15 February 1941, quoted in E. Leiser, *Deutschland, erwache! Propaganda im Film des Dritten Reiches* (Reinbek bei Hamburg, 1968), p. 53. Translated into *Nazi Cinema* (London, 1974), p. 61.
[14] *Institut für Zeitgeschichte* (hereafter IfZ), Munich, *Goebbels Tagebuch* (unpublished sections), entry for 15 May 1943.
[15] IfZ, *Goebbels Tagebuch*, entry for 1 March 1942.

costume films were popular. By creating an anaesthetic effect, films were able (so Goebbels believed) to manipulate the cinema-going public into the more acceptable forms of behaviour such as discipline and obedience, comradeship, heroism, and subordination of the individual will to that of the Führer. Goebbels therefore encouraged the production of feature films that reflected the ambience of National Socialism rather than those that loudly proclaimed its ideology.[16] In this way, by subtly reinforcing existing values and beliefs rather than openly declaring the Nazis' intentions, the cinema was able to move the thinking process towards such elements of Nazi philosophy as German nationalism, the superiority of the Aryan race, the Volk community, élitism, and militarism.

In the following chapters I shall be considering not only films dealing with overt political matters but also a number of the so-called *Tendenzfilme* which, without explicitly mentioning the NSDAP and its ideology, advocated various themes and archetypes commonly associated with National Socialism. My aim is to take the content (and style, where appropriate) of Nazi films, theme by theme, to illustrate how the medium of film was manipulated for political ends in an attempt to shape and direct mass feeling towards specific 'facts' in accordance with the ambitions of the Nazi Party at different periods of time. These themes, which are dictated by the films themselves, include: Comradeship, Heroism and the Party, Blood and Soil (*Blut und Boden*), the Leadership Principle (*Führerprinzip*), War and the Military Image, and the Image of the Enemy.

[16] I am indebted to Marcus Phillips for this phrase.

III

COMRADESHIP, HEROISM, AND THE PARTY

The ultimate truth is penultimately always a falsehood. He who will be proved right in the end appears to be wrong and harmful before it. . . . Meanwhile he is bound to act on credit and to sell his soul to the devil in the hope of history's absolutism.

Extract from the diary of N. S. Rubashov in Arthur Koestler, *Darkness at Noon*

SOON after coming to power the Nazis attempted to use feature films as a means of Party political propaganda. As the NSDAP began to take over film production, the original Party members expected to see their own activities and struggles against the Weimar Republic transferred to the cinema screen. These sentiments were expressed by Curt Belling, one of the Party's official spokesmen on film matters:

One of the points worked out by the Party for its film programme during the time of struggle was the demand for a completely new cinematic style through the infusion of National Socialist ideas. The spirit of our ideology must one day permeate all those who participate in German film-making. We also desire that this spirit should prevail in the cinemas throughout the world.[1]

Surprisingly enough, after their accession to power, the Nazis produced (in 1933) only three feature films which openly glorified the Party and its martyrs: *SA-Mann Brand, Hitlerjunge Quex*, and *Hans Westmar*. These films which sadly have been dismissed by contemporary critics, conform to the principles enounced in *Mein Kampf* according to which 'Propaganda should go well ahead of organization and gather together the human material for the latter to work up.' It was not sufficient for film-makers to produce merely documentary accounts of

---

[1] C. Belling, 'Film und Nationalsozialismus', in *Der Autor*, July 1937, p. 10.

their 'glorious struggle'. Rather, in accordance with Hitler's dicta, it was above all necessary to 'humanize' the new peers of the Third Reich, by scaling the propaganda content down from the general to the specific. In order to familiarize the masses with some of the heroes of the regime, and in an attempt to reduce a historical epoch to individual, human terms, the film-makers put forward some exemplary martyrs for the public to admire: the Unknown SA Mann, the Unknown Hitler Youth, and Horst Wessel (renamed Hans Westmar in the film). The rationale behind this strategy was presumably that it was easier to get the German public to identify in the first instance with the individual characters, and then, through the fictionalized drama that unfolded, with the movement as a whole. Once again this closely follows Hitlerite principles of propaganda technique.[2]

The following three films are of fundamental significance not only because of their idealization of Nazi archetypes, but also because of the *manner* in which they were presented, and the different strata of the population they were destined for. There can be little doubt that *SA-Mann Brand*, *Hitlerjunge Quex*, and *Hans Westmar* conform to the pattern I referred to earlier as the 'lie direct': that is, film is exploited entirely for propaganda purposes; there are no subtle pretensions of mixing art with politics. The audience would be under no illusion that they were witnessing anything other than a propaganda tract; from start to finish, the National Socialist ideology is loudly and unashamedly proclaimed.

SA-MANN BRAND (1933)

SA-Mann Brand was the first Nazi feature film to deal with the SA. It was passed by the German Censor (*Prüfstelle*) on 9 June 1933 and went on general release on 14 June 1933. Although the prologue to the film proclaimed that it was to present 'the glorious struggle and eventual victory of the SA' the film was undoubtedly made with the broad masses in mind. Its plot was simple and concise, it was easily understood by all who saw it, and it required very little contemplative thought. *SA-Mann Brand* was produced in Munich by Bavaria Film on a tight budget and was directed by the little-known Franz Seitz.

[2] A. Hitler, *Mein Kampf* (London, 1939), p. 474.

The low budget of the whole venture is evident from the cast which featured virtually unknown actors. However, a certain continuity with the Weimar screen was maintained by the appearance of Otto Wernike and Wera Liessem, who had earlier appeared in Fritz Lang's *Das Testament des Dr Mabuse* (*The Last Will of Dr Mabuse*, 1933).

The story begins in the period before Hitler's ascent to power. After the opening credits, we are told that this is 'a picture of life in our own time'. Germany is divided into two camps, the National Socialists and the Communists. The unfolding conflict is personalized through Fritz Brand's family, which represents a schematic portrait of German public opinion: Brand's father is a Social Democrat, Brand himself is a committed Nazi, and somewhere in between the two lies the mother. As so often in Nazi films, the mother performs a precarious balancing act between her husband and her children. However, although she is reluctant to admit it in front of her husband's blind prejudice, she has been secretly won over by the Nazis and is happy that Fritz is a member of the SA.

SA-Mann Brand is firmly entrenched in *Kampfzeit* ('time of struggle') mentality, evoking the conflicts in the last months of the Weimar Republic. From the opening shots a distinction is drawn between the disciplined, Aryan features which characterize the SA headquarters and its members, and the unruly, decadent nature of the Communist camp. Such distinctions lead to a simple equation: the National Socialists are the true Germans whereas the Communists stand for a foreign internationalism alien to the German people. The audience's sympathy for the Nazis is elicited as they fall victims to the machinations of the Communists who are intent on undermining everything they represent, namely a strident nationalism and a determination to restore Germany to a great and powerful nation.

After one of these scuffles, in which the innocent SA are trapped and shot at, Fritz returns home to engage in a heated argument with his father about the future role of Germany and the type of leadership that is needed. He explains to his mother that he can no longer live in the same house as his father and decides to lodge with a neighbour, a Nazi widow whose young son (Erich) is a member of the *Hitler Jugend* (HJ).

Soon after moving into his new lodgings, Fritz is given his cards at work and expelled from his trade union. When the bewildered Fritz asks for an explanation, he is told by a Jewish official that it is because he is a loyal Nazi. By this one isolated act, the trade unions are characterized as corrupt and profiteering.

The plot then switches to Fritz's newly adopted family and their neighbours. Once again we have a cross-section of German public opinion. The landlord is a secret Nazi dominated by a cruel wife who thwarts his generosity. The widow's son Erich idolizes Fritz and longs for a HJ uniform in order that he may join his young comrades on one of their weekend camps. In an effort to earn the money, his mother sews every night to buy him the uniform. She is assisted by the kind but weak landlord who produces some money from the covers of his treasured possession—*Mein Kampf*!

The rest of the story serves to illustrate the rapidly growing support for the Nazis: from the lifting of the ban on the SA (17 June 1932), through von Papen's suppression of the Prussian Government (20 July), and finally to Hitler's victories in the elections of 5 March 1933.

During this time the Communists have once again devised a plan to crush the SA (who, it must be remembered, are barred at this time—a severe indictment of all the political parties). However, they are foiled by Brand who hears of these plans from a girl-friend who is an ex-Communist and in love with him. Shortly after this abortive attempt, in which Fritz is wounded, he hears that the ban on the SA has been lifted. The camera pans into a newspaper headline which reads:

> Ban on SA lifted from 17 June
> 40,000 SA men march for Germany
> Adolf Hitler speaks to 60,000 in Darmstadt

Of course this is what Fritz has been waiting for; the SA can once again hold their heads high as they march proudly through the streets in their uniforms. Fritz decides that Erich should experience his first march in his new uniform. However, the occasion turns to disaster as a shot is fired, and in the chaos that follows young Erich collapses, mortally wounded. He is carried back to his mother in Fritz's arms. Erich dies like a true hero—the first film martyr of the Nazi cinema. Given the emphasis the Nazis placed on the future role of German youth, it is significant that they should invest such mystical aura on the sixteen-year-old high school student. The death scene is imbued with an almost religious quality; the lighting is suitably subdued and the young Hitler Youth appears to experience the presence of some spiritual agency. With his last ounce of strength, Erich proclaims the new-found faith of the Third Reich: 'I go to the Führer in Heaven.'

The murder of the Hitler Youth is seen as a catalyst in the struggle for power in the Weimar Republic and leads to the climax of the film. Following Erich's murder and other outrages perpetrated by the Communists there is an upsurge of nationalist sentiment which sweeps the Nazis to power. When the results are known there are scenes of tremendous rejoicing throughout Germany. As an act of retribution, Communist agitators are rounded up (including the Communist officials who had earlier dismissed Brand), and trade union offices and assets are seized on behalf of the Labour Front. The film ends with a torchlit parade of the SA troops. This time they are rapturously received: the crowds chant *Sieg Heil*, their arms raised in salute and thousands of Nazi flags hang from the windows overlooking the streets. The final shot is a close-up of Fritz (leading the SA) juxtaposed with the Nazi swastika; the sound-track takes up the SA marching song and the Nazi flag gives place to the marching columns of the SA:

The flag high, the serried ranks –
The SA marches with firm, measured steps . . .

Despite its open glorification of the Party, *SA-Mann Brand* met with a mixed response. It was not helped by a disastrous opening night at the Gloria Palast in Berlin. In an attempt to display their appreciation of the film, thousands of SA and SS members lined the streets leading to the cinema; they also made up the packed audience inside the auditorium. However, as the *Frankfurter Zeitung* reported, a contretemps occurred which was quite unforeseen:

On Friday evening on the occasion of the première of the film *SA-Mann Brand* an accident occurred at the beginning of the performance. SA

Group Leader Beckerle informed the public that the publicity posters were designed by a Polish artist. In view of the fact that the owners of the Gloria Palast had refused to remove them, he ordered the SA and SS members to leave the cinema. Those present carried out this demand immediately, at which point the showing was cancelled.[3]

Surprisingly enough, *SA-Mann Brand* was not even appreciated in the 'official' Nazi press. On the eve of its première, a review appeared in *Der Angriff*, which if not actually written by Goebbels, was certainly supervised by him. It claimed that the film did little justice to the heroic efforts of the SA and that it was cheaply produced and badly researched:

. . . the director, Franz Seitz, has attempted to produce an epic account of the Unknown SA Mann, and in doing so, to re-recreate the glorious myth of the SA for the cinema screens. Unfortunately, Seitz and his team have neither the talent nor the competence necessary for a film of this importance. To capture the epic qualities of the SA requires a vision of the grandest scale.[4]

We should not be misled by this criticism for it must be remembered that Goebbels had little to do with either the commissioning or the production of the film. At this stage he was still in the process of establishing his own position in the *Filmwelt* and gaining its confidence. *SA-Mann Brand* was essentially an act of faith on the part of Seitz, who obviously thought he was producing the type of propaganda that would please the new masters of the Third Reich. In his efforts to capture the milieu of the SA in the 'time of struggle', the director was only giving cinematic expression to the thoughts on the future role of film, which Goebbels had expressed on more than one occasion in 1933. Indeed, taking their cue from the Propaganda Minister a whole series of articles appeared in the German press and in published works substantiating Goebbels's views. For example:

The German film must become pure and true to life. That sense of an evening's entertainment and relaxation after the burdens of the day which patrons rightly expect from the feature film, should no longer be exclusively reflected in the opium of luxurious opulence and the myth of lucullan delights. The feature film must instead show us life based on our own experiences, fates, and environments, that are not unreal

[3] *Frankfurter Zeitung*, 18 June 1933, quoted in J. Wulf, *Theater und Film im Dritten Reich* (Berlin, 1964), p. 351.
[4] *Der Angriff*, 14 June 1933.

and mendacious, but which – be they funny or serious – captivate us completely.[5]

Despite the fact that *SA-Mann Brand* failed to captivate its audience in this fashion, it is none the less an interesting film for a number of reasons. Not only was it the first political propaganda feature film produced in the Third Reich but, perhaps more importantly, it was conceived before Goebbels and the RMVP had had time to dictate film policy. *SA-Mann Brand* was a crude attempt to reach as wide an audience as possible by means of a story-line that aimed at the lowest level of intelligence, concentrating on such basic emotional elements as love and hatred. This is the type of film propaganda that Hitler envisaged. He also maintained that one of the key functions of propaganda was 'to bring certain subjects within the field of vision of the masses'. In *SA-Mann Brand*, the public is directed towards a number of such themes. Of particular interest are: 'to sacrifice oneself for Germany', the image of the enemy, the hero or martyr figure, and idealization of the NSDAP—the People's Party. I shall analyse these themes in turn.

Like the other two films in this genre which were made in praise of the Party, *SA-Mann Brand* is concerned with establishing the religious quality associated by the Nazis with the myth of sacrifice. When Germany entered the Second World War this quasi-religious notion of sacrifice became an increasingly important part of the National Socialist hagiography. The idea that standing up for one's beliefs involves an element of danger and self-sacrifice is invoked from the beginning of the film, which opens with a Bolshevik mob stoning the SA Headquarters, the police being unwilling to become involved. This of course only serves to increase the SA's determination. Soon after this incident Fritz is reading *Der SA-Mann* at his parents' house. There is a look of concern on his face, the camera pans to the headline which reads: 'Murdered by the Red Menace!' Another comrade has sacrificed himself. Not surprisingly, Fritz's mother is concerned for her son's safety, and this gives Fritz the opportunity to expound

---

[5] K. Kuastz, 'Sauber und Lebenswahr', in *Deutsche Film in der Deutschen Kultur-Wache* (Berlin, 1933), vol. 10, p. 12.

his faith in National Socialism, even if it means that he too may die:

MOTHER. Fritz, be reasonable. Is this 'association' worth gambling your life for?

FRITZ. It's not an 'association' mother. It's a movement — yes, a Freedom Movement. Our fight concerns something very important — Germany's freedom. A life doesn't count for much where a whole nation is concerned.

Both Hitler and Goebbels would surely have approved of these sentiments. The sacrifice of one's blood would, in Nazi mythology, ensure eternal life and inspire Germany in the future centuries of the Thousand Year Reich. 'To die for Germany' was just one theme in Nazi propaganda, but it was to become increasingly important as the war drew nearer.

The antithesis of the 'hero figure' willing to die for his country is of course the enemy. The 'image of the enemy' was of crucial importance to film propaganda in the Third Reich, because it was the enemy that would effectively become the scapegoat for the ills within German society and the rationale for extending their frontiers. The dual areas which were given the most attention were the anti-Semitic and the Communist campaigns. Apart from casting the weak and unsympathetic employer, Herr Neuberg, as a caricature Jewish figure too feeble to oppose the corrupt trade unions over the matter of Fritz's dismissal, *SA-Mann Brand* concentrated on the conflict with the Communists.

There were legitimate grounds for the animosity that existed between the Nazis and the Communists. They had fought each other for many furious years on the streets and as Z. A. B. Zeman has pointed out: 'the National Socialists found themselves, during the economic crisis, in direct competition with the Communists for the favours of the industrial workers, who were deserting the SPD. By grossly exaggerating the Communist threat, the Nazi propagandists forged an effective political weapon.'[6] Thus Hitler was portrayed as Germany's saviour, and it did not require a great leap of faith to see that what he had achieved in Germany could just as easily be gained in Europe. However, that was in the future; in the mean time films had to limit their scope to the battles that had raged in the

[6] Z. A. B. Zeman, *Nazi Propaganda* (London, 1973), p. 95.

streets of Germany. On a superficial level, the distinction between the two camps was drawn by the depiction of the respective headquarters. The NSDAP camp is comprised of 'true Nordic Aryan Germans' who are impeccably dressed in their uniforms. Their HQ is clean and tidy with flowers adorning the rooms. The overall impression is one of unity and discipline with a total commitment to the movement's ultimate goals. This reminds one of some of the striking Nazi coloured posters of the time, which were hammering home election slogans. The most famous, and probably the most effective because of its simplicity was a drawing of the profiles of three grimly determined Storm Troopers with the text: 'National Socialism, the organized will of the nation'.[7]

In contrast the Communists' HQ is dirty and run down, the Communists themselves are unshaven, they are seen drinking a great deal, and they tend to walk around with their hands in their pockets. On a personal level there is Frau Hubner (the landlord's wife), cruel and unsympathetic to Frau Lohner (Erich's mother), and selfish and dictatorial in manner. She never actually expounds her political beliefs—she never has to; her actions speak louder than words. However, at the end of the film Frau Hubner votes for List 6 and thus her actions are drawn to their logical conclusion and explained when she casts her vote for the Communists. By contrast the metamorphosis of the kindly Wert Hubner is revealed through the coming of the Third Reich; after the election results are announced he suddenly discovers his courage and begins to assert himself in the household—a new order has emerged.

The depiction of the Communist adversaries in these early Party films illustrates an important aspect of propaganda which is often overlooked. That is, the widely held belief that propaganda is solely concerned with the art of persuasion, of influencing or changing opinions on particular issues. Thus propaganda is seen as a means of conversion of one kind or another. However, it should also be remembered that it can be used as a means of maintaining the status quo, of reinforcing already held beliefs, by way of various psychological defence mechanisms. In *SA-Mann Brand* there is an interesting example of this type of propaganda. The extent to which the caricature

[7] Zeman, p. 30. See also A. Rhodes, *Propaganda* (London, 1976), pp. 9–64.

of the Communists reflects the Nazis' own mentality can be illustrated by a short extract taken from a conversation between a Communist agent and a Party member in a bar:

AGENT. If there is really such freedom . . . it could potentially be very useful for the Party.
PARTY MEMBER. How do you mean? I can't imagine that.
AGENT. It isn't important that you understand. Thinking is a matter for leaders. 'Heil Moscow' [*with clenched fist salute*].

Such a conversation could well have taken place between two National Socialists, and this is precisely the point. It was a common ploy of the Nazi propaganda machine to attribute attitudes or behaviour to their enemies which they could not admit to themselves.[8] If Goebbels's propaganda was to remain effective in a police state, it was vital that the German people should not be allowed or be encouraged to think for themselves. Only the Führer, the true bearer of a genuine *Weltanschauung*, could assume such a task. These thoughts were expressed by Rudolf Hess at the National Socialist Party Congress of 1934, which was filmed by Leni Riefenstahl under the title *Triumph des Willens*:

My Leader, around you are assembled the flags and standards of National Socialism. When these are but dust then alone will men be truly capable of looking back and recognizing the greatness of our time and realizing what you, my Führer, mean to Germany. You are Germany; when you act, the nation acts, when you judge, the people judge. In recompense we vow to stand by you in good and evil times, come what may . . . You have been our guarantee of victory, you are our guarantee of peace. Heil Hitler! Sieg Heil![9]

Closely linked to the idea of self-sacrifice was the hero, or martyr figure. German films celebrating the Party in the early 1930s created the prototypes for future utilization and modification. The importance of such figures and the manner in which they were dramatized will be discussed in greater length at a later stage. Essentially their appeal was twofold: heroic sacrifices were intended to set an example for the masses, and, through the unfolding story, audiences were encouraged to identify with their faith and exploits, experiencing both their

---

[8] Perhaps the most famous example of this was the anti-British film *Ohm Krüger* (1941) which will be discussed in some detail later.
[9] *Der Kongress zu Nürnberg vom 5. bis 10. September 1934. Offizieller Bericht* (Munich, 1934), pp. 142.

frustrations and triumphs. Thus they served as a means of personalizing the Party's programme. However, once Goebbels had begun to shift his operations on to a wartime footing, the early type of Party hero was no longer necessary. Although with the coming of the *Blitzkrieg* the dramatization of the hero figure changed, his essential qualities and what he represented remained the same. In *SA-Mann Brand* there are two characterizations representing different aspects of this phenomenon. Fritz Brand is clearly not just the protagonist; he is imbued with certain qualities of the true leader of men. Similarly young Erich Lohner represents the loyal follower who, in Nazi terminology, is not so much killed but rather sacrificed for the cause. It is interesting to note that in the two other films in this genre (*Hitlerjunge Quex* and *Hans Westmar*) the hero figures are deified through dying heroic deaths for the Movement. In this, the earliest of the films, Fritz does not die, although he does come near to death on one occasion. Apart from this distinguishing factor, Fritz possesses all the qualities of the traditional Nazi martyr figure: he is a true Aryan German with ascetic features and a Nordic profile, he is clean-living, untainted by any sexual involvement, and displays the exceptional qualities of a charismatic leader. A contemporary critic, who could find little else to enthuse about, wrote:

SA-Mann Brand . . . cheerful events, jolly national types . . . are mixed together in the dramatic moving story of Fritz Brand, Erich Lohner, and the masculine Troup Leader Smith . . . who again and again risk their lives until the banners of the new Germany bear the news of victory over the whole Reich.[10]

This quotation also highlights another important aspect of Nazi film propaganda, namely, the symbolic attachment to Nazi icons such as the flag, the banner, and the uniform. The most revealing scene in *SA-Mann Brand* manages to incorporate many of these propaganda points.

The scene begins shortly after Erich has returned from a Hitler Youth excursion. Under a picture of her late husband in military uniform taken during the First World War, Frau Lohner lays out her son's new HJ uniform. When Erich sees it

[10] O. Kalbus, *Vom Werden deutscher Filmkunst. Teil 2: Der Tonfilm* (Altona-Bahrenfeld, 1935), p. 119.

he is overjoyed. His mother hands him a letter written by his father shortly before he died fighting in the war. It commands him to stand up for the cherished ideals that he and his comrades were prepared to die for, and to work for the glory of the Fatherland. At this point, Fritz enters the room and presents Erich with a picture of Adolf Hitler. The camera pans back to the Hitler Youth wearing his new uniform, standing in front of two pictures of his father and his Führer, both in military dress. The implications of this scene are obvious: without any recourse to dialogue this one frame conveys a crude, yet powerful Nazi interpretation of German history, its past, present, and future. Moreover, it also serves to prepare the audience psychologically to accept Erich's death and eventually to rejoice in his martyrdom.

As with the other two films in this genre, death is associated with the promise of paradise. Thus Erich dies fighting Communism, but like all Nazi martyrs, his last moments are sweetened by a vision of the future. Erich's last words collectively link Germany's past with the present; for like his father before him, 'to die for Germany' is not only a duty but also the supreme honour:

ERICH LOHNER [*his last words to his mother before he dies*] : Please don't cry mother. You yourself have often said: 'One must be able to die for one's Fatherland. Like Father.'

From the look in Erich's eyes we already know that he has glimpsed the millennium. His last words are deliberately ambiguous, invoking the quasi-religious myth of salvation in faith and sacrifice. The ambiguity relating to the word 'Führer' (was it God or Hitler?), would surely not have been missed by a Nazi audience which had been indoctrinated with such comparisons. Thus, as Erich dies he gasps to his mother and to Fritz Brand: 'I go to the Führer.'

For reasons which I shall outline later, *SA-Mann Brand* was not popular with Goebbels and the RMVP. Writing a few years afterwards a Party spokesman on film policy gave some indication of this displeasure. In an explicit reference to the emotional impact of the film he wrote:

Just because people weep and sob in the stalls does not necessarily mean that it is a good film, as this reaction can be induced by any 'sham' art.

The spokesman appears to be attacking the film for its cheap emotionalism. Prima facie, this would appear to be a strange objection given the fact that one of the tenets of Nazi propaganda was that the masses were stirred not by rational argument but by just such appeals to their emotions and passions. The truth of the matter was that the Propaganda Minister was dissatisfied with the quality of the production and wished to assert his own position regarding all future productions. However, despite Goebbels's reluctance to promote the film, *SA-Mann Brand* was accorded some official recognition when it was later awarded the *Prädikate* 'artistically especially valuable' and 'valuable for national education'.

HITLERJUNGE QUEX (HITLER YOUTH QUEX, 1933)

As we have seen in Chapter I, the film industry was in a state of turmoil in the early stages of Nazism. Commercially, it was fighting for survival but, as *SA-Mann Brand* demonstrated, it was unsure of exactly what kind of films the new 'overlords' were looking for. The only indication the *Filmwelt* had been given was Goebbels's speech at the Kaiserhof on 28 March 1933.[11] It would be totally wrong, therefore, to give the impression that all political propaganda films made at this time sprang from the initiative of the newly created RMVP. Siegfried Kracauer has shown that throughout the Weimar Republic film companies had anticipated and given expression to a number of themes that would recur in the cinema of the Third Reich.[12] Consequently, as soon as the Nazis acceded to power the film industry required very little prompting from Goebbels and was only too willing to undertake the task of glorifying the Party and its martyrs on celluloid. In addition, the industry had yet to be nationalized (despite rumours that were circulating), which created a situation where individual film companies were desperately vying for Goebbels's and his Ministry's favours. Thus Ufa's decision to produce *Hitlerjunge Quex* was taken on their own initiative without promptings from the RMVP in an attempt to compete with Bavaria Film's *SA-Mann Brand*. The Ufa committee minutes reveal that they were aware of the similarity to *SA-Mann Brand* but were convinced that *Quex* would be more artistic. A decision was taken to go ahead

---

[11] See Chapter I, pp. 16–17.
[12] S. Kracauer, *From Caligari to Hitler* (Princeton, 1947), pp. 3–11; 369–72.

with production 'unless the Propaganda Minister should declare the production undesirable'.[13]

Unlike *SA-Mann Brand, Hitlerjunge Quex* was a production on a substantially larger and more lavish scale. It was directed by one of Germany's most accomplished directors, Hans Steinhoff,[14] with a script by Karl Alois Schenzinger and B. E. Lüthge from a novel by Schenzinger based on the life of Herbert Norkus. Norkus was a young boy killed by the Communists while on an errand for the Nazi Party, and subsequently became, in a very special way, the hero and martyr of the *Hitler Jugend*.[15] The film's appeal was aimed directly at the young; it was subtitled 'A film about German youth and its spirit of sacrifice', and it was produced under the patronage of Baldur von Schirach (Leader of the Hitler Youth).

Once again the plot is set squarely in the period prior to 1933 and deals with the *Kampfzeit* legends of combat and sacrifice enabling the Nazis and their enemies to be explicitly labelled on the cinema screen for the edification of German youth. *Hitlerjunge Quex* was passed by the censors on 7 September 1933, it was shown to Hitler at the Ufa-Palast in Munich on 12 September 1933, and had its official première in Berlin on 19 September 1933.

Hitlerjunge Quex has already been analysed in some detail by Gregory Bateson.[16] During 1942 Bateson worked at the Museum of Modern Art on an extensive cultural and thematic analysis of *Hitlerjunge Quex* in an attempt to apply anthropological techniques to the examination of a fictional film. The high standard of scholarly achievement associated with this work necessitates a certain brevity in my own analysis. I shall merely outline the plot and restrict my comments to points which arise outside the scope of Bateson's analysis.

The following synopsis is taken from a National Socialist textbook written by A. U. Sander entitled *Jugend und*

---

[13] BA, *Akten der Ufa-Film GmbH in Liquidation, R1091, Ufa Vorstandsprotokoll, 1029a, No. 924*, 16 June 1933.

[14] Hans Steinhoff (1882–1945), script-writer and director in both Weimar and Nazi periods. He went on to direct fifteen more films in the Third Reich.

[15] Another book written about Norkus went through twenty-six editions in six years, testimony to the anti-intellectualism of the Nazis. See R. Rumlow, 'Herbert Norkus? —Hier!' Opfer und Sieg der Hitler Jugend (Berlin 1933).

[16] G. Bateson, 'An analysis of the Nazi film Hitlerjunge Quex', in M. Mead and R. Metraux (eds.), *The Study of Culture at a Distance* (Chicago, 1953), pp. 302–14.

Film.[17] Although only the briefest of plot summaries, it is particularly interesting for the light it sheds on how the Nazis wished German youth to view the film. In accordance with Hitlerite principles of propaganda technique, witness the stress laid on the importance of following the instincts of the heart rather than any logic of the mind:[18]

Heini Volker is a fresh, diligent boy of around 15, an apprentice in a small printers' shop in Beusselkitz. His father, forced into the clutches of the Commune by years of unemployment, enrols his son in the Communist Youth. Comrade Stoppel is pleased with the boy and wants him to align himself with the Reds. But Heini's heart belongs to the Nazis, particularly since he went on a weekend camp and had the opportunity to see the contrasting conduct of two youth groups: the clean, disciplined, happy comradeship of the Hitler Youth, compared with the atmosphere of the Communist's camp — oppressed and poisoned by big city life. Heini unerringly follows his heart and takes to the Nazi movement, first secretly then openly. He yields to no danger and makes the greatest sacrifice of all, his life.

The occasion of the film's special première in Munich was certainly a gala affair. In the presence of Adolf Hitler, thousands of Hitler Youth lined the streets leading to the cinema, where the orchestra played Bruckner's Symphony in F Major. The audience was then addressed by Baldur von Schirach who placed the film within its historical context:

My Führer, German Comrades! There is little I can say about *Hitlerjunge Quex*, for this film speaks for itself. I can only draw your attention to the young comrade whose fate will be immortalized . . . for he is no longer with us. . . . It was at the time of the worst terror, as I stood before 2,000 Hitler Youth members who had responded to the general 'call-up' in Berlin. I spoke to them of the sacrifice that was required; of the Führer and of heroism. An oppressive atmosphere hung over this assembly, we had a premonition of a terrible event. . . . I said that tomorrow there might be one whom I would not see again. And I said to him, be thankful for having had to take this fate upon yourself and for having the honour, among millions, of bearing the name of the Hitler Youth. Next morning, Herbert Norkus fell at the hands of the Marxist terrorists. In the place where the little Hitler Youth fell there now stands a Youth movement of one and a half million. Each individual knows the spirit of sacrifice and comradeship. I would like us in this hour to raise ourselves to his memory. Let us continue his battle, let us fight with his unyielding spirit. Heil Hitler!
(It becomes dark in the cinema, and the film begins).[19]

[17] A. U. Sander, *Jugend und Film* (Berlin, 1944), p. 43.   [18] Hitler, pp. 282-3.
[19] *VB*, 13 September 1933, quoted in Kalbus, pp. 121-2.

It is quite clear from von Schirach's speech that the film was made not only to glorify the HJ and to preserve the memory of Herbert Norkus, but also as a means of attracting new members who had since reached the age of recruitment and the remaining Catholic youth groups, which had managed to carry on despite harassment. As Richard Grunberger has noted: 'the Hitler Youth purloined its ethos from other youth movements, such as the *Jugendbewegung* [Youth Movement]; in addition, it cannibalised their leaders. Suppressing the *Bundische Jugend* [Youth League], the Scouts and Protestant youth groups within eighteen months of the seizure of power (the Catholics lingered on until 1939), Schirach adroitly incorporated many of their leaders into his own apparatus.'[20] The HJ, backed by the resources of the Nazi State and invested with the slogan 'Youth Leads Youth', was now in a position to mobilize German youth on a national basis. Furthermore, by the skilful use of propaganda and ideological training, the leadership was able to elicit a response that was both sacrificial and unquestioning.

These themes were also reiterated to both parents and children alike in the *Illustrierter Film-Kurier*, the programme booklet distributed at the cinemas. The plot summaries contained in them provide an extremely useful guide as to how the RMVP wished the cinema audiences to approach the film in question. The *Film-Kurier's* account of *Hitlerjunge Quex* concerns itself with the elaboration of key Nazi rituals and icons such as the flag and the uniform. As with Schirach's speech at the film's première, the *Film-Kurier* stresses the great sacrifices that the *Hitler Jugend* have made in the past and the important role they are to play in Germany's future:

The Hitler Youth is on the march. . . . thousands of shining flags flutter over Germany, flags red with blood. Young people in hundreds of thousands march in endless columns. We see from their faces that they have discovered a new energy as they follow their banner which they understand so well. They have sworn themselves to their Führer . . . proud and conscious of fashioning the Germany of today. To succeed in this, they have had to suffer, to have been hungry, to have sacrificed. They are conscious of being the Germany of tomorrow.[21]

[20] R. Grunberger, *A Social History of the Third Reich* (London, 1974), p. 351.
[21] *Illustrierter Film-Kurier*, 26 September 1933.

In terms of content the film is nothing more than a reprise of *SA-Mann Brand*, with an emphasis on the younger age-group of the HJ rather than the SA. But the quality of its overall production technique is far more impressive, the underlying message being insidiously disguised; for this reason it was an important means of propaganda and indoctrination. It is typically Ufa in style, what Lotte Eisner referred to as that 'mawkish perfection';[22] abundant use is made of mobile cameras juxtaposed against a backcloth of expertly designed studio sets, which lend a certain realism and credibility to otherwise clichéd ideas, and thus remove that 'stiffness' which characterized *SA-Mann Brand*. Indeed, in its depiction of the enemy, *Hitlerjunge Quex* would appear to have been consciously influenced by the image of the depression in the Weimar Republic seen in a number of left-wing film productions. Lotte Eisner has rightly noted that the style of *Hitlerjunge Quex* is not far removed from its political opposite, *Berlin Alexanderplatz*.[23] Furthermore (almost, it would seem, in an attempt to retain continuity with the Weimar screen), the unemployed husband and father in Steinhoff's production is played (brilliantly) by Heinrich George, who appeared as the rootless and embittered worker in *Berlin Alexanderplatz*.

This continuity with the Weimar period was made possible by the highly-qualified staff of artists and technicians who worked for Ufa and who had developed with the German film industry and were trained to such a high standard that they were unaffected by the wave of expulsions that followed the Nazi seizure of power in 1933. The break in continuity was not as marked as some writers have made out, and the same can be said for the actors themselves. Of all the film stars who emigrated between 1933 and 1939 only 32 per cent of the seventy-five most popular actors and actresses left Germany to work abroad.[24] Great talent remained in Germany and the

---

[22] L. Eisner, *The Haunted Screen* (London, 1973), p. 333.

[23] *Berlin Alexanderplatz* was directed by Piel Jutzi in 1931. Apart from Heinrich George, who was one of the most renowned stars of stage and screen in both Weimar and Nazi eras, it is worth pointing out that a number of other actors in this left-wing production found little difficulty in continuing to work under the Nazi aegis. They include Albert Florath, Käthe Haack, and Jakob Tiedtke.

[24] For the full list of film stars who emigrated between 1933 and 1939 see D. Welch, 'Propaganda and the German Cinema, 1933–45' (Doctoral thesis, University of London, 1979), pp. 41–4.

magnificent theatres in Berlin and the provinces were still able
to provide a veritable reservoir of excellent actors.

Like *SA-Mann Brand*, the plot of *Hitlerjunge Quex* centres
on the conflict in a typical lower-middle-class family. Heini
Völker's parents are rather downtrodden as a result of inflation
and the father's war wounds. The fact that Herr Völker fought
for Germany in the First World War and has become a Communist owing to his disillusionment with Weimar democracy will
later be a crucial factor in determining the sympathetic treatment he is given in the film and a rationale for his actions and
attitude towards his son. However he is still a Communist, albeit a confused and misguided one, and Communism cannot be
condoned (even by Ufa). This, together with his general des-
pondency and lack of vision, will be used as a means of comparison with the thoughtful and visionary qualities of the
Hitler Youth Leader. In the debate that follows after Heini's
mother's suicide and the child's stay in hospital, the superior
arguments of the Nazis are presented as a justification for
taking Heini away from his father.

From the propagandist point of view the fight for Heini's
soul and his conversion to National Socialism provide Steinhoff
with the ideal platform upon which to articulate a number
of Nazi prejudices relating to the German family and to the
country's arch-enemy, the Communists. A more detailed look
at these points will illustrate just how much of the Nazi mentality German film-makers had absorbed after a relatively short
period of National Socialism, and how willing they were to
transfer the Party's ideology to the cinema screens.

In the Third Reich the family was seen as the true 'germ-cell'
of the nation.[25] In his first address as Chancellor on 1 February
1933 Hitler announced that he had assumed power 'in order
to put an end to the destruction of the family, honour, loyalty
. . . wrought by fourteen years of Marxism'. Yet the purpose of
founding the HJ and the BdM was, as J. P. Stern noted, 'precisely the dissolution of the traditional authoritarian structure
of the German family'.[26] Not merely was the ardour of the SA
tamed through this emphasis, but the family was theoretically

[25] For a more detailed discussion of the family in the Third Reich see G. Mosse, *Nazi Culture* (London, 1966), pp. 30–8.
[26] J. P. Stern, *Hitler, The Führer and the People* (London, 1975), p. 172.

an intrinsic part of their racial world view.[27] Paradoxically, therefore, *Hitlerjunge Quex* and particularly Heini's conversion to National Socialism can be viewed in terms of the destruction of the family. The emphasis upon the family and, later, marriage (two extremely bourgeois institutions) highlights the fact that violence, such as that perpetrated by the SA and, to a lesser extent, the Hitler Youth, was welcomed only if directed against the enemy, who were seen at this stage as all those opposed to the Nazi Revolution. What emerged from this was the strange paradox whereby the family restrained the more fanatical elements in the Party, and yet at the same time it prevented the emergence of a truly National Socialist consciousness in the country at large.

In both *SA-Mann Brand* and *Hitlerjunge Quex* the family is seen as a reactionary force preventing the implementation of the *Völkischer Staat*. In this sense the violence referred to above was a necessary factor. As youth was given the task of leading Germany into a new epoch, inevitable undercurrents of conflict developed between the generations. In *Hitlerjunge Quex* this conflict was portrayed initially as one between a dominating, cruel Communist father and a blond, blue-eyed Aryan son, who refused to share the same political beliefs. The subsequent revolt of the son against the father is heightened from the beginning of the film. Heini has been forced by his father to go on a Communist hike. However, he is disgusted by their crude behaviour and manages to slip away in the dark to watch a company of Hitler Youth, resplendent in their magnificent uniforms, celebrating the summer solstice. He is struck immediately by their sense of fellowship ('Our flag is fluttering before us . . .') and their banners. He returns home to his mother recounting the virtues of the Nazis and sings her the Hitler Youth Song ('Our flag flutters before us . . .'). His father hears this and in a fury compels Heini to sing the 'Internationale', boxing his ears while he sings with tears rolling down his cheeks.

Thus, Heini's parents oppose National Socialism in different yet equally stereotyped ways; his father, who courts Communism out of sheer frustration, is vehemently anti-Nazi; his

[27] Cf. Ludwig Leonhardt, *Heirat und Rassenpflege: Ein Berater für Eheanwärter* (Munich, 1934), pp. 2-10.

mother, on the other hand, is non-committal but is dominated by her bullying husband. The role of the mother in *Hitlerjunge Quex* is interesting for the light it sheds on the women's role in Nazi society. As in *SA-Mann Brand*, Frau Völker is juxtaposed with her son and her husband. This is once again a completely negative role, for the mother is no family arbiter; she never attempts to remove these imposed limitations by reconciling the father and son. Within the confines of the stereotyped family she is concerned with the more mundane affairs of placating her husband while remaining sympathetic and maternalistic towards her offspring. As far as I am aware no film made during the Third Reich features a heroine as the main protagonist. Women were certainly prominent in a number of films, but they invariably took on submissive roles, generally acting as loyal comrades to their menfolk, rather than assuming heroic stature in their own right. Actresses were encouraged to represent the Germanic ideal of genuine *Völkisch* womanhood as opposed to the painted and perfumed 'degeneracy' of Hollywood. The role of women under National Socialism was adequately summed up by Goebbels in 1929:

The mission of women is to be beautiful and to bring children into the world. . . . The female bird pretties herself for her mate and hatches eggs for him. In exchange, the mate takes care of gathering food, and stands guard and wards off the enemy.[28]

A further example can be cited from *Hitlerjunge Quex* in this context because of its similarity to a scene already referred to in *SA-Mann Brand*. Heini has informed the Nazis of the Communists' plans to destroy their arsenal. When Stoppel, the Communist leader, hears of this he threatens his mother who pleads with Heini to reconcile his differences with the Reds. Frau Völker's concern is that her son should not sacrifice himself in pursuit of futile ideals. However, as with Brand, Heini realizes that he is one small cog in a much more powerful machine:

MOTHER. Heini, I beg you to come to terms with Stoppel because if you don't everything will be lost.
HEINI. But Mother, you don't understand, do you? Everything is not lost — this is just the beginning.

[28] J. Goebbels, *Michael: Ein deutsches Schicksal in Tagebuchblättern* (Munich, 1929), p. 41.

Whereas the mother in *SA-Mann Brand* is able to adjust to this new situation, Heini's mother, driven to distraction by fears for her son's safety, attempts to gas herself and her son. She dies but Heini survives and is taken to hospital. One is reminded at this point of the similar death of the heroine in Piel Jutzi's *Mutter Krausens Fahrt ins Glück* (*Mother Krausen's Journey to Happiness*), produced in 1929. In Piel Jutzi's film, one of the most celebrated of all 'realist' films in the 1920s, Mother Krausen commits suicide because she sees no further purpose in living. In her death she takes with her a frail child whom nobody cares about, wishing only to spare it the misery and degradation that she had experienced.

However, in *Hitlerjunge Quex*, the result of Mother Völker's suicide is most revealing. When Heini awakes in hospital he is confronted by a delegation from the Hitler Youth who present him with a uniform, a symbol that he has been accepted into the ranks of the Movement. Heini is now supremely happy, there is no remorse for his dead mother, he has found a substitute in the fellowship of his new comrades. Thus Steinhoff transforms a scene of great pathos, the destruction of the family through the untimely death of Heini's mother, into a ritualistic celebration of the Nazi ethos.

Frau Völker is portrayed as a reactionary force, unable, or unwilling, to take the same leap of faith as her son took. Thus there is nothing sad or distressing about her suicide. Her death represents an inevitable fate: the outcome of deep pessimism and lack of vision. Moreover it is only after her death that Heini is finally accepted into the HJ. It is not surprising, given youth's role as the vanguard of the Nazi revolution, that parents were frequently portrayed in National Socialist propaganda as rather bourgeois, reactionary forces. All those who opposed their children were depicted as either lacking vision or simply ignorant of what the younger generation were striving to achieve. From this it can be seen that *Hitlerjunge Quex* was also an attack on existing institutions and the guilt complexes of the German bourgeoisie. Hitler, of course, detested the bourgeoisie. In *Mein Kampf* he referred to them as 'narrow-minded . . . feckless . . . and lamentably supine'.[29] This aspect of the film was brought out in Oskar Kalbus's review of

[29] Hitler, p. 280.

Hitlerjunge Quex. After referring to Quex's death and his last vision of the HJ 'marching to their song, with the swastika flag above, in the light of the bright future', Kalbus wrote:

And the German bourgeois turned over lazily in bed, pulled his nightcap over his ears, murmured something about young rascals who gave him no peace and who would be better off going to school. *Non scholae, non vitae, sed morti discimus.* How often must brave youth throw itself at the breast of the enemy before the self-satisfied in the country have respect for this desire for freedom?[30]

This, then, was the rationale behind the Nazi's destruction of the family, or at least their desire to drive deep wedges into an already disintegrating family life. In order to win the hearts and minds of the people, the NSDAP needed to instil in them a new consciousness. The enlightenment of the masses by means of a new culture was the task of agitational propaganda. But given the poverty of their 'ideology' this new consciousness would inevitably demand an unquestioning faith in the regime and an urgent enthusiasm for their policies. Therefore all forms of opposition and reaction had to be replaced as quickly as possible.

In the case of Heini Völker, the question of 'where does he belong?' has still to be resolved. His mother has been conveniently removed, but his father, the main source of opposition, still has custody. Erwin Leiser has drawn our attention to an important sequence in the film which is not in Schenzinger's novel.[31] It is not possible to state with certainty whether this scene was inserted by Ufa or the RMVP, although as there are no records of any government interference in the *Ufa-Vorstandsprotokolle* (Ufa committee minutes), it is reasonable to assume that this was undertaken by Steinhoff and Ufa on their own initiative.

The sequence in question is perhaps the key scene in the film. In it, the Nazi *Bannführer* (Hitler Youth brigade leader) confronts Heini's father in an attempt to resolve the child's future. Heini is sitting between the two men, listening intently to their opposing ideologies. The conversation that follows is worth quoting at length because it provides just one example

[30] Kalbus, p. 123.
[31] E. Leiser, *Nazi Cinema* (London, 1974), pp. 36-8.

of the manner in which this 'new consciousness' was instilled in the German people through the medium of film:

YOUTH LEADER. Hello, Heini, The doctor says that you can leave the hospital now.

HEINI. But where am I to go?

FATHER. What sort of question is that? With your father, of course, where you belong.

YOUTH LEADER. But that's precisely the question. Where does the boy belong today? My parents were well-meaning, but when I was fifteen, I ran away . . . Many boys did the same. . . .

FATHER. Rascals, that's what they were, all of them.

YOUTH LEADER. Ah, but that is their nature, and it always has been. Once they reach a certain age they all want to roam. Where then does a boy belong? Why don't you ask your son?

FATHER. Well then, what have you to say for yourself? [*Heini starts to answer* . . .]

YOUTH LEADER. Tell me, were you in the war?

FATHER. Why, of course I was. . . .

YOUTH LEADER. Well then, over two million boys volunteered for action. All of them had families, fathers, and mothers. Tell me, where did they belong?

FATHER. I am a simple man of the people.

YOUTH LEADER. You've heard of the Movement, haven't you?

FATHER [*gesticulating*]. Movement! Up one, two, — Up one, two — that's the movement I understood. Until I was hit by a bullet and then the movement stopped. From then on I had to limp to the labour exchange. Week in, week out, year after year. It drove me crazy. Do you think that I got fat through eating too much? Of course not, it was because I was out of a job. Sitting around made me fat. So where do I belong? I belong with my friends, from my own class. And where I belong, my son belongs too.

YOUTH LEADER. With your own class? By that, I take you to mean the Internationale?

FATHER. Yes, of course, the Internationale.

YOUTH LEADER [*pauses*]. Where were you born?

FATHER. Why, on the Spree.

YOUTH LEADER. Yes I know that. But in what country?

FATHER. In Germany, of course.

YOUTH LEADER. Yes, of course, in Germany — in *our* Germany. Now I want you to think about that.

Heini's father needs no further persuasion: the Youth Leader has won the argument and the father subsequently allows Heini to go and live at the Nazi Youth Hostel. Thus, the destruction of the family is complete. From now on its place will be taken by the Hostel, and discipline and sacrifice will be the credos

inculcated into the minds of German youth. For as the same
Youth Leader informs Heini on his first day with his 'new
family': 'Anyone wearing this uniform will be expected to
obey orders and commit himself totally to the Fatherland.'
In the case of the family, the events portrayed in *Hitlerjunge Quex* were to prove prophetic. By 1936, the *Hitler
Jugend* had a membership of approximately six million, which
prompted Baldur von Schirach to declare: 'The battle for the
unification of German youth is at an end.'[32] One explanation
for this was the Nazi's remarkable ability to stimulate the
imagination of an alienated youth with promises of an exciting Utopia. One has only to look at the advertisements for
Schenzinger's novel to see how it came about:

What happens to a boy like this, when the great river catches him? What
is it that sweeps him along, that draws him, that inspires him, that destroys him? How does a child of fifteen come to leave his mother, to hate
his father, to despise his former friends? Norkus and Preisser [another
HJ martyr] were hardly older when they died for an idea whose greatness
they could not understand, of which they had only a presentiment.[33]

Thus for the young cinema audiences watching the exploits of
the heroic 'Quex' there could be no alternative but to become
a member of the HJ. But for their parents more sinister forces
were involved. For within a few short years, parents whose
political and religious convictions did not coincide with those
of the State, like the Völkers, would have their children taken
from them: 'The worker', as Georg Elser had complained,
'...because of the Hitler Youth is not master of his own children
. . .'.[34] The process by which this would be carried out would
be quite simple: if the authorities felt that a child was being
reared in a nonconformist manner then they would apply to
the guardianship court for the child to be removed to the local
Youth Hostel (referred to as a 'politically reliable home'). As
Richard Grunberger has noted, parental offences punishable
by such judicial kidnapping included: 'friendship with Jews,
refusal to enrol children in the Hitler Youth, and membership
of the Jehovah's Witnesses'.[35] These disturbing features were

[32] For the full speech see B. von Schirach, *Revolution der Erziehung. Reden
aus den Jahren des Aufbaus* (Munich, 1938), pp. 22-3.

[33] B. von Schirach, *Die Fahne der Verfolgten*, quoted in J. Fest, *The Face of
the Third Reich* (London, 1972), p. 334.

[34] Quoted in Stern, p. 142.   [35] Grunberger, p. 310.

also observed by an American correspondent in Berlin at this time.

Nevertheless, with children more and more removed from parental and religious influence through the HJ, evacuations into the country, and exposed to Nazi propaganda through school, books, the press, radio, and motion pictures, it was to be expected that the young were succumbing to the Nazi wishes.[36]

Returning to *Hitlerjunge Quex* it is a measure of Heini's ability and devotion that soon after joining the HJ he is nick-named 'Quex' (quicksilver) in recognition of his heroic missions against the Communists. Moreover, the speed and willingness of Quex's conversion is also seen as a total vindication of the educative process of the Youth Hostel, where service to the community is placed above the individual. The parallel between the two opposing political groups is nowhere better illustrated than in the milieu of their respective party organizations. As in *SA-Mann Brand*, the young Communists are presented as a criminal element, noisy, untidy, and disorderly; whereas the HJ are disciplined and idealistic. Thus the Communists are not simply different from the Nazis, they are the systematic opposite of the National Socialist ideal. It is this dedication and idealism that prompt Heini to volunteer to distribute NSDAP election leaflets in the dangerous Communist-held district of Berlin.

This leads into the climax of the film and to Heini's martyrdom. Alone in the backstreets of the Berlin slums, he is hunted and eventually trapped by the Communists who are sheltered by the darkness that symbolizes their intent. It is interesting to note that this simple, yet crude cinematic device by which the Nazis portrayed themselves and their enemies in terms of light and shade, was employed in each of the three Party films. Encircled by the vengeful Bolshevik mob, the Hitler Youth member takes refuge in a tent in a deserted fair nearby. Inadvertently he betrays himself by setting off a mechanical figure of a toy drummer. The enemy closes in on their victim and Heini is stabbed in the dark. As the dawn breaks (once again, the 'play' on light and shade), the Nazis arrive to find him dying. For Heini, however, death is sweetened by a glorious vision of the future. His last words are: 'Our flag flutters before us ...'.

[36] H. W. Flannery, *Assignment to Berlin* (London, 1942), p. 84.

The apocalyptic final scene is almost identical to the final scene of Luis Trenker's *Der Rebell* (*The Rebel*, 1932) which is set in the Tyrol in 1809 and describes the conflict between the Tyrolese and the French. In this film the hero (played by Trenker) is a prophet with a vision of a Pan-German nation. Although he is murdered, the final scene shows him rising from the dead (together with his two comrades, Kloz and Rakensteiner), picking up the blood-bespattered flag and marching at the head of men, women, and children to a victorious future. When Dr Goebbels introduced himself to the *Filmwelt* on 28 March 1933, he praised *Der Rebell* and cited it as the type of film that National Socialist film-makers should aspire to. Consequently, in *Hitlerjunge Quex* the flag with Heini's blood on it becomes the symbol of the Hitler Youth. When Heini utters the words of Baldur von Schirach's HJ marching song, the sound-track takes up the song and the Nazi swastika appears on the screen, to be replaced by columns of marching Hitler Youth.

At this point, Steinhoff employs montage similarly to the way Trenker used it in *Der Rebell*. In cinematic terms, this Ufa production equates Heini's sacrifice with a victorious future for Germany, by juxtaposing a ghostly 'Quex' leading an inspired division of Hitler Youth. These powerfully emotional images of rigidly disciplined columns of determined-looking young men effectively conveyed the ambience of *Deutsche-Ordnung* and the invincible might of German youth. Significantly, it was precisely these aspects that the *Illustrierter Film-Kurier* stressed in their explanatory notes accompanying the film:

This brave young soldier died a hero's death . . . He died for a cause he believed in, for his comrades, his flag, and above all, for his beloved Führer. But there are many thousands of German youth ready to raise the flag consecrated by the blood of one of the nation's great martyrs.[37]

Although not without its critics,[38] *Hitlerjunge Quex* met with a more favourable response than its predecessor *SA-Mann Brand*. One of the reasons for this, apart from Ufa's style and

---

[37] *Illustrierter Film-Kurier* (hereafter *IFK*), 26 September 1933.
[38] Walter Darre, for example, criticized Ufa for the exaggerated cost of the film 'which is said to have cost ¾ Million RM'. BA, *Dr Gottfried Traub Folder*, *No. II*.

superior production techniques, lies in the characterization of Heini. The part was played by an unidentified HJ member, which undoubtedly gave it a certain authenticity, particularly with the younger generation. However there is a certain irony here, for according to SHAEF (Supreme Headquarters Allied Expeditionary Force), the boy who played Quex was later sent to a concentration camp for being homosexual.[39] Nevertheless the story of Herbert Norkus's martyrdom was well known and extremely popular; Goebbels claimed that 'the whole population of Berlin turned out to follow Norkus to his grave.'[40] The audience could identify with Heini in that he represented what was by 1933 a familiar historical figure, and the Nazi struggle against the Communists was thus humanized. In this respect *Hitlerjunge Quex* anticipated the type of film propaganda that Goebbels would favour in later years. Indeed he appeared to recognize these qualities in the film when he publicly thanked Ernst Hugo Correl, Ufa's chief of production, in a letter that was reprinted in the *Völkischer Beobachter*:

All those at Ufa who collaborated in the making of this film have achieved great merit, not only in developing German film art, but also in the artistic presentation of National Socialist ideas. Those of us who attended the film's première and saw just how moved and shaken the audience were at the death of Hitler Youth Quex, must realize the unlimited possibilities of the truly German film, and the enormous tasks awaiting us.[41]

Hitlerjunge Quex was subsequently awarded the highest *Prädikat* 'politically and artistically especially valuable'. In 1938 it was given additional recognition by the new award of *Jugendwert* (valuable for youth), which although not strictly a *Prädikat* in that it did not carry tax relief, was none the less decisive for its selection in schools and youth organizations. These awards indicate the intentions behind the film and the degree of official approval on the part of the RMVP. Having said this, and given the fact that it was a propaganda film aimed at inspiring the Hitler Youth, one question begs to be answered: how successful was it? According to the two Austrian film

[39] *SHAEF, Psychological Warfare Division. Viewed and graded by Major F.L. Evans and H.J. Lefebre. List of impounded films with comments.* In general these comments are more perceptive than the *Allied Commission's Catalogue*, but in this instance I can find no evidence to substantiate the claim.
[40] J. Goebbels, *Vom Kaiserhof zur Reichkanzlei* (Berlin, 1934), p. 267.
[41] *VB*, 16 September 1933.

historians, Helmut Blobner and Herbert Holba: 'The impression produced by the film on young people was tremendous. As late as the 1940s it was regarded as "the film" by them.'[42] It is difficult to substantiate this claim. There was certainly no 'feedback' information at this time, as the SD (*Sicherheits-Dienst*) Reports had yet to be established. One source that is available is A. U. Sander's *Jugend und Film*, in which the author produces a list of films containing the likes and dislikes of the youth film audience. *Hitlerjunge Quex* does not appear on the list of their seventy-eight favourite films.[43] Furthermore, of the seven feature films that were made specifically for the HJ, this Ufa production was voted last.

However, this evidence can be misleading. For example, the author samples only an extremely narrow range of opinions and there is no mention of the criteria he uses in his sampling techniques. But perhaps more importantly the survey was conducted in 1944, eleven years after the release of *Hitlerjunge Quex*. Given the time lapse, it would surely come as no surprise to discover that this type of agitational propaganda failed to appeal to a new generation of German youth who were witnessing the disintegration of Hitler's 'Thousand-Year Reich' and the proclamations that brought it into being. Despite this, there can be little doubt that *Hitlerjunge Quex* was still thought to contain an important message for the younger generation. Compare for example the plot summary quoted earlier, which took great pains to draw out carefully defined responses, with Sander's concluding sentence on the contemporary value of the film a decade later: 'This film will give information to the coming generations of the spirit and sacrifice of German youth in the time of National Socialism's great struggle.'[44]

That the Hitler Youth were still expected to be inspired by young Heini's exploits in the face of manifest political, economic, and social decay says much for the intransigent nature of the tenets of Nazi propaganda and the degree to which the National Socialists' triumph in the early *Kampfzeit* was thought to provide a necessary myth for the existence of the Third Reich.

[42] H. Blobner and H. Holba, 'Jackboot Cinema' in *Films and Filming*, December 1962, p. 15.
[43] Sander, pp. 118–19.
[44] Sander, p. 43.

HANS WESTMAR: EINER VON VIELEN (HANS WESTMAR: ONE OF MANY, 1933)

The last film to be shown in this trilogy was a 'heroic contemporary film' produced by the newly founded *Volksdeutsche Filmgesellschaft*, based on the life and death of the National Socialist martyr, Horst Wessel, who was one of the earliest Nazi martyrs; his major contribution was the Horst Wessel Lied, based on the old Communist fighting chorus and later to become the battle hymn of the NSDAP. Wessel, in fact, lived with a Berlin prostitute whose protector murdered him out of jealousy in 1930. However after his death Goebbels built him up as a national hero who had been murdered by the Communists. The prevalent attitude towards the martyr was well stated by *Der Brünnen*:

How high Horst Wessel towers over that Jesus of Nazareth — that Jesus who pleaded that the bitter cup should be taken from him. High unattainably high all Horst Wessels stand above Jesus![45]

Hans Westmar was directed by Franz Wenzler and was based largely on the biography of Horst Wessel by the celebrated German novelist Hans Heinz Ewers.[46] It would appear that Hitler liked the novel and asked that Ewers be commissioned to write the scenario for the film version.[47] Assisting in the production team were the SA of Berlin under the supervision of SA-Oberführer Richard Fiedler. The music was composed by Ernst ('Putzi') Hanfstaengl, the Party's Foreign Press Chief and a close friend of Hitler.

On 3 October 1933, a week before its official première, the film was previewed before a specially invited audience which included Göring and other Nazi dignitaries. The following day it was proclaimed in the press as the 'peak of Ewers's achievment' and the French journalist Jules Sauerwein, writing in the *Deutsche Allgemeine Zeitung*, regarded the 'Horst Wessel film as one of the best he had ever seen'.[48]

[45] *Der Brünnen*, Düsseldorf, 2 January 1934, quoted in F. L. Schumann, *Hitler and the Nazi Dictatorship* (London, 1936), p. 368.

[46] Ewers had previously scripted *Der Student von Prag* (filmed in 1913 with Paul Wegener and later in 1926 with Conrad Veidt and Werner Kraus) and his novel *Alraune* (Mandrake) was filmed by Henrik Galeen in 1928.

[47] Cf. E. Hanfstaengl, *Hitler: The Missing Years* (London, 1957), p. 232.

[48] *Deutsche Allgemeine Zeitung*, 4 October 1933. Many of the details relating

The film was scheduled to have its official première at the Ufa-Palast on 9 October 1933, the anniversary of Wessel's birthday. It had still to be submitted to the *Prüfstelle* for its approval and any *Prädikate* that might be awarded. Goebbels used this opportunity to exert his authority in the *Filmwelt* and also to provoke a confrontation with various Party groups who he believed were interfering in the film industry. Goebbels had already warned of the undesirability of depicting NSDAP organizations on the cinema screen. On 19 May 1933 in a speech under the auspices of the NSBO and KdfK, he made his views on the subject perfectly clear: 'The SA's rightful place is in the streets and not on the cinema screen.'[49]

Despite this earlier warning it came as a complete surprise to everyone when, on the morning of its première, the film was banned. The *Prüfstelle* was chaired by *Regierungsrat* Zimmermann and included Daluege, who was Chief of the Prussian police, and a certain Hägert from the RMVP. The *Prüfstelle*'s hearings were still prescribed by the Reich Cinema Law of 1920. The film was banned as being detrimental to the memory of Horst Wessel and therefore 'liable to endanger vital state interests and Germany's reputation abroad'. The *Licht-Bild-Bühne* concluded an extensive rationale for the ban by stating: 'The memorial to our unforgettable Storm-Leader Horst Wessel demands only the best, and so in the interest of the whole nation it would not be just to allow a film to appear which did not portray these qualities before the eyes of the world.'[50]

It was obvious to everyone, however, that this was just a legal farce and that the film had been banned on Goebbels's orders. Dr Hanfstaengl, who apart from composing the musical score later became assistant producer to the film project, recounts what happened after the *Prüfstelle*'s decision:

I showed Hitler and Heinrich Hoffmann rough cut and they seemed to like it well, but I had reckoned without Goebbels . . . The première was arranged. The invitations had gone out. Everyone in Berlin society from the Crown Prince down was to be present and suddenly Goebbels forbade the film to be shown.

to the *Hans Westmar* affair have been taken from H. Barkhausen, 'Die NSDAP als Filmproduzentin. Mit Kurzübersicht: Filme der NSDAP 1927–1945', in G. Moltmann and K. F. Reimers (eds.), *Zeitgeschichte im Film-und Tondokument* (Göttingen, 1970), pp. 155–7.

[49] *VB*, 20 May 1933.   [50] *Licht-Bild-Bühne* (hereafter *LBB*), 9 October 1933.

This was too much. A lot of money had been tied up in the project and now ruin stared us in the face. I stormed in to see Hitler and then Goebbels, but the little man had invented a thousand excuses why it was not to be shown, although his real reason was jealousy. It was too bourgeois in approach, emphasized Wessel's Christian background too much, was not full of the National Socialist revolutionary spirit, was trite — everything was wrong.[51]

The ban shook the *Filmwelt* and the ramifications on the film economy were so great that Goebbels was forced to state his position in an interview with the *Licht-Bild-Bühne*:

We National Socialists see no value in our SA marching on the stage or screen, their place is on the streets. Such an ostensible show of National Socialist ideology is no substitute for real art. Therefore it is so difficult as to be almost impossible to make a film that is truly equal to the spirit of such an exalted organization as the SA. I have informed the film-makers who have contacted me that their films will be released only if they fulfil the claims of great art. . . . The figure of Wessel in this film did not correspond to the wonderful memory that the German public have of this great National Socialist.[52]

The case caused such an uproar in the Party that Goebbels was ultimately forced to back down. But only after he had insisted that the film's original title, 'Horst Wessel', be changed and that 'all allusions to Horst Wessel's life and death' should be avoided in the new version.[53] Two months after the original ban and with substantial cuts the film was passed with a new title, *Hans Westmar: Einer von vielen*. The film went to the *Prüfstelle* on 23 November 1933, and was finally released on 13 December 1933.

The film opens in Vienna in a manner reminiscent of the German *Kulturfilm*. In a Viennese beer cellar Hans Westmar, a handsome young student, is talking to two newly acquired friends, an expatriate German business man and his daughter Maud who have returned from America. Both ask Hans to stay in Vienna, but Hans must return to his studies and invites them to Berlin. Maud enquires if Berlin is as beautiful as Vienna. In order to answer her question the film cuts to Berlin.

In Berlin dole queues fill the streets and the special accommodation for the homeless is full. This provides us with an introduction to the Communist faction. As the Internationale

---

[51] Hanfstaengl, p. 233.
[52] *LBB*, 13 October 1933.
[53] *Hannoversche Volkszeitung*, 2 November 1933 quoted in Wulf, p. 350.

plays, two of the leaders survey a scene of terrible poverty. The younger of the two, Ross, is horrified that human beings should have to live in such conditions. The leader of the Berlin commune, on the other hand (played by Paul Wegener), looking remarkably like Lenin, views these conditions as an ideal breeding ground for Communism: 'This poverty is our greatest asset.'

Hans has meanwhile returned home. His mother tells him that two SA friends have called but clearly feels he should be spending more time on his studies and less on political activities. An example of Hans's studies follows. This is an extraordinary geography lesson in which a Jewish-looking lecturer preaches internationalism. True, he says, thousands of Germans are outside the Reich but the frontiers established at Versailles have in reality made the country borderless; Germans have at last become Europeans and there can be no more wars. 'Down with weapons,' he declares.

The answer comes once again by means of the director's editing: as two sabres appear on the screen, a voice off picture commands, 'Up with weapons!' The camera pulls back to a student fencing match. Hans gives an impromptu speech in which he insists that the real struggle is taking place in the streets and that class is irrelevant:

I'm telling you, all Germany is at stake down there on the streets. And that is why we must get closer to the people, we cannot stand aloof anymore. We must fight side by side with the workers — it's all or nothing!

One of the students retorts that the workers want nothing to do with Nazi students, because they are from a different class. However Westmar replies: 'We simply cannot talk in terms of class any more. We are workers too, but we happen to work with our heads, our place is next to our brothers who work with their hands.'

At the SA headquarters, Hans learns that Goebbels has decreed that every effort has to be made to win Berlin. He explains to his comrades that he has to escort his two guests around the town that night and so will be absent from the meeting. The expatriate German cannot believe he is back in Berlin, so much has changed. The night club they visit is extravagantly cosmopolitan; American-style décor, the signs

are in English, even German beer is not available! Hans grows
steadily more annoyed. When a Negro jazz band plays havoc
with the martial rhythms of *Die Wacht am Rhein* he loses
control and leaves declaring: 'This is no longer Germany!' A
sequence of First World War trench warfare scenes introduces
Hans and a fellow SA man communing together in a war cem-
etery. They reflect on the millions who died fighting for the
Fatherland and deplore the decadence of those whom Hans
has just left, jitter-bugging on the dance floor in the night club.

The following evening Hans attends a Communist meeting.
The speaker, a Jew called Kupferstein who is also a Communist member of the Reichstag, mocks the existing government
and denounces the capitalists who grow fat on the toil of the
workers. The Nazis are mere hooligans, an unimportant minority led by a ridiculous Don Quixote (Hitler) in the pay of
the industrialists. The streets belong to the Communists and
those who challenge them will be swept aside. He ends with
a rousing 'Long live the Fatherland of the worker. Long live
Soviet Russia.'

Hans is invited to reply to this but is not allowed to speak
freely, especially as his appeal to nationalism seems a potent
one. A riot breaks out and later one of Hans's friends is murdered by the Communists as he makes his way home from the
meeting. When the party chiefs meet to discuss the night's
work, Ross is clearly upset by this incident, but is told in no
uncertain terms to leave such worries to Moscow: 'The death
will be a warning for the brown mice!'

Some time later Hans rescues a girl. He learns that her name
is Agnes and that her drunken father (a Communist, of course)
beats her. Gallantly he gives her money and advises her to go
away for a time. This exchange is watched with interest by
Ross who warns Hans to leave the district in which he is recruiting. Ross tells him that he will never become one of the
people. However, this only inspires him to give up his studies
to become one of the workers, and he eventually secures a job
as a taxi-driver. His mother is unhappy about this but her son
quotes *Mein Kampf*: 'He who will become great must serve.'

Hans is now living in east Berlin, the stronghold of the
Communists. He is so successful that the Communists become
worried by the number of recruits he is winning. Agnes is

ordered to spy on him and both Ross and the Commune leader try to warn him off again. Hans, who is now a labourer, is eventually warned by Agnes that the Communists are determined to kill him. Hans takes her under his protection. The election campaign proper then begins. Hans addresses his fellow workers at a rally and urges them to fight for Hitler and Goebbels. During the campaign he escapes being killed by the Communists only through the direct intervention of Ross. When the election results are announced they show considerable reductions in the Communist majorities. As a direct result of his exertions Hans is taken ill and is nursed by the faithful Agnes, who, learning of another plot to kill him, persuades him to return to his mother's home. Because of this threat to his life his mother and his comrades persuade him to finish his studies at Greiswald. However, when he returns to his lodgings to collect his clothes he sees his SA Troop in the street and realizes that it is impossible for him to return to university: 'They believe in me. I can't leave them now.' But the Communists have been told of his return and they shoot him down whilst he is addressing a workers' rally.

The film cuts directly to the funeral procession, which, in its neo-documentary form and mass scenes, incorporates aspects of Nazi pageantry which were later to be exploited in *Triumph des Willens* (1935). The funeral oration casts Hans as a martyr and demands that the job he started be finished, and this blends into a triumphant vision of the future.

Hans Westmar is a classic portrayal of the archetypal NSDAP hero. The film's main concern was twofold: to record the heroic exploits of a Nazi martyr and the doctrinal themes that his life and death enshrined, and, more importantly, to win and maintain the allegiance of the working class. The support of the working classes was absolutely vital to fulfil the rearmament campaign that was to become the prime objective of German economic life and which had already begun in 1933.[54] However although the NSDAP claimed to be a socialist party, before 1930 it had failed to make the same advances among the working classes as it had achieved with the middle classes.

---

[54] This subsidized recovery began in the form of armament credits with the issue by the Reichsbank of the so-called *Mefo* bills to large plants like Siemens and Krupp. See D. Schoenbaum, *Hitler's Social Revolution* (London, 1967), p. 122.

Apart from their importance in relation to the armaments industries the workers were the largest class and politically the most dangerous breeding-ground of anti-authoritarianism in Germany. Significantly, the Nazi hierarchy banned the formation of NSDAP trade unions in 1928, a move that attracted the big industrialists but did little to endear the Party in the eyes of the workers. However when the economic slump of the early 1930s remained unabated, the out-of-work masses provided a fertile recruiting ground for the Nazis. By 1930 a third of the labour force were unemployed and the average weekly earnings of the rest had fallen by 33 per cent.[55] In effect the workers were ultimately willing to sacrifice collective bargaining for the right to work. The seduction of the worker was completed in 1933 when full employment was declared the foremost goal of National Socialist economic policy.[56]

On coming to power, one of the first tasks confronting the Party was the creation of national solidarity behind the new government. It was deemed essential to secure the co-operation, or at least the acquiescence of the working class, which had been alarmingly under-represented in the Party's ranks. The problem confronting Goebbels in his attempt to secure this solidarity was that certain groups such as the SA and the HJ saw themselves as something special, as 'Supermen' (*Übermenschen*). Not surprisingly the workers were mistrustful. Moreover, such élitism contradicted both the professed social egalitarianism and the anti-intellectualism of the Party. Thus when Hitler seized power the whole image of the worker changed in accordance with the Nazi ethos. Together with the farmers they were referred to as 'the pillars of our *Volkstum*'. Nazi propaganda was to paint an idealized image of 'the worker' in order to achieve the assimilation of the worker into the life of the nation. In pursuit of this Hitler himself took the lead. The following question and answer was part of an ideological catechism: 'What professions has Adolf Hitler had?' 'Adolf Hitler was a construction worker, an artist and a student.'[57]

[55] Cf. W. Schäfer, *Die NSDAP: Entwicklung und Struktur der Staatspartei des dritten Reiches* (Frankfurt, 1957), p. 17. See also T. Childers, 'The Social Bases of the National Socialist Vote', in *JCH*, 1976, no. 11, pp. 17–24.

[56] *VB*, 27 July 1933, quoted in Schoenbaum, p. 123.

[57] A. Röpke, *Was musst du wissen vom Dritten Reich?* (Berlin, 1935), quoted in Schoenbaum, p. 62.

It can be seen from the detailed plot summary of *Hans Westmar* that the protagonist in the film corresponds to Hitler in a remarkable way. Westmar embodies those attributes that Hitler had prized and given expression to in *Mein Kampf*. Young Hans renounces his study to lead the humble life of a worker determined to unite a class-ridden Germany. In order to give political meaning to his life it is necessary for such gifted leaders to cast all temptation aside. Westmar sacrifices close links with his mother and renounces all sexual involvement with the two women in his life, Maud (daughter of the expatriate German business man) and Agnes, the ex-Communist who falls in love with him. This renunciation of sex is particularly striking in all three of these early 'Party' films. Throughout the history of the Third Reich the cinema portrayed the Nazi martyr as a blond, blue-eyed Aryan imbued with genius and beyond criticism. In the early films, Brand, Quex, and Westmar all dedicate their lives to the Party, and by implication the nation as a whole. Given the premiss that all Nazi martyrs were flawless and totally committed to National Socialism, they had to be seen to be above emotional and physical desires. Thus the NSDAP's successes in the elections of 1933 are seen in each of these films as the triumph of the individual will, of the sublimation of sexual desires for the purity of the heroic mission.

However, of the three, it is Westmar who corresponds more closely to Hitler and the concept of the 'leadership principle' (*Führerprinzip*). In particular, he represents the young Führer in his formative years fired with ambition and determined to gain power for the Nazis. The parallels with Hitler are not drawn with the benefit of hindsight, they were clearly formulated in the programme notes distributed with the film:

Hans Westmar is shown at the beginning of the film in his happy student days in jolly Vienna. He joins the SA, builds his little troop into a mighty assault troop and subsequently incurs the wild hatred of the Communists. He sees his way more clearly: to completely win over the workers he himself must become one of them. He exchanges cap and sword for the shovel and spade. He casts all temptation for the privileged life to the wind and ignores the warnings of hatred from the Reds: he stays resolutely by his troop, true to his Führer, Adolf Hitler. The Red killers shoot him dead, but over his grave workers and students come together. Thus Hans Westmar becomes one of the symbols of the national awakening.[58]

[58] *IFK*, 16 December 1933.

Hans Westmar's death unites students and workers in a sort of ideological marriage of convenience between National Socialism and Marxism. The film is also instructive for the way the Nazis rationalized the Communist allegiance of a large number of German workers before 1933, and possibly later. All those workers who had succumbed to Bolshevism were simply dismissed as the victims of an alien Jewish conspiracy that had permeated German political and social life. In a speech on 10 September 1936, Goebbels made explicit reference to this:

What we understand by the ideals has nothing to do with what is usually referred to as 'Bolshevism'. This is merely a pathological, criminal nonsense, thought up by Jews. Under the Jewish leadership it aims at the destruction of civilized European nations and the creation of an international Jewish world domination.[59]

However, at the other end of the scale, and more obviously the antithesis of the Westmar figure, is the leader of the Karl-Liebknecht House in Berlin, played by Paul Wegener.[60] He is the typical Nazi caricature of the Communist adversary, designed to look and act like Lenin, and this remarkable physical similarity could not have gone unnoticed. Because of his impassive countenance he was referred to in the film press as the 'Asian Commune Golem'.[61] He is seen to be nothing more than a serf who takes his orders from Moscow: when the Party's finances are discovered to be low, he contemptuously dismisses alarm: 'Don't worry, Moscow is aware of its duty towards us!' He is the cold-blooded agitator (once again, a Nazi portrait), whose task it is to exploit poverty and misery, shown in the film to be important conditions for the growth of Communism.

Set against this stereotype image of the enemy is Ross, the naïve young idealist. He is horrified by such conditions and becomes progressively disenchanted with his Party's terrorist activities. When Westmar starts to recruit in the Communist stronghold of east Berlin Ross tells him that he will never

---

[59] *VB*, 11 September 1936.

[60] Paul Wegener (1874–1948) was one of Germany's greatest actors. He starred in both the Weimar and Nazi cinema. His earlier roles included *Der Student von Prag* (1913) and *Der Golem* (1914). During the Nazi era he was made *Staatsschauspieler* (State Actor) and took part in a number of propaganda films, notably *Mein Leben für Irland* (My Life for Ireland, 1941), *Der grosse König* (The Great King, 1942), and *Kolberg* (1945).

[61] *Der Film*, 16 December 1933. This was in memory of his great performance in *Der Golem* (1914).

become one of the people because 'only a proletarian can understand the proletariat'. However in the final scenes of the film when the Nazis march down the Unter den Linden, a small group of Communists, including Ross, watch this impressively large and disciplined exhibition of strength and solidarity. As the Nazis pass by, the young Communists defiantly raise their clenched fists. But the power and magic of National Socialism is already casting its spell over Ross. His clenched fist slowly, almost involuntarily, unfolds and he lowers his arm only to raise it again in the form of a Nazi salute. It is significant that the mass demonstration should have such a profound effect on Ross for it illustrates one of the principles that Hitler enunciated in *Mein Kampf* and which is given prominent expression in all three films of this genre:

What we needed then and need now is not one or two hundred daredevil conspirators but a hundred thousand devoted champions of our *Weltanschauung*. The work must not be done through secret conventicles but through formidable mass demonstrations in public. Dagger and pistol and poison-vial cannot clear the way for the progress of the movement. That can be done only by winning over the man in the street. We must overthrow Marxism, so that for the future National Socialism will be master of the street . . .[62]

There is an inevitability about Ross's conversion to National Socialism, for it symbolizes in quasi-religious terms the firmly-held belief that all 'true' Germans would eventually come together, united as it were by a unique yet inexplicable feeling of what it is like to feel and be German. Therefore by showing Ross to be a different kind of Communist from the stereotype, the audience is being psychologically moved into accepting, indeed rejoicing in his eventual conversion. The importance of this in terms of propaganda is that, on Westmar's death, the film demands that the job he started be finished. Thus Ross's brand of commitment and idealism is seen as the natural substitute for Westmar. If audiences could be manipulated into accepting a young idealist's transition from Marxism to National Socialism, then a similar rationality could be invoked to explain away the allegiance of all those workers who had supported the KPD prior to 1934.

There were other important factors here. The presentation

[62] Hitler, pp. 445-6.

of various Jewish types, for example, enabled Wenzler to excuse workers who aligned themselves to the Communist cause as victims of a Jewish conspiracy. This theme was taken up in the film press. An instruction booklet distributed to schools before the showing of *Hans Westmar* made it perfectly clear that the Bolsheviks shown in the film were 'supported by Jews spewing forth hatred; Jewish intellectuals seducing credulous workers; and Jews who were nothing more than murderous rabble, criminals, and receivers of stolen goods.'[63]

It is the Jews who were responsible for fragmenting German society by creating a rift between workers and government.[64] In this way the film avoided any imputation that workers were, and possibly still are, Communist sympathizers. By 'delivering themselves defenceless to the Jews',[65] the workers had been 'duped'. In reviewing the film, the film magazine *Der Film* concentrated on this conciliatory aspect:

> The German worker is not bad, he has been manipulated by foreign elements (Jews) and even so-called 'Germans' who have tried to force the people into a foreign *Weltanschauung*. However the worker has rediscovered his Germanness, and it is a fool who does not pardon him today. But there shall be no pardons for the intellectuals who have tried to bring about the downfall of the Third Reich.[66]

The Jews are branded as aliens, but possessing an ability to assimilate and permeate all strata of German social and political life. Kupferstein, the KPD member of the Reichstag, fits into this latter category.[67] According to Dorothea Hollstein, 'he is a Jew who speaks with a nasal Saxon accent, with a bent nose and grey frizzy hair and glinting spectacles.'[68] Addressing a large Communist meeting attended by Westmar's stormtroopers, Kupferstein attacks 'everything that is not Bolshevik and drags anger and hatred into the meeting'.[69] He mocks the existing government, denounces the capitalists who grow fat

[63] Walther Günther, *Hans Westmar. Einer von vielen. Staatspolitische Filme* (Munich, 1933), vol. 12, p. 3.
[64] Cf. Hitler, p. 459.
[65] Hitler, p. 437.
[66] *Der Film*, 16 December 1933.
[67] An example of the former would be the Jewish professor who lectures on the virtues of pacificism and international status quo.
[68] D. Hollstein, *Antisemitische Filmpropaganda. Die Darstellung des Juden in nationalsozialistischen Spielfilme* (Munich, 1971), p. 34.
[69] Günther, p. 4.

on the toil of the workers, and refers to the SA as 'that miserable pack of brownshirts financed by heavy industry'. Gesticulating wildly, he calls Hitler an 'operetta tenor' and a 'misguided Don Quixote'. As the inevitable riot breaks out between the two factions, Kupferstein crawls under the speaker's table until the police arrive. After order is restored he creeps out from under the dais and grandly introduces himself as 'Kupferstein, member of the Reichstag', and is allowed to leave unmolested.

In this way Kupferstein corresponds to the cowardly parliamentarian so despised by Hitler. The Jews became the embodiment of every ill besetting state and society in the final stage of the Weimar Republic. Intellectually, anti-Semitism was a reaction against modernity which early *Völkisch* writers such as Julius Langbehn and Paul de Lagarde had opposed. Together with other extraneous notions such as parliamentarism, rationalism, and enlightened self-interest, anti-Semitism was seen as a corrupting influence. The cowardly Jewish parliamentarian was to appear again in later Nazi films: most notably, *Bismarck* (1940), *Carl Peters* (1941), and *Die Entlassung* (1942).

Of course, the Jews were not selected indiscriminately but because they represented a traditional and culturally acceptable scapegoat in Central and Eastern Europe generally.[70] However, by identifying the Jews with Bolshevism in these films, two targets of Nazi aversion were attacked simultaneously. In doing so the film-makers hoped to justify the ever increasing anti-Semitic measures of the regime in the eyes of many Germans not previously anti-Semitic, and also to influence international opinion, which did not share the same hatred of the Jews but was frightened by the spread of Bolshevism.

Nazi propagandists were always conscious of how they were presented in foreign capitals. But they appeared to be particularly concerned with the reaction to *Hans Westmar*. The Party propagandists believed that National Socialism had been misinterpreted. *Filmwoche*'s review of the film is typical of this reaction:

Even foreign countries are beginning to understand us. When this happens they will stop listening to the venom of our opponents, which drips from

[70] Cf. G. Mosse, *Germans and Jews* (London, 1971), p. 24.

the godless lips of 'refugees', whose deceit caused those infernal street battles. Even now their deceit causes them to act as political subversives.[71]

These sentiments were echoed even more forcefully in the *Berliner Lokal-Anzeiger* on 14 December 1933:

At a time when rootless men without a country [that is, Jews] are spreading lies about the new Germany in foreign countries . . . it has become essential that a German film should demonstrate what it is to conquer Germany, what it is to be a Nazi, and what it is to be martyred, hounded, and yet in spite of everything to fight on to an ultimate victory.[72]

Certainly if the reviews are any guide, *Hans Westmar*, even in its abridged form, was an unqualified success. The critic of the *Film-Kurier* summed up the general attitude of the film press when he wrote:

This film has that ability to absorb the individual into the action, totally. The public were so gripped and moved that I saw them stand up to watch the final overwhelming scenes in which the Horst Wessel Lied rang out. This indeed is the most effective success a film can have.[73]

Goebbels of course vehemently disagreed with these sentiments but he had yet to convince everyone that he had the affairs of the film industry under control. In attempting to prevent the film from being distributed he appears to have seriously misjudged the strength of feeling within the Party. In all probability this was due to the fact that the film section of the NSDAP had put up the money for the production and quite naturally wanted some return. Moreover, the SA and the Party hierarchy appeared to be vindicated when on its second submission to the *Prüfstelle*, *Hans Westmar* was awarded the *Prädikat* 'politically and artistically especially valuable'.

However, their success was to be short-lived. The tensions between the Party hierarchy and Goebbels's Ministry over who was to control the film industry were soon to be resolved. The uproar caused by *Hans Westmar* had apparently convinced Hitler that Goebbels should run the industry without interference. Also, of course, Hitler's own relations with the SA were beginning to cool and rousing dramas about the myths of such an organization were no longer to be encouraged. Thus *Hans Westmar* was the last feature film which openly

[71] *Filmwoche*, No. 349, 15 December 1933.
[72] *Berliner Lokal-Anzeiger*, 14 December 1933.
[73] *Filmwoche*, 20 December 1933.

glorified the Party and one of its most cherished organizations, the SA.

An analysis of the early propaganda films, *SA-Mann Brand*, *Hitlerjunge Quex*, and *Hans Westmar*, reveals the recurrence of a number of common themes: the heroic death, the mystical significance of Nazi symbols such as the uniform and flag, the destruction of family life for male comradeship within the Party, and the idealization of the Aryan stereotype. However, this 'Party film' genre of paying tribute to the archetypal Party member was never to be repeated again. The reasons are enlightening not only for what they reveal about the films themselves but also for an understanding of the complex nature of the German film industry at this time.

It was during this period that the National Socialist movement was faced with the problems involved in the metamorphosis from opposition to establishment. To a certain extent these three films reflect the transition period. They represent the struggle for the German soul between National Socialism and Communism and they rejoice in the triumph of the national will. The total effect of propaganda at this stage was to create an anti-Communist psychosis inside Germany and to attempt to gain support for Hitler abroad. The Nazis were fully aware of the potential sources of their strength. In 1933 the German middle classes feared Bolshevism, economic ruin, and anarchy just as they had feared them in 1918. But within a year of taking office Hitler was confident enough to declare that he had achieved stability and maintained public order:

The nervous nineteenth century has reached its end. There will not be another revolution in Germany for the next 1,000 years.[74]

In order to achieve these ends the NSDAP needed to construct a programme of rapprochement with representatives of the old order, the civil service, army, and big business. The transition from opposition to power went hand in hand with a change in both the organization and aims of the Nazi propaganda machine. In terms of film this meant that the type of agitational productions analysed in this chapter were no longer

[74] Adolf Hitler speaking at the 'Party Day of Unity', 1934 (Nuremberg Rally).

desirable. Germany was now to be portrayed as a united and classless society and as such the opening of old wounds could only be divisive. The cleansing of extraneous factors in Germany meant that from now on the enemy would have to be shown as a threat from without, not from within. Nazi film propaganda did change after 1933-4, but not for the reasons that writers on this subject have imagined. It was not simply a question that the early films were 'unsuccessful'; within their terms of reference, that is, Hitler's dictums on propaganda, they achieved the desired effects. They had an agitational aggressiveness about them and they carried no pretensions towards art; they were simply a political statement of faith in the new regime. What they did represent, however, was a challenge to Goebbels's authority in the *Filmwelt* and his ability to stamp his own signature on all future productions. The change was dictated as much by circumstances as by Goebbels's own bid for power and his desire to control the film industry. There is no evidence to suggest that films in this genre were not commercially successful or that they had been stopped for this reason. To appreciate fully the shift in emphasis during this period we must briefly look at the conflict in the NSDAP concerning the role of film propaganda and the nature of the film industry in general.

Any analysis of these films must be seen within the context of the film industry at the time of the Nazis' seizure of power. We have already seen that the film industry was in a state of turmoil at this stage. It was not helped by conflicting statements on the future plans for the film industry given by various Party spokesmen and the fact that in the spring of 1933 Goebbels banned a prestigious new film, *Das Testament des Doktor Mabuse* (*The Testament of Dr Mabuse*), directed by Fritz Lang, whom Goebbels had praised for his work on *Die Nibelungen* (1924). Early in April the Berlin correspondent for the *New York Times* reported that work had virtually ceased in all studios pending the passage of expected film legislation.[75] This was to result in a drastic cutback in domestic film production. The annual report of the industry showed that from June 1933 to June 1934, 114 German films and

---

[75] *New York Times*, 8 June 1933, quoted in D. S. Hull, *Film in the Third Reich* (Berkeley and Los Angeles, 1969), p. 20.

92 foreign films had been shown compared to figures for the previous year of 133 and 72 respectively.[76]

The genuine uncertainty felt by producers and the depressed business confidence can be found in the records of the *Ufa Vorstand*, which reveal that members of Ufa were extremely concerned about its future viability. They were even doubtful whether their 1933-4 production programme would be approved by the RMVP, and decided to suspend the whole programme until the government advised them on the suitability (or otherwise) of these projects. However, their fears were to prove unfounded when the RMVP subsequently approved almost all of the films.[77] Goebbels appeared to be aware of this state of confusion and the damage it was inflicting on the industry because in June he issued a statement repudiating as 'absurd' the notion that his Ministry wanted only overt political propaganda films and warned certain Party organizations against interfering in film affairs.[78]

There can be little doubt that this state of uncertainty sprang from two different concepts about the role of film propaganda that existed within the Party itself. The films I have been discussing can be seen as the industry's response to this dispute. On the one hand there was the Hitlerite view which saw film as a useful weapon for depicting NSDAP organizations. It is clear that Goebbels had a different concept of propaganda and that his *Filmpolitik* was based on this alternative notion. Apart from any conceptual argument there was an important financial consideration involved. In the heyday of the German silent film, 40 per cent of the industry's revenue had come from sales abroad. Even in 1932, 30 per cent of its total sales were derived from exports, but this was to decline alarmingly in subsequent years.[79]

The decline really began to take effect in the year 1934-5, when exports accounted for only 11 per cent of total income. But from the reports being sent to Goebbels soon after taking office he would have had little indication of such a catastrophic collapse.[80] Indeed the reports suggested that exports would

[76] *Jahrbuch der Reichsfilmkammer* (Berlin, 1939), p. 199.
[77] BA, *R1091/1029a, No. 907*, 5 April 1933.
[78] *VB*, 9 June 1933.
[79] BA. *Akten des Reichsfinanzministeriums (R2), 4799*. Denkschrift über die Sonderrücklagen in der Filmwirtschaft.

soon pick up. It was important then to have some sort of exportable product but there was plainly a limited international market for films which incorporated so much of the *Bündisch* ethos as *SA-Mann Brand*, *Hitlerjunge Quex*, and *Hans Westmar*.

However, although Goebbels wanted German films to be exported abroad, he was more concerned, at this stage, to control the type of film seen by German audiences at home. Although he encountered little opposition from the film industry itself he was still conscious of rival groups in the Party who were attempting to launch an indigenous form of 'people's cinema'. It must also be remembered that behind this Party conflict a new Cinema Law, which gave Goebbels monopolistic powers, was being drafted. But before this legal endorsement was granted Goebbels decided to demonstrate the necessity of such authority by provoking a confrontation with those groups that he considered to be interfering unnecessarily in his domain.

He repeatedly warned about the undesirability of films that attempted to extol the virtues of the NSDAP through badly made, highly melodramatic images. As late as February 1934 he informed film-makers:

If I see a film made with artistic conviction then I will reward its maker. What I do not want to see are films that begin and end with National Socialist parades. Leave them to us, we understand them.[81]

Goebbels was undoubtedly referring to the *Film Hauptamt* (Film Section) of the NSDAP which had little to do with the commercial film industry, but was part of the RMVP and therefore came under the Ministry's jurisdiction. It mainly produced short political documentaries for Party meetings and organized film shows in areas where there were no cinemas. Another reason why he disliked such films was that if a scenario did concern an NSDAP organization then quite naturally the NSDAP demanded some sort of voice in the eventual production. Goebbels found this totally unacceptable; he wanted complete control over every stage of production and would not tolerate interference or criticism. This obsession was to remain with him throughout the Third Reich and there is an

[81] *VB*, 9 February 1934.

amusing and revealing account of this by Hitler's photographer, Heinrich Hoffmann:

Initially, Goebbels used to arrange for a pre-view of new films at Obersalzberg, before they were generally released. On such occasions, of course, the production would be regarded with a particularly critical eye. Eva Braun would express displeasure at some scene or person in the film, Bormann or one of the others would take exception to something else and so on: and the upshot of it all would be that Hitler would order cuts and alterations, quite oblivious of the trouble and expense involved.

Goebbels was furious and quickly stopped sending any more new films. When I told him that I was 'fed up to the teeth with seeing the same old films again and again,' he retorted: 'And I, my friend, am not in the least interested to hear critiques of my films from some stupid little flapper' – Eva Braun – 'or from a glorified butler!' – Bormann.[82]

In the end Goebbels's repeated warnings and the *Hans Westmar* affair finally put a stop to feature films about the SA. It may well have been that the German cinema-going public had already built up a resistance to such films. It is doubtful whether Goebbels really believed this but he was convinced that they contained too distinct a division between propaganda and entertainment. Despite opposition from within the Party Hitler at least appears to have been won over by these arguments. Certainly when the new Reich's Cinema Law was submitted to Hitler for his approval he passed it without major alteration. In so doing he was confirming the Propaganda Ministry's monopoly of control over the industry and Goebbels's right to run it without interference. In May 1933, Goebbels informed German film-makers: 'Let it be my concern alone that the German film should be given a respectable face.'[83]

It was not absolutely clear what he meant by a 'respectable face' but his audience could have been left in little doubt that from now on Goebbels would assume overall responsibility for German films in pursuit of his expressed desire to revolutionize the German cinema. In his speech in February 1934 he declared that the German film had the mission of conquering the world as the vanguard of the Nazi troops. He asked the

---

[82] H. Hoffmann, *Hitler Was My Friend* (London, 1955), p. 191.
[83] *VB*, 20 May 1933. See also *VB*, 20 May 1933 for an extremely detailed speech by Goebbels on his *Filmpolitik*.

studios to 'capture the spirit of the new Germany' by making the nation conscious of its *Völkisch* identity'. Only when this was achieved, he announced, 'would immortal Germany march once more over the cinema screens of the world'.[84]

[84] *VB*, 9 February 1934.

IV

BLOOD AND SOIL
(BLUT UND BODEN)

Our Party above all, by the success of its propaganda, has
shown the force of the folk idea.
Adolf Hitler (*Mein Kampf*)

WITHIN two years of taking office, Goebbels had succeeded
in excluding his rivals, thus preventing them from interfering
in film politics, and through a series of restrictive legislative
measures had secured a position of unchallenged omnipotence.
In 1935 he attended the International Film Congress organized
by Germany and held in Berlin. Addressing delegates from over
forty nations he gave some indication of how he saw the future
development of the German film industry. The speech is worth
quoting at some length for it reveals Goebbels's obsession
that German films should 'capture the spirit of the age', a task
that film-makers were to find increasingly difficult to fulfil:

The film must free itself from the vulgar mediocrity of a mob amuse-
ment, but in so doing must not lose its strong inner conviction with the
people. . . . This does not mean that it is the function of the film to serve
the purposes of a colourless aestheticism. On the contrary, it is precisely
because of its far-reaching range that it, more than all other art forms,
must be popular art in the best sense of the word. But popular art must
present in artistic form the joys and sorrows of the masses.

There is no art that is self-supporting: material sacrifices made in the
services of art bring a return in ideal values. For every government it is
a matter of course to finance great state buildings . . . theatres . . . art
galleries. . . . It must be the same with film . . . unless we are to give up
the idea of treating the film as art.

The film must, however, keep in touch with the spirit of the age in
order to have some relevance to that age. . . . If these fundamental principles are observed, the film will conquer the world as a new artisitic
manifestation. It will then be the strongest pioneer and the most modern
spokesman of our age.[1]

[1] *Film-Kurier*, 28 April 1935.

Goebbels constantly demanded that films should reflect contemporary society, but the difficulty confronting film-makers was that the Third Reich was founded on so many contradictions. How, for example, were artists to respond to a 'reality' shaped by a confusing mixture of provincial conservatism and Fascist radicalism? The answer would come from Goebbels. In striving to 'capture the spirit of the age' as he saw it, Goebbels had always to consider the tactical problem of timing his propaganda most effectively. This was a particular obstacle with film propaganda because the period from inception to final distribution might be anything up to a year. However Goebbels believed that the problem could be overcome if the propagandist possessed a degree of flexibility and agility. In his diary he stated that the propagandist must always possess the faculty of 'calculating psychological effects in advance'.[2] It follows then that if propaganda is to be successful, a theme must begin at the optimum moment but must not be repeated beyond the point at which its effectiveness begins to diminish. A case in point was the series of films evoking the *Kampfzeit* legends: once they had outgrown their usefulness, they were never repeated.

Public opinion as we understand it cannot exist in a totalitarian police state; its place is taken by an official image of the world expressed through the media of mass communications. The total impact of Nazi propaganda was to create a picture of reality shaped according to the underlying themes of the movement. Because of the inherent contradictions and the amorphous nature of National Socialist ideology these themes would change from one year to another according to the aims of the Party hierarchy. Before exploring the theme of *Blut und Boden* (Blood and Soil), the central purpose of this chapter, it is worth looking at the role feature films played under the new regime. They would not have been seen in isolation from the media; from Goebbels's point of view they were intended to supplement and reinforce each other. Moreover, because of the time-lag and the costs involved, feature films often proved an unsuitable vehicle for topical propaganda, although this was offset by the effectiveness of short documentaries and newsreels which became compulsive viewing during the early

[2] IfZ, *Goebbels Tagebuch*, entry for 11 October 1942.

part of the war. Thus, feature films often took the form of rationalizing some political, economic, or social action that had taken place, or, alternatively, of outlining the official Party view on some contemporary issue. In accordance with Hitler's dictum of orientating the masses towards specific topics, a number of *Staatsauftragsfilme* (films commissioned by the State) appeared which attempted, together with the press and radio, to dramatize particular aspects of the National Socialist programme that were deemed important. Such productions would include: *Das alte Recht* (*The Old Right*, 1934), a justification of the State Heredity Farm Law (*Reichserbhofgesetz*, 1933); *Sensationsprozess Casilla* (*The Sensational Trial of Casilla*, 1939), an anti-American film designed to ridicule the American way of life and, in so doing, discredit America's tacit support of the British war effort; *Wetterleuchten- um Barbara* (*Summer Lightning About Barbara*, 1941), a vindication of the *Anschluss*; and *Ich klage an* (*I Accuse*, 1941), an exposition of the Nazis' euthanasia campaign.

In attempting to encapsulate various aspects of contemporary German society, the films mentioned above (and there were many more dealing with other issues) were 'one-off' productions which played an essentially subordinate role to alternative, more suitable media. However there were a number of key themes that were to recur in Nazi propaganda for which the medium of film was to provide an excellent means of dissemination to the masses. Two such themes, which I have combined in this section, were *Blut und Boden* (Blood and Soil) and *Volk und Heimat* (a People and the Homeland). David Schoenbaum has noted that for the committed National Socialist, '*Blut und Boden*, the East German homestead, the superior virtue of rural life, were ends in themselves and approximations—if not realisation—of a state of nature. They appealed like little else to a certain kind of Nazi imagination, and like little else they were maintained from the beginning of the Third Reich to the end.'[3]

Thus the concept of 'a people and a homeland' sprang directly from the doctrine of *Blut und Boden* which attempted

[3] D. Schoenbaum, *Hitler's Social Revolution* (London, 1967), p. 161. See also J. E. Farquharson, *The Plough and the Swastika. The NSDAP and Agriculture in Germany 1928–1945* (London, 1976).

to define the source of strength of the *Herrenvolk* (Master Race) in terms of peasant virtues, the Nordic past, the warrior hero, and the sacredness of the German soil, the last of which could not be confined by artificial boundaries imposed arbitrarily by a treaty such as Versailles. The reason for this is clear: the so-called ideology of the Nazi revolution was based upon what were presumed to be Germanic traditions; while the revolution looked to the future, it tried to recapture a mythical past and with it old traditions which to many people provided the only hope of overcoming the chaos of the present. Therefore, the type of nationalism espoused by the National Socialist was an attempt to recapture a morality attributed to the Volk's past. It was the purpose of Nazi *Kultur* to give this morality form and substance in a manner acceptable to the Party hierarchy. In this respect film was considered to be an excellent medium for portraying traditional German virtues and beauty, not only because of the size of the audience but also because it dealt in visual images, the most powerful and persuasive of all illustrations. John Grierson, no doubt influenced by the use made of film in Nazi Germany, wrote that the propagandist had good reasons to be interested in film as it has:

. . . generous access to the public. It is capable of direct description, simple analysis and commanding conclusion, and may by its imagistic powers, be made easily persuasive. It lends itself to rhetoric, for no form of description can add nobility to a simple observation so readily as a camera set low, or a sequence cut to timebeat. But principally there is the thought that a single say-so can be repeated a thousand times a night to a million eyes, and over the years — if it is good enough to live, to millions of eyes. The seven-leagued fact opens a new perspective, a new hope to public persuasion.[4]

Goebbels, of course, was fully aware of these possibilities. On 9 February 1934 he addressed members of the *Reichsfilmkammer* and told them that he was convinced that 'film is one of the most modern and far-reaching ways of influencing the masses today.'[5] It never occurred to Goebbels, who was arguably among the least *Völkisch* and the most 'modern-minded' of all the Nazi leaders, that there might be a contradiction between the type of message he was disseminating (expressing an essentially anti-modern, romanticized belief in age-old

[4] Quoted in H. Hardy (ed.), *Grierson on Documentary* (London, 1946).
[5] Kalbus, p. 101.

habits and customs) and the manner in which it was conveyed (by means of the most popular art form of the first half of the twentieth century).

However, before such films could be produced, the film industry, like all other aspects of German life, had to be 'cleansed' by a process of *Entjudung* (removal of Jews). This was not a new phenomenon: conservatives, opposed to modernism in all its forms, had always objected to what they believed to be the Jewish domination of the industry in Germany. As early as November 1925, Alfred Rosenberg, later to become the Nazis' 'official philosopher' on cultural affairs, wrote:

Today a cinema industry has been spawned from the movie art and overwhelmingly this industry is found to be in the hands of Jews. For this reason, the film has become a means of infecting the Volk — through lascivious images and, just as clearly as in the Jewish press, there are revealed here plans for the glorification of crime.[6]

The reorganization of the film industry has already been discussed and it is clear that, despite the uncertainties of the first months of 1933, the *Gleichschaltung* period was a convenient device for eliminating Jews and other political undesirables from working in German political and cultural life. Inexorably caught up in this 'co-ordination', the film companies proved no exception to the rule. Discussing this after the war, Dr Ludwig Klitzsch (managing director of Ufa) claimed that Ufa alone was able to withstand these pressures and was consequently victimized by Goebbels for its retention of Jewish artists:

It gradually became obvious that the Propaganda Minister was trying to annihilate Ufa under the pretext of 'ideological unreliability'. Furthermore, the press were instructed to be extremely critical of Ufa films. Ufa management were accused of being pro-Jewish because they employed Jewish artists and officials and refused to dismiss them.[7]

However, Klitzsch's later arguments are mere rationalizations based on wishful thinking rather than actual events that transpired. In the first instance there is no evidence to suggest that the press were more critical of Ufa films: indeed, given the fact that all art criticism was prohibited in 1936 and reviewers were only permitted to 'describe' films, it would have been

---

[6] *Weltkampf*, November 1925, quoted in R. Pois, *A. Rosenberg: Selected Writings* (London, 1970), p. 173.

[7] BA, *Hugenberg-Nachlass*, Dr Ludwig Klitzsch, Bockholm, 17 June 1949. At the time of writing this folder was still being classified by the Bundesarchiv.

extremely difficult for a writer to criticize any German film that had been passed by the RMVP. Klitzsch's other point that Ufa alone retained Jewish artists is contradicted by the records of the *Ufa Vorstandsprotokolle*. For example, as early as 29 March 1933, the Ufa *Vorstand* recommended:

Where possible Jewish people's contracts should be dissolved. Each member of the Committee must decide which colleagues and employees in his section can be dismissed immediately and which ones must be slowly deprived of their office. Difficult cases should be carried through with some delicacy. Payment of wages after successful dismissals are to be discussed with Klitzsch.[8]

It is clear from the heading of these minutes that Ufa was prepared to dismiss not only Jews but all those who collaborated with them. Klitzsch would later publicly praise those nationalists in the film industry who had steadfastly opposed the 'Jewish monopoly' during the Weimar Republic.[9]

Throughout the 1935-6 film season the German cinemagoing public were encouraged by campaigns in the press not to tolerate non-Aryan actors and to demand that all film stars furnish evidence of their racial origins. In conjunction with this the Bureau for the Promotion of Art (*Amt für Kunstpflege*) was established and became the focus of attention for this type of enquiry. It was essentially a Party organization and worked in close collaboration with the *Filmkontingentstelle* which was under the supervision of the RMVP. The Bureau concerned itself with the personal affairs of actors, directors, producers, playwrights, and publishers and the like. Not content with investigating such people's racial origins, they were also concerned with their 'attitudes' and the company they kept. A few examples from material deposited in the Bundesarchiv will hopefully give some indication of this three-way process: in a letter from the Bureau dated 12 March 1935 to the *Filmkontingentstelle*, they requested the following information:

Our readers have been enquiring about the racial origins of the actors Friedrich Benfer, Paul Kemp, Hilde Hilderbrand, Jenny Hugo. And also whether Hans Albers is married to the Jew Hansi Burg.[10]

[8] BA, *R1091/1029a, No. 905*, 29 March 1933.
[9] Lochner, pp. 206-7. Klitzsch was awarded the Goethe Medal by Goebbels for his services to the Nazi regime.
[10] BA, *NS (Reichspropagandaleitung der NSDAP/Filmkontingentstelle), No. 138b, Amt für Kunstpflege* to *Filmkontingentstelle,* 12 March 1935.

Just over two weeks later, Auen, chief of the *Filmkontingent-stelle*, informed the Bureau:

In reply to your questions, we have discovered that Benfer, Hilderbrand and Hugo are from sound racial origins. We are still investigating Kemp. Hans Albers is *not* married to Hansi Burg.[11]

The last reply concerning Albers was a patent lie for he had married Hansi Burg in 1934 and kept her safe in Switzerland for the remainder of the Third Reich. Although Goebbels disliked him intensely for his refusal to divorce his Jewish wife, Albers was so popular with cinema audiences that there was little that he or the RMVP could do about it. In his relations with actors, Goebbels took a rather stoical view and his motto, like that of Frederick the Great, was 'artists must not be bothered'.[12]

The extent to which audiences were bound up in this inquisitorial process can be gauged by the fact that even Emil Jannings, Germany's most renowned and celebrated stage and film actor, was not beyond such investigations.[13] In response to public enquiries the Bureau asked the *Filmkontingentstelle* to investigate his racial origins and on 6 June 1935 they received the following reply:

From our conversation of 31 May 1935, we can confirm that Jannings and Holl are married. We have still not been able to establish the racial origins of Jannings's family as it is still not required by law. Enquiries are continuing but we know that they have been married for ten years. She was previously married to Conrad Veidt.[14]

Prior to this sort of inquisition, a number of articles appeared in the press in which many of the leading figures in the *Filmwelt* publicly affirmed their faith in National Socialism and the manner in which they were converted.[15] Endorsements by such prominent artists not only gave the regime more

[11] Ibid., dated 29 March 1935.
[12] Quoted in R. Semmler, *Goebbels the Man Next to Hitler* (London, 1947), p. 161. Semmler was one of Goebbels's aides in the RMVP.
[13] Emil Jannings (1884–1950), *Staatsschauspieler*. Joined Reinhardt's Deutsches Theater Berlin in 1914 and entered the cinema in the same year. To Hollywood in 1926–9, where he won the first Academy Award for his performance in *The Last Command*. Returned to act in and produce a number of overt political films under the Third Reich. Those that will be discussed include: *Der Herrscher* (1937), *Ohm Krüger* (1941), and *Die Entlassung* (1942).
[14] BA, NS 15/138b, *Filmkontingentstelle* to *Kunstpflege*, 6 June 1935.
[15] See, for example, Heinrich George's interview in *VB*, 18 May 1933.

respectability but they also encouraged the rank and file to follow suit and thus prevented any form of opposition from developing within the film industry.

The fact that the film industry was ridding itself of Jews made it all the more conscious of the need to produce truly indigenous works of art. To this end it was given a lead by the Party itself when in 1933 they produced a short documentary, *Blut und Boden*, subtitled *Grundlage zum neuen Reich* (*Foundation of the New Reich*) under the auspices of the Staff Office of Agriculture (*Stabsamt des Reichsbauernführers*). Film was thought to be a suitable medium for disseminating this type of 'ideological' propaganda, and the doctrine of 'blood and soil' was one of the very few concepts under National Socialism that displayed any sort of consistency. From the following discussion it will emerge that there were two underlying precepts behind this type of film propaganda. The first was to bring the entire nation to a common awareness of its ethnic and political unity and the subsequent need for *Lebensraum* (living space); and as a corollary, to prepare the nation psychologically to accept and rationalize future and past invasions and annexations as a justifiable liberation of oppressed German communities living abroad.

The documentary film *Blut und Boden* was intended primarily for Party meetings and lectures, although it also accompanied the main feature film in cinemas. Despite its brevity and lack of discernible style, the film is an extremely interesting example of an early attempt by the NSDAP to define and glorify the Germanic type, and as such it served as an example for all future film production in this genre. The peasant was undoubtedly the cultural hero of the Movement. Addressing an audience on the anniversary of a medieval peasant uprising, Walther Darré (Minister for Agriculture) attempted to define the mystical qualities associated with the peasant and to explain his universal appeal to all Germans:

First there was the German peasantry in Germany before what is today served up as German history. Neither princes, nor the Church, nor the cities have created the German man. Rather the German man emerged from the German peasantry. Everywhere one will find primordial peasant customs that reach far back into the past. Everywhere there is evidence that the German peasantry, with an unparalleled tenacity, knew how to preserve its unique character and its customs against every attempt to wipe them out. . . . One can say that the blood of a people digs its roots deep into the homeland earth through its peasant landholdings, from which it continuously receives that life-endowing strength which constitutes its special character.[16]

In such a way the Nazis sought a popular base for their culture and, as George Mosse has shown, there remains considerable evidence that they often found it.[17] In their pursuit of popular taste the Nazis would invariably concentrate on confirming strongly-held prejudices rather than widening popular taste. But, if the sales figures of Nazi literature and art are anything to go by, one must conclude that they discovered a common base. *Blut und Boden* also had its practical side. Farm recovery was as crucial to the Third Reich as business recovery, and agricultural productivity was still a decisive factor after the recovery of small businesses had begun. Hitler declared the farmer 'the most important participant at this historic turning-point in our fortunes'. David Schoenbaum noted that 'the very pressures the Nazi economy imposed on agriculture and particularly on farm labour required propagandistic redress.'[18] Thus the film *Blut und Boden* attempts to win over the peasantry by emphasizing the value to Germany of its land and agriculture and the special care and attention the National Socialists have given to this problem: 'the prosperity of the land is linked to a strong and powerful Germany.'[19]

After this short documentary, which proved to be a seminal work, a number of feature films were produced which dealt with various aspects of the doctrine of 'blood and soil'. They include among others *Schimmelreiter* (*Phantom Rider*, 1934), *Ich für Dich—Du für mich* (*I for You—You for Me*, 1934), *Das Mädchen vom Moorhof* (*The Girl From the Marshland Farm*, 1935), *Fährmann Maria* (*Ferry Boat Woman Maria*, 1936), *Ein Volksfeind* (*An Enemy of the People*, 1937), *Die Reise nach Tilsit* (*The Journey to Tilsit*, 1939), *Immensee* (1943), and *Opfergang* (*Sacrifice*, 1944).

[16] R. W. Darré, *Rede des Reichsbauernführers und Reichsministers* (Altenesch, 1934), quoted in Mosse, *Nazi Culture*, pp. 148–50.
[17] For numerous examples see Mosse, pp. 130–60.
[18] Schoenbaum, p. 160.
[19] For a detailed analysis of *Blut und Boden* see Welch, pp. 162–6. For a Nazi discussion of the film see *VB*, 25 November 1933.

The creation of myths and heroes was an integral part of National Socialist dogma. The peculiarities associated with racial thought were fertile grounds for the creation of such heroes and therefore the peasant provided the constant culture hero for National Socialism. As George Mosse observed, 'The flight from reason became a search for myths and heroes to believe in, and National Socialism was only too glad to provide both in full measure.'[20] Mythology of this nature was encouraged by films such as *Ewiger Wald* (*The Eternal Forest*), a semi-documentary made in 1936 which presented in poetic form the Nazi nationalist and racial mythology.

EWIGER WALD (THE ETERNAL FOREST, 1936)

Produced under the auspices of the *NS-Kulturgemeinde* (Culture Group) the film purports to cover the changing relationship between a people and its forest during the course of German history. This 'allegory of our history and life' (as it was subtitled), which evoked 2,000 years of Germanic civilization, was both a monument to the form of nationalism mentioned above and an excellent example of the Nazi Party's obsession with 'blood and soil' as symbolized by the peasant and the forest. Not only is the theme of *Ewiger Wald* central to National Socialist ideology, but it also serves to illustrate how the Nazis manipulated the doctrine of *Blut und Boden* in order to create national solidarity and the need for space in which to live (*Lebensraum*).

In terms of its effectiveness, the concept of 'blood and soil' depended on a mystical relationship between man and nature which involved the notion of 'the organic community' (*Volksgemeinschaft*). The modern world had denied to the Germans (or so they believed) the unity which they had possessed long ago; consequently, many felt that the movement for unity must draw its strength from those distant times rather than from the present.[21] In an age of industrialization and class conflict, man was to be integrated into his Volk; by this 'self assertion of the German spirit' (as Heidegger put it) his true

[20] Mosse, p. 96.
[21] An excellent synopsis of Nazi ideology can be found in J. Richards, *Visions of Yesterday* (London, 1973), pp. 288-93. For a more detailed account see G. Mosse, *The Crisis of German Ideology* (London, 1964).

self would be activated and his feeling of alienation transformed into one of belonging. Moreover, the Nazis emphasized the consolidation of 'pure' elements within the community (*Gemeinschaft*). The ideal was to be restated many times by the Nazis; compare the following extract taken from Hitler's address to the Reichstag in 1939:

A community . . . cannot primarily be created by the power of compulsion, but only by the compelling power of an idea, that is, by the strenuous exertions of constant education: National Socialism aims at the establishment of a real national community.[22]

A great deal of mysticism was involved in this line of thought, and linked to *Völkisch* philosophy was the concept of 'blood and soil' as the source of the *Herrenvolk*'s strength. Not only is the peasant important as the purest example of German blood, but he is also the most closely attached to German soil, and therefore expresses the age-old customs and habits of the German people. The connection between blood and soil can be illustrated by the importance attached to the German forests in Nazi mythology.

The idolatry of German forests was symptomatic of an antirationalism on which the Nazis could capitalize. The German penchant for trees was not dissimilar to the mountain genre that emerged during the Weimar Republic.[23] An anti-rational and anti-critical element is present in both tendencies. The concept of an organic rural idyll was not confined to the medium of film: having its roots and antecedents in German history, it pervaded all strands of German society and all means of mass communication. Joseph Goebbels's only novel *Michael*, written in 1929, is a classic example of the Nazis' anti-bourgeois and *Völkisch* thought and illustrates the mystical importance of the forest:

No oak tree grows without soil, root, and strength. No man comes out of the unsubstantial. The people are his soil, history his root, blood his strength . . . Race is the matrix of all creative forces. Reality is only the Volk. . . . A people is an organic entity. To be organic means to possess within oneself the capability of creating organic life. The forest is only

[22] Speech of 30 January 1939, quoted in D. M. Phillips, *Hitler and the Rise of the Nazis* (London, 1975), p. 18.
[23] For a personal interpretation of the 'mountain genre' see Kracauer, pp. 110–12 and 257–63. For an excellent analysis of *Ewiger Wald*, see F. Courtage and P. Cadars, *Histoire du Cinéma Nazi* (Paris, 1972), pp. 56–8.

a multiplicity of trees. I cannot destroy nations and keep humanity alive, just as I could not uproot trees and keep the forest. Trees — that is, in their totality a forest. Peoples — that is, in their totality humanity. The stronger the oak grows, the more will it beautify the forest. The more thoroughly a people is people, the greater its service to humanity.[24]

The same kind of anti-urban, anti-intellectual sentiments can be seen in the unprecedented explanatory statement issued by the *Kulturgemeinde* a day before *Ewiger Wald*'s première at the Ufa Palace in Munich on 8 June 1936:

It must be stressed that the *NS-Kulturgemeinde* is not only concerned with the encouragement and preservation of art; no, it is much more a group for the promotion of a new heroic art.
The *NS-Kulturgemeinde* will show in *Ewiger Wald* — a film about our forests — just how well prepared it is for such a task! Our ancestors were a forest people, their God lived in holy groves, their religion grew from the forests. No people can live without forest, and people who are guilty of deforesting will sink into oblivion. . . . However, Germany in its new awakening has returned to the woods. All the laws of our existence make reference to the wood. The film *Ewiger Wald* sings this exalted song of the unity that exists between people and the forest from traditional times to the present.[25]

In its conception (although not its content), *Ewiger Wald* was a rare venture on the part of the RMVP. Although a semi-documentary (a number of historical events were reconstructed), it was intended as a main feature attraction in the cinema programme. Directed jointly by Hans Springer and Rolf von Sonjevski-Jamrowski (who directed *Blut und Boden*), it featured a continuous orchestral and choral score by Wolfgang Zeller and was narrated in the same dramatically sharp, portentous tones as Aribert Mog used in the *Wochenschau* newsreels. The programme notes stressed that the film was 'interpreted and re-enacted by men and women from all over Germany'.

The tone of the film is set by a long, beautifully photographed opening sequence of the German forests and the passing of the seasons. From winter to spring the trees majestically resist the torrential forces of the elements. Shot from below and rising into the clouds the sequence is interjected with a dedication: 'To you, people trying, fighting and struggling to

[24] J. Goebbels, *Michael: Ein deutsches Schicksal in Tagebuchblättern* (Munich, 1929), pp. 118–20, quoted in Mosse, *Nazi Culture*, pp. 105–6.
[25] *Licht-Bild-Bühne*, 8 June 1936.

build the imperishable Reich!' The narrator then announces
that the Reich is indestructable, like the forest: 'Eternal forest, eternal people. . . . The people, like the forest, thrive for
eternity.'

The film traces the history of the German people back to
the times of settlement and the changing historical fate of the
German nation as reflected in the state of German forests. A
lyrical commentary underlines this joint development throughout the film: 'It's from the forest that we come, and we live
like the forest.'

After a brief excursion into prehistoric times in which the
first funeral rites and pagan dances around a tree are reconstructed, a Roman insignia is superimposed on to the image
of a crown of foliage. With their eagle standards aloft, the
Romans are seen as enemies of the countryside. The people,
sensing the danger, must fight for their existence: 'People,
do not be afraid of war! People, aspire to victory!' The battle
of Arminius in the forest of Teutoburg and the defeat of Varus'
army (9 AD) is the inevitable outcome of fierce peasant resistance. A violent wind stirs, the black clouds pass over the sky,
lightning strikes. Following the Roman retreat the dead are
cremated on the funeral pyre. As the flames bellow in front
of the screen there emerges, hardly discernible at first, the old
runic sign which, when fully transposed, becomes the SS
insignia.

The film then traces the German people through the age
of the coming of Christianity and the Crusades to the period
of the Teutonic Knights. We are now in the Middle Ages and
we are shown medieval craftsmen at work: a blacksmith, a
woodcutter, a carpenter, and the wooden fronts of the old
houses—'the glory and power of German towns built with
wood'. German artists are also seen at work: 'From the height
of these masterpieces, it's the forest, the face of Germany,
which looks upon us and which speaks to us.' A slow pan up
a Gothic church spire dissolves into the top of a tree.

After such tranquillity the Peasant War breaks out as the
German people demand recognition. The success of the peasant
uprising is followed by the planting of new trees. The narrator
declaims that 'under Frederick the Great all is restored. The
King wants new forests to stand up like soldiers.'

The transition to modern times is heralded by an impressionistic sequence of German nineteenth-century Romantic painting, and proceeds via Strauss to the twentieth century. At this
point the sky becomes dark, war is once more upon the Germans. Once more the felling of trees symbolizes the devastation
of war, only this time it is the First World War. As Christmas
passes, the German soldiers sing 'Silent Night' in the trenches.
The end of the war is represented by a panorama of wooden
crosses that stand guard over the fallen. Defeat and humiliation
are symbolized by the felling of more trees and the occupation
of the Ruhr by *coloured soldiers* of the French Army. There
are close-ups of tall pine trees being sliced and transported in
chains to France as reparations. The commentator cries out:

People, how can you bear this? How can you stand for this unthink-
able burden, my folk? We will not give in! Let the flags lead us into
battle!

The answer comes in the form of Nazi flags, adorned with their
swastikas, and a new summer forest. The camera slowly dissolves into the faces of two Aryan children, a boy and a girl.
The film ends as it began with the evocation of early pagan
rites; peasants are seen happily dancing around the Maypole
in their traditional costumes decorated for 1 May:

'The people, like the forest, will stand for ever!'

In terms of Nazi propaganda, *Ewiger Wald* is primarily concerned with awakening German nationalism and the need for
more living-space for ethnic Germans. The overall message
conveyed by the film is significant for the light it sheds on
future developments in German foreign policy. Germany is
portrayed throughout the film as a peaceful nation that had
always been threatened by aggressive neighbours (the Roman
legions of Varus, the French, and so on) and one that has been
reluctant to respond to such threats. In contrast to this, a
consistent theme in Nazi thought was the belief that struggle
was an essential part of the Movement. Hitler's contempt for
inaction is evident in this extract from *Mein Kampf*:

If in the past our ancestors had based their political decisions on similar
pacifist nonsense as our present generation does, we should not possess
more than one-third of the national territory that we possess today and

probably there would be no German nation to worry about its future in Europe.[26]

The outcome of this apparent contradiction is that although *Ewiger Wald* attempts to trace an historical interaction between a peace-loving German people and its forest, the film is continually interjected with contemporary Nazi thought which, in turn, imposes its own contradictory interpretation of past events by urging cinema audiences: 'People, be not afraid of war! People, aspire to victory!' and 'We will not surrender. Let the flags lead us into battle!' The sequence of the Peasant War in the sixteenth century serves as a painful example of what can happen when there is a lack of national unity. Thus the authoritarian measures of the National Socialist regime are rationalized by the need for collective will and action to secure freedom and national security and to obviate the mistakes of the past. There is an interesting example in the film of how this militaristic notion was linked to the concept of 'blood and soil'. With the emergence of the Nazis and the subsequent reawakening of Germany, the camera slowly moves along a row of newly planted trees in the forests. The trees are lined up one by one; as the camera passes from one tree to another it pauses, and by rapid montage, alternate images of the trees and young soldiers are juxtaposed on the screen. This association of trees and soldiers recalls the devastation that followed the Thirty Years' War and draws a parallel between Frederick the Great's measures and those implemented by Hitler after Germany's humiliation in the First World War:

'The King wants new forests to stand up like soldiers.'

Such an obvious link between the old and the new Germany, in which trees were being replanted (under Göring's personal supervision) and the military forces rearmed, would hardly have gone unnoticed with German audiences in 1936.

Ewiger Wald reflects in a lyrical, romanticized manner the National Socialist belief in a pure German race, in which the peasant represents the primordial image of the Volk—a Master Race whose roots lie in the sacred soil fertilized for centuries by the richness of their blood. Such an image of the ideal Nordic type is in direct contrast to the French Army occupying

[26] Hitler, p. 127.

the Ruhr, which is depicted as being predominantly composed of Algerian Muslim or Black Africans. The alarming results of French degeneracy through miscegenation act as a clear warning to all Germans to retain their national identity. Nazi filmmakers would later use captured American Negroes for similar purposes in the *Wochenschauen* (newsreels) to claim that such racial elements had also undermined the moral fibre of American society.

In attempting to present the Nazis' racial mythology, the producers were doing little more than complying with Goebbels's request to 'capture the spirit of the age by making the nation conscious of its *Völkisch* identity'. He wanted filmmakers to produce films with precise tendencies, 'mit scharfen völkischen Konturen' (with sharp racial contours), portraying men and society 'as they are in reality'.[27] It would be these tendencies that Leni Riefenstahl would bring to their apotheosis in such films as *Triumph des Willens* (*Triumph of the Will*, 1935) and *Olympiade* (1938). Such qualities did not escape the *Völkischer Beobachter*'s attention in their rather long-drawn-out review of *Ewiger Wald*, of which a short extract is cited below:

Our nation has always been conscious of the eternal importance of the woods in our destiny. For centuries poets have possessed this knowledge, endeavouring to fathom the mysteries of the tree of life. . . . For the first time a film has interpreted the eternal meaning of the forests . . . The impressive close-ups of the peasants' faces are unforgettable. They were shown at significant points in the film and their tranquillity achieved a most profound effect. In accordance with peasant traditions, the sequence of historical events is broken by only a few spoken words recounting important analogies.[28]

Taking up this last point, a reviewer in *Film-Kurier* thought that despite its 'masterly historical interpretation' the film was on the whole 'too strenuous an exercise'. In particular he objected to the practice of 'pressing the full text into the public's hand before the film showing'. He contended that the cinema goer, 'however much he loves art, wants to see and hear but not to read.'[29]

Although only muted, such criticism is rare in the history

[27] *VB*, 9 February 1934.
[28] *VB*, 18 June 1936.
[29] *Film-Kurier*, 17 June 1936.

of the German cinema, particularly so in this case in that it is constructive criticism. It could only have been released with Goebbels's knowledge and blessing. He probably felt that the film was too long to have the desired effect and this is borne out by the fact that after its special showing in Munich a slightly shortened version was passed by the Censor on 20 August 1936, *Ewiger Wald* having its official première at Oldenburg on 28 August 1936.

Stylistically it is an impressive production, magnificently photographed in that typically soft-centred *Kulturfilm* tradition that had been developed by Ufa since the middle of the 1920s.[30] In this respect *Ewiger Wald* is similar to the larger works of Riefenstahl. The explanation is almost certainly that a team of ten cameramen worked on the production, notably Sepp Allgeier, who supervised the photography of *Triumph des Willens*, and Guido Seeber, who was responsible for *Der Golem* (1914) and *Dirnentragödie* (*Tragedy of the Street*, 1927).

Despite the fact that the format of *Ewiger Wald* was never repeated, it is undoubtedly one of the most interesting and revealing films made during the Third Reich. Stylistically, it combined elements of all forms of Nazi film-making; from the short *Kulturfilm*, the urgency of the newsreels and documentaries, and the more stylized and constructive approach of the feature film. However, from the propaganda point of view it was too laboured and complicated (a reasonable knowledge of German history would be required for a start) to have been as effective as Goebbels would have wished. He maintained that for propaganda to be effective it must be simple and easily digested. The importance of *Ewiger Wald* is that it evokes a number of important concepts that were fundamental to the National Socialist culture: life rooted in nature and Volk, the importance of German living-space, and the demand for purity of race. Significantly, the film was later awarded the *Prädikat* '*Volksbildend*' (for national education). Closely linked to the ideal of *Gemeinschaft* (community),

---

[30] According to a 1925 Ufa brochure: 'The world is beautiful; its mirror is the Kulturfilm.' Owing to their scientific excellence and cinematic technique the Ufa *Kulturfilme* developed into a German speciality that was in great demand in the international market. 'Yet their workmanship could not compensate for their amazing indifference to human problems,' Kracauer, p. 143.

which was an important theme in *Ewiger Wald*, was the notion of Aryan superiority. Hitler frequently referred to this racial superiority in *Mein Kampf*:

The adulteration of the blood and racial deterioration conditioned thereby are the only causes that account for the decline of ancient civilisations; for it is never by war that nations are ruined, but by the loss of their powers of resistance, which are exclusively a characteristic of pure racial blood. In this world everything that is not of sound stock is like chaff. . . . The constructive powers of the Aryan and that peculiar ability he has for the building up of a culture are not grounded in his intellectual gifts alone. . . . And the world is indebted to the Aryan mind for having developed the concept of 'mankind'; for it is out of this spirit alone that the creative force has come which in a unique way combined robust muscular power with a first class intellect and thus created the monuments of human civilisation.[31]

It can be seen from the above that the National Socialists offered this Germanic myth of racial purity as the antithesis of 'corruptible alien elements'. An obscure song of the period exclaimed, 'That is the meaning of life, that God is astir in one's blood, but God is present only in pure blood.'[32] Such thought had its antecedents in the works of racist writers like Gobineau and, more importantly, Houston Stewart Chamberlain.[33] Both writers argued that the purest contemporary race was the Aryan, a race whose inward qualities were intrinsically linked to its external appearance. In the hands of Chamberlain, however, such a doctrine became a powerful instrument for racial imperialism and anti-Semitism. He saw history as a struggle between Germanic and Jewish races and held that the Teutonic race comprised those who genuinely shape 'the destinies of mankind, whether as builders of the state or as discoverers of new thoughts and original art. . . . Our whole civilisation and culture of today is the work of one definitive race of men, the Teutonic.'[34] Pure races, he argued, would evolve through a long historic process that would ultimately create a race of supermen. Thus the National Socialists found in Chamberlain's

---

[31] Hitler, pp. 248–50.

[32] The title of the song was, 'Du bist die Kette ohne Ende' ('You are the Chain without End'), quoted in J. W. Baird, *The Mythical World of Nazi War Propaganda 1939–45* (Minneapolis, 1974), p. 8.

[33] J. P. Stern controversially maintains that Chamberlain's work was not particularly anti-Semitic, Stern, p. 51.

[34] H. S. Chamberlain, *Foundations of the Nineteenth Century*, trans. J. Rees (New York 1912), vol. I, pp. lxvi–lxviii.

work the prophecy of a German *Herrenvolk* (Master Race) to come.

The link between the doctrine of *Blut und Boden* and the *Herrenvolk* principle was that the latter could only derive its intrinsic qualities, its source of strength from the 'blood and soil' of the German homelands. Goebbels wanted film-makers to capture the spirit of the new Germany by making Germans conscious of their *Völkisch* identity. One film that illustrates this attempt to bring the entire nation to a common awareness of its ethnic roots is Leni Riefenstahl's monumental documentary, *Olympiade*.

OLYMPIADE (1938): THE MASTER RACE AND STRENGTH THROUGH JOY

Olympiade is a four-hour record of the 1936 Olympics held in Berlin and is divided into two parts, Festival of the Peoples (*Fest der Völker*) and Festival of Beauty (*Fest der Schönheit*). Riefenstahl worked for almost two years on the editing, finishing in time for the film to be premièred on 20 April 1938 in Berlin as part of the celebrations for Hitler's forty-ninth birthday.

Besides being a factual diary of an international sporting event, *Olympiade* is a paean to physical prowess and youth, a film of squads of young men and women rejoicing in their health and strength. Moreover, the film reflected the ethos of the period and part of its aim was to advertise the achievements of the 'new' Germany in an international context. The film is comprised of a series of loosely connected events, and a plot summary would do little to enhance our understanding of a number of themes crucial to Nazi ideology that recur in the film. However, before these themes can be explored in detail, *Olympiade* must first be set in its historical context.

The Olympic Games were held in Berlin only a few months after the uncontested remilitarization of the Rhineland. Whereas the earlier Saarland propaganda campaign had been conceived for the purpose of German expansion, the Olympic Games were to be an exercise in national respectability. Albert Speer noted that 'Hitler exulted over the harmonious atmosphere that prevailed during the Olympic games. International animosity toward National Socialist Germany was plainly a thing of the past, he thought. He gave orders that everything should be done to convey the impression of a peace-minded Germany to the many prominent foreign guests.'[35] Even before the Games had begun, specific instructions had been given to the various media on how the event was to be covered. In January the press were warned not to publish accounts of any 'brawls with Jews or conflicts with foreigners'.[36] Signs such as 'Jews not admitted' were carefully taken down from the restaurants, hotels, and shops and Streicher's weekly newspaper *Der Stürmer* was temporarily withdrawn from the newsagents. The press was encouraged to inform foreign visitors of the excellent German culture films that were being shown in Berlin cinemas,[37] and Ufa was employing a large number of 'eloquent students' to publicize its films as well as covering billboards with film posters.[38] On 15 June editors were requested 'to use the Olympic Games and the preparations for them for extensive propaganda in Germany'.[39]

The Games were to prove an ideal vehicle for Goebbels's propaganda and his strategy was not without success. As William Shirer, the American correspondent, observed:

I'm afraid the Nazis have succeeded with their propaganda. First, they have run the Games on a lavish scale never before experienced, and this has appealed to the athletes. Second, they have put up a very good front for the general visitors, especially the big businessmen. Ralph Barnes and I were asked to meet some of them. . . . They said frankly that they were favourably impressed by the Nazi 'set-up'. They talked with Göring they said, and he had told them that we American correspondents were unfair to the Nazis.[40]

Ernest Bramsted went even further and claimed that 'seen in an historical perspective, they [the Games] formed a high-water

[35] A. Speer, *Inside the Third Reich* (London, 1971), p. 119.

[36] BA, *Sammlung Brammer, No. 82*, 27 January 1936.

[37] BA, *Sammlung Sänger (Aus der Kulturpolitischen Presskonferenz), Zsg, Bd. I*, 102/62, 6 August 1936. These were Goebbels's daily press conferences from 26 July 1936 to 30 October 1942. This collection deals partially with the film industry, although his directives were intended for the entire German press. They reveal 'official' thinking behind film production and how films should be treated in the press.

[38] BA, *R1091/1031b, No. 1156*, 21 April 1936.

[39] BA, *Sammlung Brammer, No. 577*, 15 June 1936.

[40] W. Shirer, *Berlin Diary* (London, 1972), p. 58.

mark in the successful technique of Nazi persuasion by effective mass communications, pageantry, and showmanship.'[41] It is in the light of this carefully conceived and executed propaganda campaign that Leni Riefenstahl's *Olympiade* must be analysed. The director herself, however, has maintained since the end of the war that the film was commissioned by the International Olympic Committee, produced by her own company, and made despite Goebbels's protests.[42] However, the documentary material deposited in the Bundesarchiv in Koblenz reveals a different story.[43] These records show quite categorically that the film was commissioned and entirely financed by the Reich government (a 'dummy' company under the name of Olympia Film GmbH was established because it was thought 'unwise for the government itself to appear as producer') and supervised by the RMVP at every stage of production. The Olympic Games provided the Nazis with an excellent opportunity to indulge in some clever window-dressing and, given their all-embracing preparations for this event, it would have been surprising (and uncharacteristic) if Goebbels had failed to exploit the full resources of the film industry for his propaganda ends.

Olympiade can be seen as an impressive exercise in respectability and propaganda for the National Socialist regime. But the principal themes of the film were more central to the domestic consumption of Nazi ideology, and in particular the doctrine of *Blut und Boden*. *Olympiade* was a grandiloquent celebration of various elements of the Nazi *Weltanschauung*, notably the importance of 'Strength through Joy' (*Kraft durch Freude*) and the idealization of the Aryan body.

    [41] E. K. Bramsted, *Goebbels and National Socialist Propaganda 1925–1945* (Michigan, 1965), p. 151.
    [42] Cf. 'Nazi Pin-Up Girl', *Saturday Evening Post*, no. 39, 30 March 1946; 'Leni Riefenstahl', *Film Quarterly*, XIV, no. 1, Autumn 1960; 'Leni et le loup', *Cahiers du Cinema*, no. 170, September 1965; 'Fascinating Fascism', *The New York Review of Books*, vol. XXII, no. 1, 6 February 1975.
    [43] The first dissenting voice amid a number of 'revisionist' accounts was Hans Barkhausen in *Neue Zürcher Zeitung*, 'Auf Veranlassung des Reiches', no. 218, 10 August 1974. Later published in *Film Quarterly*, vol. XXVIII, no. I, Fall 1974. I have been able to analyse the records in the Bundesarchiv, particularly folders: *R2, Akten des Reichsfinanzministeriums* and *R55, Akten des Reichsministeriums für Volksaufklärung und Propaganda*. See, for example, R55/505 *Finance of Olympia Film GmbH*. These substantially confirm Barkhausen's arguments. Indeed, Goebbels was far more generous to Riefenstahl than she will concede today.

The concepts of health and strength were essential components of the future *Herrenvolk* who embodied the ideals and aspirations of the Nazis' racial policies. In a speech in Munich in April 1929, Hitler declaimed: 'We mean to create, out of our ideology and our political will to power, documents of stone and bronze, in order to imprint again upon every German mind that it is a proud thing to be a German.'[44] One obstacle to the development of this ethnic consciousness was the Catholic Church, which, according to Alfred Rosenberg, was not only opposed to racial purity, but had actually turned Germans against the concept, as expressed in Greek culture, of healthy, natural men and women with pride in their bodies.[45] Hitler too was impressed by the achievements of Greek culture and believed that the Dorian tribe, which migrated into Greece from the north, had been of Germanic origin.[46] Albert Speer recollects a conversation with Hitler when he revealed the extent of his admiration for Greek culture: 'Hitler believed the culture of the Greeks had reached the peak of perfection in every field. Their view of life, he said, as expressed in their architecture, had been "fresh and healthy". One day a photograph of a beautiful woman swimmer stirred him to enthusiastic reflections: "What splendid bodies you can see today. It is only in our century that young people have once again approached Hellenistic ideals through sports."'[47]

Olympiade is a classic restatement of such sentiments, for in the film Riefenstahl extolls the harmony and integration of the human body in terms of the realization of some Hellenic ideal. The prologue to Part One (*Fest der Völker*) is an example of how, by means of a visual metaphor, the National Socialist ideal of beauty is seen to have its roots in antiquity. In the opening shots, the Third Reich is shown as heir to Sparta:

The Prologue
The prologue lasts for almost twenty minutes. It starts with a romantic score by Herbert Windt followed by cloud formation that completely

[44] O. Dietrich, *Mit Hitler in die Macht* (Munich, 1934), p. 195, quoted in R. Cecil, *Myth of the Master Race: A. Rosenberg and the Nazi Ideology* (London, 1974), p. 55.
[45] Cecil, p. 144.
[46] During this period a short documentary, *Germanen gegen Pharaonen* purported to prove that Egyptian civilization originated from Northern Europe and in particular, Germany.   [47] Speer, pp. 150-1.

fills the screen. Through the mist, barely discernible, vague architectural shapes emerge. As the camera pans in we see they are those of the Acropolis and the fallen columns of the temple of Zeus at Olympia. From the temples we are shown studies of sculpture which, by an interplay of light and movement, appear like living bodies in a vision of the past. The camera slowly focuses on the Myron discus thrower and by means of low-angle shooting creates the impression of power and movement. Suddenly, the Greek statue dissolves into the modern German athlete (Riefenstahl superimposed the German decathlon champion, Huber), and then slow-motion scenes of slender females symbolising the Greek temple dancers dominate the screen and eventually merge into the Olympic flame which is being carried by a solitary runner into the Olympic stadium in Berlin where the Führer is shown presiding enthusiastically over the whole spectacle. [48]

Less than a year later, in a speech at the opening of the House of German Art in Munich, Hitler referred to the Olympic Games and the physical archetype that was so important to National Socialist mythology:

The new age of today is at work on a new human type. Men and women are more healthy, stronger: there is a new feeling of life, a new joy in life. Never was humanity in its external appearance and its frame of mind nearer to the ancient world than it is today.[49]

An American correspondent in Germany noted this 'ideological nudity' and the obsession with health and hygiene:

All the newstands displayed books and magazines filled with pictures of nude men and women. You find these on the racks and counters even at the best hotels, such as the Adlon, along the streets, and at every subway counter around which people loitered. . . . Some of them had such titles as *Sunlight and Health* and *Nature and Beauty*. Others were picture stories of *My Model*. Some of these pictures masqueraded as art and were included in monthly magazines. I remember one lighted sign in a subway advertising a sun lamp, which showed several naked women lolling about on benches. Signs in the subway trains advertised 'health-ray' institutions for men and women.[50]

The correspondent, Harry W. Flannery, believed that this was planned not to make the people more moral, but solely to produce more 'cannon fodder'. This was true, but such displays of nakedness served another purpose—to exemplify the ideal racial type. As a result of Nazi racial thought, certain stereotypes emerged which were essential in transforming the

[48] See R. Mandell, *The Nazi Olympics* (London, 1972).
[49] Quoted in Baynes, p. 591.
[50] H. W. Flannery, *Assignment to Berlin* (London, 1942), pp. 84–5.

ideology into a unifying element. According to one source, the archetypal Nordic man was 'long-legged, slim, with an average height of about 1.74 metres. The limbs, the neck, the shape of the hands and feet are vigorous and slender in appearance.'[51] It was therefore the task of all artists in the Third Reich to give expression and shape to such beliefs. In this they were assisted by such 'expert' sources as the weekly *Schwarzes Korps*:

What is fundamental in the portrayal of the naked human form and Nordic racial type is the exposure, in the true sense, of an animate beauty, the discovery and artistic fashioning of an elemental, godlike humanity. Only then does it become an effective means of educating our nation in moral strength, Völkisch greatness and, last but not least, resurrected racial beauty.[52]

It followed from this that portraiture and nude studies could only be termed German if they depicted the German body. Similarly, this emphasis on racial types led Nazi musicologists into the domain of primordial musical expression.[53] Riefenstahl's films can be seen therefore as a counterpart to the sculpture of Arno Brecker and the painting of Adolf Ziegler (known throughout the art world as the 'Reich Master of Pubic Hair') which combined to erase all 'ugliness' from the popular consciousness. But *Olympiade* is much more than a film about health and strength, it is a hymn to the human body which itself is depicted throughout as the object of Riefenstahl's loving veneration. Witness a scene described by Richard Mandell in Part Two (*Fest der Schönheit*); it clearly has very little to do with the Olympic Games but a great deal in common with various aspects of *Völkisch* thought:

Then there follows one of the most spectacular sections of film footage ever assembled. First from the ground we watch three Nordic, leotard-clad, full-breasted girls swinging exercise clubs in unison. They are splendid! Accompanied by rhythmically sympathetic music, the narrative fades in, fades out successively to 6, to 20, to 100, and then to perhaps 10,000 perfect women in faultless patterns in perfect unison. As the camera angle rises the viewer is transported with aesthetic emotion . . .

[51] Hans Günther, *Kleine Rassenkunde des deutschen Volkes* (Munich, 1933), p. 24, quoted in Mosse, *Nazi Culture*, p. 64.
[52] *Das Schwarze Korps*, 25 November 1937, quoted in H. P. Bleuel, *Strength Through Joy* (London, 1973), p. 190.
[53] See J. Wulf, *Musik im Dritten Reich. Eine Dokumentation* (Gütersloh, 1963). See, also, M. Meyer, 'The Nazi Musicologist as Myth Maker in the Third Reich', *JCH*, 1975, vol. 10, no. 4, pp. 649-65.

We swoon with the instinctive grasp of the pure power of these massed Völkisch gymnasts as the camera immortalises actions.[54]

The scene is not unlike the mass orchestration of human bodies one finds in *Triumph des Willens*, for both films represent a radical transformation of reality. It has been suggested that Riefenstahl reacted to life as if it were a pageant in which we are all engaged to play particular and inevitable roles. Thus in both *Olympiade* and *Triumph des Willens* the emphasis is on symmetry and order (key principles in Nazi art) whereby individuality is sacrificed for an ordered participation on a mass scale. The film document is no longer simply a faithful record of reality, for 'reality' has been constructed to serve the image. Not only were cameras strategically placed for the most dramatic effects but Riefenstahl also had camera pits dug alongside the track as well as employing aeroplanes and a Zeppelin for the aerial shots.

Style in the Nazi documentary has been mainly associated with the works of Leni Riefenstahl, and the epic size of her projects required a certain resourcefulness on the part of her cameramen. The technical innovation needed to film actual events—hand-held or automatic cameras, the first jump-cut, the montage of sound effects together with impressionistic music—were to have a profound influence in the development of German war newsreels, probably the most powerful element of Goebbels's film propaganda. Moreover, the sportsman-cameraman formed in Riefenstahl's films later became the soldier-cameraman of the propaganda units at the war fronts.

The spectacle of an Olympic Games held in Berlin, which registered more victories for Germany than any other country, undoubtedly lent itself to Nazi myth-making. Principal among these was the celebration of the rebirth of the body and community, symbolized by the worship of an irresistible, benign leader. Even the *Sunday Times* correspondent covering the Games was moved to write: 'It is uncanny how often Adolf Hitler's entrance coincides with a German victory!'[55] But Goebbels's problem as Propaganda Minister was how to sell a documentary to an audience two years after the event depicted had taken place. He went about it by banning all

[54] Mandell, pp. 265–6.
[55] *Sunday Times*, 9 August 1936.

reporting of the film until a month before it was due to be released, hoping no doubt to capitalize on an aura of mystery surrounding the film.[56] Then, a full-scale publicity campaign was launched to promote the film. Typical of the sort of 'informed' reporting is this account from the *Hakenkreuzbanner* published the day before the film's première and entitled 'How the Olympia Film Arose':

This work of art has developed out of 400,000 metres of film. *Commissioned by the Führer and Reich Chancellor* [my italics] the Olympic Games could not have been filmed in a more splendid location. The mighty Olympic Stadium bore proof of the National Socialists' gift for design which impressed visitors from all over the world.... It is two years since Dr Goebbels gave a German woman the task of filming such an event. . . . As the première of Leni Riefenstahl's Olympic Film draws near many questions have been asked about how the film was created. But owing to her intense preparations no one has been able to ask her these questions. So her closest colleagues are going to answer them for her . . .[57]

Her 'closest colleagues' were, of course, the RMVP who proceeded to supply all the relevant information about the film. *Olympiade* proved to be a success both financially and artistically. According to the Propaganda Ministry's records the film had made a profit of RM 114,066.45 by the beginning of 1943.[58] It was also a controversial winner of the Mussolini Cup for the best foreign film at the Biennale Film Festival in 1938. In Germany, 'due to its cultural significance' *Olympiade* was incorporated into the film programme as a feature film and not a documentary. It was eventually accorded the highest honour by winning the National Film Prize (*Nationaler Filmpreis*) for 1938 as well as being awarded the *Prädikate*, 'politically valuable', 'artistically valuable', 'culturally valuable', valuable for 'national education', and 'instructional'.

The Nazis were later to make even more capital out of the Olympic Games when, in 1940, they produced *Wunschkonzert* (*Request Concert*), one of the most popular films of the Third Reich which was concerned with the unity of the front and homeland. *Wunschkonzert* was a popular Sunday afternoon

[56] BA, *Sammlung Sänger, 102/62*, 17 March 1938.
[57] *Hakenkreuzbanner*, Berlin, 19 April 1938.
[58] BA, *R2*, Memo from Ott (RMVP) to Reich Finance Ministry, 1 February 1943.

radio programme which attempted to link those in the armed forces and the civilian population (a sort of Nazi two-way family favourites!).[59] The film traces the development of a cross-section of social attitudes from the Olympic Games to the first phase of the War. It centres on two lovers who meet and fall in love in the Olympic stadium which acts as a catalyst within which their love flourishes in the presence of the Führer and the scene of great national triumph. *Wunschkonzert* reveals a respectable, peace-loving Germany, envied by the rest of the world—a country merely correcting past grievances. The importance that the RMVP attached to the whole ethos surrounding the Games and the manufactured spectacle they presented can be gauged from this directive from one of Goebbels's press conferences:

Wunschkonzert should be carefully dealt with and presented as one of the most important films of recent times. It is no mere feature film as it pursues the fate of many people from the Olympics to the war.[60]

The importance of *Olympiade* as a propaganda vehicle was not only confined to the domestic market. Later the Propaganda Ministry was to exploit the film's propaganda possibilities during the Russian campaign. From information received from Nazi officials in the captured Soviet territories, the Ministry realized that the film could be manipulated and used as anti-Russian film propaganda. In a memo to Goebbels his staff in the RMVP suggested the following course of action:

It is the unanimous wish of the military and civilian propaganda division in the new Eastern territories that Parts I and II of *Olympiade* should be shown to the population. The Soviets arc very keen on 'Volksports' and show many sports films, although they are not as good as our own Olympics film.

We expect a great propagandistic success, if something like the following is used as a foreword to the film:

'Youth of all nations of the world came together in Berlin for peaceful competition. Only Soviet youth were absent, because the Jewish–Bolshevik conspiracy deliberately prevented direct contact with other nations.'[61]

[59] *Wunschkonzert* was the tenth biggest box-office hit during the Third Reich and grossed RM 7.2 million.
[60] BA, *Sammlung Sänger, 102/62*, 20 December 1940.
[61] BA, *R55/1288*, Memo: To Reichs Minister re Introduction of Olympics film into former Soviet territories, 15 July 1942.

However, this is by way of digression. The means of Nordic self-realization were given cinematic expression in the work of Leni Riefenstahl. *Olympiade* not only portrayed the prototype athletic warrior but in so doing provided an integrated and comprehensive legacy of the Germanic past for Nazi identification. With its pagan exaltation of athletic prowess, *Olympiade* succeeded in conveying something of the mystique that National Socialism claimed to introduce into all spheres of cultural life.

ICH KLAGE AN (I ACCUSE, 1941): THE EUTHANSIA CAMPAIGN

Given the Nazis' obsession with health and hygiene, it should come as no surprise to discover the existence of their eugenics policies. Indeed, eugenic legislation was a logical outcome of National Socialist thought and propaganda which had always stressed the importance of achieving a pure and healthy race. At the Nuremberg Party rally in 1929 Hitler had cited ancient Sparta's policy of selective infanticide as a model for Nazi Germany: 'If every year Germany had one million children and eliminated 700,000–800,000 of the weakest, the end result would probably be an increase in national strength.'[62] Although Hitler's intentions were a matter of public record, he was never able to implement these ideas despite setting out the legislative machinery for such an operation should the occasion arise.

Only a few months after seizing power, the Nazis set to work to justify the eradication of inferior human material. Surprisingly enough, the first people to be exterminated were not Jews but unhealthy Aryans. On 14 July 1933, the new government approved the 'Law for the Prevention of Hereditarily Diseased Offspring' which provided for the sterilization of persons suffering from incurable hereditary disabilities, and as such prepared the basis for the euthanasia programme. In order not to jeopardize the successful conclusion of the Concordat with the Holy See, the publication of the decree was delayed until 25 July. Although in theory this measure was discretionary, in practice it had a compulsory flavour about it. It came into affect on 1 January 1934; sterilization was permitted in cases of hereditary imbecility, schizophrenia,

---

[62] *VB*, 7 August 1929.

hereditary deafness, hereditary epilepsy, manic depression, Huntington's chorea, and extreme physical malformation.[63] The *Rassenpolitische Amt* of the NSDAP (the Political Bureau for Race) produced two short films during the years 1935-6 dealing with the problem of euthanasia. They were distributed under the titles of *Abseit vom Wege* (*By the Wayside*) and *Erbkrank* (*Congenitally Ill*). These films were intended primarily for internal 'ideological' education and were not released to the general public. Both films dealt with the problem of incurable disabilities, and significantly drew an equation between fitness to survive and physical fitness. This was in part attributable to the generally anti-intellectual prejudices of the NSDAP and in part to a misapplied social Darwinism. Walther Darré, the Minister for Agriculture, drew a typical parallel between breeding horses and humans:

We shall gather together the best blood. Just as we are now breeding our Hanover horse from the few remaining pure-blooded male and female stock, so we shall see the same type of breeding over the next generation of the pure type of Nordic German.[64]

The Nazis threw their entire weight behind the existing movement in favour of increased physical training and racial instruction in schools and youth organizations. Secondary schools were required to teach heredity, racial science, and family as well as population policies. Intrinsic to each of these was an ideological instruction in biology. Witness this extract, written by a biologist on the need for a 'new biology':

Racial eugenics works in the same way, namely, the education of the student in a national sense. . . . It should be repeatedly emphasised that the biological laws operative in animals and plants apply also to man; for example, that the knowledge acquired from studying the genetics of these organisms can, in a general way, be applied to man. Thus, the teaching of animal breeding and plant cultivation can effectively prepare the way for conceptions of racial biology.[65]

In 1937 another film on the subject of hereditary diseases, *Opfer der Vergangenheit* (*Victims of the Past*) was released. It

---

[63] See Günter Lewy, *The Catholic Church and Nazi Germany* (London, 1964), pp. 258-9. See also, Bleuel, pp. 191-2.

[64] H. Grebing, *Der Nationalsozialismus: Ursprung und Wesen* (Munich, 1959), p. 65, also quoted in Cecil, p. 144.

[65] Paul Brohmer, *Biologieunterricht und völkische Erziehung* (Frankfurt, 1933), p. 72, quoted in Mosse, *Nazi Culture*, p. 88.

was an altogether more elaborate production than its predecessors and was inserted into the film programme in all cinemas
throughout the Reich. This short documentary was commissioned by Dr Gerhard Wagner (Reich Medical Leader), who
spoke at the film's première, and was directed by Gernot Bock-
Stieber. It is a clear exposition of the Nazis' argument for the
'mercy-killing' of the mentally handicapped and can be seen
as an extension of the biological instruction that was being
carried out in the schools.

The commentary to *Opfer der Vergangenheit* is most revealing; not only did it appeal for the elimination of 'inferior
human material' in quasi-moralistic terminology but once again
the analogy of animal breeding and plant cultivation is evoked:

> The prevention of hereditary diseases is a God-given command like the
> law of nature. To prevent the growth of weeds is to promote the healthy
> plants that will be of some value. . . . In nursing the mentally handicapped
> this essentially Christian law has been shamefully transgressed. Moreover,
> the money it takes to care for these people could be put to better use
> helping strong and healthy children.

The film then proceeds to show sick children in various institutions and the cost of their upkeep. It ends with a moralistic
plea: 'By humanely terminating their wretched and helpless
lives, we shall be observing our Creator's law of natural selection and order.' The inexorable consequence of such ideas
was that the very existence of the congenitally sick seemed a
threat, and that mentally ill and incurable people in need of
care were seen as an unnecessary burden on the nation as a
whole. The inference was that a healthy Reich could not afford
sick people because they were too expensive.

On 1 September 1939, the day Poland was invaded, Hitler
issued an order to kill all persons with incurable diseases, when
he signed the following decree:

> Reichsleiter Bühler and Dr Brandt are hereby instructed to extend the
> authority of physicians designated by name in such a manner that those
> who are, as far as humanly possible to judge, incurably sick may, after
> the most scrupulous assessment of their state of health, be granted a
> merciful death.[66]

The idea of compulsory euthanasia had been in Hitler's mind

[66] M. Domarus (ed.), *Hitler: Reden und Proklamation 1932-1945* (Munich,
1965), p. 1310, quoted in Bleuel, p. 192.

for some time, but he had held back because of expected objections from the Catholic Church. The start of the war seemed the most propitious moment for inaugurating this radical eugenic programme. At the Nuremberg doctors' trial, Dr Karl Brandt, the Reichskommisar for Health, testified that: 'In 1935 Hitler told the Reich Medical Leader, Wagner, that, if war came, he would take up and carry out this question of euthanasia because it was easier to do so in wartime when the church would not be able to put up the expected resistance.'[67] Such a programme would also provide much-needed hospital space for the wounded. Thus the euthanasia programme was in direct line of succession from the sterilization measures enacted in the early months of the totalitarian regime.

The first euthanasia installation opened in December 1939 and the victims were shot. As the programme expanded, gassing in rooms disguised as showers was introduced or lethal injections administered. There were several such establishments in Germany, the largest being Grafeneck in Württemberg. It is estimated that between December 1939 and August 1941 more than 50,000 Germans were disposed of in these institutions which operated under such fictitious names as 'The Charitable Foundation for the Transportation of the Sick' and the 'Charitable Foundation for Institutional Care'.[68]

The extermination of the incurably sick and the mentally handicapped prompted the most effective episcopal protest against the actions of the Nazi regime. In a sermon delivered on 3 August 1941, Bishop Galen of Münster revealed in detail how the innocent sick were being killed while their families were misled by false death notices. The next of kin were notified that the patients had died of some ordinary disease and that their bodies had been cremated. Often they received warnings from the secret police not to demand explanations and not to 'spread false rumours'.[69] Hitler had underestimated the possibility of such a public reaction and the far-reaching nature of its impact. Shortly after Galen's sermon, the euthanasia programme was officially halted by a *Führerbefehl* (command from the Führer) of which no written record has been

[67] Quoted in G. Reitlinger, *The Final Solution* (London, 1953), pp. 125-6.
[68] Case 1, Transcript 2481, No. 426 (Affidavit, Viktor Brack), *Trial of War Criminals*, vol. I, p. 810, quoted in Reitlinger, p. 129.   [69] Shirer, pp. 448-50.

found. These public protests helped to form and consolidate public opinion, contributed to the general feeling of outrage, and led to the suspension of the euthanasia programme. Thus the public conscience could still assert itself even in 1941 when lives of their own people were at stake. But the whole question of 'mercy-killings' would not rest there; realizing their mistake, and determined to keep the issue alive, the Nazis attempted to re-educate the public through the medium of film. In his definitive work on the subject, Gerald Reitlinger wrote:

Himmler, who did not always try to avoid being a common-place man and who, as Count Ciano observed, 'felt the pulse of the German people,' had never been happy about it. In December, 1940, he had recommended Brack to suppress the Grafeneck Institute, writing that it was better first to educate the public to euthanasia through films. Taking the hint Brack persuaded the Tobis company in the summer of 1941 to produce *Ich klage an*, the sentimental story of a professor who is put on trial for hastening the death of his young wife, an incurable invalid.[70]

By 1941, film companies had begun to classify their films for financial and administrative purposes under various categories. Shortly after being asked to make a film about euthanasia, Tobis referred to *Ich klage an* as a 'very difficult problem film', and then proceeded to classify it as an ordinary entertainment film![71] The film, which was directed by Wolfgang Liebeneiner,[72] was passed by the Censor on 15 August 1941 and received its première in Berlin on 29 August 1941. The following plot summary is taken from the *Catalogue of Forbidden German Feature Films*.[73] Not only is it an excellent account of the film but it is one of the rare occasions on which the Allied Commission achieved clarity without being misleading:

A young doctor (played by Paul Hartmann) and his wife (Heidemarie Hatheyer) are very happily married. At a party one evening, as she is giving a recital on the piano, her left hand suddenly fails her. The doctor

---

[70] Reitlinger, p. 132.
[71] BA, *R2/4809*, Tobis FK, Geschäftsbericht, 30 December 1940.
[72] Wolfgang Liebeneiner (1905–), scriptwriter, actor, and director. Was artistic director of the Babelsberg Film Academy from 1938–45 and head of production at Ufa from 1942 to 1945. Two films of his that will be discussed later are *Bismarck* (1940) and *Die Entlassung* (*The Dismissal*, 1942).
[73] *Catalogue of Forbidden German Feature and Short Film Production* held in Zonal Film Archives of Film Section, Information Services Division, Control Commission for Germany (BE), Hamburg, 1951, p. 44.

asks his friend (Mathias Wiemann) to examine her and he at once diagnoses multiple sclerosis. For weeks the doctor spends all his time in the laboratory, his all-absorbing ambition being to discover the cause of the disease and thus hoping to find a cure. All his efforts are of no avail and he has to watch his beloved wife slowly dying and suffering the greatest pain knowing he can do nothing to help her. At last he makes his decision and prepares a sleeping draught which gives her release. He has done it at her own request and tells his friend of his action. The friend, however, shows no understanding, condemns him, and denounces him to the police and the doctor is brought to trial.

During the course of the trial, the friend pays a visit to a hospital where he sees a ward of small children, all incurably ill and suffering the greatest pain. After much deliberation he begins to understand the doctor and offers himself as main witness for the defence. The trial continues, the doctor himself makes the final plea of self-justification and requests the court to give its verdict. Here the film ends.

According to a Secret Police Report (SD Report) on the reception of *Ich klage an*, two issues were raised in the film:

> Its main theme is a discussion of the problem of *voluntary euthanasia for people suffering from incurable diseases*. A secondary theme deals with the question of the elimination of life which is no longer worth living.[74]

The Propaganda Ministry was aware of the controversial nature of these issues and their ramifications to such an extent that before the film had been submitted to the Censor, the press was instructed not to mention that such a film was being produced.[75] Even after it had been passed by the Censor without cuts, a press directive of 21 August 1941 insisted that:

> *Ich klage an* is not to be discussed for the time being. If later, then euthanasia must not be broached. The film will be shown to representatives of the press next week. An SS Obergruppenführer will give a paper there in order to clarify the approach that is to be taken.[76]

According to Wolfgang Liebeneiner, the reason for such precautions was that the film was intended to test public reaction to a law which would legalize euthanasia.[77] Therefore every care had to be taken to provide the groundwork for such a venture and also to avoid antagonizing various sections of German society, particularly medical and religious circles. Two

---

[74] BA, *R58/168*, 15 January 1942.
[75] BA, *Sammlung Sänger, 102/63*, see directives 4 April 1941, and 18 April 1941. The latter also specifies that no pictures or notices should appear.
[76] BA, *Sammlung Sänger, 102/63*, 21 August 1941.
[77] *Der Spiegel, No. 7*, 10 February 1965. Liebeneiner has refused to be interviewed or to correspond with the author.

examples from the film illustrate how this was achieved: the first deals with the scene in which the doctor administers the lethal drug to his dying wife, and the second is the court-room discussion where the moral implications of euthanasia are rationalized.

The Death Scene

The audience has witnessed the slow and painful deterioration of Hanna, the once beautiful wife of Professor Heyt. Finally, she tells her husband that she cannot continue any longer in such pain. He goes downstairs to discuss the problem with his friend and colleague Dr Lang, who maintains that she should be kept alive even though he estimates that she may have no more than two months to live. The husband returns to his wife's bedroom and administers the fatal dose. She says that it tastes bitter but she feels 'so light and happy'. Lang meanwhile is playing Beethoven on the piano in a downstairs room. Hanna turns to her husband and whispers, 'I wish I could give you my hand.' He takes it and says, 'This is Death Hanna,' to which she replies, 'I do love you Thomas.'

The husband eventually leaves the dead Hanna and returns to the waiting Lang and gives him the news, 'I have ended her suffering.' Lang retorts, 'You murderer, you couldn't have loved her!' and rushes out of the house to inform the police.

The scene is an excellent example of myth and reality working in the cinema, and the power of film to evoke the required response. Hanna's death is a carefully constructed and highly romanticized episode aimed specifically at the heart and sentimentality (the music drifting from below, the soft lighting, and the stirring dialogue). The audience is permitted to experience a profoundly moving and private exchange between the husband and dying wife, which is denied to the hostile Lang. As such it has very little relevance to the genuine dilemma of euthanasia, and in particular to the thousands of 'mercy-killings' that were carried out in totally different circumstances and for different reasons. By depicting euthanasia as a merciful, indeed almost joyful experience, the film-makers were guilty of a grotesque distortion in the knowledge of a merciless reality that bore no comparison.[78]

[78] Tobis also made a short documentary on this theme in 1941. It was directed

The Trial

The death scene leads directly to Professor Heyts's trial and the sounding and manipulation of public opinion. However, before the trial begins the audience's sympathy is already with Thomas Heyt, for in the face of his cross-examination we alone have been witnesses to the tender and loving bedroom scene. From this point onwards it is the film's task to re-educate the people into accepting that Thomas's actions were the logical outcome of a sense of love and duty. *Ich klage an* succeeds or fails on this issue alone. The wider problems associated with euthanasia are subjugated and personalized in the form of this particular doctor and in deciding whether his actions were morally justified. This was substantiated in a secret press directive issued by the *Reichspropagandaamt* shortly after the film was released. Once again the press was instructed not to debate euthanasia, but instead, to concentrate on the fate of the fictional doctor:

Discussion of the film *Ich klage an* is now freely allowed . . . The problems raised in the film shall be neither positively nor negatively dealt with; thus the film is to be commented on in a neutral fashion. The film is about the problem of euthanasia, but this expression is not to be mentioned in any way. On the other hand, it can be stated that the problem depicted in the film is whether a doctor should be given the right to shorten the misery of an incurably sick person. In dealing with this film great tact is required.[79]

After a number of witnesses had testified in the trial, the three judges and the jury retired ostensibly to discuss the issues raised. In fact the scene serves to raise and answer a number of points that the Nazis felt were essential if their campaign was to be accepted by the majority of the German population. They expected opposition from the Catholic Church and certain members of the medical profession so the jury represented as wide a cross-section of the country as was dramatically feasible: a teacher, farmer, soldier, pharmacist, doctor, gamekeeper, and so on. The following selected extract from their

by Franz Fiedler and entitled *Wer Macht Mit? (Who Joins In?)*. The commentary begins: 'Only a healthy people can live.' The rest of the film emphasizes the need to stay healthy by keeping fit for the good of the nation.

[79] Denecke, *Pressereferent, Archiv des Instituts für Zeitungswissenschaft*, Munich, quoted in Wulf, *Theater und Film*, p. 354.

debate will illustrate how the dialogue was slanted to justify governmental thinking on euthanasia:

SCHÖNBRUNN [*teacher*]. . . . Euthanasia. It's from *Thanatos*, which means Greek for death. You see, gentlemen, the ancient Greeks and Romans permitted it.
KNEWELS [*counsel*]. Would you acquit him?
SCHEU [*judge*]. Yes, absolutely.
KNEWELS. I'm not so sure, It's such a controversial case, other doctors might start killing their patients in a similar way.
ZIERNICH [*farmer*]. That surely would be a sin.
SCHÖNBRUNN. But Professor Heyt should be acquitted precisely because he is an example to other doctors. This is a fundamental issue in our moral and social order . . . If a person is incapable of making his mind up, the State must take over the responsibility. Clearly it is not right that a doctor should be allowed to use his discretion on this issue. We must establish commissions consisting of doctors and lawyers. But we can't just watch thousands of people continuing to live in pain simply because doctors have the power to prolong their lives by artificial means.
ZIERNICK. But this is God's will. We have suffering in this world so that people will follow his Cross to eternal salvation.
DÖRING [*Major*]. I must say, with all due respect, that I cannot conceive of a God as cruel as that.
REHEFELD [*gamekeeper*]. When gamekeepers shoot an animal and it's still suffering, we put it out of its misery. Not to do so would be brutal.
ROLFS [*locksmith*]. But you are talking about animals!
REHEFELD. Yes, but sometimes man is no different from an injured animal in pain.
DÖRING. . . . The State has a responsibility to all those people who comprise the State, namely, the workers — who would not wish to continue living if they knew that they had an incurable illness. The State says that it is our duty to die for it, therefore it must also give us the *right* to die! I'm an old soldier and I know what I'm saying.[80]

Thus the Nazis managed to insert every conceivable objection to euthanasia into the film: moral, religious, medical, and still make them appear convincing. Reviewing the film a day after the première, the *Frankfurter Zeitung* reaffirmed that the question posed by the film was 'whether the killing by a doctor of somebody incurably ill is not advisable. The discussions on the screen leave no doubt that the decision in general ought to be "Yes".'[81] Public reaction

[80] The full scene can be found in Leiser, pp. 143–5.
[81] *Frankfurter Zeitung*, 30 August 1941.

to the film was described in the SD Reports as 'generally favourable':

In general it can be stated that the film has been favourably received and discussed. Characteristic of the stir which this film has aroused is the fact that in many towns which had not yet seen the film it was being described, even by the less sophisticated, as one they really must see.[82]

Interestingly enough, given the lack of action and almost continuous dialogue in the film, the working classes were more favourably disposed to the change in the law suggested by the film than the more intellectual circles.[83] If this were so then it is testimony to the director's skill as both story-teller and propagandist. According to the SD Report, the explanation for this was that the poorer social classes were more conscious of their financial burdens. Thus, they were swayed not by religious or moral arguments but by the purely materialistic consideration of whether they could afford to care for sick people. Beliefs such as these are the result of a fully integrated propaganda machine that depended for its effectiveness on over-simplification and irrationality.

However, the film did encounter some protest from the Church, although in Protestant circles the open rejection of the film was not as strongly expressed as in the Catholic Church. In fact the SD were able to elicit some positive opinions from the Church. For example, the Superintendent of Bautzen made the following statement:

It will be the State's concern to prevent abuses of the law, and to take upon itself the responsibility for seeing that this service is carried out in a kindly way for people tormented by incurable diseases. This will be a much easier task than carrying out salvation itself. As a Christian, I must declare myself in favour of this film.[84]

The medical profession, on the other hand, appeared to be delighted by the discussion that the film had promoted. An extremely interesting article was written by a group of doctors from Breslau and published in the *Film-Kurier*. It illustrates the growing importance of film as a means of propaganda, and the acceptance it had gained with all strata of the population as a trusted contemporary document:

Just how much film enters the realm of serious observation and discussion was clearly illustrated by the special showing of the great Tobis

[82] BA, *R58/168*, 15 January 1942.   [83] loc. cit.   [84] loc. cit.

masterpiece, *Ich klage an* . . . A celebrated gathering of experts were invited for this showing . . . but above all, doctors had been invited. The chiefs of Breslau's hospitals were seen together with the country's best-known specialists. This signifies that both laymen and specialists are recognizing the achievement of films, which would not have been conceivable a few years ago. The most influential circles are now fully reconciled to the belief that film must be accepted as a 'witness of our time'.[85]

These observations and the findings of the SD Reports reveal an alarming flight from reality, a willingness to delegate responsibility, and a reluctance to face the moral implications and guilt of their actions. This was captured in the SD Report's final summing-up of public reaction to the introduction of euthanasia:

The general approval finds expression in the words of the Major in the film: 'The State says it is our *duty* to die for it, so it must also give us the *right* to die.'[86]

Equating euthanasia with such heroism is indeed a travesty of what actually happened and provides no evidence of all those who had little choice in deciding their fate and the cynical methods employed by the regime to deceive them. The fact that 'mercy-killings' were only spasmodically continued after the *Führerbefehl* is attributable not only to the forceful reaction of the Catholic Church but, perhaps more importantly, the military reverses that were shortly to occur and the fact that the full-scale extermination of the Jews had begun.[87]

Ich klage an was undoubtedly one of the most insidious of all Nazi propaganda films in that it highlighted the existence of a social problem that it claimed was in the process of being solved. It is perhaps interesting to note that similar methods were employed with regard to film propaganda in order to coincide with the preliminary stages of the 'Final Solution to the Jewish Question'. The subsequent disaster which befell the Jews, the culmination of a virulent and unrelenting anti-Semitic propaganda, did not give rise to the same ostensible debate or public outcry. But more of this in a later section.

[85] *Film-Kurier*, 22 September 1941, also quoted in Wulf, p. 354.
[86] BA, loc. cit.
[87] Reitlinger argues that 3,000 adult mental patients were killed *after* August 1941, Reitlinger, p. 133.

As I mentioned earlier, two underlying considerations influenced film propaganda in this genre. The first was to bring the entire German nation to a common awareness of its ethnic and political unity, and if, in the pursuit of racial purity, this meant that the physically and mentally sick were to be exterminated, then this was the price they were willing to pay. The second factor was the desire for 'living-space' (*Lebensraum*) and the need to rationalize annexations and invasions as a justifiable liberation of oppressed German communities living abroad. Film propaganda dealing with this second theme was categorized by the film companies as *Heimatfilme*.

The incorporation of all Germans into the Reich was a positive part of racial policy and was one of the earliest features of Hitler's political thought. Hitler wrote in *Mein Kampf*:

German-Austria must be restored to the great German Motherland. And not indeed on any grounds of economic calculation whatsoever. No. No! Even if the union were . . . to be disadvantageous from the economic standpoint, still it ought to take place. People of the same blood should be in the same Reich. The German people will have no right to engage in a colonial policy until they shall have brought all their children together in one State. When the territory of the Reich embraces all Germans and finds itself unable to assure them a livelihood, only then can the moral right arise, from the need of the people, to acquire foreign territory. The plough is then the sword; and the tears of war will produce the daily bread for the generations to come.[88]

Such 'geopolitics' offered the humiliated national spirit the idea that the destiny of Germany would be decided in the East and thus added an important aspect of Nazi ideology, that of 'space', to that of 'race'. As Joachim Fest observed, 'these two ideas, linked by that struggle, constitute the only more or less fixed structural elements in the intricate tactical and propagandist conglomerate of the National Socialist *Weltanschauung*.'[89]

The first feature film to concentrate on the problem of German minorities living abroad was *Flüchtlinge* (*Refugees*), directed by the Austrian, Gustav Ucicky, in 1933.[90] It was

---

[88] Hitler, p. 17.   [89] Fest, p. 289.

[90] Gustav Ucicky (1899–1961) was one of the regime's most reliable directors. Already an established director in Weimar Germany where he made right-wing militarist films (*Das Flötenkonzert von Sanssouci*, 1930 and *Yorck*, 1931), Ucicky directed a number of political films for the Nazis: *Morgenrot* (1933), *Das Mädchen Johanna* (1935), *Aufruhr in Damaskus* (1939), *Mutterliebe* (1939), and *Heimkehr* (1941).

also the first film to be awarded the *Staatspreisfilm* set up by Goebbels to honour the most distinguished cinematic contributions to the National Socialist movement. In *Flüchtlinge*, we find another fundamental theme of the German cinema, in that it anticipates the return to the Fatherland. The awakening of memories and the feeling of homesickness for the Fatherland is a recurring theme and found expression in such films as *Ein Mann will nach Deutschland* (*A Man Must Return to Germany*, 1934), *Der Kaiser von Kalifornien* (*The Kaiser of California*, 1936), *Das Gewehr über* (*Shoulder Arms*, 1939), *Ein Robinson* (1940), *Feinde* (*Enemies*, 1940), *Heimkehr* (*Homecoming*, 1941).

The fate of German communities abroad and the use of film propaganda had always interested the Nazis. Even before they came to power the NSDAP had developed an extremely effective distribution system for their own films which were smuggled into foreign countries by means of a central group of Nazis operating in the Hamburg ports and controlled by the Gestapo. On reaching a foreign country most of their films were banned by the various governments and could only be shown at private screenings of German societies. In such a way the NSDAP was able to gain some influence among exiled Germans and the German minorities abroad.[91] Because the Weimar Republic was not concerned with this sort of film propaganda, Germany was represented in these distant areas by National Socialist propaganda alone.[92]

Even when they were firmly established in power the National Socialists did not neglect their foreign film section. In 1936 in an article entitled, 'It Carried the Homeland Across Frontiers', the *Völkischer Beobachter* outlined the RMVP's distribution of films for German minorities abroad:

Film's role is important in this respect. By such means Germans abroad can receive information about the Homeland, its aspirations and its achievements. . . . Therefore every event, indeed anything that underlines the character and spirit of our age is recorded by film cameras. As well as the foreign film service of the *Wochenschau* the head of the Foreign Film Service has decided to compile a *Filmecho* of the Homeland made up of all the reels of film available. This National Socialist

91 Emil Ehrlich, *Die Auslandsorganization der NSDAP* (Berlin, 1937).
92 See J. Hiden, 'The Weimar Republic and the Problem of the Auslandsdeutsche', *JCH*, vol. 12, no. 2, 1977, pp. 273–89.

film report (also known as *Echo der Heimat*) is distributed four times a year to wherever expatriate Germans happen to live. It offers them a lively picture of events at home and perhaps it may be the first glimpse of the Homeland.[93]

The effectiveness of Nazi exploitation of German minorities abroad should not be overestimated. According to H. A. Jacobsen, by 1937 at most 6 per cent of all Reich Germans living outside the Reich had joined the Party: 'Although others sympathized with the Third Reich, there could not be any talk, any time, of a potential power policy instrument. Looked at critically, the works of the Auslands organization abroad was therefore a brilliant failure.'[94] This may well have been so, but it does not undermine the importance of films such as *Flüchtlinge* which, although dealing with German communities abroad, were made essentially for Reich audiences. *Flüchtlinge*,[95] for example, promoted the universality of what it meant to be German, relegating the question of German citizenship to a purely formal level, regarding the ties of blood and race as the determining factors. By showing the cruel repression and exploitation of the German minorities abroad, such films also created a favourable climate within which Hitler could carry out his foreign policy in Eastern Europe. Another film in this genre which dealt with oppressed German minorities abroad and helped to eliminate opposition to Hitler's territorial ambitions was Gustav Ucicky's *Heimkehr (Homecoming)*.

HEIMKEHR (HOMECOMING, 1941)

Once again Gustav Ucicky and script-writer Gerhard Menzel return to the theme they first explored in *Flüchtlinge*. They were inspired to make *Heimkehr* by the accounts they had received from Volhynian Germans who had left Russian-occupied Poland to 'follow the Führer's call back to the homeland'.[96] The cinema-going public was informed that the film was to go into production in September 1940, several months

[93] *VB*, 9 November 1936. A fascinating article which also outlines the technical facilities that were available for NSDAP groups to make and exchange their own films.

[94] H. A. Jacobsen, *Nationalsozialistische Aussenpolitik 1933–38* (Frankfurt am Main, 1968), p. 602.

[95] For a detailed discussion of *Flüchtlinge* see Welch, pp. 207–15.

[96] *Filmwoche*, no. 11, 12 March 1941.

after the conquest of Poland and timed therefore to inflame hatred for an already conquered nation. According to the SHAEF report on *Heimkehr* after the war, the purpose behind the film was twofold:

It was to show that Germany had no choice but to save the German minority from persecution by declaring war on the Poles. The cruelties and crimes committed by them in this picture are unbelievably ruthless. They are deliberately designed to make the blood of the German nation 'boil' with hatred, and it cannot be doubted that many Germans felt justified to commit their barbarous crimes during the occupation of Poland after seeing the Ucicky and Menzel invented atrocities.

The second purpose is to give the main figures an opportunity for making Nazi speeches. When all the Germans are herded into a prison cell for the crime of being of German descent — they are told to dream of 'Heimat', where every neighbour is German, every cloud in the air, every piece of earth, grass, tree and each little bird is German ... The Poles are just getting ready to shoot all of them — the old and children, women and men, when the Stukas and German tanks arrive, proving that the Führer always acts in time.[97]

The film begins with a rousing symphonic score and the camera slowly scans the German countryside. As the music builds to a crescendo the titles reveal a dedication:

To a handful of German people, whose forefathers emigrated East many, many years ago, for there was no room for them in the homeland ... In the winter of 1939 they returned home – home to a new, strong Reich ... What they experienced is valid for hundreds of thousands who shared the same fate.

Heimkehr is essentially a series of loosely connected incidents bound together by their emotional intensity. As such there is very little plot to recount. However, *Das Programm von Heute* summed up the events as follows:

Volhynia, Spring 1939! If the Germans were unable to see that the Poles were determined to enter German land by military means then the persecutions which they have to suffer would surely make this clear. As the brutal Polish police burn down their German school the Mayor of the town is deaf to the complaints of the teacher, Marie Thomas (Paula Wessely). Therefore a deputation of Marie, Dr Mutias, and Balthasar Manz, decide to go to the provincial capital of Luzk and appeal to the Governor — who dismisses them without a hearing. England had 'guaranteed' Poland. The whole country was steeped in a fantastic drunkenness. Marie and Dr Mutias decide to visit a cinema in Luzk and are confronted

[97] *Supreme Headquarters Allied Expeditionary Force* (SHAEF), deposited in BFI Film Library, London.

by this intoxication and hatred. Unbelievable insults are the prelude to brutal deeds; Dr Mutias bleeds to death as a result of a beating and the kindly Dr Thomas is shot in a country lane and loses his sight. Martha Launhardt, a young German peasant girl, is stoned to death in the open street of their town. 'The Führer will avenge us and bring us home' — is the only hope that comforts them in their suffering.
1 September 1939! In a silent hiding place our Volhynian Germans listen to the Führer's declaration. Polish police have thrown the terrorized Germans into prison. Here even the bravest are confused. Only Marie has yet to lose her faith in ultimate victory, when death in the form of a Polish machine gun stretches out its hand through the prison bars. Over the ruins of decaying, damp prison walls which witness a never-ending suffering, German men climb to freedom. What do these troubles mean? Beyond such suffering awaits a new, finer life for everyone![98]

Between the years 1938 and 1940, Nazi propaganda concentrated on the fate of the *Völksdeutsche* (German nationals).[99] Hitler even justified the invasion of Czechoslovakia in March 1939 as revenge against the maltreatment of Germans living there. The Aryan instinct for self-preservation involved the need for space in which to live, a need made all the more pressing by the terms of the Treaty of Versailles. Hitler wrote in *Mein Kampf*:

One must not allow existing political frontiers to distract attention from what ought to exist on principles of strict justice. If this earth has sufficient room for all, then we ought to have that share of the soil which is absolutely necessary for our existence. Of course people will not voluntarily make this accommodation. At this point the right of self-preservation comes into effect. And when attempts to settle the difficulty in an amicable way are rejected the clenched hand must take by force that which was refused to the open hand of friendship.[100]

Heimkehr was passed by the German Censors on 26 August 1941 and was shown at the Venice Film Festival (where it won a prize) on 31 August 1941. It had its première in Vienna on 10 October 1941 and was finally shown to Berlin audiences on 23 October 1941. During this period, with the onset of the war, the problem of the *Völksdeutsche* was less important than actually arousing anti-Polish feelings in the Greater German Reich. In this respect *Heimkehr* was very much in keeping with current events in Germany and the campaign of hatred directed against Polish workers in the Reich. Just before *Heimkehr*

[98] *Das Programme von Heute*, No. 1792, quoted in Hollstein, p. 151.
[99] See Zeman, pp. 49–51.
[100] Hitler, pp. 126–7.

went into production, a secret conference was held in Berlin for all publishing editors with the express purpose of establishing a 'positive' attitude towards Poles and towards Germany's quest for *Lebensraum* (living-space). The following is a report of their conclusions which was issued to all publishing concerns:

Editors are referred to Volume III of *Volksdeutsche Heimkehr* and *Neue Heimat Posen.* Dr Krieg spoke of the effects of the Polish campaign. He says that it is a basic error to assume that Germans and Poles are similar. May there never be such a community as this would lead to our destruction. We must elevate the German people to a 'Herrenvolk' . . . You can see time and time again in the Protectorate that Germans either 'crack the whip' or ingratiate themselves with Czech women. Let this be changed. Let the German people be taught to keep a certain distance from the Pole. Polish POWs who are working for German farmers are not to be treated as one of the family and German women are not to fraternize with Poles. Every time German nationals mix with Poles our standards sink. Every German must work on the assumption that there are no decent Poles. The more space Germany gains, the greater the labour force needed for menial tasks. The concept of 'Polish Culture' must never be revived. In the Polish Reichsgau [region] 4 million Poles still live. We need only a small percentage of these. 200,000 German farming families must be moved there. Only 80,000 are available at present. The press are requested to cooperate in this publicity campaign.[101]

It was within such a society (which had been well nurtured by German film-makers) that the cinema-going public were to experience how the Polish 'of little racial value' were conspiring with plutocratic Jews 'to murder this minority and eventually to annihilate *all* German people!'[102] Hitler's invasion of Poland was rationalized thus: 'the wailing of women and children under the brutal grasp of the Polish 'Soldateska' highlighted the inexorable necessity of the action taken by the Reich in pursuit of its victorious end.'[103]

By concentrating on the twin themes of Polish oppression and the heroism of a small group of Germans, *Heimkehr* provided a retrospective excuse for the invasion of Poland and a call for more 'living-space'. Or, as the critic of *Filmwelt* put it: 'If there should be any lingering doubts about our final victory then *Heimkehr*, a splendid pictorial saga, would surely

[101] BA, *Sammlung Sänger 102/62*, 9 February 1940.
[102] *VB*, 24 October 1941.
[103] loc. cit.

have dispelled all uncertainty.'[104] By viewing such films as
Flüchtlinge and *Heimkehr* the film-going public learnt about
their fellow countrymen 'who were indescribably happy in
extricating themselves from the chaos imposed upon them.
Fellow countrymen who had nothing to live for apart from a
deep and unshakeable faith in their homeland—in Germany.'[105]
Heimkehr reveals the hallmarks of Nazi terror tactics, but
it twists them and explains them away as Polish provocation
and brutality. More particularly, the film makes it clear that
it is the Jew who is behind this oppression. A brief exchange
between the heroine in the film, Marie the teacher, and
Salomonsson the Jewish shopkeeper, gives some indication of
how the archetypal cowardly and rootless Jew was portrayed
in Nazi films.

In the market place where Marie is shopping Salomonsson
solicits her to buy from him. He is an old man with a hooked
nose wearing a long kaftan-like robe typical of all Jews. He
proclaims the cheapness and quality of his goods in strong
Yiddish tones, but Marie waves him away indifferently:

MARIE. No, Salomonsson, you know very well we don't buy from Jews!
SALOMONSSON. How can you speak such harsh words, Doctor, when
I enjoy trading with the Germans. And why? Because you're honour-
able! German people are great people, a proud race, and yes, the
Führer, Hitler, a brilliant man, a great man — it's only a shame he
doesn't want anything to do with us poor Jews!
MARIE. I'll write to him about it! [*She then brushes him aside and
passes on. Salomonsson retorts angrily.*]
SALOMONSSON. How can you make such fun of us poor Jews, when
I'm friendly to you and ask nothing more than to trade with you . . .
May the earth open up and divide you like Korah and his gang![106]

The Polish Jews are thus presented as the antitype of the
National Socialist ideal, which invariably means in Nazi propaganda that the attributes they are given have their psychological
roots in the Nazi character. The extent to which the caricature
of the Jews reflects the Nazi mentality can be illustrated from
one of the first sequences in the film which has its historical
parallel in the burning of the books in 1933. In a fit of blind

---

[104] *Filmwelt*, no. I, 3 January 1941.
[105] *Filmwelt*, no. 7, 14 February 1941.
[106] An excellent account of this aspect of the film can be found in Hollstein,
pp. 150-3.

rage, the Poles drag a group of German children from their school and a young Jew, encouraged by his relatives, pours petrol on the school furniture, burning all the books and equipment in the process. *Der deutsche Film* explained to German audiences the universal law behind such actions:

It is the first step in bringing deep confusion into their existence [the *Volksdeutschen*] and destroying their sacred bounty of *Volkstum*, education, and the preservation of their heritage.[107]

Of course, this was really the intent behind the Nazi measures against Jews and Poles. In such a highly politicized society, Nazi propaganda could permit itself the luxury of depicting in every detail a situation that was an analogy of the Jewish tragedy, without risking being misunderstood by a critical and unprejudiced film audience. Film-makers were not content to produce a fictional dramatization of the fate of the *Volksdeutschen* in the East, they actually claimed historical authenticity for the events that were outlined. Thus on 1 September 1939 this German community is seen huddled together in a barn listening to the Führer's speech on the radio when he tells them that he is aware of their suffering and will not stand idly by without taking retributive action.

Shortly after Hitler's broadcast they are surprised by Polish gendarmes who beat them up and transport them to the prison of Luzk, where they are all herded together in a cellar consisting of three small cells. Before the Germans are 'liberated by the roaring Stukas and the magnificent armoured columns',[108] they discuss their plight, knowing that they are to be shot the following day. In particular it is the blind Dr Thomas who reproaches his fellow countrymen for thinking only of themselves:

DR THOMAS. Where is the heart that becomes enraged that everything in the world is absurd and turned upside down? A world in which people live alongside each other but not with one another. Where is the voice that awakens the world from its sleep of death?

---

[107] *Der deutsche Film*, 6 July 1941. Goebbels must have been unsure about the advisability of such propaganda before the showing of the film because a month later he banned all discussion of the film until after its première, BA, *Sammlung Sänger, 102/63*, 21 August 1941.

[108] *Berliner Lokalanzeiger*, quoted in A. Weidenfeld and D. Sington, *The Goebbels Experiment. A Study of the Nazi Propaganda Machine* (London, 1942), p. 212.

Such questions could well have prompted undesirable reflections on the part of German audiences, but so that they would not feel that they were the target for such an attack Marie immediately replies: 'In Germany! In Germany!: Her father then reassures his audience of the necessity for Hitler's expansionist foreign policy:

DR THOMAS. Yes, of course, in Germany. You're right my girl, such a voice is heard all over the world now. It's shaking people now, and it is indeed tragic that it has to speak in terms of guns and Stukas. But believe me, there is no other way. You see otherwise nobody would listen to the message that we must put a stop to this wretched selfishness . . .

The climax of the film is Marie's speech to her fellow-prisoners which attempts to rouse their spirits by invoking a vision of what life will be like when Germany attains her rightful place in the sun:

MARIE. Don't worry friends, we'll get home somehow, of that there can be no doubt. Everything is possible. Back home in Germany people are no longer weak and afraid. Just think of what it will be like when only honest Germans are around us. And when you go into a shop they will not be speaking Yiddish or Polish, but German. And it won't just be the village that is German, everything will be. And we will be in the heart of Germany . . .

This repudiation of the foreigner is not only a reaction to the ill-treatment they had received but it is a necessary concomitant to that particular form of patriotism which evoked a longing for a mystical reunification with the homeland:

MARIE. . . .We'll soon be living again in the good old warm soil of Germany — in our country . . . For not only do we live a German life, but we die a German death. And dead we remain German and part of Germany. A clod of soil for our grandchildren to grow corn on. And from our own hearts the vines will grow heartily in the sun — the sun, my friends, which does not burn or harm them, but gives them their sweetness. And all around the birds are singing and everything is German.

This desire for 'living-space' was one of the determining factors in Hitler's foreign policy. By the time *Heimkehr* had been made, the 'home' Marie refers to had already extended to Austria, Czechoslovakia, Poland, and was soon to incorporate Russia. In September 1939, barely eight months after Hitler had reaffirmed his intention of honouring the 1934

Non-Aggression Pact with Poland, he condemned the Versailles Treaty for stripping Germany of the port of Danzig and granting a large area of Eastern Germany to Poland. His claims could have been written for one of the main characters in *Heimkehr*:

> For months we have been suffering under the torture of a problem which the Versailles Diktat created . . . Danzig was and is a German city. The Corridor was and is German. Both these territories owe their cultural development exclusively to the German people. . . . As in other German territories of the East, all German minorities living there have been ill-treated in the most distressing manner. More than 1,000,000 people of German blood had in the years 1919–1920 to leave their homeland.[109]

However, this was 1939 when concern in Germany over the fate of German minorities abroad was at its height. Three years later when *Heimkehr* was released the German population had other, more immediate problems to consider: instead of the *Auslands-deutsche* they were now faced with Allied bombing raids, food shortages, and the campaign on the Eastern Front. Not surprisingly perhaps, *Heimkehr* was not the popular success that had been anticipated, despite the fact that Goebbels had ordered a big press coverage and awarded the film the *Prädikate* 'politically and artistically especially valuable', 'valuable for youth', and the rarely bestowed *Film der Nation*. The failure to attract popular support (it certainly had the critical acclaim) can also be attributed to psychological factors such as the omission of a strong story-line and the curiously weak cast. The film did however have some lasting effect on the younger cinema audience. A. U. Sander's 1944 survey of the likes and dislikes of German youth revealed that *Heimkehr* was in their six most popular films.[110]

Heimkehr is undoubtedly the classic cinematic statement of the *Volk und Heimat* (people and homeland) theme and, as such, it reveals the manner in which the concept of a 'people and a homeland' sprang directly from the doctrine of 'blood and soil' and the superiority of the Aryan race. By 1942, however, Goebbels appreciated that the sort of verbose, insistent propaganda that eliminated all entertainment value was no

---

[109] *Documents concerning German–Polish Relations and the Outbreak of Hostilities between Great Britain and Germany on September 3, 1939*, Cmd, 6106 (HMSO, 1939), p. 161.

[110] Sander, pp. 118–19.

longer achieving the desired goals. Thus, towards the end of the year he had already decided that, in future, entertainment films would be given priority: 'It really seems to me that we should be producing more films, but above all, lighter and more entertaining films which the people are continually requesting.'[111]

Heimkehr was the last of the major film productions dealing with the plight of the *Volksdeutsche* and the 'return to the homeland' theme. Even if the theme was out of date, its propaganda, detailing a compassionate government sending forth liberating troops, was quite in keeping with wartime propaganda. From now on, however, Nazi film-makers would no longer dramatize the suffering of others—for such realities of war were becoming increasingly familiar to the German people.

The renaissance of the Volk was built upon the foundations of the 'new man' symbolized by the peasant rooted in the soil. Goebbels's cleansing of the film industry (indeed of all art) was designed to cater for a taste which would represent the 'healthy instincts of the people'. The instincts, like the ideology that incorporated them, were conservative and all-pervasive. But how successful were the policy-makers in implementing such reforms?

The regime was of course incapable of implementing any of its fantastic schemes for a Germanic Utopian community of the 'Master Race', if only because its agricultural policy on which the doctrine of 'blood and soil' rested turned out to be the least effective of its measures of reform.[112] In fact the social revolution that did take place had little in common with any *Völkisch* or Aryan ideas. At the same time, as the euthanasia campaign illustrated, it destroyed all due process of law. In order to exhalt the virtues of the peasantry, the propaganda machine insisted on the primacy of inherited characteristics, described by the race theorist Hans Günther as 'blond, tall, long-skulled, with narrow faces, pronounced chins, narrow noses with high bridges, soft fair hair, widely spaced

---

[111] IfZ, *Goebbels Tagebuch*, entry for 12 November 1942.
[112] Stern, p. 170. For a concise and well-argued account of this point of view, see Schoenbaum, pp. 159–86.

pale-coloured eyes, pinky-white skin colour'.[113] These features were so repeatedly undermined by the appearance of most of the leading National Socialists that such a racial image could not have been seen as too obligatory. Such discrepancies were sardonically noted by a former Nazi:

> Seven of my ten Nazi friends had heard the joke — it originated in Germany during Nazism — had enjoyed it: 'What is an Aryan?' 'An Aryan is a man who is tall like Hitler, blond like Goebbels, and lithe like Göring.' They too had smiled at the mass Aryanisation, first of the Italians and then the Japanese. They all knew 'Aryans' who were indistinguishable from Jews and Jews who were indistinguishable from Nazis. Six of my ten friends were well below middle height, seven of them brunet, and at least seven of them brachycephalic, of the category of head breadth furthest removed from the 'Nordic longheadedness'.[114]

The failure to implement such a 'Utopian community' can be gauged by the fact that towards the end of the war 'ethnic Germans' throughout the Greater Reich rediscovered their regional identifications and tried desperately to hide their Germanness. The failure of the Nazis' racial policies as the war came to an end can be linked to a fundamental weakness of Nazi propaganda in general. I have argued that one of the main objectives of the National Socialist programme was to unify the German people with a single thought and purpose. This in turn became a weapon used against their enemies; that is, the invincibility of a united and determined nation. We have seen that by appealing to a certain racial myth, Goebbels gave the German people a superiority that was permanently denied to others. In this sense, film had an educational role, in that it presented the nation in a positive way. Thus the spectator learnt how to behave as a 'good' citizen, and he did this even more willingly when he sensed that he was already a valuable member of the community (*Gemeinschaft*). But Goebbels also emphasized the importance of co-ordinating propaganda with other activities. 'There must be absolute certainty that words are followed up by corresponding events,' he once stated.[115] In this context, propaganda films such as *Flüchtlinge*, *Ewiger Wald*, *Olympiade*, and *Ich klage an* could successfully

[113] Quoted in Fest, p. 154.
[114] M. Mayer, *They Thought They Were Free* (Chicago, 1966), p. 41. This is a revealing account of ten former Nazis reviewing their past.
[115] IfZ, *Goebbels Tagebuch*, entry for 28 November 1942.

achieve their desired goals while the regime's credibility was high. Alternatively, as the failure of *Heimkehr* demonstrated, Goebbels's propaganda campaigns were so closely tied to German military success that defeat found propaganda in a difficult position.

V

THE PRINCIPLE OF LEADERSHIP (FÜHRERPRINZIP)

Where he comes from, no one can say. From a prince's palace, perhaps, or even a labourer's cottage. But everyone knows: He is the Führer, everyone cheers him and thus he will one day announce himself, he for whom all of us are waiting, full of longing, who feel Germany's present distress deep in our hearts, so that hundreds of thousands picture him, millions of voices call for him, one single German seeks him.

Kurt Hesse (*Feldherr Psychologos*, 1922)

IN his study *Behemoth*, which was published in 1942, Franz Neumann pointed out that the Third Reich was no totalitarian dictatorship in the sense of a 'monolithic, authoritarian system inspired by a unified policy'.[1] Despite all the revolutionary slogans, the old social order and traditional ruling class remained. Neumann showed that the National Socialist regime had not created a totalitarian state but a form of direct rule over the suppressed masses, which was without any rational legality and which was dependent upon four largely autonomous groups, each pressing its own administrative and legal powers. These groups were the Party, the army, the bureaucracy, and industry.[2] But towering above all the rival groups was the symbolic figure of the Führer, the head of state who was not subject to any constitutional limitations. The cult of the leader is central to an understanding of the appeal of National Socialism, and is a recurring theme in the Nazi cinema.

Just as National Socialism needed its enemies so it also required its heroes, for no revolution, even if only a cultural one, has succeeded without its heroic leaders. For their concept of

---

[1] F. Neumann, *Behemoth* (London, 1942), pp. 382-9.

[2] Had he written the book when more information was available he would surely have included the SS.

the heroic leader the Nazis turned once again to *Völkism* and the *Führerprinzip*, a mystical figure embodying and guiding the nation's destiny. In practical terms this meant that decisions came down from the top instead of being worked out by discussion and choice from below. The roots and antecedents of such a concept are more complex and derive from many sources: the Messianic principle of Christianity, the thaumaturgic kings of the Middle Ages, and the Nietzschean 'superman' of *Völkisch* mythology.[3]

However, the Nazi belief in the *Führerprinzip*, as it found expression in Germany after 1933, stemmed partly from the distaste which the Germans felt towards the nineteenth century for the determining of policy by the counting of votes, and partly from the way in which Nazi philosophers such as Alfred Bäumler had reinterpreted Nietzsche's concept of the 'triumph of the will' by individual genius. The *Führerprinzip* was to be based on a very special personality which had the will and power to actualize the *Volksstaat* (the State of the People). By implication it would be the antithesis of democracy. The true will of the German people was realized in the person of Adolf Hitler, as Ernst Huber, the Nazi political theorist, outlined:

The Führer is the bearer of the people's will: he is independent of all groups, but he is bound by laws inherent in the nature of his people. In this twofold condition, independence of all factional interest but unconditional dependence on the people, is reflected the true nature of the *Führerprinzip*. . . . He shapes the collective will of the people within himself and he embodies the political unity and entirety of the people in opposition to individual interest.[4]

In analysing the way in which the *Führerprinzip* was dramatized in the Nazi cinema, I would like to concentrate on these two overlapping aspects: the anti-parliamentarianism of such a concept and the projection of the individual leader of genius.

As Hitler embodied the true will of the German people there was no limit to his imagined protean capacity. This posed certain problems for Nazi film-makers. Any dramatization of

[3] Neumann, pp. 81–3. Cf. J. P. Stern, pp. 56–65, F. Stern, *The Politics of Cultural Despair* (Berkeley, 1961).

[4] *National Socialism* (U.S. State Department Publication, no. 1864, Washington DC, 1943), pp. 34–7, reproduced in D. M. Phillips, *Hitler and the Rise of the Nazis* (London, 1975), p. 26.

such a God-like figure on the cinema screens would be considered blasphemy. Instead, they chose great figures in Nazi history to project the Hitler prototype. Thus during the Third Reich, a number of extravagant historical films were produced which were intended to strike a familiar chord with Nazi audiences. The great historical figures that were dramatized in this way were: poets (*Friedrich Schiller*), sculptors (*Andreas Schlüter*), scientists (*Paracelsus*), explorers (*Carl Peters*), industrialists (*Der Herrscher*), statesmen (*Bismarck*), and kings (*Der grosse König*). All of them can be seen as a projection of Hitler, who was exalted in Nazi propaganda as an amalgam of such geniuses.

TRIUMPH DES WILLENS (TRIUMPH OF THE WILL, 1935)

One exception to this rule was *Triumph des Willens*, commissioned by Adolf Hitler and featuring him. The Führer had personally requested that the documentary film of the 1934 *Reichsparteitag* be directed by Leni Riefenstahl and he coined the title himself. Indeed, after most of the important details had been made he went to Nuremberg 'to give the final instructions'.

In December 1941, at the height of Germany's military success, Goebbels modestly informed his officials in the Propaganda Ministry about the services he had rendered over the years towards the Party's current triumphs. Two factors that he stressed were, first: 'the style and technique of the Party's public ceremonies. The ceremonial of the mass demonstrations, the ritual of the great Party occasions', and, secondly, that through his 'creation of the Führer myth Hitler had been given the halo of infallibility, with the result that many people who looked askance at the Party after 1933 had now complete confidence in Hitler.'[5] Referring to the leader cult in National Socialism, Walter Hagemann has said that the relationship between the leader and those he leads can be 'that of a father, of a comrade, of a despot and of a demi-god'.[6] This total identification of the led and their leader was the main objective

[5] R. Semmler, *Goebbels, The Man Next to Hitler*, entry of 12 December 1941, pp. 56-7.

[6] W. Hagemann, *Vom Mythos der Masse* (Heidelberg, 1951), p. 63, quoted in Bramsted, p. 203.

behind Goebbels's manipulation of the Führer cult in Nazi propaganda throughout the Third Reich.

It is ironic therefore that *Triumph des Willens*, the most powerful film depicting this relationship, was produced against Goebbels's wishes in direct opposition to his repeated call for more subtle methods of film propaganda. In her published account of the filming, Leni Riefenstahl revealed that 'the preparations for the Party Convention were made in connection with the preparations for the camera work.'[7] Siegfried Kracauer concluded that 'this illuminating statement reveals that the Convention was planned not only as a spectacular mass meeting, but also as spectacular film propaganda.'[8] Riefenstahl's staff consisted of sixteen cameramen, each with an assistant. Thirty cameras were used to film the events together with four complete sound-equipment trucks. Altogether, 120 assistants were assigned for the filming, and new techniques of wide-angle photography and telescopic lenses were employed to scan the crowd's reactions. The result was a transfiguration of reality which purported to assume the character of an authentic documentary. Not only were scenes rehearsed beforehand but it was not a direct record as the sequence of events in the film are manipulated in order to build up an image of leader worship. Its political mission was to show, as the *Völkischer Beobachter* put it, 'the order, unity, and determination of the National Socialist movement . . . a documentary record of the unanimous loyalty to the Führer and therefore to Germany'.[9]

The ritual of the mass meetings was an important element in the projection of the Führer cult. They also served as means of demonstrating the sense of national community and the desire for order. Hilter knew this, as the extract from *Mein Kampf* shows:

Mass assemblies are necessary for the reason that, in attending them, the individual . . . now begins to feel isolated and in fear of being left alone as he acquires for the first time the picture of a great community which has a strengthening and encouraging effect on most people. . . . And only a mass demonstration can impress upon him the greatness of

[7] L. Riefenstahl, *Hinter den Kulissen des Reichsparteitagfilms* (Munich, 1935), p. 84.

[8] Kracauer, p. 301.

[9] *VB*, 2 September 1933. This included an interview with Riefenstahl.

this community. . . while seeking his way, he is gripped by the force of mass suggestion.[10]

The importance of the visible display of power as an intermediary between the persuasiveness of emotional appeals and pressures through the evoking of fear is reflected in the Nuremberg rallies.[11] For in a totalitarian state, as Ernst Bramsted observed, 'it is not enough to have power, it has to be advertised continuously. In other words, the possession of power is nothing without its display.'[12] Eugen Hadamovsky, who was later to become the Third Reich's National Broadcasting Director, wrote in 1933: 'All the power one has, even more than one has, must be demonstrated. One hundred speeches, five hundred newspaper articles, radio talks, films, and plays are unable to produce the same effect as a procession of gigantic masses of people taking place with discipline and active participation.'[13]

Triumph des Willens was eventually released in 1935 and in its completed form ran for 120 minutes. It received approval from the *Prüfstelle* on 26 March 1935 and opened at the Ufa-Palast in Berlin three days later where among the guests of honour were foreign diplomats, army generals, and top Party officials. The following description of the events captured in the documentary are taken from the *Illustrierter Film-Kurier*, the programme that accompanied the film. It is instructive for the way in which the RMVP wanted the film audience to worship Hitler:

Introduction:
'The film writes history, the days of Nuremberg.'

Happy Morning:
Sunlight floods the land of the Germans. Clouds gather into clusters, rise up to form gigantic mountains surrounded by silver and golden rays, they subside, flow, scatter . . . like a fantastic eagle, an aeroplane glides through the air. Spreading its wings wide, it plunges forward, its propellers grinding themselves howling into the wind. It is the aeroplane that carries the Führer towards the city, in which the great, proud, heart-stirring spectacle

[10] Hitler, pp. 397–8.
[11] The stage-management of the Party Congresses has been well analysed by H. T. Burden, *The Nuremberg Party Rallies, 1923–39* (London, 1967).
[12] Bramsted, p. 451.
[13] E. Hadamovsky, *Propaganda und nationale Macht, Die Organisation der öffentlichen Meinung* (Öldenburg, 1933), p. 2.

of a new Germany will be consummated. Onwards rushes the mighty machine. The roaring rhythm of the motor shouts into the wind: 'Nuremberg . . . Nuremberg . . . Nuremberg . . .'
Far below the city is radiating. Boundless masses of people stare into the sky. There! — as close as the clouds, on the sun-golden firmament, the speeding shadow becomes larger, approaches. Thundering, it circles over the city. An aeroplane. *The* aeroplane! The Führer is arriving.

Festive Day:

As the gigantic bird finally hovers over the airfield, loses altitude, approaches, stops, the tenseness of anticipation of thousands has reached its peak and is released in joyful, enthusiastic shouts. The Führer gets out of the plane. Here and there a brief, firm handshake, a friendly word, a glance of recognition. On the faces of those who were able to be there is the light of grateful confidence. With roaring cheers from all sides, the Führer rides into the city. The streets tremble with the shouts of loyalty, of love, of faith! Nuremberg greets the Führer of the Germans in the proud exaltation of this festive, sun-filled day!

Joyful Evening:

In front of the Führer's hotel the crowd pushes forward in the dark night. The army marches up. Torches and searchlights break through the evening darkness. In large, beaming lights a welcome shines from the hotel: 'Heil Hitler!' The army band groups in a ceremonious circle, the grey of the steel helmets gleam in the dazzling light. The conductor raises his baton. On up to the starry sky there rise the festive melodies of the tattoo. Again and again the Führer appears at his window, again and again he is cheered by the cheerful and exalted people on this festive, happy evening.

Parade of the Nation:

A new day dawns. The soft light of the morning sun lies on the roofs, flickers about the centuries-old towers of this most German of German towns. Bells are heard in the countryside. The old, beautiful city in the colourful decoration of billowing flags, in the cheerful ornaments of its beautiful baroque monuments and figures of the venerable churches, awaits the grandiose spectacle. And thus the festival continues to show in rapid, concise succession the events that become history:

> Opening of Party Congress in the Congress Hall.
> March past of 52,000 men in the Labour Service.
> March past of the Youth Workers.
> Parade of National Costumes of Farm People.
> German Youth before their Führer.
> Honouring of the heroes in the Luitpold Grove.
> Dedication of the units with the 'Blood Flag'.
> March past of SA and SS.
> Clustering of flags of the officials of the Labour Front.
> March past the Führer.

The Führer. As Shown in this Film:
With what heartfelt kindness the Führer steps up to the peasant women who came to Nuremberg in their old national costumes, grasps the hands extended in a shy and hesitant manner, laughs, smiles, and speaks with the women. . . . What solemn force, what manly earnestness is expressed in his features when he reviews the line of standard bearers, how very different here, almost symbolically sacred in manner, is the handshake! How very much this nation belongs to the Führer, how very much the Führer belongs to it! In every glance, in every handshake, there is expressed the confession and the vow: 'We belong together, in eternal loyalty together.'[14]

Triumph des Willens was a combination of reality and stylization, but, above all, it was a masterpiece of timing. The documentary film-maker, Robert Vas, has argued that what makes a propaganda film truly great is this recognition of the right moment, the precise point at which it can assert itself most forcefully.[15] In projecting the image of the strong leader to an audience that had come to associate the Weimar Republic and the Treaty of Versailles with national ignominy, *Triumph des Willens* represented the triumph of self-realization over the hegemony imposed by foreigners. Hence, the opening of the film begins with a slow fade-up of the German eagle and the title *Triumph des Willens*, with the caption:

Twenty years after the outbreak of the First World War,
Sixteen years after the beginning of Germany's time of trial,
Nineteen months after the beginning of the rebirth of Germany,
Adolf Hitler flew to Nuremberg to muster his faithful followers . . .

The Nazi ethos was, as we have seen, anti-individualist and therefore anti-democratic. *Völkisch* thought had always been preoccupied with myths and symbols. The irrationality that was central to *Völkisch* experience led to a belief in magic, represented by the old German gods of the *Volk*.[16] The leadership ideal became part of this complex *Völkisch* thought, in which a revolutionary leader would emerge and bring about a *Völkisch* revolution. According to Hitler, this meant that the nation should also make 'sacrifices for their great men as a matter of course. It's the great men who express a nation's

[14] *IFK*, no. 2302, 1935, this is reproduced in *Film Culture*, Spring 1973, p. 168.
[15] R. Vas, 'Sorcerers or Apprentices. Some Aspects of Propaganda Films', *Sight and Sound*, Autumn, 1963, pp. 199–204.
[16] For a more detailed discussion see, Mosse, *Nazi Culture*, pp. xxvii–xxviii.

soul.'[17] The strength of the nation was therefore seen to lie in the submergence of the individual will in the will of the nation, as expressed by Adolf Hitler. William Shirer witnessed the 1934 Nuremberg Rally and noted the willingness of the audience to surrender their independence of thought and action:

'We are strong and will get stronger', Hitler shouted at them through the microphone, his words echoing across the hushed field from the loudspeakers. And there, in the flood-lit night, jammed together like sardines, in one mass formation, the little men of Germany who have made Nazism possible achieved the highest state of being the Germanic man knows: the shedding of their individual souls and mind — with the personal responsibilities and doubts and problems — until under the mystic lights and at the sound of the magic words of the Austrian they were merged completely in the Germanic herd.[18]

Leni Riefenstahl has stated that the 'triumph' depicted in the film was twofold: the triumph of a strong Germany and the triumph of the will of the Leader.[19] These themes were conveyed by distinct stylistic device, each commanding the guise of documentary 'reportage'. The text of the film consists of policy speeches made by Hitler and his Party Leaders and oaths of loyalty from his faithful supporters. The other aspects to note are the visual compositions employed by Riefenstahl and her assistants. To some extent one can compare the ornamental organization of mass scenes with Fritz Lang's *Die Nibelungen*. The monumental style of *Triumph des Willens* was meant to show Hitler, in Erwin Leiser's words, 'as a new Siegfried and his supporters as extras in a colossal Wagner opera, an anonymous mass completely under his sway'.[20]

Although the sequence of events was changed, *Triumph des Willens* is structured in the literal documentary narrative and yet it avoids the monotony of describing such uniform events. By her skilful use of ordinary cinematic devices, Riefenstahl successfully orchestrates the motifs that are to be highlighted. These motifs include: ancient buildings, statues, icons, the sky and clouds, fire, the swastika, marching, the masses, and Hitler. As one critic has observed, the central theme they develop is that 'Hitler has come from the sky to kindle ancient

[17] H. Trevor-Roper, *Hitler's Table Talk, 1941–44* (London, 1973), p. 206.
[18] Shirer, p. 25.
[19] Riefenstahl, p. 102.
[20] Leiser, p. 25.

Nuremberg with primeval Teutonic fire, to liberate the energy and spirit of the German people through a dynamic new movement with roots in their racial consciousness.'[21] The opening sequence of the film celebrates the apotheosis of Hitler. It is worthy of particular attention as it is a statement of the key theme in *Triumph des Willens*. Through a break in the clouds we see an aeroplane waving through the white masses and suddenly appear in a clear sky. Medieval Nuremberg with its towers and spires wrapped in the mist appears below. As the plane becomes more defined the overture to *Die Meistersinger* slowly merges into the Horst Wessel Lied, just as the old Germany has given way to the new. By means of magnificent aerial photography the streets of Nuremberg are lined by thousands of marching Germans all in perfect formation, creating the first geometric pattern of humanity to be shown in the film. The plane eventually makes contact with the earth and taxis to a halt. The German people await their leader. Hitler emerges, in uniform, to acknowledge the cheers of the crowd who surge forward to greet him.

Throughout the film, Hitler is always seen in isolation photographed from below so that he appears to tower above the rest of the proceedings. Furthermore, it is not without symbolic meaning that the features of Hitler invariably appear against a backdrop of clouds or sky. The triumphant journey from the airport through Nuremberg is used to juxtapose the essential loneliness of the Führer with shots of the masses. The camera is placed behind Hitler, concentrating on his arm extended in the Nazi salute. There follows a montage sequence of Hitler's arm and individual faces that are picked out of the crowd together with the close-ups of Nuremberg's great statues looking on approvingly. As if to reinforce the message that the Saviour has descended from the heavens and is among his people, Hitler's car stops for a mother and her little girl to present flowers to the Führer.

Whenever Hitler is shown in the film he is depicted as a lone figure whereas the individuality of the people is submerged in the symmetry and order that characterizes the mass scenes. Riefenstahl conveys this idea of *Ordnung* (Order) by a whole

[21] See, K. Kelmann, 'Propaganda a Vision — Triumph of the Will', in *Film Culture*, Spring, 1973, p. 162–4.

series of rigidly straight columns of marching units surging across the screen in a succession of different patterns and combinations. An important element in the creation of this ritual is the use made of banners and flags in Nazi pageants. Throughout all the ceremonies flags proliferate, but there is one scene of special significance that encapsulates the mysticism and the linking of past and future that was so typical of the Movement. It concerns the ceremony of the 'blood flag', the official flag stained with the blood of the Nazi martyrs during the abortive Munich beer-hall *putsch* of November 1923.[22]

The ceremony starts in the Luitpold Stadium where columns of the SA (97,000) and the SS (11,000) form giant rectangles beneath a sea of banners and flags. The camera is placed high up on one of the special towers constructed for the film. Stephen Roberts, who was in the stadium, observed what happened next:

Before addressing them, Hitler solemnly marched up to the sacrificial fires that paid homage to those who had died for the movement. It was the only moment of quietness in the whole week. For what seemed an interminable time, three men — Hitler, Himmler, and Lutze — strode up the wide path that clove the brown mass in twain and, after saluting the fire, marched back. It was a superbly arranged gesture. Those men represented individualism as against the solid anonymity of the massed Brownshirts; they stood for leadership as against the blind obedience of the people.[23]

Considering that the rally was taking place only a few months after the Röhm purge, in which the SA were brought to heel, it is not surprising to discover that the occasion was used to emphasize the unity of the Party. At this solemn moment Lutze (the new head of the SA) moves towards the rostrum on which Hitler is standing and reiterates that the Party's troubles are now over:

LUTZE. My Führer, just as in the old days we carried out our duties, so we shall wait upon your orders in the future. And we cannot do anything other than follow the orders of our Führer and thus prove that we are the same as we always were. Our Führer, Adolf Hitler, Sieg Heil! Sieg Heil!

---

[22] The 'blood flag' was in fact the bullet-riddled flag that Andreas Bauriedl had allegedly held until he was struck down at the Feldherrnhalle in 1923.

[23] S. Roberts, *The House that Hitler Built* (London, 1937), p. 140.

Hitler then speaks. He stands alone on the rostrum, silhouetted against the sky:

HITLER. Men of the SA and SS, a few months ago a black cloud rose over the movement, but our Party knew how to overcome it as it knows how to overcome everything else. So it will be with every rift that appears in the fabric of our movement. It stands as solid as this block of stone and there is nothing in Germany that can break it . . . Only a madman or a confirmed liar can think that I or anyone else could have any intention of destroying the links that we joined over the years with such difficulty. No, comrades, we stand firm together here in Germany, and we must stand firm together for Germany. Now I hand over the new flags to you, convinced that I am handing them over to the most faithful hands in Germany . . . And so I greet you as my old, faithful men of the SA and SS. Sieg Heil!

The ceremony comes to an end with the consecration of rows of banners and flags as Hitler solemnly touches these new flags with the old 'blood flag'—a form of ritualistic baptism. Cannons are fired as he presents each new flag to the storm-troopers. The scene ends with a seemingly endless procession of flags passing down the stadium and up past both sides of the rostrum where Hitler stands saluting them.

What is so remarkable about this episode with the parade of flags, and also a similar scene where they are borne into the Congress Hall for the final speeches, is that one rarely glimpses those people who are bearing them. Close-up plunges the viewer into the midst of the forest of flags that seem to move of their own accord, and in the longer shots the camera angle obscures any human presence. Furthermore, this feeling of being caught in almost constant motion has an hypnotic effect. An impartial British observer at the Rally later wrote: 'It was at times a struggle to remain rational in a horde so surcharged with tense emotionalism.'[24]

On the previous evening the Party leaders came forward to pay their tribute to Hitler. Goebbels's speech is of particular interest because it reveals his attitude towards propaganda and elucidates his fear that such films (like *Triumph des Willens*) could crystallize latent opposition to the manifest crudities of National Socialism:

GOEBBELS. May the bright flame of our enthusiasm never be extinguished. It alone gives light and warmth to the creative art of modern

[24] E. Amy Buller, *Darkness Over Germany* (London, 1943), p. 166.

political propaganda. It arose from the very heart of the people in order to derive more strength and power. It may be a good thing to possess power that rests on arms. But it is better and more gratifying to win and hold the heart of the people.

Bismarck once stated that 'enthusiasm cannot be pickled like herrings', but he did not foresee the extent and power of the mass demonstrations that the Nazis incorporated in their art of pageantry. Intrinsic in the ritual of the mass demonstrations were the quasi-religious liturgical responses. An excellent example of this can be found in *Triumph des Willens* in the sequence where 52,000 *Arbeitsdienst* (members) have gathered on the Zeppelin Field, holding spades, to affirm their faith in Hitler. Marshalled in ranks beneath the great German eagle mounted over the stadium, the ceremony is conducted like a religious service:

HIERL [*leader of the Labour Front*]. My Führer, I announce that 52,000 workers have answered the summons.
HITLER. Hail, worker volunteers!
CORPSMEN. Hail, Our Leader! Corps, Take up arms! [*drumrolls*]
CORPSMEN. Where do you come from, comrade? — I come from Friesia.
And you, comrade?
From Bavaria.
And you? From Kaiserstuhl.
And you? From Pomerania . . . from Konigsberg, Silesia, Baltic, Black Forest, Dresden, Danube, from the Rhine, and from the Saar . . .
CORPSMEN [*in unison*]. ONE PEOPLE, ONE FÜHRER, ONE REICH!
ONE. Today we are all workers together and we are working with iron.
ALL. With iron.
ONE. With mortar.
ALL. With mortar.
ONE. With sand.
ALL. With sand.
ONE. We are diking the North Sea.
ALL. We greet you, German worker.
ONE. We are planting trees.
ALL. Forests everywhere.
ONE. We are building roads.
ALL. From village to village, from town to town.
ONE. We are providing new fields for the farmer.
ALL. Fields and forests, fields and bread — for Germany!
SONG. We are true patriots, our country we rebuild. We did not stand in the trenches amidst the exploding grenades but nevertheless we are soldiers.

VARIOUS. From one end of Germany to the other. Everywhere, in the north, in the west, in the east, in the south, on the land, on the sea, and in the air. Comrades, down with the Red Front and reaction.

ALL. You are not dead, you live in Germany!

HITLER. My comrades, you have now presented yourselves to me and the whole German people in this way for the first time. You are representatives of a great ideal. We know that for millions of our countrymen work will no longer be a lonely occupation but one that gathers together the whole of our country. No longer will anybody in Germany consider manual labour as lower than any other kind of work. The time will come when no German will be able to enter the community of this nation without first having passed through your community. Remember that not only are the eyes of hundreds of thousands in Nuremberg watching, but the whole of Germany is seeing you for the first time. You are Germany and I know that Germany will proudly watch its sons marching forward into the glorious future.

SONG. We are the soldiers who work.

ALL. Sieg Heil!

This affirmation of faith in the Führer reaches its crescendo in the closing ceremony held in the Conference Hall. Once again the camera links the crowd to the key icons in Nazi ritual and to Hitler himself. This technique is used throughout the film to relate the masses to specific symbolic objects. Riefenstahl frames the crowds which are dominated by huge banners and then moves deftly from the swastikas to eagles and then back to the people. The effect is one of total identification between leader and led. A massive demonstration of individuality submerged in wave after wave of fanatical devotion. In his final speech of the Rally, Hitler builds up his audience to a point of exultant fanaticism; he is both calm and impassioned: 'The nervous century has reached its end. There will not be another revolution in Germany for the next 1,000 years.' He is loudly acclaimed as the camera pulls back to reveal waves of outstretched arms hailing their Führer. Rudolf Hess, the Deputy Leader, comes forward, waiting for the applause to stop. Eventually he brings the 1934 Rally to a close by declaring: 'The Party is Hitler. But Hitler is Germany, just as Germany is Hitler. Hitler! Sieg Heil!'

Banners are raised once again and the Horst Wessel Lied swells up on the sound-track. *Triumph des Willens* ends with a dissolve from a large swastika to marching storm-troopers who represent its power incarnate. The marching columns are shot from an angle which juxtaposes them not merely against the sky, but leading up into it. The final image is the subliminal ascension of the German nation to the heavens from which the Führer came in the beginning. It symbolizes the final consummation of the triumph of the will, and in the process Leni Riefenstahl achieved the definitive obliteration of the division between myth and reality.[25]

Despite his misgivings about such a project, no doubt inflamed by the fact that Hitler had commissioned the film, Goebbels appreciated the artistic quality of *Triumph des Willens* and recommended that it be awarded the National Film Prize. One month after the film's première on 1 May 1935, he presented Riefenstahl with this award and commented on the choice:

> The film marks a very great achievement amongst the total film production for the year. It is topical, in that it shows the present: it conveys in monumental and hitherto unseen images the stirring events of our political life. It is a magnificent cinematic vision of the Führer, seen here for the first time with a power that has not been revealed before. The film has successfully avoided the danger of merely a politically slanted film. It has translated the powerful rhythm of this great epoch into something outstandingly artistic; it is an epic, forging the tempo of marching formations, steel-like in its conviction and fired by a passionate artistry.[26]

Even though a peculiarly indigenous National Socialist artefact, *Triumph des Willens* actually won the Gold Medal at the 1935 Venice Film Festival and the Grand Prix at the Paris Film Festival, 1937.[27] The film continued to be shown during the Third Reich even though it was made at a time when the Party was attempting to establish itself internationally. To the rest of the world *Triumph des Willens* was a terrifying picture of a newly emerging Fascist state, but to Germans themselves the film had a more specific intention; it celebrated the

---

[25] Cf. Kelmann, p. 164. It is ironic therefore that such a powerful film could be ridiculed as easily as it was in Charles Ridley's Movie-Tone newsreel, *Germany Calling* (1941).

[26] *VB*, 1 May 1935.

[27] Much to the surprise of the RMVP, who were also gratified to discover that it had not even been referred to as a 'propaganda film' by the French press. BA, *Sammlung Sänger, Zsg, 102/62*, 18 November 1937. The film was banned in Holland because, according to Ufa, their subsidiary 'Bioscoopbund' was governed by Jews. BA, *R1091/1031a, No. 1129*, 13 December 1935.

Führerprinzip together with an overall display of the strength and health of the German people and its youth.

Uniforms, bands, flags, and symbols were all part of the Nazi propaganda machine to increase the impact of strong words with powerful deeds. This is the fundamental rationale behind the constant display of Nazi symbols in a film like *Triumph des Willens*. The determination to be and feel united was not enough; the Nazis had to give public testimony to this unity. The Nuremberg Rallies were carefully staged theatrical pieces devised to create such an effect. 'I had spent six years in St. Petersburg before the war in the best days of the old Russian ballet,' wrote the British Ambassador to Germany, Sir Neville Henderson, 'but for grandiose beauty I have never seen a ballet to compare with it.'[28] The nature of the Nazis' message was such that concrete demonstrations of physical strength gave a visible reinforcement to the spiritual message the propaganda was trying to instil. Such emotional manipulation worked best at these ceremonies where the individual participant in the ritual, fanatically moved by Hitler's rhetoric and swayed by the crowd, underwent a metamorphosis—in Goebbels's famous phrase—'from a little worm into part of a large dragon'.[29]

DER HERRSCHER (THE RULER, 1937)

After *Triumph des Willens* there was no need to make another film about Hitler, and none was commissioned. He had been presented once and for all the way he wanted to be portrayed and no actor was asked to play him. However, there were a number of variations on the leadership theme. Generally these featured characters from German history presented in the Führer's image, although occasionally a contemporary figure was used whose life provided analogies to Hitler's career and teachings. The most notable film in this latter category was *Der Herrscher*, directed by Veit Harlan[30] and starring Emil Jannings as Matthias Clausen, leader of an industrial dynasty

---

[28] N. Henderson, *Failure of a Mission* (London, 1940), p. 71.
[29] Goebbels, *Der Kampf um Berlin*, p. 18.
[30] Veit Harlan (1899-1964). Started out as an actor but during the Third Reich directed mainly overt propaganda works: *Mein Sohn, der Herr Minister* and *Der Herrscher* (both 1937), *Jud Süss* (1940).

clearly modelled on the Krupps dynasty.[31] The story was a free adaptation of Gerhart Hauptmann's play *Vor Sonnenuntergang* (*Before Sunset*), with script-writers Thea von Harbou and Curt Johannes Braun providing the Nazi interpretation.

Although ostensibly about a widowed industrialist whose family try to have him certified insane when his ideas and love for a young secretary threaten their inheritance, the importance of the film lies in the characterization of Matthias Clausen. Whereas in Hauptmann's play the gentle art collector is destroyed by the conflict, in Veit Harlan's film he renounces his family and becomes a powerful figure in rebuilding Germany by bequeathing his factory to the community. *Der Angriff* referred to this conflict of interests in the Clausen dynasty:

> The characters in the film are not only people who speak, but people who act as well... The factory does not represent the old capitalist ethos. Matthias Clausen leaves it to the State and it is from the factory that the new leader–worker emerges, whose duty it is to administer it for the entire body of workers... One may wonder if it was necessary to push the 'antithetic' characters so strongly to the limits of caricature... Yes, it was necessary. They are nothing less than pathetic little egoists![32]

The moral of the story was that if one submitted unconditionally to absolute authority such loyalty and obedience would be rewarded by final victory. Nazi racial concepts and the idea of *Gemeinschaft* presented little conflict to the Nazis, for individual rights would be willingly forgone for the sake of the whole community. This demand for individual sacrifice was established in one of the opening scenes in the film.

After the funeral of his wife, Clausen decides to tour the factory. He informs Erhardt, head of the company's research department, that he wants to leave something of more lasting value than just the factory. He learns from Erhardt that in his absence some of the directors have decided that the company should cease to subsidize the research unit. Clausen immediately calls an emergency board meeting. He upbraids the board for stopping the subsidy, saying that the research should help to make the German steel industry independent of foreign

---

[31] Harlan maintained that he and Jannings studied newsreels of the Krupp family in order to reproduce their mannerisms on the screen. All references are from the French edition, Veit Harlan, *Le Cinéma allemand selon Goebbels* (Paris, 1974), p. 44.

[32] *Der Angriff*, 18 March 1937.

resources. He says he is proud that he can help the State in this way and he refuses to retire because none of the board are capable of carrying out his ideals. The following exchange between Clausen and his board, acted out under a portrait of Hitler, is a typical Nazi harangue about individual responsibility:

CLAUSEN [*to his directors*]. My doctor has urged me to take a long holiday. It would be the first holiday for many years. I wanted to have a talk with you to decide if I could afford to have it. I can't have it! None of you are capable of even taking my place for six months.
SON-IN-LAW. Not even I, Father?
CLAUSEN. No! It's not just a matter of a paltry sum of money. It's your outlook on life. Your boundless egoism is exposed with every word you utter and what's more, you show a profound lack of understanding of the urgent problems confronting this country. At such a time, all you can do with your handsome director's salary is whine about not getting a large enough share of the profits.

As we have seen, the Führer cult exalted the national interest and called for submission in the name of the people. These sentiments were never more explicitly expressed than in Clausen's closing speech to his directors in the same scene. It is a threatening justification for the regime's existence, couched in the sort of stirring rhetoric that was to prepare Germany for the blind sacrifice that was soon to be demanded of her:

CLAUSEN. Gentlemen, we are here to provide work and bread for millions of people. We are here to work for the community of the nation. The aim of every industrial leader conscious of his responsibility must be to serve this community. This will of mine is the supreme law which governs my work. All else must be subordinated to this will, without opposition, even if in doing this I lead the firm into ruin. He who does not submit himself to this supreme law has no place in the Clausen factories! Thank you, gentlemen.

Clausen's call for total obedience even if it meant financial ruin was remarkably similar to Hitler's speech to the Reichstag on 1 September 1939, when he claimed he had 'never learned the meaning of the word surrender' and demanded that the German people join him in the nation's glorious struggle or die a proud death with him in the attempt. The circumstances may have been different, but both speeches illustrate the radical precepts of Nazi ideology which knew only victory or death.

According to Veit Harlan the recurrence of typical Nazi

phrases like 'popular community', 'individual sacrifice', and 'the intellectual and the manual worker' were written into the script by Goebbels and Walter Funk, who at this time was Under Secretary of State in the Propaganda Ministry and later became Minister of Economics.[33] Pursuing a theme that runs throughout his autobiography, Harlan attempts to dissociate himself from the Party by arguing that he asked to be removed from *Der Herrscher* as he felt that too many political changes had been made to the original play. However Goebbels insisted that he remain, and posted Arnold Räther, Vice-President of the *Reichsfilmkammer*, to the set as an official Party observer in order that the Nazi interpretation should remain.[34] Clausen's final speech in the film, in which he talks about his past struggles and finally bequeaths his factories to the State, is alleged to have been completely rewritten by Goebbels and Funk:[35]

The courts have ruled in Clausen's favour. His family's attempts to have him certified as insane have failed. Clausen walks through the steel works alone. By the time he reaches his office he has made his decision:

CLAUSEN [*talking to Wultke, his old friend and secretary*]. . . . One must undergo the refinement process to push forward for final victory. Only then does one become steel — though you must not be afraid of the furnace!
WULTKE. Herr Clausen, you have around you many more faithful men than you think.
CLAUSEN. That ought to make me happy for these men — for loyalty is its own reward — and so is disloyalty!

Wultke leaves and Clausen requests a shorthand typist to take down his testimony. It is Inken, the girl he loves. He begins to dictate, unaware of her presence . . .

CLAUSEN. To the workers and employees of the Clausen works. Prevailed upon by the responsibility I have for the factory I have been building for generations, I declare the following . . .
I dissociate myself from my children in law. They are not worthy of taking over my inheritance and are incapable of administering it. I present the factory that I have created to those who helped me in this: I present it to the workers of the Clausen works. I am certain

[33] Harlan, p. 49.
[34] Ibid., p. 47.
[35] Ibid., p. 50.

that from your ranks a man will rise to continue my work. No matter whether he comes from the furnace, the drawing board, from the laboratory, or the work bench! I will teach him what little one who is departing can teach one just arriving. For the born leader needs no teacher other than his own genius. [*End of film.*]

National Socialism looked to a strong leader, steeped in German myths who would take charge of the interests of the nation and race. *Triumph des Willens* highlighted the emergence of the new 'homo germanicus'—a man of destiny with a clearly defined mission. *Der Herrscher* rationalizes the apparent contradiction in Nazi thought between individual freedom, collective responsibility, and the *Führerprinzip*. Therefore it served the twofold purpose of reconciling the need for an all-powerful leader with its corollary, the loyal follower.

The conclusion to be drawn from the film was that under a weak democratic form of government the Clausen works, and Germany's industry in general, had been controlled by foreign interests to the detriment of the German people. Whereas under the guidance of the individual leader of genius, embodying the will of his people, the true spirit and economic well-being of the nation is actualized. *Der Herrscher* can be seen as an explicit lecture from the RMVP on precisely what the State expected from its citizens. Goebbels, who according to Harlan, considered Hauptmann a Communist, was delighted with the film and enthused: 'After what we did to *Der Herrscher* it had very little to do with Hauptmann's play. It is because we did not follow Hauptmann that we have struck such a receptive chord with the masses.'[36]

On 18 March 1937, Goebbels attended the film's première and sat next to Jannings and Marianne Hoppe (who played Inken). Two days previously he had awarded the *Prädikat,* 'politically and artistically especially valuable'. Less than two weeks later, on 1 May 1937, *Der Herrscher* was accorded one of the highest accolades bestowed in the *Filmwelt* when it won the National Film Prize. This afforded Harlan and Jannings an invitation to the Chancelry where they were greeted by Baldur von Schirach, Goebbels, and Hitler, who congratulated them on 'a great artistic achievement which has brought

[36] Ibid., p. 55.

much honour to Germany'.[37] In a confidential directive issued to the press and film industry, they were reminded that the film had scored a notable success at the Biennale: 'This was not only due to the fact that such typical German character traits are highly regarded in Europe, but also because it was recognized, in a period of uncertainty, as a "committed" film'.[38] It was suggested that this should serve as a basis for future film production.

THE HISTORICAL ANALOGY

It was Goebbels's constant endeavour to demonstrate that the Führer's will was the true reflection of the people's wishes. In the Nazi *Weltanschauung*, parliamentary democracy does not express popular opinion. Hitler saw certain dangerous features in democratic government and in *Mein Kampf* he outlined his objections:

One truth which must always be borne in mind is that the majority can never replace the man. The majority represents not only ignorance but cowardice. And just as a hundred blockheads do not equal one man of wisdom, so a hundred poltroons are incapable of any political line of action that requires moral strength and fortitude.[39]

Because of this contempt for democratic institutions, Nazi propaganda was constantly at odds with parliamentary representation and never ceased in its efforts to promote the necessity of the *Führerprinzip*. Therefore anti-parliamentarianism and leadership by an individual of genius went hand in hand. It would appear from the great quantity that were produced that Goebbels felt that the film set in an historical context was the best medium for conveying such a political message. Dr Fritz Hippler, the director and *Reichsfilmintendant* between 1939 and 1943, wrote in *Betrachtungen zum Filmschaffen* (*Reflections on Film-Making*):

The essential requirement for a historical film is that it should possess authenticity on a grand scale. The only possible subjects for successful historical films are personalities and events from the past with which people of the present are familiar or with which they can identify. In other words, it must show meaning to life by means of the timeless

---

[37] Harlan, p. 56.
[38] BA, *Sammlung Sänger, Zsg, 102/62*, 19 August 1937.
[39] Hitler, p. 81.

authenticity of particular historical events, situations, and personalities.[40]

Historical films for the Nazis were only relevant if they exploited contemporary themes in a historical context concentrating on the 'great men' in Germany's past who embodied aspects of the National Socialist *Weltanschauung*. This allowed for flexibility and easy manipulation of the themes to be disseminated. More importantly, such films invited comparisons with the present and encouraged the audience to identify with Hitler. There is some evidence to suggest that this genre proved popular with film audiences, particularly with young people. In a survey carried out among the Hitler Youth in 1943, children were asked to list their reasons for liking a film. Invariably, the fact that it was a 'historical film' was their answer.[41]

As far as Goebbels was concerned the 'Führer-type' biography need not necessarily restrict itself to leaders as such but could centre on any historical figure whose life provided analogies to Hitler's. Thus the biographies of the inventor Diesel (*Diesel*, 1942), the sculptor and architect Schlüter (*Andreas Schlüter*, 1942), or the alchemist Paracelsus (*Paracelsus*, 1943) were all intended to show that intuitive genius could not be replaced by a 'hundred blockheads'.

Friedrich Schiller (1940)

One of the earliest films in this genre was *Friedrich Schiller*. Made in 1940, following Hitler's victory in the West, it was released under the subtitle *Der Triumph eines Genies* (*Triumph of Genius*). The film tells of the romantic *Sturm und Drang* years of the great writer when he was a Cadet at the military academy of Duke Carl Eugen von Württemberg, at Stuttgart. He is fundamentally opposed to military discipline and the philosophical ideas of his times. It is the interplay of these conflicting ideas in his relationship with the Duke which forms the basis for the political message that the film was to convey. The conflict between the young poet (Horst Casper) and the Duke (Heinrich George) is seen as a trial of strength between the genius to whom ordinary laws do not apply and the rigid conformity of the academy. An early exchange illustrates

---

[40] F. Hippler, *Betrachtungen zum Filmschaffen* (Berlin, 1942), p. 94.
[41] Sander, p. 121.

Schiller's intuitive genius and rebellious nature as opposed to the Duke's formal learning. The scene is a class-room where the Duke is conducting a lecture on 'Is the genius born or made?':

ABEL. The world derides a genius, perhaps because he will not submit to its rules, or perhaps because he doesn't notice the dust on his clothes.

DUKE. Abel, keep to the point. Now my sons, what was it? Ah yes, are great minds born or taught?

CLASS. Taught, your serene Highness.

SCHILLER. Born, your Highness, not taught!

DUKE. Well now, an opponent. We'll debate. Great minds are taught not made!

SCHILLER. Great minds are only born, never made.

DUKE. If great minds were just simply born, you would have geniuses all over the place. Even amongst the most primitive tribes on earth. [*laughs*]

SCHILLER. The Genius, as we refer to a great mind, is not just born of his mother, but of his whole people.

DUKE. Excellent! but the State directs him on his way to perfection in its schools.

SCHILLER. No! Genius can find its own way to fulfilment. He does not need imperfect institutions like schools.

DUKE. Do you really think the genius is as perfect as that?

SCHILLER. Genius is simply a term ordinary people use to describe an extraordinary man — it is a yardstick that the world has created for him.

DUKE. Yes, but if the genius is as perfect as you say, then surely he must recognize this himself.

SCHILLER. All the Genius knows is that it must be as it is. He has no option to behave other than the way he does.

DUKE. Must he be then as he is?

SCHILLER. Yes.

DUKE. And he must behave accordingly?

SCHILLER. Always!

DUKE. And have you accomplished anything in the nature of a genius?

SCHILLER. I don't know — I would like to.

DUKE. You would like to — ha ha — Yes, but I think the genius has to! [*shouting*]

SCHILLER [*shouting back*]. I want to!

DUKE. What?

SCHILLER [*softly*]. I want to!

At first glance the film might seem to be an appeal for freedom of opinion and against the suppression of free speech, and therefore a classic anti-Nazi parable. However, by contrasting

Schiller's Pan-Germanism with the Duke's blind opposition to German unification, the director, Herbert Maisch,[42] was to present the poet as a prophetic genius in an age marked by the despotism of antiquated princedoms and ignorant rulers. Thus the Duke of Württemberg is not maligned for his lack of vision; Schiller is merely presented as a prototype Hitler, imbued with exceptional gifts of seeing beyond the limits of his age. Even so, Goebbels was not entirely convinced that German audiences would grasp the point. On 13 November 1940 he ordered trial showings of the film in Stuttgart and Strasbourg to gauge the reaction of the people from Schiller's homeland. All press reports and previews were banned.[43] These showings, in fact, proved to be a notable success and eventually, on 17 December 1940, *Friedrich Schiller* was given its première at the Capitol am Zoo in Berlin, and thereafter distributed throughout the country. However Goebbels's cautious policy was vindicated by a generally favourable response from the public, as indicated by the following extract from the SD Report on *Friedrich Schiller*:

The reception of the film has been generally favourable with a few, minor, exceptions . . . it is reported that the film has made a strong impression with all levels of society. Many people are saying that Schiller, who for many people is a hazy figure from their school days, has come to life, and that the film has successfully brought one of the leading figures of the past closer to the present. This impression is even confirmed in rural areas where the title of the film aroused little interest at first. From the kind of remarks made after people had seen the film, it is apparent that people regard Schiller as representing gentle criticism of the 'regimented education of the young people'. At the same time, it is of course recognized that the Charles' School was a product of antiquated principalities. Amongst regular cinema-goers, it was recognized as a positive feature that the protagonist was played not by an established star but by an actor of the coming generation.[44]

Bismarck (1940)

On 6 December 1940, Wolfgang Liebeneiner's *Bismarck* was released. Like *Friedrich Schiller* it was concerned with a leader of genius and his attempts to unify Germany. The story begins

---

[42] Herbert Maisch also directed *Andreas Schlüter* (1942). Earlier he directed *DIII 88* (1939), a strong militarist film about the Luftwaffe.
[43] BA, *Sammlung Sänger, Zsg, 102/62*, 8 November 1940.
[44] BA, *R 58/157*, 27 January 1941.

with Bismarck as the newly appointed Prussian Prime Minister who defeats Austria at war, outwits France, and brings about the proclamation in 1871 of Wilhelm I of Prussia as Emperor of Germany. The unification of a strong and united Germany marks the triumph of Bismarck's indomitable will. The film makes it clear, however, that this was achieved not by consensus politics and the parliamentary process, but by 'iron and blood'. Addressing the Landtag at the beginning of the film, Bismarck outlines a theme that is to recur again and again: 'The great questions of the present will not be solved by speeches and parliamentary decision, but by iron and blood.'[45] Like all great leader figures, Bismarck knows what is best for Germany. In his *Table Talk* Hitler referred to the importance of these men of genius:

I shall not cease to think that the most precious possession a country can have is its great men. If I think of Bismarck, I realise that only those who have lived through 1918 could fully appreciate his worth. One sees by such examples how much it would mean if we could make the road smooth for men of talent.[46]

The historical parallel with Hitler is emphasized throughout the film. Like Hitler, Bismarck, on assuming power, immediately builds up a strong modern army to secure a lasting German Empire. In order to achieve this he informs King Wilhelm that Germany must change her attitude towards Austria and that a military pact with Russia is necessary to protect Prussia's eastern flank. When the King objects to this new alliance Bismarck retorts: 'By the time the grumblers in parliament get around to doing anything about it, we will be ready and mobilized!' Nazi film audiences were quick to spot this analogy between Bismarckian diplomacy and the Nazi-Soviet Non Aggression Pact. The SD reported:

Also well received were those parts of the film showing Bismarck's struggle to convince King Wilhelm of the validity of his policies and of the necessity of applying them at that time to the realities of the situation. When Bismarck made clear to the King the necessity of a change in attitude towards Austria, speaking of it as a matter of 'politics and diplomacy', the film audience applied this to the current relationship

[45] It was also reinforced in the special booklet, 'Bismarck', which accompanied the film. It cost 10 Pf. and contained the most important propaganda points that the RMVP wanted disseminated as well as giving brief biographies of the film stars involved. Werner Stephan, *Bismarck: Aktuelle Filmbücher* (Berlin, 1940).
[46] *Table Talk*, p. 325.

between Germany and the USSR. The reference to the fact that in foreign policy one had to be a little 'two-faced' was well understood.[47]

But the main intention of the film was to reinforce the message that the *Führerprinzip* was an essential prerequisite for the unity and greatness of the Reich. Once again a simple analogy is drawn between the two leaders. Just as Hitler protected the country from an international Jewish–Bolshevik threat by means of the Enabling Act, so Bismarck is shown dissolving the Landtag and imposing press censorship in his efforts to unite Germany's forty states under a single all-powerful rule. The impotence of the Landtag and its inability to recognize Bismarck's greatness as a politician is revealed in the following exchange prior to the dissolution of Parliament between the Iron Chancellor and Professor Virchow who is the spokesman for his opponents:

BISMARCK. In our country everyone who has achieved something in his own field thinks he can make his voice heard in politics. Professor Virchow would scarcely allow a banker to amputate the arm of a sick man, but he would like to meddle amateurishly in politics even though he knows no more about it than a banker! . . .
[*Great unrest in the Landtag*] . . . That knot that prevents Germany from fully expressing herself will never be undone with love — only military action can achieve this. So we are compelled to carry out the reform of the army in any case, whether you are in agreement or not! [*Camera shows MPs jumping up and gesticulating wildly — pans faces of Jewish-looking members, including Loewe.*]
JAKOBY. We're going to bring in a motion to make the Minister answer for these remarks with his head and his power.
BISMARCK. I'll willingly take on this responsibility, for in my politics neither my person nor my power enters into it. I intend to dissolve this Parliament, which has caused so much disorder and confusion, by order of the King until the conflict is resolved and Prussia is out of danger.
VIRCHOW. You are violating the constitution — the King is slandered!
[*Uproar, Bismarck attempts to speak many times, then pulls newspaper out of his pocket and begins to read back to the MPs. Eventually order is restored.*]
BISMARCK. Gentlemen, it is you who are violating the constitution by your doctrinaire attitude. You have made an agreement between Parliament and the King unworkable, therefore the constitution is suspended. But the machinery of government must continue, the trains must run, the Post Office must deliver the mail, the civil servants must draw their salaries and you gentlemen, your allowances. Who is

[47] BA, *R58/157*, 27 January 1941.

to look after all this? You? No! We shall have government by the King, who alone has the responsibility and power for this task.

VIRCHOW. Gentlemen, this is a black day in the history of our Fatherland. In this struggle for the ideals of liberty and progress Prussia has been thrown back into the darkness of the Middle Ages. No, gentlemen, let us go no further down this path. We are a nation of poets and thinkers, and we are proud of this!

BISMARCK [*jumps up*]. But don't you see the irony in the words 'a nation of poets and thinkers'? While you sit here dreaming, others are dividing up the world for themselves.

VIRCHOW. I demand that you do not interrupt me. We don't want the world, all we want is freedom in our own country.

BISMARCK. But you haven't even got that! There is one country between Calais and Marseilles, and six frontiers between Hamburg and Munich.

VIRCHOW. The unity of heart and spirit is far greater than any law. This unity has already been achieved.

BISMARCK [*to Roon*]. 'German Michael' has to be forced to accept his good fortune.

VIRCHOW. Herr von Bismarck and Herr von Roon may smile at my words. They are men for whom, in their own words, might is greater than right.

BISMARCK. I did not say that. Kindly do not twist my words!

VIRCHOW. I thank Mr Chairman, I value facts — not words. Herr von Bismarck and Herr von Roon are enemies of the people and devoid of patriotism . . . but one thing I'll assure you of and establish in the face of history, you won't succeed in preventing the unification of Germany.

BISMARCK. It's an honour for me to be called an enemy of the people by Virchow. Herr Virchow does not know the people at all! He really meant 'enemy of the Landtag!' In fact I desire the hatred of the Landtag.

CHAIRMAN. The Minister for War has the platform.

ROON. The President is not sitting here like I am, in uniform. He can't react differently to Dr Virchow's accusations, but I can. To deny patriotism to a Prussian officer is perfidious, unashamedly vulgar, which I object to . . .

CHAIRMAN. I won't allow you to express such opinions . . .

BISMARCK. The Minister is the King's representative in this House. So you are forbidding the King to have the floor. Everybody can express his opinion except the King. The King's Ministers *will* speak here, you can believe that. They'll speak as long as they wish and if you dare forbid the King to take the floor, then you are breaking the constitution . . . [*Bismarck gropes in his pocket and pulls out a piece of paper which he holds in front of the Chairman's nose*] . . . Bismarck dissolves Parliament. [*Chairman tries to speak*] . . . You didn't finish your sentence — before you did I closed the Landtag. The King will decide when it shall be summoned again.

Virchow symbolizes 'German Michael', the confused dreamer who is unable to grasp the political realities of the time. Although his argument may appear extremely reasonable in print, the use of camera movement and lighting and the assured characterization of Bismarck together with the predisposition of the Nazi audience renders the debate innocuous. The SD discovered that this scene had the most profound effect on the people:

. . . those unfamiliar with history were able to find direct parallels between Bismarck's struggle to establish a united German Reich and the unifying work of the Führer. The two-hour-long film is described again and again as a 'history lesson' with the greatest relevance to the present day. Especially appreciated were the scenes in Parliament ('It's a good thing that we haven't still got such prattlers in Germany today!').[48]

Bismarck was an undoubted box-office success in Germany. The SD attributed this success to the 'extensive discussions on the fundamental problems of historical films' which had been taking place on the radio and in the press.[49] The RMVP had obviously been preparing the groundwork for the historical film cycle by 'educating' film audiences into visualizing history in terms of great leader figures who shaped Germany's destiny.

Die Entlassung (The Dismissal, 1942)

As a result of the public's demand for a sequel to *Bismarck*, Wolfgang Liebeneiner directed *Die Entlassung (The Dismissal)*, which was released on 6 October 1942. The film opens in 1888 with the deaths of Wilhelm I ar.d Friedrich Wilhelm III and the accession of the arrogant Wilhelm II. The ageing Bismarck (played by Emil Jannings) is persuaded out of retirement to assist the new King (who has antagonized the rest of Europe), with his superior knowledge and experience of political diplomacy. However, a new breed of bureaucrats have appeared on the political scene and begin to intrigue against him. A charge is trumped up that he has withheld certain important documents from the Kaiser and so kept him in ignorance. Wilhelm is enraged and Bismarck is forced to hand in his resignation.

The fall of Bismarck was a strange choice to include in the historical film cycle. It is the only film in which a Great Leader

[48] BA, *R58/157*, 27 January 1941.   [49] Ibid.

symbol is defeated. Moreover, after Bismarck's resignation, Germany fails to renew the Reinsurance Treaty and is ultimately committed to a war on two fronts. It is difficult to tell exactly what Goebbels hoped to achieve with this film, although it was probably meant to be an indirect attack on the state bureaucracy. When the old statesman comes out of retirement he enjoys some initial success, but is finally forced to resign by the conspiracy of jealous bureaucrats. A postscript to the film and the fact that it was released with the subtitle *Schicksalwende* (*Change of Destiny*) tends to substantiate this interpretation. The postscript declared:

Germany's misfortunes between 1890 and 1933 can be traced back to this one great disaster, which opened the door to the political dilettantes Bismarck so despised and paved the way for Versailles. The fate of a nation rests not on its institutions but on its personalities.

The diplomat, Ulrich von Hassel, felt that the film was antimonarchist: 'I dipped into history and saw the very superior film on Bismarck. It again confirmed my conviction that films must falsify history . . . Many believe it works against the monarchist idea.'[50] Whatever his motives, Goebbels fully appreciated the delicacy of the situation. As late as 3 November 1942, he wrote in his diary:

The scenes are very discreet and tastefully done, and in no way do they sink to caricature. But in spite of this I have my doubts whether this is the right time to release this film publicly.[51]

Goebbels may well have thought when he sanctioned the film that the war in the East would be over by the time *Die Entlassung* was finished. However by mid-1942 the implications of the film, with its implicit attack on state bureaucracy and its warning about the inadvisability of conducting a war on two fronts, started to reverberate throughout the Party and the RMVP. The shooting of the film began in a blaze of publicity but by the time it was completed Goebbels had instructed the press not to mention the film.[52] As it became increasingly obvious that Russia was not about to capitulate, every Party organization with a vested interest demanded that they be allowed to preview the film and register their opinions before

---

[50] U. von Hassel, *The von Hassel Diaries 1938–44* (London, 1948), p. 244.
[51] IfZ, *Goebbels Tagebuch*, entry for 3 November 1942.
[52] BA, *Sammlung Sänger, Zsg, 102/63*, 4 April 1942.

Die Entlassung should be considered for general distribution.[53] Goebbels was eventually forced to seek Hitler's advice on this matter. It would appear that the Führer·was too busy to see the film himself; instead he instructed Bormann to view it and report back his impressions. Hitler was, however, aware of the controversy surrounding the film and on the evening of 20 August he discussed the wider implications of Bismarck's dismissal:

A question which is frequently put to me is, should we now release the film 'Bismarck'? I know of no more trenchant criticism of the Kaiser than that given in the third volume of Bismarck's memoirs. When I read it I was appalled . . . had he possessed the virtues of his grandfather, he would have kept Bismarck close to his side, he would have won the affection of his people, and Social Democracy could never have become the power it did. This dismissal of Bismarck undoubtedly shattered the nation . . . for Bismarck was the symbol of national unity.[54]

It was decided to show the film in the small German town of Stettin on 15 September 1942 when only the local press would be allowed in to report the audience's reaction. A few days later, Rosenberg sent Bormann a comprehensive letter outlining his reasons why the film should not be released.[55] There were three main points to his argument: it gave the impression of German war guilt because it omitted the intrigues of Russia and England; it would add fuel to Allied propaganda, and it would burden the German people with the unfortunate policies of Kaiser Wilhelm II and the cause of the First World War. Rosenberg concluded: 'As far as foreign policy is concerned this film is a ghastly mistake and it will do nothing to enhance domestic policy.' Despite Rosenberg's protest, Goebbels had already described the experiment as 'a brilliant success' and requested that the film be shown to the rest of Germany.[56]

Die Entlassung eventually received its première in Berlin on 6 October when, strangely enough, the press were ordered not to draw historical parallels but to emphasize instead the differences between Wilhelm II's system of government and

---

[53] BA, *NS 18/283*, 27 July 1942. For the complete cross-section of opinions see, Welch, 'Propaganda and the German Cinema', pp. 474–8.
[54] *Table Talk*, pp. 646–7.
[55] BA, *NS 18/283*, 25 September 1942. In fact it had been decided to use Stettin and to restrict reviews to the local press towards the end of August. BA, *Sammlung Sänger, Zsg, 102/63*, 28 August 1942.
[56] IfZ, *Goebbels Tagebuch*, entry for 23 September 1942.

that of the Third Reich.[57] Despite opposition from a number of government departments, *Die Entlassung*, like *Bismarck*, proved popular with the German public. This is not surprising given the predisposition of Nazi audiences for cinematic allegories on Adolf Hitler's greatness. And despite press censorship, they could not fail to draw anything but this conclusion from Bismarck's final speech shortly after he had resigned from office:

[*Bismarck is alone in his room beneath a picture of the proclamation of Wilhelm I as Emperor of Germany. Close-up as he begins to speak ...*] BISMARCK. Twenty years ago I stood there . . . and now? Where do I stand now? But this is of no importance. For what survives me is the Reich, my Reich — Germany. [*The screen is now covered by the picture of Kaiser Wilhelm's proclamation. Off-screen, Bismarck's voice can be heard*] . . . Princes come and go, people die, but the nation is eternal. States blossom and crumble, institutions change like summer and winter. What must remain is the Reich, if people and Reich become one, then the Reich too will be eternal. . . . My work is done. It was only a beginning. Who will complete it?

The moral is clear; Bismarck's work is left unfinished, awaiting the emergence of a new Führer. That leader is, of course, Adolf Hitler, whose rise to power is seen as the fulfilment of Prussia's destiny. By the time *Die Entlassung* was released, Bismarck's legacy had passed to Hitler. The film was subsequently awarded the honorary prize, 'Film of the Nation', and the *Prädikate*: 'politically and artistically especially valuable', 'culturally valuable', 'nationally valuable', valuable for 'national education', and 'valuable for youth'. Together with *Kolberg* (1945), it was to receive more awards than any other film made during the Third Reich.

DER GROSSE KÖNIG (THE GREAT KING, 1942)

Frederick the Great was the other great Prussian leader to be placed in the same category as Bismarck. The German cinema had shown a preoccupation with the seminal Prussian hero figure dating back to Arzon von Cserepy's *Fridericus Rex* (1922).[58] As in *Bismarck*, the moral of the 'Fridericus' films

[57] BA, *Sammlung Sänger, Zsg, 102/63*, 5 October 1942.
[58] The other two films were *Das Flotenkonzert von Sanssouci* (*The Flute Concert of Sanssouci*, 1930) and *Barberina, Die Tanzerin von Sanssouci* (*The King's Dancer*, 1932).

was that the community should submit unconditionally to absolute authority. Not surprisingly, this warrior hero was ideally suited to the cinematic portrayal of the prototype Führer figure. The Nazis were quick to seize the 'Fridericus' cycle and to rewrite their films so that they fitted in with contemporary events, thus making the historical analogies even more powerful. In 1933, *Der Choral von Leuthen* (*The Hymn of Leuthen*) was directed by Carl Froelich (later to become President of the *Reichsfilmkammer*) and portrayed Frederick as the courageous military leader who, against the advice of his generals, insists on fighting the Austrians at Leuthen where he wins the battle. Once again this film emphasizes the radical elements of Nazi ideology in which the consequences of the Führer's decisions are either victory or ruination. Oskar Kalbus noted that Frederick was 'a man possessed of supernatural powers of determination whose intuition leads to either total victory or death'.[59]

Between 1935 and 1936, two more films in the cycle appeared: Hans Steinhoff's *Der alte und der junge König* (*The Old and the Young King*) and Johannes Meyer's *Fridericus*. Both films showed a Germany encircled by enemies and whose only hope lay in the determined genius of Frederick's leadership. *Fridericus* in particular anticipates the military language that was to be employed later in the documentary 'campaign' films and the feature films with strong militarist themes. The whole 'Fridericus' cycle was a concerted attempt to familiarize the German masses with the idea of a Führer. Indeed, in an attempt to maintain continuity with the Weimar cinema, Hitler insisted that the actor Otto Gebühr should continue to portray Frederick under the Nazi regime.[60]

Der grosse König was the last and most elaborate treatment of the career of Frederick the Great. By 1942 historical events were being deliberately manipulated to suggest a contemporary parallel. As final victory seemed less certain, propaganda struck a new note of heroic resistance and stoicism, and absolute faith took the place of the earlier arrogant enthusiasm. The

---

[59] Kalbus, p. 75.
[60] When Harlan decided to cast Werner Krauss as Frederick, Hitler personally intervened and insisted that Gebühr should continue in the role that he had specialized in all but one of the Fridericus films. Harlan, pp. 181–2.

idea of producing another version of the heroic attitude of Frederick II during the critical phases of the Seven Years' War was therefore most attractive. Its message was particularly suited to a distressed nation which had encountered military reverses for the first time. Goebbels believed that such a message would greatly lift morale. In his diary he noted:

With this film we can make politics, too. It is an excellent expedient in the struggle for the soul of our people and in the process of creating the necessary German resistance needed to see us successfully through the war.[61]

The film was in fact commissioned by the Propaganda Minister and although Goebbels did not actually write the screenplay, he ordered a number of scenes to be rewritten.[62] Directed by Veit Harlan, *Der grosse König* was one of the most expensive films made during the Third Reich with elaborate sets and a high-quality cast including Otto Gebühr as Frederick the Great. Although similar in many ways to its predecessors, it contained a number of different features. It placed more stress on the superiority of Frederick's judgement over that of his generals and also emphasized the sufferings of the Prussian people during the Seven Years' War and the faith they kept with their leader. The Great King is clearly modelled on Hitler. Indeed, certain lines in the film sound like quotations from Hitler's speeches, although the prologue upholds the historical authenticity of the film by stating that 'what Frederick says in the film has been taken from his own writings'. In an essay entitled 'History and Film', Harlan wrote that in *Der grosse König* he tried: 'To bring credibility to the character of the King. I avoided any kind of heroic pose, since I wanted to show the harassed face of a man who after his defeat had almost collapsed under the weight of responsibility he had shouldered.'[63]

Despite Harlan's claims, the Frederick he portrayed was merely an historical ruler who could equally have been Adolf Hitler, on whom the German nation was now resting its hopes. Like all the historical leaders who pre-figure Hitler, Frederick is revealed to be a man of Fate. Thanks to the hand of Providence, he escapes an assassination attempt after the disaster

[61] IfZ, *Goebbels Tagebuch*, entry for 19 February 1942.
[62] Harlan, pp. 184–8.
[63] Quoted in Leiser, p. 113.

of Kunersdorf, thus enabling him to rally his forces and prevent his brother (whom he had chosen in his will to succeed him) from making a peace settlement. It is this knowledge that he has been specially chosen that gives him the will to continue:

FREDERICK II [*to his brother*]. If I had fallen at Kunersdorf — and that nearly happened twice — then you would have been the King of Prussia today as I declared in my will. Providence, however, did not want this to be. I have been chosen to fulfil Prussia's hour of destiny.

The leader who sacrifices all in pursuit of such a goal is therefore entitled to demand great sacrifices. He discusses with his generals the retreat under pressure of the Bernburg regiment. The generals advise the King that the odds were too great and that he would be·wise to seek a peace settlement. He interrupts impatiently and informs them that the regiment is to lose its standard and is to be stripped of its stripes because: 'At Kunersdorf they preferred life to victory. . . . instead of deserting they should have built a wall for me out of corpses, a wall of Prussian corpses!'

Goebbels was convinced of the propaganda value of *Der grosse König*. He also saw the film as a means of criticizing the OKW by furthering his 'total war' campaign. Following the King's outburst quoted above, his generals still insist that the war is lost and that a peace settlement should be negotiated immediately. The King decides to take over the supreme command from Count Fink and to continue the war against his generals' wishes. He challenges their patriotism and calls for a vote of confidence. When the film was shown to an invited audience towards the end of January 1942, representatives of the OKW were most alarmed by scenes such as this. Goebbels noted their reaction with some interest:

There were many gentlemen from the OKW there who were somewhat benumbed by the film. They were fully aware of the sharp criticism made in the film of the generals' defeatism. They obviously notice this aim — and are annoyed by it![64]

Throughout the following month the controversy continued at the Führer HQ. The generals were disconcerted by the film's suggestion that Frederick the Great had been abandoned in his

[64] IfZ, *Goebbels Tagebuch*, entry for 28 January 1942.

hour of need. Goebbels recorded in his diary that it was only Keitel's intervention that succeeded in mollifying the disaffected general staff.[65] However it was only after a routine visit towards the end of March[66] to confer with Hitler about his proposals for intensifying the war effort (and after the film had been on general release), that Goebbels discovered that the problem of *Der grosse König* had been decided by Hitler:

I came to know of the hard fight which has broken out in the Führer HQ over the Frederick the Great film. In the end the Führer resolved the matter. Although he had not seen the film he had so many details explained to him that he was able to make quite a graphic image of it. How benevolent this characterization of the great King has been to him. He asks me to place a copy of the film at his disposal. He intends sending it with an accompanying letter to the Duce. Of course, in such an atmosphere, my suggestion for radicalizing our efforts has a very positive effect on the Führer.[67]

Goebbels clearly saw this as a personal victory and a major boost in his propaganda campaign for the sacrifices demanded by 'total war'. Besides discrediting the OKW by stressing the old King's superior judgement over his generals, the film concentrated on the loneliness and dedication of the Leader figure. Once again this aspect served to reinforce a similar campaign that Goebbels was conducting in the press and on the radio at this time. Just over a month after the film's première Goebbels referred to the enormous burden borne by the Führer: 'He stands alone facing his and our fate in order to battle out to a victorious conclusion the titanic struggle imposed on us for the life of our nation.'[68] Interestingly enough, whereas audiences did not respond to the unreliability of Frederick's generals, they were conscious of the tragic solitude of the great King. This also marked a departure from previous 'Fridericus' films. The SD reported that:

The film had managed to remove the romantic smokescreen, the patriotic pathos and the bourgeois morality from Prussian history and to give our people some idea of the lonely, glacial atmosphere surrounding a head of state responsible for a nation's destiny.[69]

[65] Ibid., entry for 2 March 1942.
[66] Lochner, pp. 87–95.
[67] IfZ, *Goebbels Tagebuch*, entry for 20 March 1942.
[68] J. Goebbels, *Das Eherne Herz* (Munich, 1943), p. 290.
[69] BA, *R58/172*, 28 May 1942.

The SD also noted that many people 'recalled seeing a newsreel in which the Führer is also seen alone in his headquarters'. This is not surprising since Goebbels specifically asked that the most recent newsreel which contained this very image, should be included in the film programme with *Der grosse König*.[70] The solitude in which mighty leaders live and work is continually stressed. They are sublimely indifferent to personal happiness or misery. In *Der grosse König*, Frederick is often seen alone, even in the midst of the many battles. There is one scene where he forgets about his responsibilities and dreams he is in Sanssouci playing the flute and reading Plato and Voltaire. His state duties even prevent him from being at his son's bedside when he dies of smallpox. Instead he is seen reading Sophocles —a present to his son Prince Heinrich many years ago. The camera pans in to the opening page to reveal the dedication 'To my dear son'. But *Der grosse König* is not concerned with Frederick the philosopher–artist of the Enlightenment, but Frederick the warrior–hero. Even when Prussia celebrates total victory, Frederick returns to Kunersdorf, where he had suffered his worst defeat. The King's example has inspired his country which has been severely weakened by the war. New life appears out of the ruins and in the midst of this new life only the Kings remain alone. An exchange between Frederick and the wife of his dead Sergeant-Major is revealing for the manner in which it brings together a number of the film's major themes.

The scene was incorporated at the insistence of the *Reichspropagandaleitung Amtsleitung Film*.[71] In many reprints this dialogue has been substantially edited. In its unexpurgated form, the scene attempts to rationalize Frederick's harsh measures, reiterate his essential loneliness, and to symbolize the rebirth of a Prussia which has won the war and is recovering from its sacrifices:

FREDERICK. Are you alone?
[*The WOMAN kisses her little baby.*]
FREDERICK. I am also alone.
WOMAN. His Majesty is not alone though!

[70] BA, *NS 18/342*, Note from RMVP to Tobis dated 10 March 1942.
[71] BA, *NS 18/342*, this is a folder on *Der grosse König*. This exchange of dialogue is undated.

FREDERICK. Oh yes.

WOMAN. But the Prussian people . . .

FREDERICK. Hate me! They have even pronounced it — here in this house!

WOMAN. Does my child hate me if it doesn't understand me?

FREDERICK. Do my people know how I love them?

[*The WOMAN nods silently.*]

FREDERICK. And do they understand that I was only waging this war to secure their future?

WOMAN. What we can't grasp with understanding, our hearts tell us.

FREDERICK. Yes, the heart. I will think of that when I feel lonely again.

WOMAN [*looking at the King, says to her child*]. He needs us — our strong hearts!

Der grosse König ends with this image of a country rebuilding itself after war. We are shown windmills being built, citizens ploughing fields and sowing corn, and bountiful crops. The last shot is a montage sequence consisting of cloud formation, the Prussian flag, and the King's face staring resolutely out from all this. The moral is unmistakable: the battle has been won and the intuition of a Führer has proved superior to normal reasoning. Peace and prosperity are the rewards for the sacrifices that the King demanded. In the illustrated brochure that accompanied the film, Goebbels wrote:

It is up to us whether this war is a curse or a blessing. It demands complete sacrifice, but it will also provide all we shall need for our future as a nation. Given the choice, which one of us would exchange the present for other less significant times? The day will come when we too shall hear the bells ringing for the end of the war and for victory. That will be our reward. But every individual will have to account for what he has done and what he has failed to do, and then collectively we shall be judged by history.[72]

Goebbels did his utmost to promote the film. He was closely involved with every stage of the film's production. At its première in Berlin on 3 March 1942 before a selected audience of wounded soldiers and armaments workers, Goebbels bestowed the title 'Film of the Nation' on it and by permission of the Führer announced the elevation of Otto Gebühr to *Staatsschauspieler*.[73] Furthermore, all *Gaupropagandaleiter* were ordered to 'celebrate' local premières with their personal

---

[72] *Aktuelle Filmbücher* (Stephan).

[73] This had been decided early in February but Goebbels refused to allow the press to announce it lest it destroy the dramatic effect of the première. BA, *Sammlung Sänger, Zsg, 102/63*, 6 February 1942.

attendance and to 'energetically promote the message contained in the film on a wider basis', because:

. . . this film, of whose excellence the press have already been informed by the Führer and Goebbels personally, is not only a great artistic achievement, but it is the best weapon we have for persuading the people of the need for self-discipline and sacrifice at the present time.[74]

However Goebbels instructed the press not to draw parallels with Germany's present situation or with the Führer.[75] But according to the SD Report this message was not lost on the German audience:

Large numbers of people talk of a *mirror image of our own age* in the film. The collective judgement of the audience is that this film is second only to the Bismarck film, which they regard as the finest cinematic treatment of an historical theme.[76]

On 19 April 1942, Goebbels gave a radio address to mark Hitler's fifty-third birthday. He referred to *Der grosse König* and praised its moving qualities and then posed the question: 'what is the lesson to be learnt from the film?'[77] He argued that it was not economic resources or military potential, but superior leadership that decided wars, a belief firmly established in German hearts until Stalingrad. At a time when German forces were encountering the miseries of a Russian winter, and the German population at home was forced to reappraise the omnipotence of its Führer, *Der grosse König* formulates with a view to Stalingrad one of the first expressions of the need for endurance throughout the war. A slogan that is repeated throughout is 'Prussia will never be lost as long as the King lives.' Despite Goebbels's pretence to the contrary, such slogans were clearly meant to apply to Hitler. They were to remain effective until the end of the war. An example of this is the newsreel (*Deutsche Wochenschau*) released in April 1944 to celebrate Hitler's fifty-fifth birthday.[78] It was to be one of the last appearances that Hitler made in the German newsreels. At an NSDAP concert on the eve of his birthday (where Beethoven's 'Eroica' is played), Goebbels offers the

[74] BA, *NS 18/342*, 3 March 1942 and 4 March 1942.
[75] BA, *Sammlung Sänger, Zsg, 102/63*, 2 March 1942. See also Boelcke, p. 287.
[76] BA, *R58/172*, 28 March 1942.
[77] Goebbels, *Das Eherne Herz*, p. 289. See also Bramsted, pp. 222-3.
[78] *Deutsche Wochenschau* No. 712. This is available for hire at the Imperial War Museum.

Party's congratulations to Hitler and reaffirms the nation's faith in him: 'We want to assure him that he is able to rely on his people absolutely in this great struggle—that he is today as he always was—our Führer!' The scene in the concert hall is followed by shots of a bomb-damaged Berlin recovering from an Allied sortie. In the background, just visible, slogans can be seen daubed on the ruins and on banners hanging from windows. As the commentator says that this is the German people's gift to Hitler, the camera pans in to reveal a demonstration of the nation's unbending will: 'Our walls may break but our hearts do not—as long as the Führer lives!'

Der grosse König was to be the last feature film until Kolberg (1945) to deal with the Führerprinzip and the need for discipline and obedience. As shown in the next chapter, the cult of the Führer was intensified in the final year of the war to coincide with the release of this film. During this time Hitler was portrayed in Goebbels's propaganda as a leader superior to any other in world history, who, following the dictates of Providence, would lead the nation into 'a new epoch'.[79] At the same time, Goebbels launched into another of his discourses on Frederick the Great. It was the same message that is found in Der grosse König: if only Germans would fight as the Prussians had done during the Seven Years' War. He even quoted a letter from Frederick to his sister Amalia written in 1757, in which the King commented that 'victory or death were the only alternatives'. Goebbels promised that if the German people kept faith with the Führer, Hitler would produce a 'similar victory'.[80]

Both Goebbels and Hitler were obsessed with the historical parallels to be found with Frederick the Great. According to his own account, Goebbels consoled the despondent Führer by reading aloud to him from Carlyle's History of Frederick the Great, choosing the chapter that described the difficulties the King encountered in the winter of 1761-2:

Carlyle is an ardent admirer of Frederick the Great and the picture he draws of his life is that of an heroic epic. From this account one can judge the critical situations in which the great Prussian King was sometimes

[79] J. Goebbels, 'der Führer', in Das Reich, 31 December 1944. An analysis of this revealing article can be found in Baird, pp. 241-3.
[80] Quoted in Bramsted, p. 448. Cf. Baird, p. 249.

placed, the lofty relaxed frame of mind in which he met them and the admirable stoicism with which he overcame them. He too sometimes felt that he must doubt his lucky star, but, as generally happens in history, at the darkest hour a bright star arose and Prussia was saved when he had almost given up all hope. Why should not we also hope for a similar wonderful turn of fortune![81]

The obsessive lure of historical parallels illustrates the extent to which German propaganda had retreated into mythology: myth, after all, need not be reconcilable with the truth. As Joachim Fest pointed out, 'The tendency to seek signs and portents outside reality extended far beyond books as the end came closer; here once again the irrationality of Nazism was revealed.'[82] And yet a few days before Hitler and Goebbels were both to commit suicide, the Führer's presence in Berlin was still apparently delaying the end of the war. Der Panzerbär defiantly proclaimed: 'Where the Führer is—victory is!'[83] It would appear from such pronouncements that towards the end even the German people were unable to divorce myth from reality. The Führerprinzip continued unabated until the end.

The significance of the Führerprinzip in the National Socialist movement was in the appearance of a charismatic leader as the saviour of a disillusioned and alienated mass. The Führer cult constituted one of the few consistent aspects of Nazi ideology and remained a potent force right up to Hitler's death. The need to identify with and obey a strong leader had been one of the most important factors contributing to the rise of National Socialism and to the maintenance of Hitler's power once it had been obtained. This absolute, almost mystical relationship to the leader gave the Nazis a sectarian character and distinguished them from other political ideologies such as Liberalism and Marxism. As we have seen, for example, in Triumph des Willens, this self-identification with the Führer gave the German people a sense of superiority that was permanently denied to others. In fact, one of the most important tasks of Nazi films in this genre was to contrast the need for a strong leader with the confusion inherent in parliamentary democracy (Der Herrscher, Bismarck, Carl Peters, Die Entlassung).

[81] H. Trevor-Roper (ed.), The Goebbels Diaries (London, 1978), p. 215. Cf. Bullock, pp. 780–1.   [82] Fest, p. 734.
[83] Der Panzerbär 29 April 1945, quoted in Baird, p. 255.

The legitimation of the leader was founded not on the power of the State but on the superior insight of the Führer as the executor of the 'common will of the people'. Thus the essential factors which these films reveal are the overriding importance of untutored genius over formal learning and of determined intuition over pedantic reasoning (*Triumph des Willens, Friedrich Schiller, Bismarck, Der grosse König, Kolberg*).

It is no coincidence that most of the films discussed in this section are historical, and are set in a time when one historical period is giving way to another,[84] and that the leader figure has the ability to see beyond the confines of his age. This not only encouraged audiences to equate the great men of German history with the Führer, but it also served to reiterate the leader cult in that it reminded them that historical change came about through the will of the leader of genius and not through the twin evils of Liberalism and Marxism. In other words, it is great leaders who make history, not history that makes great leaders. In December 1943, Wolfgang Liebeneiner and Veit Harlan, two of the finest exponents of the National Socialist historical epic, gave a press conference to discuss the implications of historical authenticity in films. According to *Film-Kurier* the questions were resolved as follows:

At the outset Professor Liebeneiner had asked whether films in historical costume were ever justified, i.e. films that are set in a period when there were as yet no films. Only later did we appreciate that one of the principal tasks of the film is its capacity to transmit to posterity a true picture of the past and, seen in this light, all the films that we are making today will one day be truly 'historical'. Should a historical film therefore attempt to remain true in all respects to the history that has been handed down to us? In a sense, yes, for the film should not falsify history. But art, and film art in particular, consists to a great extent of omission. And so a historical film can only ever show a part, a small chapter of history that should nevertheless remind us of the great events.[85]

The question of 'omission' and 'inclusion' is essential to an understanding of this genre. Nazi film-makers manipulated history to project the Leadership Principle by means of the historical films with *contemporary* implications. The names they use are historical, but the ideas are contemporary. The

---

[84] I am indebted to Marcus Phillips for this observation.
[85] *Film-Kurier*, 21 December 1943, quoted in Wulf, p. 397.

historical film to the Nazis was therefore not a museum piece —it was only relevant if it added meaning to the present. The impact of this genre should not be underestimated. In the only nation-wide film survey conducted during the Third Reich, it was discovered that among the Hitler Youth the six most popular films were, in order of preference: *Der grosse König*, *Bismarck*, *Die Entlassung*, *Friedrich Schiller*, *Heimkehr*, *Ohm Kruger*.[86] With the exception of *Heimkehr*, the other five films project a Great Leader within an historical context.

The extent should also be noted to which these films incorporate elements of the *Bündisch* ethos, particularly the twin precepts of charismatic leadership by the exceptional few and the sublimation of sex in pursuit of some higher, heroic mission. However it is interesting that apart from *Friedrich Schiller*, these archetypal leaders are not imbued with classical Aryan features. Their importance lies in the fact that they pre-figure Hitler. They are examples of great German patriots whose geniuses and pioneering work were left unfinished, to be completed by Hitler (hence the relevance to the present). The overriding purpose of these political reconstructions was to demonstrate the theme of the individual creating his work in the face of opposition from a pedantic and uncomprehending society, but always fully conscious of his moral obligation to the German collective spirit. Reflecting the more important facets of *Völkisch* thought, the historical film in this genre always resolves itself in a celebration of German nationalism, of the individual's submission to the well-being of state and community.

[86] Sander, p. 118.

VI

WAR AND THE MILITARY IMAGE

Big and small people, the rich and the poor compete with each other to devote themselves completely to the task of enabling the nation to fight out its gigantic struggle for survival victoriously. In two and a half years we have become a nation of warriors.

Joseph Goebbels (Speech of 25 January 1942)

THE outbreak of war provided Goebbels with a new impetus and he increased his efforts to improve the artistic level of German films, believing that war would act as a catalyst by providing the emotional and artistic stimulus needed for such a 'revolution'. In practical terms this meant commissioning a number of extremely expensive political films and increasing the vigilance of the RMVP.

Initially, war presented the Nazis with few problems as it was inexorably linked to their ideology and therefore easily disseminated by propaganda. However, because of the precarious fortunes of war and the fact that their propaganda was so closely tied to military success, Goebbels had to vary his film productions from the overtly militaristic film to the pure escapist musical. As the war dragged on, he relied less on the political films and more on the escapist element to be found in entertainment genres. Films with a political message were still made, and even in the last two years of the war the most expensive productions were the political or historical epics. However the RMVP preferred to concentrate on a few large-scale, prestigious, but inevitably expensive propaganda films. The decline in the number of political films may be put into perspective at this stage by outlining two important factors that determined all film production during the war.

The first point to note is that during the Third Reich, and

particularly throughout the war, the number of films produced declined rapidly as Table 6 clearly demonstrates.

Table 6 *Feature Film Production, 1933-45*

Production year	'33	'34	'35	'36	'37	'38	'39	'40	'41	'42	'43	'44	'45	Total
Number of films	114	129	91	112	92	93	107	85	67	58	76	60	6	1,090

Source: A. Bauer, *Deutscher Spielfilm-Almanach, 1929-1950* (Berlin, 1950).

Not only were fewer films being produced but the average costs during the first two years of the war were rising by 68 per cent, of which the overt political films were accounting for a good deal of this increase.[1] For example, in 1940 Tobis FK were informed by Goebbels that half of their production programme for 1940-1 would consist of political films.[2] Thus in the firm's 1942 Annual Report we duly find that they produced eight political films and eight ordinary feature films. However, the political films exceeded their budgets by over 25 per cent, whereas the other films exceeded their estimated costs by less than 7 per cent (in terms of average costs this worked out at RM 2,157,000 against RM 883,000).[3] Apart from being exempt from the budgetary restrictions imposed on other films,[4] such political films, because of the importance and delicacy of the subject-matter, also had to suffer continual supervision and interference by the RMVP.[5] Therefore, given all these factors and the costs involved, it is surely not surprising that the numbers declined as the war dragged on.

The period between the outbreak of war and the first reverses in Russia marked the highest concentration of overt

[1] BA, *R2/4791*, 9 September 1941. As I mention in Chapter I this document would be used by Goebbels to justify his nationalization of the film industry in 1942.

[2] The document of 23 April 1940 is quoted in Albrecht, p. 143.

[3] BA, *R2/4809*, 30 June 1942. Cf. also a report by the Supervisory Board of the RMVP on 31 March 1940. It notes that 'great energy is being devoted to political films', but also points out that 'rising costs are creating a situation whereby films are reaching the limits of feasibility'. BA, *R55/4809*, 31 March 1940.

[4] Cf. BA, *R1091/1034b, 1477*, 8 January 1942: 'Von Reichmeister informed the firm recently that the maximum cost for feature films has been set at RM 1 million. Only state-political films will be allowed to surpass this figure.'

[5] Boelke, p. 219. See also Albrecht, p. 526.

Nazi political propaganda in feature and documentary films during the Third Reich. Quite definite types of films may now be noted in the film schedules of the various companies, partticularly the use of large-scale Nazi documentaries, as the RMVP increasingly dictated the themes and methods used. This chapter concentrates on those films that encouraged an aggressive militarist spirit by showing a distorted and romanticized vision of modern warfare. In confining myself to three films (*Pour le Mérite, Feuertaufe, Kolberg*), and an examination of wartime newsreels, which I feel represent a fair cross-section of wartime film production, my aim is to explore the changing nature of film propaganda and the manner in which Goebbels justified the war, extolled the invincibility of German military might, romanticized its heroes, and, as Germany's military position became more desperate, mythologized the nation's *Götterdämmerung*.

POUR LE MÉRITE (1938)

War was an important aspect of Nazi mythical ideology and as such Goebbels experienced little difficulty in shifting his operation on to a wartime footing. As Jay Baird noted, 'the movement had a dialectic and teleology of its own which was expressed in the symbols of combat.'[6] However, both Goebbels and Hitler appreciated the burden that a war would place on the RMVP. Hitler in particular was dismayed by the lack of marked enthusiasm during the Sudeten crisis in August and September 1938.[7] On 10 November 1938, he summoned 400 of the regime's leading journalists and media experts to Munich and instructed them in their future role in the coming war:

It is absolutely necessary gradually to prepare the German people psychologically for the coming war and to make it clear to them that there are some things which only force, not peaceful means, must decide.[8]

The main point of Hitler's message was that it was the task of propaganda to instil in the German Volk an absolute obedi-

---

[6] Baird, p. 8.

[7] For a discussion of Nazi propaganda during the Sudeten Question, see Bramsted, pp. 167–77.

[8] W. Treue (ed.), 'Rede Hitler vor deutschen Presse', 10 November 1938, *Vierteljahrshefte für Zeitgeschichte*, vol. VI, April 1958, pp. 175–91, also quoted in Baird, p. 23.

ence, a willingness to die, and an unshakeable belief in final victory. Film was particularly suited to this type of 'appeal *with* emotion'. The whole notion of 'self-sacrifice' inevitably evokes emotional rather than intellectual responses. It is prompted by a polarity of emotional extremes that ranges from universal despair to a blind faith in the rightness of a particular cause. What it invariably lacks is a middle ground of rational thought. The obsession with the nobility of self-sacrifice and an heroic death prevailed throughout the films of the Third Reich. In *Unternehmen Michael* (*Operation Michael*, 1937) which depicted the daring exploits of a German company during the First World War, and is representative of this genre, a commanding general explains to the major in charge of a suicidal assault unit: 'Posterity will remember us not by the greatness of our victory but by the measure of our sacrifice!'

The finest exponent of the militarist feature film set in a contemporary context was Karl Ritter. Such films came to be referred to as *Zeitfilme* and it was Ritter who was largely credited with creating the genre. In an interview with *Filmwelt* in 1938 he attempted to outline what the term meant to him:

The pure entertainment film is only one aspect of our *Weltanschauung*. The *Zeitfilm* is about tanks, aircraft, and the troops at the front. It must bear the characteristics of contemporary Germany, it must be heroic, as our fate at this time demands. At the same time it must show humour and a positive attitude to life in accordance with our new found beliefs.[9]

Pour le Mérite, a Ufa production directed by Ritter, corresponded to these conceptions. It was passed by the Censor on 7 December 1938 and received its première on 22 December 1938. Made just before the outbreak of the Second World War, it dealt with the fate of several air force officers, holders of the 'Pour le Mérite' order, between the years 1918 and 1933. Apart from obviously being conceived as a tribute to the Richthofen Squadron (and therefore Hermann Göring) it was, more importantly, an unequivocal endorsement of the illegal German rearmament.[10]

The call for rearmament comes towards the end of the film, but what precedes it is a typical Nazi harangue against all those

---

[9] *Filmwelt*, no. 20, 13 May 1938.
[10] For a detailed discussion of this film see, Welch, pp. 235–40.

factors that the National Socialists claimed had combined to destroy Germany: the treachery of the *Dolchstoss* ('stab in the back'), the conspiracy of the Communists, and the inherent weakness of Weimar democracy. But Ritter's main purpose was to rationalize and strengthen faith in German military rearmament and to psychologically prepare the spectator for the coming war. As the Nazi-Soviet Pact was at this time being negotiated, it was difficult for film propaganda to stake a claim in defending Europe from Bolshevism. Therefore, prior to the invasion of Poland, they had to prepare the audience for the campaign ahead by concentrating on the past and in particular on the evil of democracy. This was achieved by clearly delineating villains and heroes respectively as those who gave tacit support or profited from the Weimar Republic, and those who fought heroically to subvert it. In such a way, Ritter was able to make all those who had lived through the Weimar era feel guilty of a spineless treason against German nationalism. In this sense, *Pour le Mérite* can be compared with the early 'Party films'—*SA-Mann Brand*, *Hitlerjunge Quex*, and *Hans Westmar*.

In a society where Jews and Communists are seen as the Nazis' main adversaries, war veterans meet only to discover that they are wearing the same Party badge under their lapels, for as one of them explains: 'The time has not yet arrived when we can openly and honourably display the symbols that represent all that "true" Germans hold sacred.' Addressing a Weimar court after being arrested, the leader of the Squadron, Captain Prank (played by Paul Hartmann) declares:

I have nothing whatsoever in common with this country, because I detest democracy like the plague! Whatever you do I will personally try to disrupt and destroy wherever I can. We must restore a Germany that represents the ideals of the soldiers that died at the front. I consider it my life's work to achieve this. And I shall go about it as a soldier would.

In an obvious reference to these early Party nationalists, the *Völkischer Beobachter*'s review of the film continued:

As in life, Ritter's films always appeal to the latent moral strength in our people, between good and evil, or the essential worth or worthlessness of an individual. Thus the soul of the real German manifests itself through the actions and words of the individuals in *Pour le Mérite* who act as inspiration in the fight for the heart of the nation.[11]

[11] *VB*, 23 December 1938.

Hitler was also at the première of the film and he publicly congratulated the director and declared the film a 'great success, the best film of contemporary history up to now'.[12] Hitler's reaction is not surprising given the manner in which Ritter manipulates his audience with crude appeals for an excessive nationalism and monumental heroism. Karl Ritter was a personal friend of the Führer's and as such he was not subject to Goebbels's dictates on propaganda. The ending of *Pour le Mérite* can therefore be viewed as a classic restatement of Hitlerite principles of propaganda applied to film.

Pour le Mérite concludes with Hitler's Proclamation to the People of 16 March 1935, in which conscription was reintroduced and the Wehrmacht established. As Germans all over the country pay homage at memorials to those who died during the Great War, young men and old men alike can be seen in military uniforms armed with new weapons and resolutely determined to take up the fight. Captain Prank returns to a rebuilt Luftwaffe under the leadership of Hermann Göring. As Prank inspects his new squadron the voice of Goebbels reading Hitler's Proclamation can be heard over the noise of engines and the Luftwaffe singing: 'We are the black hussars of the air!'

THE WAR NEWSREELS

Despite the persuasive qualities of a film such as *Pour le Mérite* its effect was circumscribed by the political exigencies of the time. Certainly, by concentrating on feelings of guilt, such films might stir a German audience into demanding rearmament and condemning parliamentary democracy—but it could not, in the final analysis, manipulate public opinion to the extent that when war was declared, Germans would greet the announcement with universal enthusiasm. As Albert Speer noted:

From the start the populace took a far more serious view of the situation than did Hitler and his entourage . . . The atmosphere was notably depressed; the people were full of fear about the future. None of the regiments marched off to war decorated with flowers as they had done at the beginning of the First World War . . . The streets remained empty.[13]

---

[12] Ibid.
[13] Speer, pp. 240-1.

Whether by means of direct political instructions or by covert use of entertainment genres in an attempt to create a false sense of security or normality, feature films throughout the war years attempted to counteract the negative opinions held by the population. In this respect they were greatly enhanced by the newsreels and documentaries. Both the newsreel and the full-scale documentaries that were made from newsreel materials were an excellent vehicle for portraying the invincible might of the armed forces. They did indeed succeed in reinforcing a feeling of security and reassurance on the part of a reluctant German audience. Compare for example this SD Report shortly after the outbreak of war on how the audience responded to a newsreel (*Wochenschau*) dealing with military operations in Denmark and Norway:

Great Applause.
The *Wochenschau* undoubtedly increased confidence in victory. From *Breslau*: 'by means of this *Wochenschau* it was thrillingly paraded before the people's eyes how strikingly strong and quick as lightning our armed forces are . . .'. Total silence in cinemas – people had to pull themselves together afterwards. From *Dresden*: reports that *Wochenschauen* are awakening an understanding of the geographical difficulties the military are experiencing in Norway and it was suggested that for propaganda purposes, more use should be made of maps in the newsreels to highlight the distances that the Luftwaffe travel and the scale of their achievement in occupying Norway.[14]

Until the outbreak of war there were four newsreels operating in Germany, *Ufa-Tonwoche*, *Deulig-Woche*, *Tobis Wochenschau* (which developed in 1938 out of *Bavaria-Tonwoche* which in turn developed from *Emelka-Woche*), and *Fox tönende Wochenschau* which was American-owned. A fifth newsreel, *Ufa-Auslandswoche*, distributed German home news abroad. It was the task of the Propaganda Ministry to coordinate these newsreels into a powerfully controlled and stringently organized propaganda weapon. Initially this was achieved by establishing a German 'news-bureau' (*Wochenschaureferat*) under the chairmanship of Hans Weidemann of the RMVP in an attempt to combine all newsreel reports into one 'official' version of contemporary Germany.[15]
As the political ideas and authoritarian claims to the film

[14] BA, *R58/150/2*, No. *83*, 29 April 1940.
[15] BA, *R1091/1030b*, *1079*, 14 May 1935.

1. *Hitlerjunge Quex* (1933), based on the life of Herbert Norkus, hero and martyr of the Hitler Youth

2. Emil Lohkamp in the title role in *Hans Westmar* (1933)

3. *Olympiade* (1938), the prototype Aryan warrior-sportsman

4. The death scene in *Ich klage an* (1941)

5. *Triumph des Willens*
(1935), Hitler alone,
juxtaposed against the
sky at Nuremberg

6. *Friedrich Schiller*
(1940), the triumph of
untutored genius.
Horst Casper as the
poet Schiller

7. *Der grosse König* (1942), Otto Gebühr as Frederick the Great

8. *Stukas* (1941), comradeship and self-sacrifice in war

9. *Kolberg* (1945), the heroism of death in combat; Napoleon's
troops driven back by the citizens of Kolberg

10. The Bolshevik: drunken Red Army soldiers in *Friesennot* (1935)

11. Andrews Engelmann as the murderous Bolshevik Commissar in *GPU* (1942)

12. British hypocrisy: priests distributing bibles and
rifles to the natives in *Ohm Krüger* (1941)

13. British oppression: starving Boer women in a British concentration camp (*Ohm Krüger*)

14. British brutality in Ireland: the torture by water sequence in *Mein Leben für Irland* (1941)

15. The Jew: Werner Krauss as the archetypal Jew in *Jud Süss* (1940)

16. Jew Süss (Ferdinand Marian) seeks to seduce the Aryan heroine (Kristina Söderbaum)

industry became more pervasive so the newsreels became less and less the product of journalistic enquiry. Even before 1933, Alfred Hugenberg, who owned Ufa, had used Ufa newsreels to gain support for the National Socialists. After 1933 the aim of the newsreel was to create mass intoxication and to obtain mass approval for the projected deeds of the regime in both domestic and foreign affairs. A special style appeared in structure and documentary sequences which had little connection with objective reporting. Newsreels increasingly became a formalistic, carefully planned artistic transformation of reality in an attempt to achieve the propaganda intentions of the Nazi regime. An American correspondent, John McCutcheon Raleigh, noted an excellent example of this practice:

One day, returning from the Rundfunkhaus after a broadcast, I saw a group of Hitler Youth posing with shovels and picks for an official cameraman. They shovelled industriously while the camera whirred. When the cameraman had sufficient material the group formed into squads and marched off, singing in unison. Later in the week I saw the same pictures released for propaganda in the current newsreels. The commentator proudly announced that the Hitler-Jugend was bending its back to clear away the snow. All winter this was the only time I saw youths in Hitler-Jugend uniforms wielding shovels.[16]

In order to achieve the most effective final results, cameramen were given special facilities for effective filming together with the most detailed instructions on the staging of a particular event.[17] They were assisted in this by legislation, notably the so-called 'Newsreel Law'—*Gesetz zur Erleichterung der Filmerichterstattung* (*'Wochenschaugesetz'*), which was introduced on 30 April 1936 in order to ease the problems of distribution and copyright. Two years later in October 1938, legislation was passed which made the showing of a newsreel compulsory at every commercial film programme, and also reduced the number of editions from fifteen to eight.[18] The system of hire charges was also changed so that it was no longer cheaper to hire old newsreels. These reforms ensured not only that film audiences would see the very latest newsreels (which

[16] John McCutcheon Raleigh, *Behind the Nazi Front* (London, 1941), pp. 247-8.
[17] For an interesting example of just how detailed these instructions were see F. Terveen, *Die Entwicklung der Wochenschau in Deutschland. Ufa–Tonwoch, No. 451/1939 — Hitlers 50. Geburtstag* (Göttingen, 1960).
[18] Tackmann, 31 October 1938.

was not the case before 1938), but also that propaganda material could be dispersed as widely as possible.

As the authorities began taking the newsreel more seriously and the propaganda aims of the RMVP became increasingly defined, this was obviously reflected in the content of prewar newsreels. Politics represented almost 50 per cent of all Ufa newsreels in the season 1935/6.[19] Writing in 1937, Fritz Hippler, later President of the RFK, outlined the importance of the newsreel and hinted at the new instructional use that was being made of the medium:

> The present task of the weekly newsreel is not only to be a mirror of our age, in objectively reflecting contemporary society, but it must facilitate a recognition of our present needs and the tasks that still have to be achieved in the future.[20]

Not surprisingly, a propaganda weapon as important as the newsreel was subject to a certain control before being distributed. Censorship was exercised by the *Wochenschauzentrale* (having replaced the *Wochenschaureferat* in 1938) which was directly subordinate to Goebbels. By 1939 when Hippler had taken over control of the *Wochenschauzentrale* (from Weidemann), its responsibilities included not only routine matters of liaising between the four newsreel companies but, more importantly, 'the arrangement of film reports according to the political and cultural points of view of the State'.[21] Furthermore, Hippler's responsibilities extended to the supervision and production of much longer documentary propaganda films. Thus in August 1939 Hippler directed *Der Westwall*, a forty-five-minute documentary on the building of the Siegfried Line. Newsreels were replaced altogether to accommodate a film which stressed Germany's military preparations against an attack from the West. The commentary claimed that the 'Westwall' made war less likely as it would act as a deterrent: '1914 encirclement but undefended boundaries—today?—encirclement but invincible boundaries!' In this respect the film echoed the sentiment of the time that was expressed in the propaganda slogan, 'He who wants peace must also prepare for war.'

[19] K. W. Wippermann, *Die Entwicklung der Wochenschau in Deutschland: Ufa-Tonwoche No. 410/1938* (Göttingen, 1970), p. 21.

[20] Quoted in *Der deutsche Film*, August 1937, p. 52.

[21] H. J. Giese, 'Die Film-Wochenschau im Dienste der Politik', Diss. (Leipzig, 1941), p. 59; reproduced in Wippermann, p. 19.

Throughout 1939 the newsreels had continued in this manner, attempting to prepare the nation psychologically for the coming war by increasing their emphasis on military subjects. In the Spring of 1939 they reported on the war in Spain and took great delight in recording the exploits of the Condor Legion. A few months later the newsreels were already giving the impression of a Germany at war, provoked, as it were, by Polish atrocities. On 29 August, Ulrich von Hassell noted in his diary:

Last night I saw in the movies a disgusting example of how human misery is exploited for purposes of propaganda. Weeping women and children are shown and in voices choked with tears they describe their sufferings in Poland.[22]

The *Film-Kurier*, reporting on the same newsreel prior to the invasion of Poland, commented: 'This newsreel on the sad fate of German refugees fleeing from Polish barbarities had a profound effect on German audiences.'[23]

After the outbreak of war the RMVP merged the newsreel companies to form a single war newsreel. On 21 November 1940, the *Deutsche Wochenschau GmbH* was founded and all other newsreel companies were dissolved.[24] Goebbels ordered that in future the war newsreel should simply be referred to as *Deutsche Wochenschau*. Until this time the public were largely unaware that the newsreels were state controlled as very little was known about the *Wochenschauzentrale*. From Goebbels's point of view such a revelation would have reduced their effectiveness and therefore no hint was given. But this reticence was to change so radically after 1939 that a Propaganda Ministry spokesman declared:

Deutsche Wochenschau bears little relevance to the weekly newsreels up until now. It has a totally different structure both in terms of its content and form. It must be seen as a new type of cinematic creation under the personal influence of the Propaganda Minister. Its producers achieve every week a new, exciting compilation of the war experience.[25]

[22] Von Hassell, p. 64.

[23] *Film-Kurier*, 25 August 1939. The last newsreel released prior to the outbreak of war (*Ufa Tonwoche* 469, 30 August 1939) depicted German troop mobilization and lampooned Allied politicians.

[24] BA, *R 55/504* (Gründung bei Deutsche Wochenschau GmbH: 1940-2).

[25] H. Traub, *Die Ufa. Ein Beitrag zur Entwicklungsgeschichte des deutschen Filmschaffens* (Berlin, 1943), p. 110.

War invariably produced an excess of good propagandist material, and Goebbels had control over the cameramen whose responsibility it was to capture it. Such a concentration of resources permitted speedy and economic reporting of events both at home and abroad. War reporting was the responsibility of the PK Units (*Propaganda Kompanie Einheiten*) which were formed in 1938. They were appointed by the RMVP but at the front they operated under the command of the *Oberkommando der Wehrmacht* (OKW). However, all film shot was at the exclusive disposal of the Propaganda Ministry. The material shot by the PK Units was further used in the prestigious 'Blitzkrieg' documentaries: *Feldzug in Polen* (*Campaign in Poland*), *Feuertaufe* (*Baptism of Fire*), *Sieg im Westen* (*Victory in the West*). In fact only a small percentage of newsreel footage was used in the *Deutsche Wochenschau*; the rest was stored in the National Film Archive and preserved as historical documents to be revealed after the war.

The importance of the newsreel was that it offered the propagandist all the advantage of a modern communication medium in that it was topical, periodical, and universal. Its success, particularly during the early war years, depended on the ability of the cameramen to capture topical and exciting events and on the skill of the editor in selecting and manipulating an intensive linkage of moving pictures in order to create what was believed to be a 'factual' reportage of reality. And of course this was reinforced by its conscious placement in the film programme and the manner in which it was contrasted with the more 'theatrical' feature film which followed it. However, Goebbels was conscious of the need to ensure that the disparate elements were not sacrificed for artistic unity thus stressing the aesthetic quality of newsreels.[26]

The war newsreel undoubtedly contributed to the increase in cinema audiences. As Table 4 illustrates, by 1940 cinema attendances had almost doubled within two years. They proved particularly successful in the rural areas where the peasants were not regular cinema-goers.[27] Goebbels responded to this by providing 1,000 mobile cinemas which travelled continuously around the country, ensuring that Germans saw a film

[26] Cf. Boelcke, p. 368.
[27] Boberach, p. 116.

show (with a newsreel) at least once a month.[28] One reason for this popularity was that after 1939 the war in the West was presented in such an immediate way that the public were fascinated by these reports. As a result of this response, Goebbels ordered that special newsreel shows be established in the Spring of 1940. Initially these were for Saturdays only when screening of past and present newsreels would be shown continuously. Admission charge was 30-40Pf., soldiers and children payed half price, but the theatre owners were expected to contribute 20 per cent of the costs.[29] After 1940, newsreels were also incorporated into the schools and Hitler Youth programmes with great success.[30] On 20 June 1940, the SD reported on the reception of the fifth war *Wochenschau*. The Report reiterates the undoubted success of the newsreel at this time in presenting military victories and it also mentions how the promotion of the *Führerprinzip* had been received:

Allenstein, Münster, Halle, Breslau, Stuttgart, Lüneburg — just some of the areas that have confirmed an enormous success. Many reports state that this is the best *Wochenschau* yet — a peak has been reached with cinemas reporting overflowing auditoriums. . . . The conquering of Dunkirk made an overpowering impression and was followed breathlessly by spectators. . . . Reports from Brunswick; spectators want to wreak destruction above all on England in order to gain revenge for the crimes she has committed against Germany. Shots of the Führer . . . according to reports from all over the Reich, spectators applauded and there were shouts of 'Heil'. Applause however halted to a pregnant silence when these shots were followed by pictures of Hitler moving to the map table with his Generals. Every move of the Führer's was followed with rapt attention. The people discussed, above all, the tired and serious features of his face. Reports from Aachen speak of relief in the auditorium when 'Adolf' laughed — the people are very concerned for his health and safety . . .[31]

Another important factor contributing to its early success was the length of the newsreels. In May 1940, it was announced that all German newsreels would last for forty minutes.[32] This enabled the RMVP, by means of a continuous and uniform repetition, to illustrate the fighting attitude of Germans abroad

[28] BA, *Sammlung Sänger, 102/63*, 13 June 1941.
[29] BA, *R1091/1034a, 1412*, 16 May 1940.
[30] BA, *R58/155*, 24 October 1940.
[31] BA, *R58/151*, 20 June 1940.
[32] *Licht-Bild-Bühne*, 23 May 1940.

and also to reinforce firmly held prejudices at home. Goebbels believed that a propaganda theme must be repeated, but not beyond the point of diminishing effectiveness. This posed various technical and artistic problems for the newsreel editors: how, for example, were they to accommodate the enlarged format and still make it interesting and exciting? While German armed forces were still registering victories this did not pose too great an obstacle—a skilled editor needed only to compose subsequent scenes by stressing similar 'facts' (that is the invincibility of German military might) to ensure the desired interest and response. According to the SD Reports, this was still proving a successful formula well into the summer of 1941:

According to reports from all over the Reich, the strong interest of the population in the newsreels from the Eastern front continues undiminished. Numerous reports speak of overflowing cinemas at special newsreel performances. It is often commented that the new kind of newsreel has achieved the almost impossible by reaching the same standards as its predecessor. It is generally emphasized that the film sequences, despite their length, are not at all tiring, but extremely varied and exciting. According to some reports, people consider the extended format to be more successful in that it allows for greater flexibility.[33]

In the midst of such euphoria German audiences would certainly not question domestic policies and thus under the pretext of 'historical truth' and 'factual reportage' the newsreel could openly and effectively reinforce prejudices. Witness the following response, reported in the same SD Report, to the anti-Semitic campaign being whipped up by Goebbels at this time:

The pictures showing the arrest of Jews involved in murder were enthusiastically received, and people commented that they were still being treated too leniently. The film sequences showing Jews being forced to do clearing-up work was greatly appreciated. The 'lynch justice' meted out by the people of Riga on their tormentors was greeted with shouts of encouragement![34]

According to Siegfried Kracauer, early Nazi newsreels were distinguishable from their British and American counterparts by their much greater length, their use of sophisticated editing, the utilization of music for emotional effect, and a preference for visual images at the expense of the spoken commentary. In Kracauer's view these pointed to a greater understanding

---

[33] BA, *R58/161*, 24 July 1941.   [34] Ibid.

of the film medium and an awareness of the importance of newsreels as an effective instrument of war propaganda.[35] Certainly Goebbels believed in the supreme importance of the war newsreels. Explaining why he immediately provided the *Wochenschauzentrale* with emergency headquarters after a particularly heavy air raid towards the end of 1943, he said: 'It costs much trouble to assemble the newsreel correctly each week and to make it into an effective propaganda weapon, but the work is worthwhile; millions of people draw from the newsreel their best insight into the war, its causes, and its effects.'[36] And in an earlier speech to the *Reichsfilmkammer* he expressed regret that feature films had still to match the power of the *Wochenschauen*:

In fact the most striking evidence revealing the deficiencies of the old type of films was that the cinemas were filled, not because of the films, but because of the newsreels. (Loud applause.) On many occasions it was noted that people left the cinemas after the newsreels because they knew that the films could not bear comparison with the broad sweep of the *Wochenschau*.[37]

There can be little doubt that stylistically the *Deutsche Wochenschauen* are impressive examples of film propaganda. But as the war dragged on they suffered, as did all Nazi propaganda, through their close association with German military success. Indeed, their effectiveness depended on their ability to report the victories that German leaders promised. While confidence in the Führer was high, the contradictions of Nazi propaganda mattered little. Attitudes could easily be altered as long as the regime exuded strength. However, this was all to change towards the end of 1941. The time of striking and easy victories was over and the enemy (and what it said) had to be taken more seriously.

The newsreels also had to adapt to the changed circumstances; there were no more sensational marches into enemy

[35] S. Kracauer, 'The Conquest of Europe on the Screen. The Nazi Newsreel, 1939–40', *Social Research*, vol. 10, no. 3, September 1943, pp. 337–57.
[36] L. W. Doob, 'Goebbels' Principles of Propaganda', in D. Katz *et al.* (eds.), *Public Opinion and Propaganda* (New York, 1954), p. 513.
[37] Full speech (15 February 1941) reproduced in Albrecht, pp. 465–79. Hitler is reported to have remarked in 1941: 'I've been thrilled by our contemporary news-films. We are experiencing a heroic epic, without precedent in history.' Trevor-Roper, *Hitler's Table Talk*, entry for 25/6 September 1941, p. 43.

territory and German audiences had to be content with the mundane affairs of war. In the knowledge that there would be be no speedy end to the war, Nazi propaganda increasingly depended on irrational themes at the expense of factual war reporting. One can detect the deliberate evasion of material problems such as food shortages, labour difficulties, and air raids. By prescribing what could and could not be shown or mentioned in the mass media, the Nazis betrayed how little they were concerned with reality. On 10 June 1940, Goebbels issued a directive for film, press, and radio to the effect that while the severity, magnitude, and sacrifice of war could be shown, any excessively realistic representation, likely to arouse a horror of the war, had to be avoided at all costs.[38] A month before this directive, the OKW issued instructions to cameramen and editors that pictures should not be used which 'are apt to produce fear, horror, or revulsion' of the war, 'unless they acquire documentary value for this reason'.[39] These principles were followed to the end of the war with the result that newsreels never showed the war in its true frightfulness and murderous intent. The early *Wochenschauen* in particular give the impression of an invincible military machine sweeping forward against the enemy without the loss of a single life or machine. This abolition of death from all newsreels was a peculiarity of Nazi propaganda.[40]

After Stalingrad, disillusionment set in and audiences started to question previous assumptions and the banality and lies they were witnessing in the weekly newsreels. Only a month after the Propaganda Minister addressed the RFK and proclaimed the supreme importance of the *Wochenschau*, the SD reported that Germans were now lingering outside the cinemas until the newsreels were over.[41] Goebbels responded by closing all cinemas during the showing of the newsreel, so that if a patron

[38] Boelcke, 10 June 1940, p. 132.
[39] Ibid., 24 May 1940, p. 129.
[40] The effect was achieved by skilful editing. Cf. Shirer, p. 267. The correspondent recounts viewing uncensored newsreels in the Propaganda Ministry which showed quite clearly death and destruction.
[41] BA, *R58/158*, 27 March 1941. One explanation supplied by various *Gauleiter* to the RMVP was the fact that Hitler was not appearing frequently enough in these newsreels. From Munich it was claimed that when the Führer was not shown 'morale sank — but when he appeared a new desire and will for victory emerged'. BA, *NS 18/341*, 6 August 1942.

wanted to see the feature attraction he was forced to sit through the newsreel as well![42]

By 1943 this disillusionment was clearly reflected in the reception given to the war newsreels. No longer were Germans willing to comment spontaneously on the content of the *Wochenschau* as the following SD Report illustrates:

Reliable reports have revealed that the newsreels have been unable to regain their former popularity. It had been confirmed from wide sections of the population that people no longer want to go to the cinema just to see the newsreel. It is only seldom now that people make spontaneous comments about newsreels. Observations of this kind are confirmed constantly, and as a result, wide sections of the community are not allowing themselves to be influenced by the newsreel.[43]

After the defeat of Stalingrad, German propaganda had shed all agitational pretensions; instead, it limited itself to strengthening the community spirit in the struggle for 'total war'. The aim of such propaganda was the indoctrination of fear. Writing in 1943, H. Herma noted:

The concept of propaganda had been redefined by National Socialism. It has been closely linked to the totalitarian organisation of society and may more aptly be called 'psychological management' than propaganda. It does not want to persuade or convince. It introduces the element of fear, and aims at the elimination of rationality.[44]

The development of the *Deutsche Wochenschauen* details the gradual retreat of National Socialist propaganda into myth from 1939 to 1945. By invoking the *Untergangsmotif* (theme of destruction) and declaring that war was an ideological struggle, a 'fight to the death', Goebbels was once again appealing to German fears of the barbaric Bolshevik that he had employed so successfully in 1933. In this sense fear may become an intrinsic part of propaganda and eventually the two become interchangeable. An outline of the contents of one Nazi newsreel in the last phase of the war will demonstrate this. I have chosen *Deutsche Wochenschau* No. 45-6, which was released towards the end of 1944 and illustrates the

[42] Boelcke, p. 652. It would appear that by 1943 *Gaupropagandaleitung* were ignoring these instructions. Goebbels was forced to remind them of this directive and the need to impose it rigorously. BA, *NS 18/341*, 9 July 1943.

[43] BA, *R58/1148*, 4 March 1943.

[44] H. Herma, 'Goebbels' Conception of Propaganda', *Social Research*, vol. 10, no. 2, 1943, p. 217. Cf. also BA, *NS 18/341*, 23 June 1943.

fear tactics employed as the Russian troops advanced on Berlin.

Deutsche Wochenschau No. 45-6, 1944

Introduction: Trumpet fanfare, bells ringing, and the Nazi version of the German eagle.

1. *Food substitutes*: ash berries when harvested and pressed produce a floury substance which can be refined and bottled. It is claimed that 2 cupfuls of these berries equal 7 lemons in Vitamin C.

2. *Volkssturm*: 'The hour of battle has arrived for us all. Men and women between the ages of 16 and 60, regardless of class or occupation, enrol all over Germany to save the nation.' 18 October – it is the 131st Jubilee of the Battle of Leipzig. Himmler proclaims the Führer's instructions for the Volkssturm: 'Our accursed enemies must come to realize that an invasion of Germany, were that possible, would cost them dearly and that the national spirit would be aroused to the utmost resistance.'

Service of dedication at the Annaberg Memorial. A mass *Volkssturm* rally is held at Leipzig — 'hundreds of thousands have volunteered from the eastern regions and are ready to defend the Fatherland with their blood.' A local *Gauleiter* is seen addressing the rally and the *Volkssturm* recruits receive rifles and anti-tank weapons. The Hitler Youth march behind ('they are ready to fulfil their oath').

3. *The Stone Lion at Belfort*: Metz Cathedral, the Moselle valley and Trier have all been under air attack 'but the people of these areas have learned to accept this with courage and stoicism'.

4. *West Front*: German reserve divisions move up to the front, 'the enemy have severely extended themselves through their mistaken belief in Germany's impending collapse!' At Geilenkirchen, pupils of the Officers' School in Julich take over the defence of the city and demonstrate the effectiveness of their anti-tank missile in repelling an American attack. The commentator refers to the American prisoners (whose battle-soiled faces are shown in close-ups and include a number of negroes) as 'these gum-chewing liberators of Europe who only prove that they spring from the same stock as Stalin's hordes from the Steppes!'

5. *East Front*: The battle areas in East Prussia — naval detachments provide support for the army in the Baltic near Memel and defence positions are formed near Goldap and Gumbinnen.

Nemmersdorf: the Wehrmacht have discovered evidence of Bolshevik atrocities 'no restraint is placed upon Bolshevik soldiers and this resulted in women being raped, old men beaten to death, and children murdered. The whole countryside is ravaged by death. This Testimony of brutal bestiality may be the last warning to Europe.'

6. *Final Sequence*: Air and tank battles on the Eastern Front. The commentator claims that the Russians have lost over 80 per cent of their equipment in just a few days and that the German people now have a 'fervent determination to save their country from Stalin's murderous hordes!'

The newsreel ends with the commentator screaming: 'Even in this final critical stage, German soldiers behave as if Hitler had given each one of them a personal order to hold out to the last!'

In the final year of the war 'heroism' and 'sacrifice' often appeared in the newsreels, where there was no mention of surrender. As the newsreel quoted above demonstrates, when other methods of persuasion failed, terror was invariably employed as the antidote to cowardice. Furthermore, as Jay Baird observed:

When at the end of their rope, Hitler and Goebbels made one final, frantic effort to survive — they blurred the distinction between Party and nation in an attempt to convince the people that the demise of the one guaranteed the destruction of the other.[45]

In other words, Germans were no longer fighting an ideological battle for National Socialism, but rather for the survival of Germany. Although the German people's response to this may suggest that Goebbels enjoyed some limited success in 1945, it owed little to any ingenious use of propaganda techniques but rather to traditional German patriotism and to a people intuitively defending their country.

FEUERTAUFE (BAPTISM OF FIRE, 1940)

From the speeches that he made between 1939 and the reverses in Russia, it is quite clear that Goebbels believed the war provided the cinema with an important challenge. In his address to the RFK in 1941 he reaffirmed this belief:

When the war broke out, there were some voices, even in leading German circles, saying that now was no time for concerning ourselves with culture, that the war affected the most elementary conditions of our national life, and that culture was only a matter for peaceful, happy times. . . . I strongly oppose any move to bring our cultural life to a standstill. . . . I have stated my view that the war should present a challenge for the German cinema (loud applause).

Goebbels went on to say that he thought German film-makers had responded to this challenge:

I was promised that efforts would be made to meet this new challenge. Therefore I decided not to convene a meeting of the RFK in 1940 because I was convinced that these new films were on their way, I thought

---

[45] Baird, p. 11.

they were not yet ready, and I didn't want to develop a programme without the factual evidence to substantiate my claims. All this is in the past. The breakthrough which was made between September–October 1939 towards the creation of a great national cinema, can be regarded now as having succeeded (stormy, lengthy applause). That this breakthrough has also been acknowledged by the German nation can be seen from the fact that the attendance figures rose from 700 millions in 1939 to 1,000 millions in 1940. (Applause.)[46]

According to the Propaganda Minister, one reason for this was that German film-makers had rejected 'colourless dialogue which was of little value and had concentrated instead on the depiction of action'. Often in Nazi propaganda the action referred to is supplemented by a large measure of intimidation and fear. Goebbels believed that propaganda must not only be supported by force but that propaganda content itself should incite violent action. In his diary he stated that, 'a sharp sword must always stand behind propaganda, if it is to be really effective.'[47] Eugen Hadamovsky, the chief of German broadcasting, wrote that 'propaganda and terror are not opposites. Violence, in fact, can be an integral part of propaganda.'[48]

Terror and fear are one of the oldest forms of psychological warfare and can be traced back to the feathers and paint of warring tribesmen. It is not surprising then that the warrior spirit of the Nazis made full use of this concept. Propaganda was able to advertise military victories and indirectly help to prepare an atmosphere, or expectation, for new ones. In this sense the propagandist could support military campaigns by creating a confident and aggressive spirit at home and by deliberately challenging enemy leaders to reveal their military prowess in the arena of combat. Thus, during the period of lightning German victories in Poland, Scandinavia, and France, German belief in an early termination of the war had been strengthened by a propaganda campaign that included a number of large-scale documentaries compiled from newsreel material, all made with the intention of illustrating Germany's military superiority and the futility of resistance.

Feature-length war documentaries, which were an attempt to educate the nation about the magnitude of Hitler's Blitzkrieg success, now figured prominently in Goebbels's film

---

[46] Goebbels's speech of 15 February 1941, see above, note 37.
[47] Lochner, p. 370.   [48] Hadamovsky, p. 22.

schedules. *Feldzug in Polen* (*Campaign in Poland*) was produced by Fritz Hippler and released in February 1940. It concentrated on the part played by the German army in the Polish campaign. Two months later, *Feuertaufe* (*Baptism of Fire*) depicted the annihilation of Poland and her capital by the Luftwaffe. Nine months after the fall of France, the relentless advance of the Wehrmacht across Europe was meticulously chronicled by Goebbels's cameramen in the third of the series, *Sieg im Westen* (*Victory in the West*).

Feuertaufe was directed by Hans Bertram, a former air ace and script-writer and author.[49] In 1939, much to the annoyance of Goebbels who disliked interference of any kind, Göring had sponsored a film about the Luftwaffe entitled *D 111 88* which turned out to be an unqualified financial success.[50] Although the film was directed by Herbert Maisch, Bertram had written the script and directed the airborne sequences. His experience in aviation and in film production thus made him an obvious choice as director of the film about to glorify the role of the Luftwaffe in the Polish campaign. The result was *Feuertaufe*, drawn from over 230,000 feet of newsreel material, and arguably the most impressive of the full-length campaign films in its successful dissemination of Nazi propaganda. The importance of this film both in terms of its content and style and as an example of the Nazi documentary warrant a detailed analysis of its structure. Such an analysis should reveal the National Socialist rationale for the invasion of Poland (and therefore the beginning of the Second World War) and also the extent to which the symbols of combat became such an important aspect of the Nazis' mythical ideology. In *Feuertaufe*, as in most Nazi militarist films, war is depicted more or less as a sporting event devoid of human suffering.

The film opens with a series of credits against a background of gently floating clouds. The people involved in the film participated 'on behalf of their Führer and their Fatherland'.

[49] Hans Bertram was born in 1906; he was an author of a number of books and wrote the screenplays for several films including *Frauen für Golden Hill* (*Wives for Golden Hill*, 1938) and the anti-British film set in Ireland, *Der Fuchs von Glenarvon* (*The Fox of Glenarvon*, 1940).

[50] The film made a net profit of RM 1½ million and was cited in Goebbels's 1941 speech to the RFK (quoted above) as an 'irreproachable film of national destiny'.

Another drawn-out sequence shows all branches of the Polish armed forces passing under the benign eye of Marshal Rydż-Smigly. In sarcastic tones the narrator points out that her *peacetime* strength amounts to thirty divisions and two million men! There follows an animated map of Germany and Poland, with the Polish border, in heavy inking, flowing into German territory. 'These people wish to penetrate the Reich and carry the frontier line far beyond the Elbe, and annex it for eternity.' The Poles' first target is Danzig, 'But Danzig is German, was German, and will always remain so.' (Shots of Danzig—a typical German town. Houses are gaily decorated with swastikas and the German eagle; Nazi posters are seen from every building.) *Gauleiter* Albert Forster proclaims to the people of Danzig: 'However much we are provoked by threats of war, we shall stand firm and Danzig will remain calm.'

(A montage sequence of frontier incidents; German homesteads are burnt and thousands of refugees can be seen fleeing to safety in the Reich.) Suddenly Hitler's voice is heard over these distressing pictures:

During the past weeks we have done our utmost to ward off any on-slaught of any kind against Danzig. But the German army is standing by and is prepared to fight for the freedom of the Greater German nation.

(The camera pans to reveal resolute-looking soldiers presumably marching towards Danzig, and a tracking shot of the training ship, 'Schleswig-Holstein', entering the port and being given a rapturous welcome by the people of the ancient Hanseatic town.)

And our young Luftwaffe is poised like a sword in the sky, ready to give battle, determined to fight and annihilate those who may attempt to destroy peace in Europe.

(The announcement that Germany is only interested in maintaining peace is followed by a montage sequence of foreign newspaper captions all proclaiming the same headline, 'The Reich threatens world peace'. But as if to give the lie to this we are shown the machinations of the Allied Governments who are goading Poland into war with Germany so that they may prosper themselves:

Attention please! This is London calling. We are broadcasting a news bulletin in German. Lord Halifax has made the following statement in the House of Lords: 'Our guarantee still stands; we are ready to intercede whenever Poland desires. The Royal Navy is on alert, ready to sail in a matter of hours. British citizens are leaving German territory.'

(Shots of London, feverish political activity as Cabinet Ministers meet to decide their strategy. European newspaper headlines intended to reveal the hypocrisy of British politics run throughout these takes . . .)

NARRATOR. London is the centre of the warmongering fever. Between Downing Street and the Houses of Parliament the plutocrats are manipulating their puppets. Soon England will give Poland a free hand.

NEWSPAPER HEADLINE. 'Berlin threatens Warsaw!'

NARRATOR. The hysteria of Germany's democratic enemies knows no bounds.

HEADLINE. 'The Reich threatens world peace!'

NARRATOR. Prompted by England, Poland attacks Germany. But Germany will strike back.

HEADLINE. 'Nazis provoke Europe!'

NARRATOR. This is your doing Mr Chamberlain. You have made the man in the street believe that . . .

HEADLINE. 'Hitler wants war!'

NARRATOR. But what does it mean, 'Hitler wants war?' Poland wanted war, they took the first step. Poland is already in a state of war, and to prove it, the homes of the *Volksdeutsche* are already ablaze . . .

    [*Flashback to the earlier scenes of burning homesteads and columns of fleeing refugees.*]

. . . Here the defenceless are being slaughtered. In their thousands they seek refuge in the Reich. Old folk, women, and children, who lay in hiding in the woods, slip secretly over the border. What indescribable hardships these people have suffered, simply because they are Germans.

The first part of *Feuertaufe* outlines Polish provocation, expands the theme of 'British plutocracy' (which was to play a leading part in Nazi propaganda until Hitler decided to turn his attention eastward in 1941), and draws attention to the moral superiority of Germany's retaliation. The second half of the film concentrates on this response and establishes the myth of German victory through Blitzkrieg methods. In the process *Feuertaufe* illustrates the extent to which the Nazis' need for vengeance found an outlet through images of terror by means of various symbols of combat.

The Nazis' preparations for the strike on Poland are slowly and lovingly detailed, one by one. The mood changes from one

of dutiful restraint to unchecked jubilation as the annihilation
of Poland is celebrated in an orgy of violence.

The Luftwaffe have switched their bases to the airfields of
East Prussia and the Baltic coast. (As the morning breaks, an
airfield is just discernible through the early mist. Solemn strains
of a military march can be heard in the background . . .)

NARRATOR. Any moment may bring the order to attack. All strategic
targets are now under the protection of our armed forces. On the
aerodromes our planes are being camouflaged to safeguard them from
hostile attack.
[*Shots of aeroplanes being manoeuvred into the woods and covered
with branches etc.; ammunition crates are unloaded, bombs are attached to the planes*] . . .
Bombs are loaded. It is not unlike a smooth-running military
manoeuvre — except that now the bombs are lethal. These weapons
are destined to destroy all opposition.

(There follows a long sequence about the invaluable technical
work of the ground crew as they service the planes and install
the ammunition. The last of the bombs is loaded and the bay
is slowly closed.)

NARRATOR. If it reopens over enemy territory, woe betide! Germany's
airforce is standing by. He who wants peace must be prepared for war.

(Shots of the *Bündisch* spirit that exists in these bases. The
camp-side atmosphere pervades throughout as pilots and
ground crews are shown happily socializing and undertaking
their individual duties.)

NARRATOR. At the eleventh hour the Führer makes one more attempt
to avoid war. The whole world waits with eager anticipation . . .

(Montage sequence showing newspaper headlines on the progress of the conflict. Music enhances the gravity of the situation
by rising to a crescendo. Hitler arrives at the Kroll Opera. Later
a tense crowd is shown listening to the Führer's speech in the
Reichstag which is broadcast over the loudspeakers . . .)[51]

HITLER. For the first time today, Poland, deploying regular soldiers,
opened fire on our territory. Since 5.45 we have been returning their
fire. From now on we shall retaliate, bomb for bomb.

(A burst of solemn music followed by a flourish of trumpets

[51] Hitler's speech of 1 September 1939 is taken from the booklet accompanying the film: *Feuertaufe. Der Film vom Einsatz der deutschen Luftwaffe in Polen.*

and a roll of drums. The Luftwaffe squadrons stand by for their first operational flight. Suddenly, the music is drowned by the roar of engines! Whole rows of planes take off and fly in perfect formation. As the camera scans the faces of the pilots and turns to reveal other planes seemingly gliding through mountain-like cloud formations, the song of the Luftwaffe strikes up . . .)

LUFTWAFFE SONG. Up in the heights, we feel in the East wind the day's daring venture. We reach up for the sun, leaving the earth far below. Comrade, comrade, all the girls must wait. Comrade, comrade, the order is clear, we're ready to go. Comrade, comrade, the slogan you know: 'Forward at the enemy, forward at the enemy — bomb the land of the Poles.' .

NARRATOR. First sortie over enemy territory. The German spear-head strikes deep into the heart of Poland. Turret and rear gunners lie in readiness behind their machine guns. Like flying fish the fighter planes streak alongside the bombers.

(Close-up inside the Heinkel III, of pilot, co-pilot, and gunners. The noise of the engine is drowned by the lyrical strains of a violin.)

PILOT. Look out! Troop road ahead. Stand by! Small cloud straight ahead. Flak. Just you wait! We'll soon pay that back with a few bombs! . . .
    [A glance at the map to make sure they have the right target, and then . . .]
    Bombs away!

(A loud burst of music. Bombs are seen being released from inside the Heinkel. As they fall to the ground the sonorous music gives way to a strangely soothing orchestral score which creates the impression that the procession of bombs are falling in slow motion. This curiously unreal scene is broken by the explosions on the ground and columns of smoke drifting from the pulverized roads.)

NARRATOR. In a shower of missiles, the concerted and invincible might of the Luftwaffe had unleashed its fury. Mission over. Back home to base. Like noble greyhounds, our pursuit planes gambol over the conquered areas.

(The first sortie ends with an impressionistic sequence of aerobatics and tracking aerial shots which reveal the extent of the damage; bomb craters along the railway lines, smoking ruins, etc.)

The film then continues to outline the Luftwaffe's incessant bombing of Poland for seventeen continuous days until only Warsaw is able to offer any sort of resistance. The third part of *Feuertaufe* concentrates on the final capitulation of Poland and the preparations for the forthcoming attack against Britain.

September 18: The last day of the decisive battle as the Luftwaffe arrive to support the army again. (Luftwaffe song starts up again.) As the camera pans the smiling faces of the young pilots, we see thousands of tons of bombs falling on Poland's capital. Within a short time Warsaw surrenders. Shots of deserted streets, ruins, and the expanse of debris. After days and nights of misery and suffering, the starving population slowly emerges from its cellars. Amidst the city's ruins the German army distribute soup and bread to the people. As if to leave the cinema audience in little doubt of the futility of such resistance, the Narrator explains that the Luftwaffe are to fly over Warsaw once again—only this time not to release bombs but to survey the extent of the damage. More shots of smouldering, gutted buildings and a report of the bomb damage; factories, railway depots, civic buildings, and roads. The camera zooms in to take close-range shots of the wrecked city . . .

NARRATOR. What have you to say now, Mr Chamberlain? Here you can see the catastrophe for yourself . . . the ruin into which you plunged the Polish capital. Aren't you afraid of the curse of the nation you betrayed? Here you can see the results of your cold-blooded war-mongering. All this is your work! One day you will answer for your sins at the Last Judgement! And remember; this is what happens when the German Luftwaffe strikes. It will also strike its blow at the really guilty ones!

[*A further, slow montage of aerial shots of the devastation.*]

NARRATOR. Our plane casts a shadow over the coach in which the talks of surrender are taking place, where, at this very moment, the curtain is being drawn on the last act of the Polish tragedy.

(The capitulation document is signed. Through the carriage windows, Hitler and his General Staff are seen in earnest conversation with the Polish negotiators. After signing, the Poles are led away under escort. 130,000 prisoners are marched out of the city. Happy, cheerful music emanates from a group of young soldiers.)

NARRATOR. The reason for these soldiers' high spirits is easier to understand once you realize that they are *Volksdeutsche* students who have been forced to serve in the Polish army.

(The surrender document is read out to the incoming German troops. A victory fanfare follows. A brief shot of a military parade is interjected with captured, dispirited Polish soldiers in barbed POW camps. Cut back to the parade and Hitler reviewing the whole gamut of German military strength. The parade ends with a Luftwaffe formation flying overhead.)

HERMANN GÖRING [*full-face, speaking into the camera*]. With great force and emphasis this film shows the German people what a remarkable impression was made by the Polish campaign and in particular the great achievement of our Luftwaffe. This air force and its exploits will go down in history.

It is mainly due to the Luftwaffe's contribution that we owe the defeat and annihilation of the enemy. When this great weapon was taken away from Germany at Versailles, no one suspected that under the leadership of Adolf Hitler, this force would rise up again, mightier and more impregnable than before . . .

[*As Göring continues to speak, aerial shots above the clouds.*]
. . . Now we stand at the end of the first phase of this great battle. What the Luftwaffe has shown in Poland it will fulfil in the coming battles in England ánd France. In other words, it will strike in these countries too — it will conquer and annihilate the enemy!

[*Trumpet fanfare and the roar of Luftwaffe planes in threatening low-flying formations and the familiar sound of their song, 'Bomben auf England'.*]

LUFTWAFFE SONG. Thus our youngest weapon has been baptized and tempered in the flames. Now the winged host reaches out to the sea, we are ready for battle. Forward against the British lion, for the last, decisive blow. We sit here in judgement of a crumbling Empire — for which purposes German soldiers are fighting.

Comrade, comrade, all the girls must wait. Comrade, comrade, the order is clear, we're on our way. Comrade, comrade, the slogan you know; forward at the foe, forward at the enemy — bombs on England! . . .

[*As the final chorus of the song is reached the screen is taken up with animated clouds.*]

LUFTWAFFE SONG. . . . Do you hear the password? Forward, onward to the enemy! Do you hear the password? Onward to the enemy! Onward! Onward! Bombs on England! . . .

(The clouds now open up to reveal a map of the British Isles. The camera swiftly pans in towards it accompanied by the penetrating sound of a diving Stukas. There is a loud explosion and the map of Britain is destroyed. The film ends on this symbolic annihilation with the last line from the Luftwaffe Song.)

Bombs, bombs, bombs on England!

Film is the one propaganda medium that rarely allows itself to threaten its audience. However, as the film historians Furhammar and Isaksson noted, 'this rule has a single exception in the way the Nazi Government used newsreels of its army offensives at the beginning of World War II.'[52] One of the main functions of the campaign films such as *Feuertaufe* and *Sieg im Westen* which were compiled from newsreel footage, was to illustrate the lightning speed and devastating power of the German armed forces. Such films could be exploited as a psychological weapon against those countries that were due to be attacked next (or thought they were). Thus in 1940, *Feuertaufe* was shown by many German embassies in neutral countries with a view to intimidating foreign diplomats. E. K. Bramsted succinctly stated how the Nazis hoped this would be achieved: 'they [campaign films] illustrated that resistance to the mighty German armies, up to date in their weapons, was equivalent to committing suicide.'[53]

However, the point should be stressed that even these campaign documentaries were intended primarily for the German audience at home where they served to reinforce a jubilant military self-confidence. The impression left by such films was that Hitler had launched a relentless drive and that German success was assured because of the technical and moral superiority of their war aims. In promoting the myth of these Blitzkrieg methods the RMVP and the OKW had to establish the worthiness or credibility of their enemy. This was established in *Feuertaufe* after the decisive battle of Vistula on the eighteenth day, when the narrator makes it quite clear that German armed forces were opposed by a fully-equipped modern army and that the magnitude of their victory can only be judged on those terms:

NARRATOR. After only eighteen days, the Polish army is destroyed in the battle of Vistula. But this eighteen-day battle was not the defeat of a small, badly-equipped force by a modern, monster army. The German soldier fought a well-equipped enemy, and often battled against superior forces.

Despite the stress that was placed on this point in the illustrated booklet accompanying the film, the SD Report noted that

---

[52] Furhammar and Isaksson, p. 188.
[53] Bramsted, p. 67.

audiences still felt that 'too little had been shown of Polish defensive forces. As a result, people received the impression that there had been no serious resistance.'[54] In celebrating the Nazi 'fighter stereotype', whether the Luftwaffe in *Feuertaufe* or the Wehrmacht in *Feldzug in Polen*, the campaign films invoked almost every aspect of the Nazi mythology of war. *Feuertaufe*, in particular, not only by its promotion of Blitzkreig but also by its elaborate use of technique and stylization, set the tone for a whole series of military educational films (*Wehrerziehungsfilme*) directed specifically at the youth audience.[55] For example, Hans Bertram was asked to fictionalize the attack on Poland in *Kampfgeschwader Lutzow* (*Squadron Lutzow*, 1941) which used newsreel material and incorporated Luftwaffe songs first used in *Feuertaufe*. The early films of this genre portrayed war as the hero's struggle for liberation and as such they were part of an older, epic tradition.[56] To take the example of the war songs, their importance in terms of psychological warfare was that they allowed for self-identification and also clearly registered the enemy. In *Feuertaufe*, whenever the songs occur, the camera is inside the plane capturing the comradeship and determination of the young Luftwaffe pilots. It was a device, moreover, which allowed the Nazis to ease the tension of the campaigns and depict war as a form of sport devoid of human suffering in which various teams (in this case, the Luftwaffe, represented by their own song) could participate. However it would appear that this deliberate misrepresentation of the reality of war produced an ambivalent attitude in cinema audiences. According to one SD Report on *Feuertaufe*:

It was apparent from the way Feuertaufe was received, and the same applies to all war films, that it is impossible to achieve a uniform reaction from every member of the audience. While one section wanted even more action with live war scenes, others, especially women,

[54] BA, *R58/184*, 14 May 1940.

[55] As well as being 'politically and artistically valuable', *Feuertaufe* was also designated an 'educational' film and exhibited at the compulsory performances of the Hitler Youth.

[56] Such films would include: *Drei Unteroffiziere* (*Three Non-Commissioned Officers*, 1939), *Jakko* (1941), *Kadetten* (1941), *Kopf hoch Johannes!* (*Chin-Up John!*, 1941), *Blutsbrüderschaft* (*Blood-Brotherhood*, 1941), *Himmelhunde* (*Sky Dogs*, 1942). Interestingly, these early war films are the only genre that the Nazis felt confident enough to present in a contemporary context.

expressed sympathy for the Poles, and faced with the sight of Warsaw in ruins, the feeling was one of depression and anxiety about the 'horrors of war', rather than one of heroic pride.[57]

On the other hand, they discovered, not surprisingly, that the film had been enthusiastically received in Lower Styria where the 'Slovene country population witnessed their own experiences of Polish terror in the scenes where the German farms were burning in Poland.'[58]

War songs were also important in that they clearly delineated heroes and villains. In the first part of the film the Luftwaffe pilots sing of the sacrifices that have to be made in order to destroy the Polish enemy and, once this has been achieved, the same song sets out their new objective: 'Forward against the British lion, for the last decisive blow.' Similarly in *Stukas* (1941), Karl Ritter's film about comradeship and self-sacrifice, there is a famous scene where Captain Bork, the squadron leader, lines his pilots up and tells them of the danger involved in their forthcoming attack on England. We then see the young Aryan pilots assembled in their Stukas, and the camera zooms in to reveal their faces and then dissolves into cloud formation. At the juxtaposition of the two images the ecstatic pilots begin to sing 'Stukaslied':

> Always prepared and ready to attack
> [*track-in to happy, smiling faces and a Stuka formation*] . . .
> We the Stukas, Stukas, Stukas.
> We dive from the sky
> [*more resolute, but happy faces*] . . .
> We advance on — to defeat England![59]

Such songs also compensate for the lack of dialogue in all these militaristic films. The purpose of this type of propaganda was to popularize the Nazi ethos of blind obedience and self-sacrifice by sublimating the will of the individual to the collective consciousness. German soldiers on the cinema screen were never seen to express personal feelings or attitudes towards war in general; they were only vehicles to be manipulated by being given artificial speeches quite alien to the common experience. In *Stukas*, as in numerous other war films, it was

---

[57] BA, *R58/184*, 14 May 1940.
[58] BA, *R58/160*, 15 May 1940.
[59] For an extremely amusing analysis of this film, see H. K. Smith, *Last Train from Berlin* (London, 1943), p. 134.

common after the death of an ordinary soldier for a comrade
suddenly to recite (for example) 'Hölderlin':

> For the Fatherland, to bleed the heart's blood . . .
> Now heralds of victory descend, the battle
> Is ours! Live on high, O Fatherland,
> And count not the dead! For you,
> Beloved, not one too many is fallen.[60]

Such stilted dialogue was intrinsic to Nazi film-making and
it is illustrative to compare *Feuertaufe* with contemporary
British propaganda films, *Target for Tonight* (1941) and *Listen
to Britain* (1942), where aviators, soldiers, and civilians speak
frankly about their feelings towards the war and the enemy.[61]
Because there was an element of defensiveness in British film
propaganda ('London can take it'), the Germans had to reject
this style as it did not correspond to their idealization of the
Nazi fighter stereotype. Moreover, it emphasized individuals
and individual expression at the expense of sublimation and
the community. Referring to his 1941 film *Über alles in der
Welt* (*Above All in the World*) Karl Ritter encapsulated what
could have been the credo of almost all Nazi film-makers:

The ultimate purpose of all National Socialist films is to show the test
of an individual within the community — for the individual's fate only
has meaning when it can be placed at the service of the community,
whereupon it becomes part of a people and nation.[62]

Feuertaufe was part of this tradition of film-making and
for this reason alone was an important part of the war effort.
It projected and celebrated the image of the German warrior
as the brave, fearless Aryan, willing to sacrifice his life for
Führer and Fatherland. The SD Report on the reception given
to *Feuertaufe* appears to substantiate Goebbels's enthusiasm
for the film and in particular the expensive advertising campaign that was undertaken to promote it. Furthermore, confidence in the invincibility of the Luftwaffe would never be
higher.[63]

Stylistically, the majority of feature films that dealt with

---

[60] Quoted in Leiser, p. 33.
[61] See A. Lovell and J. Hillier, *Studies in Documentary* (London, 1972).
[62] *Der deutsche Film*, vol. 10, April 1941. For a detailed analysis of the film
see Hollstein, pp. 123-7.
[63] BA, *R58/184*, 14 May 1940.

militaristic themes were not artistically innovative, although they were invariably of a high technical standard. However, *Feuertaufe* probably came closer to achieving the distinctive Nazi style that Goebbels desired, although it ultimately lacked the broad imaginative leap or ideological commitment which would have revolutionized the German cinema in the same way that Eisenstein's *Battleship Potemkin* changed Soviet film-making.

Films such as *Feuertaufe* encouraged an aggressive militarist spirit, particularly among young people, by presenting a distorted and romanticized vision of modern warfare. To a large extent this explains the appeal of the film. The careful selection from the vast footage shot produced a record of German indomitability and testified to the Nazis' grasp of documentary film propaganda based on the axiom that the 'camera never lies'. A detailed analysis of *Feuertaufe* reveals how careful Nazi film propagandists were to evade reality, although always eager to convey an *impression* of reality. By presenting Western democracies as evil, plotting powers intent throughout history on destroying Germany, the film gives the impression that Hitler's triumph was the culmination of an historical mission. Anyone seeing the film now would be amazed at the relentless reiteration of the central message, but in 1940, with the campaign in Poland over, Goebbels was able to unite the country behind Hitler by linking politically aggressive film propaganda with the Germans' highly mythical notion of their military tradition and with symbols which, as we saw in the last chapter, they traced back to Frederick the Great. Goebbels, however, was soon to discover that the dissemination of such propaganda proved easier in victory than in retreat.

GERMAN FILM AUDIENCES IN WARTIME

Given the all-embracing nature of the *Gleichschaltung* of the film industry and Goebbels's desire for some kind of feedback in the shape of SD Reports, it is surprising to discover that the RMVP failed to undertake a comprehensive and systematic survey of the age, sex, and social status of German film audiences (or even the audiences in occupied territory). As a result, very little reliable data are available, although one can reasonably assume that in wartime women and children would make up the majority of the audience.

For ideological reasons, relatively few women were employed in Germany during the war compared to Britain and Russia.[64] One reason for this was that the allowances paid to soldiers' wives were so generous that it was often more economic for them not to work. In times of rationing, hardship, and loneliness, sitting in a warm cinema was an obvious way for such women to spend their time and their money. Precisely how many women visited the cinema on a regular basis is unknown, but as early as 1938 the *Film-Kurier* felt obliged to refute a suggestion made in the *Hamburger Tageblatt* that women comprised 70 per cent of the average cinema audience.[65] Although an obviously exaggerated claim, there can be little doubt that women did constitute the majority of the regular cinema audience during the war. Goebbels, in fact, only once acknowledges the preponderance of women in wartime audiences[66] and it is difficult to speculate just how much they influenced film policy, although women probably had some bearing on Goebbels's decision to commission more escapist entertainment films after 1942. But given their importance as regular cinema-goers, it is indeed surprising that women did not noticeably influence RMVP policy. This would tend to suggest that Goebbels was more interested in appealing to another section of the populace—the youth audience.

There is evidence to suggest that the trend among young people to attend the cinema on a regular basis, which began when the Nazis assumed power, continued to increase during the war. The total population of Germany in 1939 was 79.4 million, of which 57.1 million were over eighteen years of age and 22.3 million under eighteen.[67] At the beginning of the war the average German over fifteen years of age visited the cinema 10.5 times per year; by 1943 this had risen to 14.4 times per

[64] See A. S. Milward, *The German Economy at War* (London, 1965). The most comprehensive studies of the role of women in Nazi Germany, see J. Stephenson, *Women in Nazi Society* (London, 1975) and *The Nazi Organisation of Women* (London, 1980).

[65] *Film-Kurier*, 3 June 1938, quoted in Phillips, M.S., 'The German Film Industry', p. 246.

[66] IfZ, *Goebbels Tagebuch*, entry for 13 December 1942.

[67] Figures taken from *Das Statische Jahrbuch für das Deutsche Reich, 1937–42* (Berlin, 1942).

year.[68] A survey among fourteen- to eighteen-year-olds conducted by Alois Funk in 1933 revealed that 16.6 per cent
visited the cinema on a weekly basis (fifty times or more),
48.9 per cent on a monthly basis (at least twelve times), and
34.5 per cent seldom went at all (nine times or less).[69]
Funk's research was based on a questionnaire circulated to
the parents of this age-group. However, in 1943 another questionnaire was circulated by the *Führerdienst der Reichsjugend-
führung* to 686 boys and 1,260 girls aged between ten and
seventeen. It discovered that 22.05 per cent visited the cinema
at least once a week; 71.73 per cent went on a monthly basis,
and only 6.22 per cent saw less than nine films a year.[70] It also
revealed the surprising statistics that 26.82 per cent of the boys
and 11.91 per cent of the girls visited the cinema on average
once a week.[71]

It must also be remembered that this wartime increase in the
average cinema visits by the young was further supplemented
by the compulsory weekly visits to the Youth Film Hours
(*Jugendfilmstunden*), where even less choice was exercised on
the part of the young generation. Goebbels knew full well the
importance of this age-group, for it was these boys who were
encouraged to fight and die for their Führer. The all-embracing
and masterly arrangement of the military educational films
(*Wehrerziehungsfilme*), ensured that their appeal to the younger
generation aroused a passionate commitment and taught
them to believe in National Socialism, obey Hitler's orders,
and die gloriously for the Fatherland. Goebbels's consum-
mate skill as a propagandist rested on his ability to tap German
youth's idealism by stressing the importance of the collective
body taking precedence over the individual. From the early
'Party films', comradeship and self-sacrifice (which were interchangeable) represented the very essence of German masculinity. Paradoxically this same masculinity, or comradeship,
can be seen as a pervasive though unacknowledged form of
homosexuality. The antecedents of such homosexuality are
found in the concept of the *Bund*, the tightly knit all-male
community that corresponds to the notion of the heroic

[68] See Table 4.
[69] A. Funk, *Film und Jugend* (Munich, 1934), vol. II, pp. 47–9.
[70] Sander, p. 54.   [71] Ibid., p. 116.

leader.[72] Thus, by extolling the Spartan virtues of worldly abstinence, the *Zeitfilme* series formed an integral part of the ideological chauvinism that pervaded all aspects of National Socialist thought. In the cinema, as in most spheres of Nazi society, women were required to accommodate the all-male ethos. The neglect of women patrons to the cinema runs parallel with the chauvinism found in the content of Nazi films. The armed forces themselves were extremely conscious of the manner in which film-makers depicted fighting men to the young audience. There is a celebrated entry in Goebbels's diary which illustrates this sensitivity. It concerned the popular German film of 1942, *Die grosse Liebe* (*Great Love*), in which a Luftwaffe lieutenant spends the night with a famous singer while on leave.[73] Even though the aviator returns to duty and the singer entertains the troops in occupied France, the OKW failed to recognize the propaganda qualities of the film and complained bitterly to Goebbels about the way in which soldiers on leave were portrayed on the cinema screen.[74] Goebbels, however, discovered some unlikely support from Hermann Göring:

I had a telephone conversation with the Reich Marshal. He complained about the OKW's protest against the new Leander film;[75] this shows an aviator spending the night with a famous singer. The OKW consider itself insulted morally and insists that a Luftwaffe lieutenant wouldn't act in that way. Göring, on the other hand, correctly considers that if a Luftwaffe lieutenant didn't make use of such an opportunity, he simply wouldn't be a Luftwaffe lieutenant. Göring pokes great fun at the sensitivity of the OKW. That's fine grist for my mill, since the OKW creates many difficulties for me anyway in my film work.[76]

Although the film industry and the RMVP welcomed the increase in the number of times that the younger generation were visiting the cinemas this was not without its problems. Certain official channels, for example, associated this predilection for

[72] For a discussion of the *Bund* concept, see Mosse, *The Crisis*, pp. 204-9.

[73] *Die grosse Liebe* can be compared in terms of style and content with *Wunschkonzert* and was even more popular.

[74] The moral tone for such films was set by Ritter's 1937 film, *Urlaub auf Ehrenwort* (*Leave on Word of Honour*) about a group of soldiers on their way from the Eastern to the Western Front in August 1918.

[75] Zarah Leander was a Swedish actress who starred in the film. Together with the two other Swedish actresses to emerge after 1933 (Söderbaum and Kirsten Heiberg) she was extremely popular with German film audiences.

[76] Lochner, p. 173.

the cinema with the growing rate of juvenile delinquency, or claimed that children were taking cinema seats at the expense of munition workers and soldiers on leave. In March 1940 police in some parts of the Reich banned children from the cinemas after 9 o'clock unless they were accompanied by adults.[77] This practice was finally taken up in the rest of the country in July 1944, although it would prove impossible to implement.[78] German youth, on the other hand, complained of the lack of suitable films and the archaic censorship laws which disqualified them from seeing 'adult' films until they were eighteen. In a speech to a Hitler Youth audience in 1941, Goebbels did even condemn censorship which restricted certain films to 'adults only' and went on to state that such a classification had been responsible for the disreputable nature of the film industry before 1933.[79] However, the practice was continued until the end of the war despite vociferous criticism from *Gauleiter* all over the Reich. They claimed that prohibited films inevitably attracted German youth, resulting in a conflict with the law, 'especially as they know that in Czechoslovakia the age limit is 16 not 18.'[80] As far as the *Gauleiter* were concerned, the only answers were either to increase the number of films aimed specifically at children, and abolish films 'for adults only', or reduce the age limit as 'young men undertake military service at 17 and girls are allowed to marry at the same age'.[81] The so-called 'Law for the Protection of Youth', which was introduced in 1940 and banned unaccompanied young people under the age of eighteen from all public places, highlighted the contradictions and double standards of the Third Reich. The frustration it subsequently fostered in the younger generation was registered in a complaint by Hitler Youths that was frequently heard in 1944 and must cast serious doubts on Goebbels's whole policy of film censorship: 'We are good enough to become soldiers at fifteen or sixteen and get ourselves killed, but we're not allowed into cinemas to see "adult" films until we are eighteen.'[82]

However, despite censorship and classification difficulties

[77] BA, *R55/343*, file on 'Übermässiger Kinobesuch von Kindern, 1940'.
[78] *VB*, 22 June 1944.
[79] Speech reproduced in Goebbels, *Das Eherne Herz*, pp. 37–46.
[80] BA, *NS18/343*, 9 June 1943 ('Suitable films for the young').
[81] Loc. cit.   [82] Quoted in Grunberger, p. 348.

and complaints from all sections of the community, who by 1942 had their own ideas about the sort of films that should be exhibited, audiences continued to increase during the war as they also did during the First World War. The reasons for this are numerous and complicated but are intrinsically linked to the changing military situation. Until the first setback in Stalingrad, there can be little doubt that Germans visited the cinema in order to have their own National Socialist ideas reinforced, and in this respect Goebbels was able to give them what they wanted to see and hear. Later, with military defeats and a deteriorating domestic situation, entertainment was in short supply and the cinema offered one of the few safe and relatively inexpensive forms of escaping from reality and economizing on fuel.[83] Commenting in 1943 on the length of the queues forming outside cinemas immediately after a series of particularly severe air raids, Goebbels wrote in his diary: 'People crave recreation after the gruelling days and nights of the past week. They want solace for their souls.'[84] Whatever the reasons, the continuing increase in cinema attendances and the receipts that resulted allowed the Propaganda Ministry to maintain production of extremely expensive but prestigious propaganda films despite rising production costs.

KOLBERG (1945)

By 1942 Goebbels had become the principal spokesman for the regime. It is interesting to note that in his speeches he adopted a posture similar to Winston Churchill; he made no secret of the difficulties ahead, admitted that a German defeat was possible, and called for total involvement in the war effort. However, this apparently realistic approach did not extend to films—in fact, he demanded more purely escapist entertainment films supplemented by a number of extremely expensive historical epics which became increasingly mythical as the end of the war drew near. His one concession, partly a response to pressure from angry *Gauberichten*, was to ban advertisements

---

[83] Although in the last year of the war cinemas were badly destroyed by allied bombing, Goebbels had successfully established up until that time a system of air raid shelters in the cinemas themselves. BA, *R1091/1034a*, 1414, 29 May 1940.
[84] Lochner, p. 440.

in the cinemas for all luxury products and for products in short supply.[85]

The final period of National Socialist propaganda is characterized by the attempted indoctrination of fear. Compare this extract from Goebbels's 'Total War' speech in the Berlin Sportspalast, 18 February 1943, as it was presented to German cinema audiences in the *Deutsche Wochenschau*:

COMMENTATOR. The mighty demonstration in the Berlin Sportspalace. Reichsminister Goebbels speaks. He declares: 'In this winter, the storm over our ancient continent has broken out with the full force which surpasses all human and historical imagination. The Wehrmacht with its allies forms the only possible protective wall. [*Applause.*] Not a single person in Germany today thinks of hollow compromise. The whole nation thinks only of a hard war. The danger before which we stand is gigantic. Gigantic, therefore, must be the efforts with which we meet it. [*Shouts of Sieg Heil.*] When my audience spontaneously declared its support for the demands I made on 30 January, the English press claimed that this was a piece of theatrical propaganda. I have therefore invited to this meeting a cross-section of the German people . . .'

The Minister then put ten questions to this representative gathering . . .

GOEBBELS. The English claim that the German people are resisting Government measures for total war.

CROWD. Lies! Lies!

GOEBBELS. It doesn't want total war, say the English, but capitulation.

CROWD. Sieg Heil! Sieg Heil!

GOEBBELS. Do you want total war?

CROWD. Yes! [*Enthusiastic applause.*]

GOEBBELS. Do you want it more total, more radical, than we could ever have imagined?

CROWD. Yes! Yes! [*Loud applause.*]

GOEBBELS. Are you ready to stand with the Führer as the phalanx of the homeland behind the fighting Wehrmacht? Are you ready to continue the struggle unshaken and with savage determination, through all the vicissitudes of fate until victory is in our hands?

CROWD. Yes!

GOEBBELS. I ask you: Are you determined to follow the Führer through thick and thin in the struggle for victory and to accept even the harshest personal sacrifices?

CROWD. Yes! Sieg Heil! [*A chant of 'The Führer commands, we follow'.*]

GOEBBELS. You have shown our enemies what they need to know, so

---

[85] BA, *NS 18/346*, 17 March 1942. This file lists all items that were to be banned in the future; they include leather shoes, handbags, toothpaste, chloroform for false teeth!, cosmetics, etc.

that they will no longer indulge in illusions. The mightiest ally in the world — the people themselves — have shown that they stand behind us in our determined fight for victory, regardless of the costs.
CROWD. Yes! Yes! [*Loud applause.*]
GOEBBELS. Therefore let the slogan be from now on: 'People arise, and storm, break loose!' [*Extended applause.*]
CROWD. Deutschland, Deutschland über alles, über alles in der Welt....[86]

Goebbels was one of the few Nazi leaders to realize that by 1942 final victory could only be achieved by a full mobilization of German resources which would incorporate every citizen. The Propaganda Minister envisaged a radical departure from the measures that other leaders like Bormann had established for civilian defence. For Goebbels, success could only be achieved by the complete mobilization of the home front in order that Germany should become one fighting body, united under a powerful leader.[87] He informed a group of German journalists in April 1943 that 'To applaud a blitz campaign needs no toughness. But I have the feeling that this war will not come to an end quickly. So we must prepare our minds and hearts for bitter experiences.'[88] This meant a change of propaganda policy from the buoyant, almost arrogant claims of the previous three years. In particular, Goebbels attempted to create toughness in the civilian population by resorting to one of the oldest techniques of persuasion—the indoctrination of fear. Fear of the subhuman Bolshevik 'beast–man' endangering Western civilization became the leitmotiv of his propaganda in the winter of 1943. In his 'Total War' speech outlined above, total sacrifices and participation are put forward by Goebbels as the only alternatives to the type of total destruction that only the Wehrmacht were preventing.

Goebbels appreciated that total war meant increasing hardships on the part of the civilian population and he adjusted film propaganda accordingly. He rationalized (given his express desire to 'revolutionize' the cinema) this switch by arguing that as both front-line soldiers and home-front civilians would be 'living' National Socialism then there would be less need to

---

[86] For an excellent analysis of this newsreel see K. W. Wippermann, *Die Entwicklung der Wochenschau in Deutschland: Die Deutsche Wochenschau No. 10/651, February 1943* (Göttingen, 1970), pp. 36–41. See also Bramsted, p. 266.
[87] Hitler, however, would never completely mobilize the homefront, despite repeated requests by Goebbels.
[88] Semmler, p. 73.

express the ideology in films. Entertainment films, well made, would enhance the regime's cause by providing relaxation and escapism.[89]

As the war dragged on it became necessary to provide the domestic cinema audience with more than just good entertainment films. With the military situation becoming increasingly desperate, Goebbels somehow had to link his fear campaign with the need for endurance in the face of overwhelming odds. Since the future was uncertain and the present unbearable, Goebbels turned to history for the reassurance he needed to offer, particularly the hagiography of Frederick the Great. As I pointed out in the last chapter, the Prussian King had always been a significant symbol in German history, but it was only towards the second half of the war that this figure came to represent the apotheosis of the indomitable spirit who refused to accept defeat. In fact, Wilfred von Oven, observing the exceedingly large number of portraits of Frederick the Great scattered throughout Goebbels's Ministry remarked sardonically: 'It would appear that old Fritz is the protector of Goebbels's intellectual world altogether.'[90]

From 1943 onwards, Nazi propaganda continued to insist that final victory was assured however great the difficulties. The response of the film industry to military setbacks which threatened the fighting morale of the people is of particular interest. Certainly the agitational kind of propaganda that characterized the early 'Party films' had by now disappeared; there were a few political works that portrayed various themes that had been important in previous years. *Germanin* (1943) attacked British colonialism; *Paracelsus* (1943) was a thinly disguised exposition of the *Führerprinzip*; *Junge Adler* (*Young Eagles*, 1944) addressed itself to the German army of the future and stressed the need for obedience and discipline. But on the whole, the film industry abandoned political and military subjects in favour of love stories and operettas—a combination which may well have had an important propaganda function in that it gave the people what they wanted, but one that failed to capture the contemporary experiences of the masses undergoing total war.

[89] Lochner, p. 64.
[90] Von Oven, p. 27.

At this stage Goebbels was continually looking for a sign that would persuade the people to believe in final victory. The thrust of his message was that if only the German people stood firm, a miracle might yet save them, like 'the miracle of the House of Brandenburg' in 1759. In January 1943 he informed his staff:

It ought to be the mission of all German propaganda to create a myth from the heroism of Stalingrad, a myth which can become a precious ornament in German history.[91]

He must have decided that the cinema was the most effective medium for such an important and emotional task, for five months later he commissioned Veit Harlan to direct what was to be the last Agfacolor film, *Kolberg*, loosely based on the events that occurred in the town of Kolberg in the Franco-Prussian War of 1806/7:

I hereby commission you to produce the epic film Kolberg. The film is to demonstrate, through the example of the town that gives it its title, that a people united at home and at the front will overcome any foe. I authorize you to request whatever assistance you feel necessary from all Government, Party, and military agencies.[92]

The story concerns a rather obscure historical incident that took place in the city and fort of Kolberg on the Baltic coast during the Napoleonic war of 1806/7. In 1806, after the battles of Jena and Austerlitz, Napoleon attempted to obliterate Prussia. Only the fortress town of Kolberg prevented a complete victory for the French. The local government and army are represented as defeatist and corrupt because, realizing the inevitability of the French advance, they decide to surrender the town. But under the inspired leadership of the Mayor, the citizens decide to defend their territory by resisting, to the end if need be, the invading French forces.

Goebbels's overriding problem in producing *Kolberg* was that despite the Kolbergers' courageous resistance they were eventually overwhelmed by the French. It is a measure of how far Nazi propaganda had become entrenched in a mythical

---

[91] Boelcke, '*Wollt Ihr den Totalen Krieg?*': *die Geheimen Goebbels-Konferenzen 1939–43* (Stuttgart, 1967), p. 333.

[92] In his autobiography, Harlan quotes the following entry from his wife, the actress Kristina Söderbaum's diary on 5 October 1943: 'How horrible, we've been informed that Veit has to make *Kolberg*, "*Hic incipit tragoedia. Que faire!*" Harlan, pp. 257–8.

world that the Propaganda Minister ordered Harlan to disregard historical fact, even when it revealed such heroism, and to invent a love story in order to give the scenario a human dimension![93] However, the importance of *Kolberg* is that it brings together archetypal themes that pervaded the Nazi cinema: the *Führerprinzip*, national idealism, obedience, and sacrifice, and the indomitable spirit of the 'real Germans' (*Echtdeutsche*). It also offers a unique insight into the behaviour of a totalitarian police state and its response to imminent collapse.

Goebbels wanted to show that resistance to Napoleon came from the people and not from the military. He saw the civilian militia as the prefiguration of the *Volkssturm* and told the director that he wanted him to symbolize the continual conflict between the SA and the Waffen SS, with the former depicted as the true heroes.[94] In the film, this conflict is presented in terms of the Kolbergers under the leadership of Nettelbeck (played by Heinrich George), and the ageing Colonel Lucadou, the commandant of the fortress, who is determined to surrender without resistance. In this sense one can draw an analogy between Lucadou and the Wehrmacht officers who Goebbels believed as early as 1943 were unwilling to fight and were burdening Hitler with talk of surrender.[95]

The corruption and inability of the military to understand the patriotic feelings of the ordinary people is established early in the film. As the prologue informs us that the story is based on historical fact, a heavenly choir is singing:

CHORUS. With a death-like mood the great morning breaks. And the sun, cold and bloody, lights our bloody way. Within the next few hours the fate of the world lies, and the weak are already trembling and the dice are cast. Who is cowardly, remaining idle? People rise up! People rise up! The storm is breaking!

It is 1813, and in the royal palace at Breslau Wilhelm von Gneisenau is attempting to persuade the Prussian King, Friedrich Wilhelm III, to enlist the aid of the people in the cause of war. The King is depicted as a timid reactionary afraid of the masses. He refers to Gneisenau as 'a fantasizer, a German

[93] Ibid., pp. 257-8.
[94] Ibid., pp. 258-9.
[95] Cf. Lochner, p. 220.

dreamer'. Unperturbed, Gneisenau relates the story of Kolberg to substantiate his point:

GNEISENAU. I know reality, your Majesty. I looked it in the face that time in Kolberg, when our armies were falling and Napoleon was driving through all Germany, when one fortification after another was crumbling — then it was the citizens who saved the Prussians. Your Majesty, speak to the people. That time in Kolberg the idea of a people's army came to me. In Kolberg I experienced the dawn of German freedom, when Princes and Kings had deserted their people.

By means of flashback, the story proper begins with Nettelbeck discussing the threat of Napoleon and the need to stand up and fight. In an attempt to emphasize Goebbels's call for a last-ditch resistance, a parallel conflict is constructed between Colonel Lucadou (Paul Wegener) and Nettelbeck over the preparations for the defence of Kolberg and between Lucadou (Horst Caspar) and Major von Schill (Gustav Diessl) regarding the training of a civilian militia. In both scenes Lucadou and his subordinates are represented as distrustful of the people and apprehensive about the war. They embody the mythical world of Goebbels's propaganda, the reactionaries of 1806 and the defeatists of 1944.[96] Witness the latter scene, where von Schill is drilling the citizens of Kolberg into a credible fighting force. It is Lucadou who voices the criticisms of Goebbels's opponents who argued against a civilian militia and it is left to Major Schill to give a passionate retort that could have come straight from one of Goebbels's speeches:

LUCADOU. People, go home, leave this foolish playing at war—what will you gain by it? And as Officers do you support it? These good people perhaps meant well by this gesture but do you expect it to be of any military significance? On the contrary, as soon as things 'hot up' this civilian guard will only add to the confusion. Or do you disagree Major?
SCHILL. If I may say so, yes I do. These people want what is right.
LUCADOU. But just look at them! What do they want?
SCHILL. That everybody should be capable of fighting. They want to become a people of soldiers; we can use that Colonel. The salvation

[96] In March 1945 the commandant of Kolberg had wanted to surrender the city to the Russians without a fight. Hitler immediately replaced him with a younger officer. On 5 March 1945 Goebbels wrote in his diary: 'Have these degenerate generals no sense of history or responsibility? Does a present-day Military Commandant of Kolberg nurture the ambition to emulate a Lucadou rather then a Gneisenau?' Trevor-Roper (ed.), *Goebbels Diaries. The Last Days*, p. 52.

of the Fatherland lies with the people. It all depends on their mood and attitude. If a fortification is besieged, then there can be no difference any more between civilians and soldiers.

LUCADOU. Ah, but waging war is a craft that has to be learnt.

SCHILL. Learnt, yes, but a craft Colonel, it's not that. It's something that comes from the heart and the citizens of Kolberg have got that. They love their corner of the earth, and for this reason they'll be even better defenders than the soldiers . . .

Kolberg is full of involuntary ironies that demonstrate the schizophrenic nature of Nazi propaganda. For example, Napoleon's reactions to the news of Kolberg's defiance is supposed to represent Churchill's policy of saturation bombing, but it also evokes Hitler's wish that Russian cities should be destroyed for their obstinacy:

NAPOLEON [*in French*]. Kolberg — Graudenz — nests of mud that one could crush under one's foot. Who dares to stand up to my Governors and who dares to refuse to swear the oath of allegiance? They'll submit to my will eventually!

LOISON. Sire, allow me!

NAPOLEON. Speak, Loison!

LOISON. It is foolish, but such patriotism dies hard with these people. [*In German*] . . . The ghost of their great king has not died yet.

NAPOLEON. The spirit of Frederick the Great? This is ridiculous! . . . Kolberg! . . . What is this place Kolberg, anyway? [*In German.*] The ghost of Frederick the Great? Small-minded people! They want to turn their back on history — a cavalry squadron will bring them to their senses.

TEULIE. Sire!

NAPOLEON. Move the army to Kolberg and raze it to the ground! Weaken the morale of the people with your cannons. I'll name you Duke of Kolberg on the day you report to me the fall of Kolberg.

Although Harlan is credited with writing the script in conjunction with Alfred Braun, he admitted in his autobiography that Goebbels did in fact write many of the speeches himself.[97] Kolberg's simple response to Napoleon's attack was to reply with its own cannons. Nettelbeck's speech, in which he encourages the people to take action, is a classic propaganda device often employed by Goebbels. The call is for some great sacrifice or suicidal action; it is presented in terms of apparent honesty in that the magnitude and even the irrationality of the act is clearly stated. But the challenge is softened by a reference

[97] Harlan, p. 260. The complete screenplay of the film *Kolberg* has been translated by the author and can be found at the British Film Institute, London.

to some mystical (or mythical) 'high goal' that only Germans are capable of aspiring to:

NETTELBECK. Ah, you need reasons to remain an upstanding fellow — yes, there are reasons why a fortification shouldn't be given up. For example, the best French cannons, of which you were speaking of earlier — we could hold on to them here in Kolberg so that they can't be used against our troops in Danzig, Tilsit, or anywhere else. That's one reason to start with. Yes, there are many pertinent reasons, but also what you might call irrational ones as well. For example, what might become of a Prussian who said, 'You, Napoleon, are so much stronger and mightier — come and devour us, we can't stop you.' What would become of these people who could think and speak like this? They'd soon exterminate themselves and wouldn't deserve a better fate.

For the counter-offensive to have any chance of success, one farm has to be burnt to the ground because it is in the line of the Kolbergers' fire and part of the town has to be flooded to deny the French easy access. The stoicism that these people show in the face of such hardship is clearly meant as an example for contemporary Germany. But just how intentional was the parallel with the Nazis' policy of 'scorched earth' in this scene is less easy to say.

One of the highlights of the film is the scene where Nettelbeck sends his niece (Kristina Söderbaum) to the King of Prussia with a message requesting a replacement for Lucadou. Maria is received by Queen Luise of Prussia who is deputizing for the absent King. The exchange between the two women gives ultimate cinematic expression both in terms of style and symbolism to a number of key themes that recur in Nazi propaganda. Maria is portrayed as the archetypal Aryan woman; blond, big-boned, stoical, and dressed in peasant costume, she is seen throughout the film as the upholder of traditional peasant values associated with the doctrine of *Blut und Boden*. For example, at the beginning of the film she is seen sitting at her loom singing:

> The year is half over
> The farmer is cutting the corn
> Many have lost their hearts in summer-time
> The sea bears many ships. They come from far away
> For someone who may come — someone who may come
> I'll keep my heart free.[98]

[98] This, and other songs in the film, were composed by Norbert Schultze who was best known for Lili Marlene.

But Maria also embodies virtues of strength and courage. By the end of the film she has lost her father, two brothers, and her beloved, Major von Schill. Yet her spirit is undaunted for she believes completely in the rightness of Kolberg's fight. After their triumph she is comforted by Nettelbeck who salutes her sacrifice:

NETTELBECK. Yes, you have sacrificed everything you had, Maria — but not in vain. Death is entwined with victory. The greatest achievements are always borne in pain, and when a person takes all the pain on herself then that person is indeed a great person. You helped us to win, Maria, you are great too!

Such an uncompromising attitude was essential to the success of Goebbels's total war strategy, and as this entry in his diary illustrates, Maria could well have been modelled on his wife, Magda:

She is in pretty good shape again and takes an interest in everything that is happening in the outside world. I am very happy that she is absolutely uncompromising and radical on the question of total war. If all Nazi women thought as she does, total war would be much more of a reality.[99]

Queen Luise (Irene von Mayendorff), on the other hand, incarnates the *Landesmutter* of Prussian tradition. She is portrayed as the mother of the Fatherland, its protector under the weak Frederick William III. The scene between the two women is one of the most sentimental episodes in the cinema of the Third Reich: a simple farmer's daughter is granted an audience by the Queen:

MARIA. I come from Kolberg.
FRAU VON VOSS [*Queen's servant*]. From Kolberg. You have come from Kolberg?
MARIA. Yes, I've brought a letter from the citizens' representative from Kolberg.
FRAU VON VOSS. The Queen is expecting his Majesty the Tsar Alexander of Russia, but perhaps she still has time to hear news from Kolberg. I'll try.
    [*She is granted an audience.*]
MARIA [*to herself*]. Your Majesty, your Majesty, graciously receive this letter. The citizens of Kolberg want to be a shining example for all the citizens of Prussia. How did Nettelbeck put it? — The citizens of

[99] Lochner, p. 195.

Kolberg would rather let themselves be buried under the rubble than be untrue to the King and the country. . . .
[*She is ushered into the Queen's chamber. Celestial music. Scene filmed through filter achieving 'hazy' effect.*]
QUEEN. Good day, my child — what brings you to us from Kolberg?
MARIA. Your majesty . . .
QUEEN. Come here — now tell me, what's in your heart? [*Embraces her.*]
MARIA. I can't . . . [*Overwhelmed.*]
QUEEN. I have reports daily from Kolberg. You can be very proud of your home town. You wish to give me something for the King, don't you? Give it here, I'll give this letter to the King — today — I promise you.
SERVANT. His Majesty the Tsar has arrived. . . .
QUEEN [*to Maria*]. Thank you. I'll press Prussia and Kolberg to my heart. There are but two precious jewels left in our crown. Kolberg is one of them.

Maria's hero-worship and absolute faith in her Queen (an encouragement to adopt a similar attitude to Hitler) are rewarded when Gneisenau is sent to the beleaguered town. Gneisenau will go right to hell 'with a man who loves his town and his land of birth more than his own life'. On his arrival in Kolberg there is an exchange of dialogue that is reminiscent of Goebbels's speeches at *Volkssturm* rallies. The sentiments expressed in this scene are crucial to an understanding of the central message of the film, and indeed offer an insight into the state of Goebbels's mind at this point and the propaganda motif of 'holding-out' (*Durchhalten*):

GNEISENAU. 35,000 men, Nettelbeck, and 500 cannons, all aimed at this town. There's no point any more, we can't hold the town. Do you understand what that means? Everything we've experienced so far will be child's play in comparison!
NETTELBECK. Commander!
GNEISENAU. It's all over, Nettelbeck, there's no point any more.
NETTELBECK. And what is to happen?
GNEISENAU. We'll have to surrender.
NETTELBECK. Ah, like Magdeburg, Erfurt, Stettin, and Spandau. All has been in vain . . . a disgrace.
GNEISENAU. It's no disgrace, if the soldiers have shot their last bullets. Even Blücher had to capitulate.
NETTELBECK. But we haven't fired our last bullet yet! and Blücher didn't have to forfeit his birthplace, and you weren't born in Kolberg. You were ordered to Kolberg, but we grew up here. We know every stone, every corner, every house. We're not letting it go even if we have to claw into the ground with our bare hands. In our town we don't

give up. No, they'll have to cut off our hands to slay us one by one. You can't disgrace me by surrendering our town to Napoleon. I even promised our King that we would rather be buried under the rubble than capitulate. I've never pleaded to anyone, but I get down on my knees, Gneisenau. Kolberg must not be surrendered!
GNEISENAU. That's what I wanted to hear from you, Nettelbeck. Now we can die together.

The importance of *Kolberg* as an historical document is that it reflects the National Socialist logic of collective suicide and destruction that found expression in a perverse idealism. The theme is of death in combat, the pre-eminence of obeying orders until the last instance, a nihilistic affirmation of the national ideal.[100] The most evocative scenes are those where despair and bravado are dominant. The moral tone of *Kolberg* is the German cult of death in preference to surrender and the *Nibelungentreue*, the Germanic faithfulness of the followers. In reality, Kolberg fell to Napoleon, but in the film Napoleon, alarmed at the losses he has sustained, orders his cavalry to pull back. The flashback ends and we return to the royal palace at Breslau in 1813. By invoking the courageous stand of the Kolbergers in 1807, Gneisenau persuades the King to sign his famous proclamation 'To my people':

GNEISENAU. That is the page of glory in the history of the Prussian people. You knew then that where there was danger there was also a way to victory. And if today in 1813, the citizens should rise up again, then it is because they are inspired by that secret strength and the example of the people of Kolberg. . . . The people are rising up for the coming battle of nations, your Majesty, the storm is breaking![101]
THE PEOPLE'S SONG. Horrifying, death-like, the great morning breaks, and the cold and bloody sun lights our bloody way. Within the next few hours the fate of the world lies. The weak are trembling and the die is cast.
Behind us in the grey of the night lies disgrace and shame — the outrage of foreign domination.
And the German oak broke.
Our language was disgraced, our temple collapsed. Our honour is in need of redemption.
Brothers, redeem yourselves!
In our town there is hope and a golden future. The whole sky is open,

---

[100] Cf. entry from Goebbels's diary of 31 March 1945. Trevor-Roper, p. 289.
[101] Goebbels liked to identify himself with Gneisenau. Compare this speech by Gneisenau with Goebbels's 'total war' speech of 18 February 1943. The Minister ends with 'People arise, and storm, break loose.' See above, note 86.

The holiness of freedom blossoms.
German art, and German songs, women's favours and happiness in
love,
May all the great things return as beauty itself returns.
Who like a coward is holding his hands in his lap [repeat]
The people are rising. The storm is breaking! [repeat]
WILHELM III. You are right Gneisenau. To my people!
GNEISENAU. 1813. In the year of freedom — from the ashes and rubble
a new people will rise like a Phoenix, a new Reich.

The message that Goebbels is disseminating is quite clear;
by the falsification of historical parallels he is saying 'be firm
now, hold out—you may die in the process—but you will enter
into the realms of national immortality'.[102] The example of
1807 inspired a resurgence of strength in 1813; similarly, an
heroic struggle in 1944 will inspire future generations. It was
with these hopes that on 30 January 1945, the day of the
film's première in Berlin and the twelfth anniversary of the Nazi
seizure of power, a print of the film was flown into the beleaguered fortress of La Rochelle. Goebbels obviously thought
that it would lift morale for he also sent the commandant,
Vize Admiral Schirlitz, the following telegram:

The film is an artistic hymn of praise to courage and ensure in the defence
of a people and homeland. It will therefore have a worthy première to
mark the close relationship between those fighting at the front and at
home who are revealing to the whole nation the virtues embodied in
this film. My hope is that the film will be accepted by you and your
courageous soldiers as a document of the unwavering will of a people,
united in this world struggle, prepared to emulate the great feats of its
glorious history. Long live our Führer![103]

Schirlitz's reply was broadcast on German radio the same day:

The première of the colour film 'Kolberg' took place in La Rochelle be-
fore soldiers of all units in our defence corps.
Deeply moved by the artistic presentation of the heroic action of the
Kolberg fortress, we add our gratitude for the despatch of the film on
30 January and our pledge to emulate the courageous struggle at home
. . . Long live Germany, Long live our Führer![104]

The expense lavished on *Kolberg* testifies to the importance
of the project and the extent to which Goebbels's propaganda

---

[102] R. E. Herzstein, 'Goebbels et le Mythe Historique par le Film', in *Revue
d'Histoire de la Deuxième Guerre* (Paris, January 1976), no. 101, p. 59. This is an
extremely interesting and perceptive analysis.
[103] *VB*, 31 January 1945.
[104] loc. cit.

had lost touch with the military situation. A budget of RM 8½ million was allocated (twice the normal budget for a film of this importance). And at a time when Soviet forces were crossing the East Prussian border, Goebbels withdrew 187,000 soldiers and 4,000 sailors from active duty in order that the film could be completed on time.[105] The director, Veit Harlan, has stated that both Hitler and Goebbels were 'convinced that such a film was more useful than a military victory'.[106] Although *Kolberg* ran for only a few days in Berlin and appears to have been shown mainly in Party circles, it was awarded the important prize of 'Film of the Nation' together with six *Prädikate*. However, on 19 March 1945 Goebbels recorded in his diary:

We have now had to evacuate Kolberg. The town, which had been defended with such extraordinary heroism, could no longer be held. I will ensure that the evacuation of Kolberg is not mentioned in the OKW report. In view of the severe psychological repercussions on the Kolberg film we could do without this for the moment.[107]

The explanation for this extraordinary behaviour lies in Goebbels's continual obsession with dramatic effects. As Joachim Fest observed, 'to the end, he was what he always had been: the propagandist for himself.'[108] On 17 April Goebbels summoned his staff in the RMVP together. Some fifty of them were there, many demanding to be released in order to escape from the encircled Berlin. Goebbels spoke to them about *Kolberg* and its message of heroic resistance. Then he mentioned another even more splendid film which would be shown a hundred years hence. It would be a film of the Twilight of the Gods in Berlin in 1945:

Gentlemen, in a hundred years' time they will be showing another fine colour film describing the terrible days we are living through. Don't you want to play a part in this film, to be brought back to life in a hundred years' time? Everybody now has a chance to choose the part which he will play in the film a hundred years hence. I can assure you that it will be a fine and elevating picture. And for the sake of this prospect it is worth standing fast. Hold out now, so that a hundred years hence the audience does not hoot and whistle when you appear on the screen.[109]

---

[105] These figures are taken from Harlan, pp. 262–3.
[106] Ibid., p. 263.   [107] Trevor-Roper, p. 167.
[108] Fest, p. 151.
[109] Semmler, p. 194 (entry of 17 April 1945).

Clearly, Goebbels was happy to accept *Kolberg* as his testament to future generations and to preserve a niche for himself in history by his Führer's side. His staff, however, were not so impressed by these heroic gestures. They looked at him incredulously and concluded that he had gone mad! Kolberg itself is now Kolobrzeg, on the Baltic coast of Poland.

It is perhaps ironic that a society which placed so much emphasis on the cult of the young, highly-trained warrior, should leave as its testament a film glorifying the heroic resistance of an ageing civilian militia. It would be too simplistic to suggest that such a parallel could be extended to the history of the Third Reich.

I have attempted in this chapter to outline the broad development of film propaganda with military themes during the war years. It can be seen that although the trend was towards mythology, the central message of self-sacrifice, comradeship, and heroic death in battle remained the same. 'War', wrote J. P. Stern, 'in the mythology of National Socialism, represents the consummation of all manly virtues, it is the area of "authentic experience" . . . the true proving ground of men and nations.'[110]

The films discussed in this section, together with the newsreels, illustrate different aspects of this mentality, or war ethos. But again they all share a typically Nazi outlook—their romanticization of modern warfare with its approbation of killing and force, coupled with callousness. At the same time as *Pour le Mérite* was being made, Baldur von Schirach wrote in the *Völkischer Beobachter*: 'We wish to give meaning to our lives: the war spared us for war!'[111] Such sentiments were being reinforced by the aggressively militaristic films that German youth in particular were forced to see in the *Jugendfilmstunde*. Films like *Pour le Mérite* helped prepared the nation psychologically for war by endorsing illegal German rearmament, glorifying past military heroes, and perpetuating old myths and German nationalism. The newsreels served to whip up enthusiasm for the war as well as providing an important information service. During the two years of the Blitzkrieg,

110 Stern, p. 177.
111 *VB*, 7 February 1937.

Feuertaufe and the other 'campaign' films increased the belief in Germany of an early end to the war and the futility of resistance in the face of Germany's military superiority. The propaganda films made during this period of Nazi ascendancy in Europe reflected the mood of elation and triumph. Such films went hand in hand with an educational curriculum that prescribed as follows:

> From an early age youth must be able to face a time when it may be ordered not merely to act, but to die; it must simply learn to think like our ancestors again. A man's greatest honour lies in death before the enemy of his country.[112]

Behind such embattled clichés lay a romantic attitude that was construed as heroic, when in truth it was little more than a nihilistic affirmation of what it was to be German. In *Kolberg* a member of the citizens' council asks Nettelbeck: 'why do we have to sacrifice ourselves, for what purpose and to what end?' Nettelbeck retorts: 'Ah, you need reasons to stay a decent fellow!'

Goebbels once remarked that, 'the essence of propaganda consists in winning people over to an idea so sincerely, so vitally, that in the end they succumb to it utterly and can never again escape from it.' By this criterion, films with a military theme undoubtedly failed, for in the final analysis they were unable to instil in the German population what Coleridge termed a 'willing suspension of disbelief'.

However, in the last year of the war Goebbels made one last desperate attempt to radicalize the German cinema. In June 1944, he appointed Hans Hinkel as *Reichsfilmintendant*. Hinkel was a fanatical member of the SS and former head of the *Berlin Kampfbund für Deutsche Kultur*. Almost immediately he attempted to change film policy within the RMVP by encouraging the active participation of the SS in film matters and ordering script-writers that in future they should concentrate on producing 'politically and nationally worthy themes'.[113] Shortly afterwards, he compelled cinemas to show repeats of films dealing with military and nationalistic subjects.

---

[112] Cf. also this speech by *Obergebietsführer* Stellrecht: 'We wish in the course of the year (1937) to reach a point where the gun rests as securely in the hand of German boys as the pen.' Both speeches quoted in Fest, pp. 350–1.

[113] Hinkel was particularly concerned that the SS become involved in youth film propaganda. BA, *R58/1248*, 5 December 1944.

These films were mostly made in the period 1940-1 which marked the highest concentration of political film propaganda in the Third Reich. This was a complete reversal of the previous policy of the RMVP whereby the need to boost morale took priority over ideological indoctrination. Just how successful Hinkel's efforts with film audiences were is difficult to calculate owing to the absence of documentation and the fact that in the last few months of the war many cinemas were closed or destroyed.

The outbreak of the war undoubtedly provided Goebbels with an opportunity of revolutionizing film propaganda. With the exception of the 'Blitzkrieg documentaries' the result was a gradual retreat into National Socialist mythology at the expense of a genuine ideological commitment. However, it would seem that Goebbels was satisfied with the prestigious political films of 1940-1 and was optimistic about future prospects.

VII

THE IMAGE OF THE ENEMY

The cult of hatred and xenophobia is the cheapest and surest
method of obtaining from the masses the ignorant and savage
patriotism which puts the blame for every political folly or
social misfortune upon the hand of the foreigner.

L. Woolf (*Principia Politica*)

PERHAPS the most outstanding stylistic device in film propaganda is the use of contrasts. Not only do strong contrasts contain a greater emotional intensity than the more subtle nuances, but they also guide the audience's sympathies with more certainty. This aspect of film propaganda is full of confrontations between good and evil, beauty and the beast, order and chaos; in each case the contrast serves to force the individual into the desired and firmly established commitment. In this ultimate purpose, propaganda is aided by man's psychological need for value judgements in simple black and white terms. This is particularly so if a country is in a state of crisis, or war, when there is an increasing need for a simplification of the issues. In such a situation, as the Swedish writers Furhammar and Isaksson noted, 'the other side becomes totally malevolent, one's own cause indisputably just, and everyone gathers around the symbols of unity'.[1]

Political propaganda is at its most effective in times of uncertainty, and hatred is generally its most fruitful aid.[2] In any society a people cannot be kept too long at the highest level of sacrifice and conviction. Even under National Socialism and the relentless fanaticism demanded by such a regime, some form of diversion was needed. Hatred of the enemy was manipulated to fulfil this need as it is probably the most

[1] Furhammar and Isaksson, p. 201.
[2] These thoughts owe a great deal to Ellul, pp. 72–4.

spontaneous of all reactions, and in order to succeed, it need only be addressed to the most simple and violent of emotions and through the most elementary means. It consists of attributing one's own misfortunes to an outsider. A frustrated people needs to hate because hatred when shared with others is the most potent of all unifying emotions. Heine wrote, 'What Christian love cannot achieve is affected by a common hatred.' Whether the object of hatred is the Bolshevik, the Jew, or the Anglo-Saxon, such propaganda has its best chance of success when it clearly designates a target as the source of all misery or suffering, providing the target it chooses is not too powerful. The aim of propaganda is to provide the object of this hatred in order to make it a reality. Moreover, as Jaques Ellul observed: 'propaganda points out enemies that must be slain, transforming crime into a praiseworthy act . . . it opens the door and allows him to kill the Jews, the bourgeois, the Communist, and so on, and such murder even becomes an achievement.'[3]

One of the most striking means by which the cinema has influenced social attitudes—changing or reinforcing opinions —has been through the use of stereotypes. By that I mean conventional figures that have come to be regarded as representative of particular classes, races, and so on. Walter Lippmann developed the term 'stereotype' to describe the knowledge men thought they possessed. That is, knowledge based on myths or dreams. Lippmann believed in the power of the myth or stereotype to arouse popular enthusiasm. He argued that abstract ideas and concepts like national pride are more real to the masses than actual realities.[4] In this context, propaganda gives the individual the stereotype which he no longer takes the trouble to work out for himself; it furnishes them in the form of slogans or labels. The recognition of stereotypes is an important part in understanding the use of anti-symbols and the portrayal of the enemy in Nazi propaganda. The enemy is of great importance in film propaganda for not only does it provide a target than can be attacked, but it also offers a scapegoat, the easiest means of diverting public attentions from genuine social and political problems at home.

[3] Ellul, p. 152.
[4] W. Lippmann, *Public Opinion* (New York, 1945).

THE IMAGE OF THE BOLSHEVIK

The anti-Bolshevik concept was central to the Nazi *Weltanschauung*. The movement had developed and finally emerged from a struggle in which the Communist together with the Jew formed the main target of Nazi violence and invective. Indeed Jewry was equated with Marxism in Nazi ideology—an equation that one can trace to Hitler's experiences in Vienna.[5] The *Herrenvolk*, so the National Socialists believed, was predestined to rule the world. As Hitler wanted to be regarded as the defender of Western civilization, most forms of anti-Soviet activity suited his objectives perfectly. Russia, therefore, figured not only as the centre of world Communism, but could be easily identified as the repository of international Jewry. By 1924 anti-Communism was firmly established as one of the major themes of Nazi propaganda as Hitler increasingly began to regard himself as the crusader against Jews and Marxists.[6] It was a belief that remained with Hitler, even when all was lost in 1945.[7] As *Gauleiter* of Berlin, Goebbels directed his propaganda during the Third Reich's last days in a manner that rationalized the regime's existence and lent coherence and credibility to Hitler's ideological posture. The Führer's death was broadcast on the evening of 1st May to the solemn accompaniment of Wagner and Bruckner followed by the Horst Wessel Lied: although he took his life cursing the German people for their weakness, the impression left by Goebbels's propaganda was that of a hero's death, fighting to the last against Bolshevism.

Stereotypes invariably come ready-made, having evolved, whether consciously or subconsciously, over a considerable period of time. In the context of this work they frequently attach themselves to myths associated with other nations, races, or groups.[8] This was particularly the case with the anti-Bolshevik motif in Nazi propaganda. In 1933 the National

[5] In *Mein Kampf* Hitler related how in pre-war Vienna he first equated the Jews with Marxism. Hitler, pp. 30–66.

[6] Ibid., p. 66.

[7] He referred to the 'Jewish–Bolshevik' motif for the last time on 15 April 1945 in his final appeal to his troops and the German nation. *Deutsche Allgemeine Zeitung*, 17 April 1945.

[8] Cf. Fürhammar and Isaksson, p. 201.

Socialists were fully aware of the sources of their strength. By discovering the Jewish–Bolshevik conspiracy the Nazis not only found a scapegoat for the defeat of·the German army in 1918 and the vindictive Versailles treaty, but they also managed to appeal successfully to long-standing fears of the German middle classes by portraying the Bolshevik as the bar-barian *Untermensch* (subhuman). As I mentioned in Chapter III, the Communists form the principal enemy in feature films during the *Kampfzeit* and the period of Hitler's consolidation of power. Films such as *SA-Mann Brand, Hitlerjunge Quex*, and *Hans Westmar* present the enemy as contemptible, deca-dent, and totally subservient to the wishes of Moscow. How-ever the interesting aspect of the anti-Bolshevik campaign, compared with the anti-Semitic campaign, was that although it was never far from the centre of Nazi propaganda, it had to be continually suspended or modified according to the demands of the diplomatic relations with the Soviet Union.

Apart from the series of 'Party films' made in 1933, the first feature film openly to attack Bolshevism in terms of its insidious threat to Germany and to Western civilization was *Um das Menschenrecht* (*For the Rights of Man*, 1934). After the war the Allied Commission summarized the film as follows:

1918, the end of the war, there is not yet peace in Germany, but Revol-ution. Four comrades have returned from the Front, embittered and disillusioned. They go to their respective homes and the rest of the film deals with their efforts to understand and deal with the new situations that continually arise in post-war Germany. Two join up with the Com-munists, one with the Freikorps, the fourth retires to his farm. The bar-ricades are put up in the streets and the Bolsheviks plunder, murder and loot. The three friends meet again as enemies, they realise the futility of all they are trying to do, that none of the political parties are worth any-thing. The two Communists flee to their friend's farm, but all three are caught there. They finally decide to emigrate as there is nothing left for them in Germany.[9]

This is not a particularly impressive film and from Goebbels's point of view as Minister of Propaganda, explicit feature films that perpetuated the myths and legends of the *Kampfzeit* were no longer necessary or desirable in 1934. Goebbels had already decided to widen his propaganda to incorporate the ideologi-cal imperialism of Marxist-Leninism rather than to depict

[9] *Catalogue of Forbidden German Films*, p. 77.

Bolshevism purely in terms of a power struggle that occurred within post-war Germany. Moreover, it was now felt to be damaging to portray German Communists even if their existence could be explained away by the bankruptcy of the Weimar Republic. In order to achieve his aims, Goebbels needed to delineate a target for hatred more precisely. This could only be achieved by juxtaposing German with Russian or in terms of racial stereotypes: blond Aryan with subhuman Slav. This is clearly the intention of the next film with an anti-Bolshevik theme, *Friesennot* (*Frisians in Peril*, 1935).

Friesennot (*Frisians in Peril*, 1935)

By 1935, the *Antikomintern*, which had been founded under Goebbels's patronage in 1933 with the expressed intention of undermining the Communist International, had extended its activities to incorporate broadcasting and film production. The important political film of the year was Delta-Film's *Friesennot*, based on the novel by Werner Kartwig and directed by *Reichsfilmdramaturg* Willi Krause under the pseudonym of Peter Hagen. *Friesennot* was one of the few films to be distributed directly by the Party. This enabled the *Gaufilmstellen* (Party film centres) to give the film the widest possible distribution and incorporate the most remote villages by means of the Party's mobile cinema units.

Friesennot recalls the problems of the Volga Germans living in Russia during the Revolution and starred Inkijinoff (the hero of Pudovkin's *Storm over Asia*) as the brutal Russian Commissar. In many respects it can be compared with *Flüchtlinge* and *Heimkehr*; in all three films either the Russians or the Poles are shown to be responsible for the oppression of cultural and national minorities, treating ethnic Germans in the same fashion as the Germans were to treat the Poles and Russians when they occupied Eastern Europe. The plot can be outlined as follows:

Centuries ago Frisian Germans emigrated to Russia and settled on the lower reaches of the Volga. They were a peaceful, self-contained community, but good subjects of the Tzar. The Bolshevik Revolution changes everything. Soon, a 'Red' Commissar with a contingent of troops arrives and imposes heavy taxes and ensures their collection quite ruthlessly. Fighting breaks out between the Bolsheviks and the Volga Germans when

Mette, daughter of a Frisian, flirts with the Russian Commissar. As soon as the people are aware of this they drive the girl out of the village into the woods, where she perishes in the boggy moor. Before she dies, Mette realizes her sin and the price she must pay. The Frisians are only maintaining their own strict, moral code, but the primitive Bolsheviks fail to understand this. As soon as Chernov, the Commissar, learns of her death he and his men indulge in a drunken orgy during which they plunder the Frisians' church and their homes and which culminates in the brutal rape of one of the German girls. Wagner, the leader of the Frisians, has done his best to keep the peace but this is the final straw. The film ends with a blood-bath in which all the soldiers are slaughtered. The Frisians then pack their few belongings, burn down their homesteads, and start their trek across the steppes to find a new home.

Friesennot was passed by the Censor on 15 November 1935 and received its première in Berlin on 19 November 1935. Although the Nazis were not to launch their concerted anti-Communist campaign until the 1936 *Parteitag*, the release of *Friesennot* towards the end of 1935 was timed to prepare the nation for the forthcoming attack on Bolshevism. The use of film for this purpose, to prepare rather than to justify, was a new departure in propaganda techniques and indicates the confidence of the new regime.

The Bolsheviks are clearly the Nazis' major adversary during this period; but unlike the earlier anti-Communist propaganda, the emphasis is now no longer on the Bolshevik at home but instead on the danger of the world Communism and its threat to Western civilization. Thus in *Friesennot* the Bolsheviks are not just physically unattractive (they have Asiatic features, they are unshaven, and they are given to drinking vodka almost incessantly), but they also represent dangerous ideas. In *GPU* (1942), probably the most vehement of all anti-Bolshevik films in the Nazi cinema, the propaganda message is essentially one of an ideological war against alien beliefs and behaviour. In 1935, Bolsheviks were still 'subhumans' but the first elements of ideological conflicts begin to be disseminated by means of the feature film. There is a scene in *Friesennot* that illustrates both these aspects of anti-Bolshevik propaganda: the barbarian *Untermensch* and Soviet atheism.

Soon after the Red Army arrive in the village they embark upon a prolonged bout of gorging and drinking which leads to the rape of a German girl and the destruction of the village church. Throughout the film the vices of the Bolsheviks are contrasted with the virtues of Volga Germans. The manipulation of stereotypes by means of their behavioural habits is employed and reinforced. Examples of such habits are the frenzied manner in which the Bolsheviks eat and drink, their lack of personal hygiene, and their wild dancing and primitive, animalistic chants to the accompaniment of strange-looking instruments. When the soldiers dance and sing around their camp fire, the peasants, who are looking on impassively, proudly render a traditional German folk-song that recalls life and customs in Germany while the camera closes in on the grotesque faces of the soldiers as they gorge great chunks of meat obliviously. The soldiers are now in a torpid state of drunkenness and decide to draw obscene pictures of women and then post them on the walls of the village. They then force an old man to drink vodka, plunder the villagers' homes, and finally force their way into the church where they smash a figure of Christ. Exhausted by their exertions, the soldiers fall into a noisy sleep on the floor of the church, when once again the debauched faces of the Bolsheviks are juxtaposed with the saintly images on the stained-glass windows and then finally the broken figure of Christ.

Interposed with this behaviour is a revealing exchange between Wagner and Chernov, the Russian Commissar. Wagner protests at the high taxes that are being levied. Outside the Commissar's office he notices the obscene anti-religious posters drawn by the drunken soldiers, and in *four* languages an inscription which reads 'THERE IS NO GOD'. The following conversation takes place:

WAGNER. You have been lying to me about the new regime! Those pictures outside, what do they mean?
CHERNOV. I did not lie to you. What has the truth got to do with the pictures my men put there?
WAGNER. But that's blasphemy!
CHERNOV. You don't understand, there is no God in Russia.
WAGNER. So there's no God in Russia. Who says so? Who can suddenly abolish him?
CHERNOV. The Authorities.
WARNER. But don't you see that all authority comes from God. How can you abolish God?

CHERNOV. It's easy if you can capture the souls of the masses.[10]

It is typical of the Nazis' disregard for truth that in a country which compelled religious groups to accept a constitution designed to force the Church under state control, the Communists should be portrayed as anti-Christ. The atheistic Chernov is a continuation of the barbaric soldiers in *Flüchtlinge* (1933). It is furthermore ironic that Chernov's remark about 'capturing the souls of the masses' could be applied equally to the rise of National Socialism and highlights the extent to which the caricature of the Bolsheviks reflects the Nazis' own *Weltanschauung*.[11]

In contrast to the way the Communists behave among themselves in the film, the Frisians, in the tradition of their daily lives and by their strict adherence to a moral code, are shown to be the custodians of a deeply-rooted Germanic culture that transcends geographical boundaries. The *Illustrierter Film-Kurier* referred to them as 'those heroic Germans whose sturdy skulls and generous hearts are allied to an unshakeable faith and an indomitable ability for endurance.'[12] If propaganda which intends to portray an image of an enemy is to be successful then it must facilitate the displacement of aggression by clearly stating the target that is to be attacked. In *Friesennot* this is achieved by means of stereotypes and contrasts which culminate in the brutal rape of a German woman by the Bolsheviks and the wanton destruction of the Frisians' Church. Thus by slowly reinforcing the stereotype image of the Bolsheviks through behavioural traits, their final slaughter while asleep in the Church should be a psychological blunder since it could arouse compassion for the soldiers. But an audience which had already chosen the Bolshevik as Germany's major adversary would regard the mass slaughter as a symbolic act (divine retribution), and enjoy it as revenge.

A German critic writing in 1938 referred to *Friesennot* as a classical example of a *Tendenzfilm*, a term used to describe films that showed strong National Socialist 'tendencies'. The importance of such films, according to the critic, 'was that

[10] For an analysis of this film cf. Leiser, p. 41, and F. Courtade and P. Cadars, *Histoire du cinéma nazi* (Paris, 1972), pp. 212-13.

[11] Cf. Hitler's views on the 'enslavement of the masses', Hitler, pp. 158-60.

[12] *Illustrierter Film-Kurier*, no. 3101, 1935.

from the very beginning they attempt to lead the audience in the direction of certain ideas, not by the use of crude symbols, but by the strength and conviction of the artists' inner experiences that find expression through the medium of film'.[13] The central idea in *Friesennot* was the desire to prove the sound racial instincts of the Frisian Germans in their dealings with the Bolshevik, the subhuman *Untermensch*. As such, it only served to reinforce a process of *Entjudung* that was being carried out at this time in all aspects of German life. The film was awarded the *Prädikat*: 'politically and artistically especially valuable'. Reviewing *Friesennot* after the war, the Control Commission for Germany dismissed the film as: 'Fair production, the acting is rather melodramatic and "hammy" with typical "blond" Germans and "Asiatic" Russians, the entire film is very heavy and slow moving, full of German nationalist and anti-Soviet propaganda.'[14] However, Goebbels must have felt that the film was of sufficient importance, because shortly after the German–Soviet non-aggression Pact in 1939, he banned the film from all further distribution.[15]

1936 saw an increase in the anti-Communist campaign, indeed, the *Reichsparteitag* in September was devoted to it. Two treaties were signed in late 1936 in quick succession. Germany and Italy signed a treaty (the Rome–Berlin Axis) and, with Japan, both signed the Anti-Comintern Agreement. The anti-Communist pact was seen by Hitler as a rallying point for other powers to resist the spread of world Communism. The Civil War in Spain also provided Goebbels and Hitler with a further opportunity to exploit this theme by dividing international opinion into the desired polarity: the evil forces of Jewish Bolshevism on the one hand, who resisted the champions of Western civilization on the other. As Z. A. B. Zeman has pointed out, the powerful propaganda onslaught on the Soviet Union launched in 1936 was designed 'to create an anti-Communist psychosis in Europe in the same way as it had created one inside Germany in the years 1932 and 1933'.[16]

However this new propaganda campaign did not include the medium of feature film. German newsreels utilized the Spanish

---

[13] Eckert, pp. 19–25.
[14] *Catalogue of Forbidden German Films*, p. 41.
[15] BA, *Sammlung Sänger, Zsg. 102/62*, 7 October 1939.   [16] Zeman, p. 102.

Civil War for propaganda purposes in the manner outlined above, but there was only one feature film with an anti-Bolshevik theme released in 1936, *Weisse Sklaven* (*White Slavery*), a small-scale production directed by Karl Anton which looked at the plight of White Russians during the Bolshevik Revolution.[17] Geobbels came under increasing pressure from local Party officials to use feature film in the struggle against Bolshevism. As a result, a number of articles appeared in the press publicizing the Government's forthcoming cinematic attractions that were intended to contribute to the ideological battle. What is interesting about this campaign is that they invariably named films that were never to be made. For example, the *Neue Abendzeitung Saarbrücken* under the heading 'Film warfare against Bolshevism' mentioned six films that Ufa planned to produce in the coming year (1937/8). Three of the films were intended to 'highlight the Bolshevik menace':

Staatsfeind Nr I is planned: this will reveal Bolshevism unmasked and will expose the methods of the most evil threat to civilization of our time.
Blutregiment Bela Khuns: is a caricature of Bolshevism.
Boris und Trina: tells the story of two people who manage to escape from the 'Red hell'.
The film *Mein Sohn, der Herr Minister* is a satire of parliamentarianism.
Unternehmen Michael and *Feibeuter* depict heroic exploits during the war.[18]

Reaffirming public interest in 'state-political films', the article concluded by lamenting the fact that since 1933 feature films had not been fully utilized as a weapon against Bolshevism but promised that in future this would be rectified.

Such articles reveal not only the frustrations of local Party officials but also provide an example of how Goebbels could appease them in many instances by simply feeding them false information. Of the six films mentioned above, only two— *Unternehmen Michael* and *Mein Sohn, der Herr Minister*—were ever made. *Unternehmen Michael* was a *Staatsauftragsfilm* that glorified heroic death in war and has already been mentioned. *Mein Sohn, der Herr Minister* (1937), a loose adaption of the French comedy *Fiston* by Andre Birabeau, was directed by

[17] For a synopsis of *Weisse Sklaven*, see *Catalogue of Forbidden Films*, pp. 41-2.
[18] *Neue Abendzeitung Saarbruchen*, 19 November 1936. See also BAK, NS 15/165, which provides numerous examples of similar demands by *Gaupropagandaleitung*.

Veit Harlan. Set during the time of the Popular Front in France, the main contention of the film was to equate parliamentary democracy with Communism.[19] It can be seen then that the projected anti-Bolshevik campaign by means of film propaganda did not materialize. In fact neither the records of the film companies nor those of the RMVP suggest that such films were ever seriously considered. The most likely explanation is that Goebbels, aware of the growing demand for a more ideologically orientated cinema, simply gave the officials the information they wanted; by the time they realized that such films were not being made, it was too late.

Goebbels must have decided (for there is no recorded evidence) to continue this campaign through the other media at his disposal, although he did release one other film prior to the outbreak of war in 1939. This was *Kameraden auf See* (*Comrades at Sea*, 1938). Directed by Heinz Paul, it attempted to present the Spanish Civil War as a Communist uprising against the legal government of the country.[20]

This film apart, no other feature films attacking Soviet Russia or any other form of Communism were made in the Third Reich until 1942, when *GPU* was released. Indeed, after the Russo-German Non-aggression Treaty, anti-Bolshevik caricatures disappeared. Goebbels was confronted with serious problems in interpreting this treaty and J. W. Baird has argued that there is 'a good deal of evidence demonstrating that he was unable to convince Germans that the pact was not a tactical manoeuvre which in time would be reversed.'[21] All films with an anti-Bolshevik motif, including *Flüchtlinge* and *Friesennot*, were immediately banned from distribution as they proved embarrassing to the Nazi regime.[22] In 1940 two feature films appeared that actually presented the Russians in a sympathetic light: Gustav Ucicky's *Der Postmeister* and Wolfgang Liebeneiner's *Bismarck*. The latter was timed to lend credence to the treaty by drawing on historical parallels from a period

---

[19] It is interesting to note that almost all Veit Harlan's films were banned by the Allies after the war. However, because *Mein Sohn, der Herr Minister* had an anti-Russian theme, it was allowed to be distributed in Germany.

[20] For a synopsis of this film, see *Catalogue of Forbidden German Films*, pp. 80-1.   [21] Baird, p. 147.

[22] BA, *R1091/1033c*, 6 October 1939, and *Sammlung Sänger, Zsg. 102/62*, 7 October 1939.

when relatively cordial relations existed between the two countries. However, Goebbels was not helped by the fact that, owing to bureaucratic incompetency when *Bismarck* was being premièred banned films such as *Flüchtlinge* were still being shown.[23] A year later the situation was reversed. Though the declaration of war against Russia was not greeted with enthusiasm, the German people 'accepted the decision as inevitable'.[24] Previously banned anti-Bolshevik films such as *Flüchtlinge* and *Friesennot* were now distributed widely throughout Germany. *Friesennot* was retitled *Dorf im roten Sturm* (*Red Storm Over the Village*) and Goebbels instructed the film press to discuss the implications of the film but to leave out all *Volkstümlich* questions.[25]

Initially, the Nazis rationalized the invasion of Russia as a defence measure against an imminent attack from barbaric Slavs from the East. In this way they were able to link the fear and salvation motives intrinsic to the crusade against Bolshevik 'subhuman' beings. On 10 July 1941, the RMVP received a message from the *Führerhauptquartier* that:

The Führer wants shots of Russian cruelty towards German prisoners to be incorporated in the newsreel so that Germans know exactly what the enemy is like. He specifically requests that such atrocities should include genitals being cut off and the placing of hand-grenades in the trousers of prisoners.[26]

In the same month the SD were to report that the propaganda campaign waged in all media against the racial inferiority of the Slav and the 'cruel deeds of the GPU and the Bolshevik soldier towards the civilian population', was proving to be particularly successful with cinema audiences:

It is apparent from all reports that the focus of attention was the film of the Bolshevik prisoners of war. Again and again, the people were outraged by the pictures of these criminal types with their barbaric features. The atrocities of the GPU and the Bolshevik military rabble against the civilian population were discussed heatedly and at length.[27]

Feature films also contributed towards this campaign. In

[23] BA, *R58/144*, 23 October 1939.
[24] A. Fredborg, *Behind the Steel Wall* (New York, 1944), p. 27.
[25] BA, *Sammlung Sänger, Zsg. 102/63*, 21 August 1941.
[26] BA, *NS 18/282*, 10 July 1941.
[27] BA, *R58/205*, 24 July 1941.

1941 Karl Ritter directed *Kadetten* (*Cadets*), which told the story of the Russian invasion of Berlin in 1760. Interestingly enough, by contrasting the 'Asiatic' features of the 'subhuman' Russians with those of the Aryans, the invading forces were presented not as an ideological threat but rather a contaminating racial menace.

Towards the end of 1941 a number of short films were inserted into the film programmes which stressed the horrors of life under Bolshevism and how the Russian population welcomed the German troops as liberators. A typical example of this type of film propaganda was *Das Sowjetparadies* (*The Soviet Paradise*), a film that was banned after the war by the Allied Commission for the following reasons:

> In the form of newsreel shots by German photographers accredited to the German Armed Forces which were taken in Russia after the invasion in the last war, the Soviet 'paradise' is shown as it was then really found to be. We are shown the primitive living conditions of Russian peasants; how the old people were neglected by Russian authorities, the neglect of young orphans who formed dangerous and unscrupulous marauding bands and finally the welcome is shown that was given to the liberating German armies by the Russians. Average production and photography, intended solely as anti-Russian propaganda.[28]

GPU (1942)

By 1942, a discernible shift can be seen in propaganda as the Nazis attempted to revive and adapt the traditional pre-1939 anti-Bolshevik propaganda to the needs of war. In a series of articles printed in *Das Reich* Goebbels proclaimed that the invasion of Russia was a timely strike against an enemy intent on destroying European civilization. In a less belligerent mood he wrote of this task in his diary on 21 March 1942:

> In the evening I saw the Russian Bolshevik picture, *Suvorov*. It is a strongly nationalistic film, in which the Bolsheviks try to establish a connection between the Russia of today and the old heroic history of the country. Certain passages are as naïve as if a twelve year old child had shot the scenes. Others, again, are of extraordinary vitality. There are lots of possibilities latent in Russians. If they were organised really thoroughly they would undoubtedly represent the most tremendous danger possible for Europe. Preventing that is an objective which we must attain during the coming offensive. May God grant us success.[29]

[28] *Catalogue of Forbidden German Films*, p. 111.
[29] Lochner, p. 99.

After a brief flirtation with the *Untermensch* line at the height of Germany's military success, Goebbels was ready to put an end to this type of propaganda and instead to dramatize the Reich's war against Bolshevism rather than the Russian people. Realizing the inadvisability of Hitler's *Ostpolitik*, Goebbels appreciated that not only were they demoralizing Russians employed in German defence industries but they were also alienating various Russian national groups who were sympathetic to the Nazi regime. Thus, even towards the end of 1941, he had ordered Ufa to make four films all with a number of Russian dialects for the expressed intention of 'enlightening the Russian population about life in Germany'.[30]

In rejecting the *Untermensch* theme Goebbels was returning to his original mission of safeguarding Europe from the 'Jewish-Bolshevik conspiracy'. Reflecting this shift was Karl Ritter's virulent anti-Bolshevik film *GPU* (1942). Interviewed by *Filmwelt* while making the film, Ritter outlined the basic propaganda message that was to be disseminated: 'That the German Armed Forces had destroyed the terror organization of the GPU which had been established by Jewish-Bolshevik "criminals" intent on planting the vile seeds of Bolshevik revolution throughout the world.'[31]

GPU came from an original idea by the actor Andrews Engelmann who starred in the film and wrote the script together with Ritter and Felix Lützkendorf. Production was started in December 1941 and it had its première in Berlin on 14 August 1942. The following synopsis is taken from the Allied Commission's *Catalogue of Forbidden German Feature Films*:

Olga, a White Russian refugee from Bolshevik terror, has joined the Bolshevik GPU Secret Police in order to find the man who killed her parents. After many years she at last meets him in Riga and then in Kowno in the summer of 1939. He is Bokscha, one of the chief agents of the GPU in Europe, instigator of numerous assassinations, uprisings, acts of sabotage etc. Bokscha falls in love with her, she goes with him to many countries. At last in France she feels the time is ripe, denounces him to Moscow as a traitor and he is liquidated. She goes to Moscow, refuses the decoration offered to her, discloses her real reasons for joining the GPU and she too is liquidated. Interwoven is the story of a young

---

[30] BA, *R1091/1034a*, *1474*, 6 November 1941. The themes to be covered were: Farmers, Factory workers, Forest Workers Camp, the Führer, and his People.
[31] *Filmwelt*, no. 13/14, 1 April 1942.

Baltic couple whom Olga befriends; in Rotterdam they are arrested by the GPU and imprisoned in the cellar of the Commercial Attache of the UDSSR, and the film ends with the victorious advance of the German Army into Holland in May 1940 when the two young people are at last released.[32]

The film is intended to reveal the Jewish influence behind Bolshevism and the brutality of the GPU. In the prologue to the film, GPU is translated as *Grauen* (horror), *Panik* (panic), *Untergang* (destruction). So as not to leave the audience in any doubt, the *Programm von Heute*, which accompanied the film, stressed the insidious nature of the GPU in a language reminiscent of that used to describe Jews: 'It is mid-1939. Like the threads of a spider's web the GPU spreads out beyond the Soviet "paradise" to engulf many unsuspecting lands.'[33] In fact the term 'GPU' was no longer employed in the USSR; it had been replaced in 1934 by NKVD (People's Commissariat for Domestic Affairs). But of course this did not affect Goebbels's anti-Bolshevik propaganda. The GPU was so firmly embedded in the minds of Germans as the symbol of Russian barbarism that it had to be perpetuated regardless of whether it existed or not. Moreover, the Russian Secret Police are presented as a Jewish-directed Communist organization. This is established in the first scene where Olga Feodorovna is giving a violin recital for the International Women's League in Riga. Introducing Olga, the Chairwoman maintains that the organization was established to further international co-operation and is 'totally unpolitical'. But an old man interrupts and claims that they are in fact organized and financed by Jewish interests in Moscow. He maintains that he has proof that they had sent greetings telegrams to the Jewish politician Litvinov-Finkelstein.[34] The Chairwoman repeats that the organization is concerned only with promoting peace and freedom for all people. But the old man will not be interrupted:

OLD MAN. Don't interrupt! I said, financed by Moscow! The conclusive evidence is the presence of this gentleman, who calls himself a Soviet

---

[32] *Catalogue of Forbidden Films*, p. 41.
[33] *Programm von Heute*, no. 1837, 1942. Cf. Hollstein, pp. 156-60.
[34] Maxim Litvinov (1876-1951). From 1930-9 he was Soviet Ambassador in America. The Nazis gave him the name Finkelstein and the category 'Jew' in a press directive. BAK, *Sammlung Brammer Zsg. 101/375*, quoted in Hollstein, p. 339.

Diplomat. Do you know who this Consular Attache Smirnov is? He is the murderer Bokscha, GPU agent ... yes, GPU agent! The blood of hundreds of thousands of poor people clings to his hands. Yes, I have evidence. I also have evidence that he murdered my son ... [*struggle*] ... You will not keep me quiet! Not you! Look at him, this representative of peace and freedom! He should be caught. ...

The fact that the old man was seen to be violently removed from the hall by GPU agents and subsequently murdered tended to substantiate his allegations. Other scenes served to highlight Jewish participation in the GPU and the manner in which the Russian Secret Police carried out their subversive activities in other countries. Invariably, Bolshevik meetings would take place deep underground where they would dispassionately plot sabotage and murder beneath portraits of Lenin and Stalin. In Moscow Bokscha is shown plotting the downfall of foreign politicians and the sabotage of allied shipments from Sweden. Action is needed in Finland; we are told that Molatov is waiting for a chance to give an ultimatum and then invade the country. Bokscha is sent to Helsinki where GPU agents are conspiring with Jews to find an appropriate excuse for a Russian invasion. Once again the meetings take place in cellars where the Bolsheviks can seek refuge in the shadows:

BOKSCHA. I have a very amusing plan; an assassination attempt on Soviet employers and Soviet citizens in Helsinki. This would precipitate an ultimatum and then an invasion.
JEW. And who will carry out these assassinations?
BOKSCHA. Funny question! We will, of course, our people.
ANOTHER MAN. So you mean we should kill our comrades?
BOKSCHA. Yes!
JEW. Do they know about it up there?
BOKSCHA. Of course not, they would report to Moscow in noble indignation.
JEW. [*laughing*]. Yes, that's certainly very funny.
 [*They all start laughing and Bokscha closes the meeting. As they leave, one turns to the Jew ...*]
ANOTHER MAN. That's a wonderful plan!
JEW [*throws his hands in the air*]. Oh, wonderful, wonderful!

The Jewish-Bolshevik conspiracy is invoked by the fact that Bokscha is prepared to engage Jewish agents in his subversive activities. Such scenes are intended to reveal the alien beliefs and behaviour of the GPU who are prepared even to murder their own comrades. The moral appears to be that the ends justify the means—a philosophy that could be equally applied to National Socialism. It is interesting to note in comparing these two different political systems that at no time in Nazi film propaganda is Bolshevism discussed in terms of Marxist-Leninism, although ideological comparisons are implicit throughout. Rather, Bolshevism is equated with certain brutal types that recur in the Nazi cinema under different guises, ranging from the barbaric Chernov in *Friesennot* to the cynical murderer Bokscha in *GPU*.

If the Nazis were not prepared to enter into an ideological debate then they had to specify a target for hatred. The stereotype employed in *GPU* is, of course, Nikolai Bokscha. Yet he is not an amalgam of either the *Untermensch* line or the deeply committed Communist; he is neither a racially inferior Slav nor a misguided Party member. Instead, he symbolizes the opportunism of Bolshevism and its alienation from Western civilization. He is referred to in the film as 'one who has made a career for himself without being either a Jew or a proletarian'. Olga summed up his value to Moscow as a 'good executioner who is worth a great deal to the Central Bureau'. In another scene with Olga in the Soviet Embassy in Helsinki a portrait of Lenin is drawn to his attention, and he replies: 'Oh yes! It was the era of proletarian revolution. A dark age! Fortunately one forgets!'

In *GPU*, Asiatic features have largely disappeared from the stereotype image of the Bolshevik enemy. He is now portrayed in collusion with conspiratorial Jews. In fact in Nikolai Bokscha we have the archetypal bourgeois, albeit a brutal and cynical one. *Filmwoche* referred to him as 'the bourgeois after his acre of land', and a 'manipulator of chaos for his own enrichment'.[35]

Goebbels once remarked that if film propaganda was to be successful it 'must make use of painting in black and white, since otherwise it cannot be convincing to people'.[36] This is particularly so when producing an image of the enemy. For the stereotype to be effective it must be contrasted with some kind of 'opposite' figure that an audience can identify with

---

[35] *Filmwoche*, no. 33/34, 9 September 1942.
[36] Quoted in Doob, p. 519.

and positively respond to. In *Friesennot*, Wagner, the leader of the Volga Germans, is contrasted with Chernov the Red Army Commissar, and in *GPU* Bokscha is contrasted with the beautiful young Aryan couple, Peter and Irina, who are imprisoned in Rotterdam and eventually liberated by Nazi troops. However in *GPU*, Ritter portrayed the enemy in such a transparent and unreal way that even German cinema audiences failed to be convinced. It is an indication of the displeasure felt by the RMVP that they not only refused to award the relevant *Prädikate* for such a prestigious film, but they actually banned *GPU* from being shown to German youth. Certainly the dramatization of the GPU torturers fabricates clichès which are so simplistic that the propaganda loses all credibility, while the actors' wildly exaggerated gestures are totally unconvincing.

There is also another explanation linked to the political and military situation that may account for *GPU*'s lack of success. In August 1942, the month of *GPU*'s première, the SD reported that the stories of Russian atrocities were having a 'profound effect on the German population':

The Soviet people are shown to be animalistic and bestial . . . they are simply 'subhuman'. Reports of atrocities which were given in the first months of the Eastern campaign have strengthened the opinion that the Red Army and their agents are 'beasts' that have to be rooted out and destroyed.[37]

This may well have given a false impression about the success of such propaganda and probably reflected the political views of the *Gauleiters* and their agents rather than the population in general. For only two months later the SD had to report that as a result of the personal contact with Russian workers, and since soldiers on leave from the Eastern front were returning with different opinions about the Red Army, Germans were questioning previously held views of the 'subhuman' Russian. The report concluded that as people were re-evaluating their opinions then the 'anti-Bolshevik propaganda had failed in its purpose'.[38]

The failure of *GPU* to attract official approval also illustrates the contradictions and cynicism of Goebbels's attitude towards

[37] BA, *R58/309*, 17 August 1942.
[38] BA, *R58/325*, 12 October 1942.

film propaganda. On assuming power in 1933 he declared that he wanted German film-makers to 'capture the spirit of their age', However, if *GPU* is anything to go by, he did not mean this to be taken too literally. Karl Ritter was renowned for creating the *Zeitfilm* genre, which reflected various (usually militarist) aspects of contemporary society under National Socialism. Despite statements to the contrary, Goebbels was against such films for he appreciated the danger of setting a Nazi film in a contemporary milieu. In a 'closed' society like the Third Reich, both information and propaganda had to be carefully selected and all other sources prevented from reaching the German population. For this reason Goebbels could perpetuate myths surrounding Frederick the Great and heroic resistance at Kolberg with a good deal of certainty, given the difficulty in reappraising any historical myth. The problem with a film such as *GPU*, especially after the military setbacks in Russia, was that it invited discussion and allowed the German public to question the validity of the propaganda message being disseminated. If the message contradicted their own experiences, then the propaganda currency was lost. Not surprisingly, then, *GPU* was not a satisfactory vehicle for Goebbels's propaganda campaign against Bolshevism and was soon phased out of film programmes.[39]

Towards the end of 1942, shortly after the release of *GPU*, Goebbels changed his propaganda campaign once again to indulge in a kind of *post festum* gloom. After the fall of Stalingrad his task was to inform the German public of the Russian disaster without alarming them too much, yet at the same time retaining the fear and salvation motives that were so important. He therefore launched a major propaganda campaign based on gloom and fear of Bolshevism which became the theme of Nazi propaganda from the winter of 1943 until the end of the war.

Although the image of the Bolshevik enemy provided a permanent basis for the 'strength through fear' campaign, it is revealing to note that after *GPU* Goebbels rejected feature films with anti-Bolshevik leitmotivs. He chose instead newsreels

---

[39] On the day of its première, the press were instructed 'not to evaluate the film as documentary evidence of Bolshevism, but rather as an ordinary adventure film'. BAK, *Sammlung Sänger, Zsg. 102/63*, 14 August 1942.

and short documentaries to implant fear in cinema audiences and preferred feature films to concentrate on historical material in order to boost morale.[40] One explanation for this was that his anti-Bolshevik campaigns changed so frequently that it was not possible for feature films to reflect these subtle shifts. Another reason may well have been the technical difficulties in portraying the 'subhuman' Slav. In terms of make-up and the like, it was much easier for German actors *en masse* to give a convincing performance of, for example, Jews in ghettos, than large numbers of 'Mongol hordes' in the Red Army.

THE IMAGE OF THE BRITISH

Indoctrination through the cinema is most successful when there is an element of excitement in the presentation, for this provides the illusion that the spectator is making his own discoveries or drawing his own conclusions. This lack of excitement was one of the reasons why the anti-Bolshevik films were sterile and unconvincing. Another point that should be made is that by producing an element of excitement in the medium of film one is inevitably manipulating visual and sound images.

The cinema of the Third Reich reflects almost every phase in the relationship between Great Britain and the National Socialist State. It reveals a love-hate relationship symbolized by the myth of 'British plutocracy' which until Germany's *Drang nach Osten* in 1941 came to represent an amalgam of respect and jealousy. Traditional clichés of the English national character which were to determine Goebbels's propaganda in years of peace and more intensely in years of war can be traced back to an anglophilia that existed in German minds long before 1918 or 1933.[41] However, even Goebbels had to admit on one occasion that 'English rule has something really phenomenal about it. I have always felt myself drawn to the English

[40] An excellent example of this would be *Im Wald von Katyn* (*In the Forest of Katyn*, 1943), a short documentary which Goebbels released to coincide with the discovery of the Katyn massacres in February 1943. Accusing the Red Army of the crimes, the film highlights the threat posed by Bolshevism and is particularly interesting because, following Stalingrad, it reflected German opinion at that stage of the war. For synopsis, see *Catalogue of Forbidden Films*, p. 110. For Goebbels's reaction to the film, see Lochner, pp. 257-8.

[41] An informative account of anglophilia and anglophobia that dates back to the eighteenth century can be found in Bramsted, pp. 403-5.

world.[42] Hitler also shared these sentiments; his admiration for the British super-race was amply justified, so he believed, by their ability to control with relatively small forces the vast spaces and numerically superior species of the world.[43] As Milan Hauner has noted, 'a sentiment of Nordic solidarity, a sort of "racial internationalism"—bound Hitler in spirit with the English.'[44] It was precisely because of this ambivalent attitude toward the English that the Nazis unequivocally vented their frustrations and anger when the final break came.

Initially, however, the Nazi cinema displayed signs of admiration and envy. Between 1934 and 1936 a number of *Staatsauftragsfilme* were commissioned which reflected this precarious relationship. In 1934, for example, Paul Wegener directed *Ein Mann will nach Deutschland (A Man Must Return to Germany)*, and Herbert Selpin *Die Reiter von Deutsch-Ostafrika (The Riders of German East Africa)*. Both films are set in the First World War and despite the fact that the British are German's main adversary, they are a worthy enemy that has to be respected. In *Ein Mann will nach Deutschland* the honourable British prison camp commander informs his German captives that such internment is offensive to him 'both as an officer and a gentleman'! Ironically enough, the film was banned in February 1940 for its pacifism but after protests from Ufa that they were sacrificing considerable profits, Goebbels re-released it in March.[45] With the signing of the Anglo-German Naval Treaty the following year, the British were drawn in an even more sympathetic light in Gerhard Lamprecht's *Der höhere Befehl (The Higher Order)*. Set in 1806, Britain is shown to be Prussia's ally in the fight against the French usurper Napoleon. In 1936, Karl Ritter's annual propaganda exercise, *Verräter (Traitor)* would appear, *prima facie*, to have reappraised the naval pact with Britain, as the British Secret Service are accused of being the main opponents of German rearmament. However as Erwin Leiser observed, 'the film makes a clear distinction between the British patriot who spies for his country and his German associates who betray

---

[42] Von Oven, p. 181, 27 January 1944.
[43] Cf. F. Hesse, *Hitler and the English* (London, 1954).
[44] M. Hauner, 'Did Hitler Want a World Dominion?' in *JCH*, vol. 13, 1978, p. 26.
[45] BA, *R1091/1033a No. 1407*, 6 March 1940.

theirs.' *Verräter* is an excellent example of how the RMVP used what they believed was a successful propaganda film to indoctrinate the German masses. After it was passed by the *Filmprüfstellen* on 19 August 1936, it was decided to give the film its première at the opening of the Nuremberg Party Rally on 9 September 1936. A month later Ufa were inundated with requests from *Gaufilmstellen* who were at the Rally and who wanted the film incorporated into the schools' programme. The film was subsequently re-edited with cuts so that a 'Jugendfrei' *Prädikat* could be awarded, and a specially edited narrative text with stills was distributed to teachers so that the need for rearmament could be inculcated in the minds of young Germans. A similar procedure was adopted with the educational divisions of the armed forces.[46]

Verräter was to be the last film with a British theme to be made in the Third Reich until after the war. Between 1936 and 1939 when Germany's military expenditure accounted for 16.5 per cent of the country's GNP (twice that of Britain and France),[47] Hitler attempted to pacify British politicians and to divert their attention from his efforts to conquer Europe.[48] It is surely no coincidence that the absence of such films should coincide with such well-laid plans. Given the ease with which films can be misinterpreted, it was more likely a calculated move in order that Hitler's gesture of reconciliation should not be undermined.

In the months prior to the war Goebbels made the timely discovery of the 'clique of plutocrats'. The term 'British plutocracy' with its anti-capitalist connotations was used by the German propaganda machine to indict not the English but only the ruling élite. In one of the earliest press directives given shortly after the outbreak of war a clear distinction was to be made between the British people and their misguided leaders:

In the leader articles for the next few weeks you should exhaust the points raised in the Führer's reply to England: there should be no difficulty with this material. The weight of the argument should initially be against England and not France. Do not attack the English people, but the leading individuals in British society who have guided England into

[46] Information taken from, BAK, *R1091/1031b*, 1173 (28 July 1036); 1179 (26 August 1936); 1190 (20 October 1936).
[47] B. Carroll, *Design for Total War* (The Hague, 1968), pp. 179-90.
[48] See, K. Hilderbrand, *Foreign Policy in the Third Reich* (London, 1973).

the encirclement policy. Attack particularly the Jews, international capitalism, and the financial interests.[49]

During the summer and autumn of 1940 propaganda against Britain reached a new crescendo with the feeling in Germany that the country was on the verge of collapse. In April, the Propaganda Ministry commissioned Ufa to produce a short documentary 'depicting the international warmongering leaders of Britain— Churchill, Chamberlain, and Eden'.[50] I have been unable to locate this film but a year later a documentary with similar intentions entitled *Gentlemen* was released under the auspices of the *Deutsche Wochenschau GmbH*. Although only a short documentary, *Gentlemen* is of particular interest because it managed to embody a number of different anti-British themes that Goebbels had employed since the beginning of the war. It achieved this by simply editing a mass of diverse archive footage together so that it formed an aggressive attack on the ethics of the English gentlemen at war. This idea formed a major theme of Goebbels's propaganda in 1939 which he expressed in slogans such as 'the decadent "Haves" (British ruling class) encircling the healthy "Have-Nots" ' (Germany and her quest for *Lebensraum*). In order that German hatred could be conserved specifically for the British, this line of argument excused France and implied that she had been duped into joining the war to defend British interests.[51] Such propaganda was also intended to drive a wedge between the Allies. By concentrating on individual leaders, particularly Churchill, the film also makes an important distinction between the British people and their Government. But the overall impression given is of Britain the 'perfidious Albion'—a decaying nation surpassed in unreliability only by the Jews.

The theme of the weakness and increasing decadence of the English ruling class was expressed in a unique short documentary film released in 1941 entitled *Die englische Krankheit* (*The English Sickness*). It is designed both as propaganda and/ or health instruction since it deals with the prevention and treatment of rickets and how the British deliberately spread the disease in Germany during the First World War. Banned by

[49] BA, *Sammlung Sänger, Zsg. 102/19*, 3 September 1939.
[50] BA, *R1091/1034a, 1410*, 24 April 1940.
[51] Cf. Bramsted, pp. 239–40.

the Allied Commission after 1945 for its virulent anti-British propaganda the following plot summary is taken from their analysis of the film:

The commentary starts by emphasising that rickets originated in England in the 17th Century. It claims by means of the reproduction of an article from a British newspaper that Britain intentionally ensured that this disease should spread to Germany during and after the '14–'18 war intending in this way to destroy the vitality of the German people. In diagrams we then are shown the effect of rickets on children and adults and how it can best be prevented, how in some cases it can even be healed. It shows what the Nazis do for the towns' population in the winter by providing for them artificial sun-ray treatment. Average production and photography, beginning of film virulently anti-British propaganda.[52]

Although, with the benefit of hindsight, we may laugh at these absurd suggestions, it is important to remember that we are reacting to historical events shaped by our knowledge of their outcome and not to the blinding illusions of propaganda. *Die englische Krankheit* succeeds in attacking the British and providing health instruction both at the same time. Not only is Britain reinforced as a target for hatred, but it is achieved in such a way that the British, by their dastardly deeds, are shown to be a decadent and negative force, whereas the measures taken by the Nazis reveal National Socialism to be a truly progressive and positive political system. Once again Goebbels, who took a personal interest in the film,[53] was manipulating value judgements in simple black and white terms in an attempt to force the individual into the desired and firmly established commitment. If the SD are to be believed, they confirm that, in the early part of the war at least, Goebbels achieved some measure of success with his anti-British propaganda.[54]

It can be seen from the films already mentioned that the image of the British oscillated from that of a worthy and respected opponent to a cowardly plutocrat intent on denying the Reich its need for living-space by encircling it into subjection. However, it was only after the fall of France and the unexpected resolve of the British to continue the war after their cities had been blitzed that Goebbels attacked the English on racial grounds as being the 'Jews among the Aryans whose

[52] *Catalogue of Forbidden Films*, p. 109.
[53] See Boelcke, *Kriegspropaganda 1939–41*, p. 266, and pp. 722-3.
[54] Cf. SD Reports, 27 May, 20 June, and 4 July 1940. BAK, *R58/151/152*.

teeth one has first to knock out before one can talk to them sensibly'.[55]

By now the term 'plutocracy' in German propaganda meant the oppressive and sinister rule of the few. Goebbels had defined the 'plutocrats' in a rally in Münster on 28 February 1940 as a 'kind of political and economic leadership, in which a few hundred families rule the world'.[56] On 16 June, in his *Das Reich* editorial he made the quintessential racist statement of the war against England: 'The English are firmly convinced that God is an Englishman. In their character mélange of brutality, mendacity, sham piety, and sanctimonious Godliness, they are the Jews among the Aryan race.'[57] Such sentiments were soon to be incorporated into a series of inflammatory anti-British films. By the Propaganda Ministry's own admission, large-scale propaganda films attacking the British had been at a standstill since the beginning of the war.[58] This was due, no doubt, to the fact that Hitler was still making conciliatory overtures towards Britain. However, in 1940 *Die Rothschilds* was released amidst a wave of expectancy generated by the mass media, and became the first film to combine anti-Semitism with an anti-British bias.

Die Rothschilds Aktien von Waterloo (The Rothschilds' Shares in Waterloo, 1940)

Directed by Erich Waschneck, who had made a number of films during the Weimar era,[59] the screenplay was jointly written by C. M. Köhn and Gerhard Buchholz from an idea by Mirko Jelusich. *Die Rothschilds* was passed by the *Filmprüfstelle* (Censor) on 16 July 1940 and had its première in Berlin a day later. It is part of a trilogy of films, all made in 1940, designed to prepare German audiences for more stringent measures against Jews (*Jud Süss* and *Der ewige Jude* will be discussed later). I have included *Die Rothschilds* in this section because it was rewritten a year later and re-released under

---

[55] Goebbels, *Die Zeit ohne Beispiel*, p. 304.
[56] Ibid., p. 248.
[57] Quoted in Baird, p. 121.
[58] BA, *Sammlung Sänger, Zsg. 102/26*, 8 July 1940.
[59] Erich Waschneck (born 1887) made his reputation with *8 Mädels im Boot* (*Eight Girls in a Boat*, 1932) and *Abel mit der Mundharmonika* (*Abel and the Mouth Organ*, 1933).

the new title *Die Rothschilds Aktien von Waterloo*. In its final form the film is as virulently anti-British as it is anti-Semitic and illustrates the extent to which the content of films in Nazi Germany was determined by political considerations. The following plot summary, which is taken from SHAEF, is an analysis of the re-released version:

In 1806 the 'Landgraf' of Hesse escaping Napoleon has to entrust his fortune of £6,000,000 to somebody for safekeeping. He deposits the money with the Jewish banker, Meyer Amschel Rothschild in Frankfurt. The abusive use of this money becomes the foundation for the power of the Rothschilds. Amschel Rothschild sends the money to his son Nathan in London who is not respected by his business rivals. But Nathan ruthlessly outwits all of them. He gets money to Wellington in Spain with the help of his brother in Paris — Nathan is the first to receive news that Napoleon has escaped from Elba and the only one to gamble all he possesses on the reinstatement of Louis of Orleans. He is a joke in Society — nobody takes him seriously but his Jewish hirelings and the British Minister of Finance. 'Lord' Wellington is again sent to fight Napoleon. He has very little time to prepare for the war — the ladies keep him busy! But he has time enough (just as Fouche has in Paris) to confer secretly with Rothschild who implies that Wellington will be well rewarded if Rothschild is the first to know the outcome of the battle. The moment Rothschild hears that Napoleon is beaten he spreads news that the English cause is lost. A panic follows — everybody sells Government Bonds — Rothschild buys them. The poor lose their money. The few honourable rich Englishmen (one of them is pictured as extremely decent due to the fact that he is married to an Irish woman!) lose all they own. The star of David lies over England — over the part of the world that Nazi Germany fights.[60]

A twofold purpose can be gleaned from *Die Rothschilds*: it attempted to explain the rise to power and wealth of the Rothschild family and the emergence of the 'Jewish–British Plutocracy'. It also robbed England of the glory of having won the battle of Waterloo, claiming that victory was due to the Prussians under Blücher.[61] The *Illustrierte Film-Kurier* referred to these two themes as being based 'wholly on historical facts' and continued: 'the Rothschilds' fortunes were built on the blood of German soldiers, sold as mercenaries to the

---

[60] SHAEF, *List of Impounded Films* (Deposited in BFI Film Catalogue Library), p. 217. For a detailed description of the film, see Hollstein, pp. 65-75.

[61] SHAEF were extremely annoyed by this slur on British military honour. In their remarks, following the plot summary, they commented rather indignantly: 'Furthermore, *four* times it is repeated that not Wellington but the Prussians won the victory of Waterloo!' SHAEF, p. 218.

British.'[62] By revealing the 'historical fact' that Jewish financiers had profited from the death of German soldiers, *Die Roths-childs* was consistent with the argument which rationalized the extermination of the Jews that Hitler had first expressed in *Mein Kampf* and subsequently repeated on numerous occasions. Compare the following speech delivered in the *Reich-stag* in 1939: 'Today I will once more be a prophet: if the international Jewish financiers in and outside Europe should succeed in plunging the nations once more into a world war, then the result will not be the bolshevization of the earth, and thus the victory of Jewry, but the annihilation of the Jewish race in Europe!'[63]

The audience, of course, still had to make this conceptual link and draw a parallel between the measures undertaken by the Nazis against the Jews and the Rothschilds' speculation on the battle of Waterloo at the expense of German blood. First of all, it must be remembered that the film would not have been viewed in isolation from the widespread propaganda campaign being waged at this time; secondly the main thesis was augmented by the role of the British in this affair. Interestingly enough the film reveals how, even in 1940, the curiously ambivalent attitude towards the British which I have already discussed remains, as Waschneck obviously felt compelled to distinguish between the decent and the unscrupulous type.

The first scene in the film is an exchange between Amschel Rothschild (Erich Ponto) and his son Nathan (Karl Kuhlmann); it will establish the moral standard of the Rothschild family for the rest of the film. Amschel is opening a safe containing the money deposited with him for safe keeping. He intends to abuse this trust by sending the money to England and establishing the family empire there. He tells his son: 'You can only make a lot of money with a lot of blood!'

Despite referring to himself as 'an English Gentleman', Nathan is despised and ostracized by the English financiers who regard him as something of an alien upstart. But Wellington is in desperate need of money for his campaign in Spain. Herries, the scheming Minister of Finance (Walter Franck), persuades Nathan to contribute to the expedition. It is decided that the

---

[62] *Illustrierte Film-Kurier*, no. 3120, 1940.
[63] Reproduced in D. M. Phillips, pp. 21–2.

money should be sent to Spain via Paris where another relative
lives. One of the hirelings charged with escorting the money
asks if the scheme is fraught with danger, to which Nathan
retorts: 'You will be going where there are Jews—it's never
dangerous!'

As the detailed plans are carried out for the export of this
money a caption appears on the screen: 'International Judaism
goes to work!' The price that Nathan demands in exchange for
his financial assistance is that Wellington should establish a
system of couriers to supply him exclusively with advance information about the outcome of the battle. When asked why
by the puzzled Wellington, he replies: 'News is money!'

As the battle gets under way and Nathan puts his plan into
action, a caption appears once again on the screen:

Everything for money. While soldiers bleed to death on the battlefields,
gigantic speculations are being prepared on the London Stock Market.

With such an arrangement Nathan Rothschild is the only specu-
lator to learn of Napoleon's defeat at Waterloo ('Like God, I
know everything!'), but he spreads the rumour that Wellington
has been defeated, causing a panic on the Stock Market. In
accordance with the propaganda aim, the whole film is structured around the theme of Stock Exchange manœuvres in
which English bankers and the Rothschilds speculate at the
expense of brave soldiers. Nathan, who by now has a leading
position in England, discovers that he has made eleven million
pounds and exclaims: 'My Waterloo!'

The British characters in the film, particularly the bankers,
politicians, and generals, are presented in such a way that they
are supposed to reinforce Goebbels's claim that the 'English
are the Jews among Aryans'. England is shown to be a decaying
society dominated by Jews, but a society that deserves to be
robbed by the Jews. For example it is Herries, the Minister of
Finance, who provides Nathan Rothschild with his entrée into
British high society.

'Lord' Wellington is portrayed as a cowardly hedonist who
not only betrays the Prussians in the struggle against Napoleon
but is more concerned with his numerous mistresses than fighting. In a conversation with Nathan Rothschild regarding the
Spanish campaign, a scantily clad mistress suddenly appears

from the bedroom and entices Wellington in. Such a crude denigration of a figure that loomed large in British history was to be typical of the methods employed by the Nazis.

However, it is also important to stress that Nathan's acceptance into British high society does not come readily; he is mocked for calling himself an 'English Gentleman'. Despite his pretensions he is openly ridiculed by his fellow bankers for his accent and Jewish appearance. In one scene, Nathan decides to give a magnificent ball to mark his entrée into high society in which all the leading British financiers are invited. But in a nearby hotel these bankers deliberately insult the Rothschilds by attending a much smaller affair. As they gaze at Nathan's lavish 'folly' one turns to another and says: 'They may have to deal with us but they can't join us!'

The camera switches to a sullen Nathan Rothschild seated alone at a vast table surrounded by an untouched banquet. He is joined by his secretary Bronstein who tries to rationalize the situation:

BRONSTEIN. Nathan, will you finally realize that you can't obscure the fact that you were born in the Jewish alley in Frankfurt. I tell you [*spoken with a Jewish accent*], as you climb higher and higher, as you become an important person in England, you will still remain a big lad from the Jewish alley in Frankfurt.

NATHAN. Bronstein, look here, you look like a beggar, you're miserable and not very clean — but your son will call himself a Gentleman and your grandson can even perhaps be a Lord in this country, and everything that accompanies such a title. This can all be achieved with money.

The English underestimate such determination and treachery. Interestingly enough, it is the decent English banker and his Irish wife, who have tried to expose the Jewish menace, who are ruined by him. The moral is that by allowing the Rothschilds to prosper, the Jews and the English plutocracy were worthy of each other. The honest British couple are imprisoned and finally decide to leave the country where 'God is a business partner' to discover a 'new place where one can breathe freely'. As they prepare to leave, Nathan Rothschild's name is mentioned, to which the incorruptible banker retorts: 'You say Rothschilds'—I say England—It's the same thing!'

If German audiences failed to grasp the appropriate message, the final scene in the film, in which Nathan demonstrates to

Herries the extent of Rothschild power, heavily underscores it. He uses a map of Europe to illustrate the centres of Rothschild power and draws a family tree, which, when its branches are drawn together, forms the Star of David. The film concludes with the flaming star superimposed over a map of England and a final caption that declares:

As this film was being completed, the last members of the Rothschild family are leaving Europe as refugees and escaping to their allies in England. The fight against British plutocracy continues!

In *Die Rothschilds*, Jews are seen to pose an economic as well as a racial threat. British plutocracy, based on the capitalist ethos, is shown to be dependent upon Jewish financial support. By rejecting such an economic system and by exterminating Jews, the film highlights the fundamental conflict between Germans, Jews, and the British, and suggests that under National Socialism these two enemies of the Reich are receiving their just deserts.

Although in some ways a well-constructed film, *Die Rothschilds* was not an unqualified success. This was to some extent due to the uncertainty that surrounded the political arena at this time, which was to have a profound effect on the final shape of the film and its distribution. Writing in the *Völkischer Beobachter* in 1939, the Austrian Mirko Jelusich, who provided the idea for the film, indicated that the first working script contained a strongly anti-British bias.[64] But as the political situation changed it is clear that this bias was tempered with a more sympathetic dramatization of certain British characters that were to appear in the film. Even on the day of its première the political situation regarding Germany's relationship with Britain was still extremely uncertain. One day before, on 16 July 1940, Hitler had issued the now famous Directive 16 which set 'Operation Sea-Lion' in motion and prepared the way for the invasion of Britain. However, three days later he summoned the Reichstag to listen to his final conciliatory offer of peace to Britain.[65]

Two months after its première, *Die Rothschilds* was withdrawn from circulation. It had only been shown in Berlin and a few other towns where, according to the SD Reports, it had

---

[64] *VB*, 26 December 1939.
[65] Domarus, pp. 1540-59.

caused a 'flurry of excitement'.[66] Despite the fact that it was 'eagerly anticipated everywhere', it was to take another year before the film was to be shown widely throughout the Reich. On 2 July 1941, the RMVP finally gave Ufa permission to release a re-edited version of the film with the subtitle *Die Rothschilds Aktien von Waterloo*, and in order to emphasize the much stronger anti-British theme that was now required, the final caption outlined above was also added. Goebbels must still have been dissatisfied with the film for the press were forbidden to discuss it in detail and no *Prädikate* were ever awarded.[67]

Die Rothschilds is an example of film propaganda within a totalitarian police state that badly misfires. Because of the changing political situation and the pressure exerted by the RMVP that the film should reflect National Socialist policy, the director and the script-writers were never sure whether they were making an anti-British or an anti-Semitic propaganda film. As we have seen, one of the fundamental tenets of any form of propaganda based on hatred is that the enemy must be simply and clearly portrayed. Fritz Hippler, the *Reichsfilmintendant*, wrote in a pamphlet entitled 'Reflections on Film-Making': 'In the cinema, the spectator must know, with greater certainty than in the theatre, "whom should I love and whom should I hate!"'[68] By showing Englishmen to be either partners or victims of the Jews, *Die Rothschilds* consequently produced an ambivalent response to the anti-British campaign. In other words, it failed to create a 'them' and 'us' mentality in which attitudes and prejudices could be formed or reinforced.

Although *Die Rothschilds* was not liked in official circles it was decided to use the films first released as a way of promoting the forthcoming film programme for the season 1940/41, a period which marked the highest concentration of political film propaganda. There can be little doubt that as German military successes multiplied, film propaganda became increasingly aggressive and agitational—a shift that German film audiences generally welcomed after the lull that had existed

---

[66] BA, *R58/155*, 10 October 1940.
[67] BA, *R1091/1034b, 1461*, 2 July 1941.
[68] Hippler, *Betrachtungen*, p. 92.

since the beginning of the war. The SD noted that the public wanted even more political films ('on Jewish warmongers, British lying Lords, etc.'). They concluded that 'the main interest is now in the subject which is being treated, while previously it had often been confined to the actors appearing in the film.'[69]

The fact that relatively more overt political films were being produced and that audiences were choosing films to see on the basis of their content and not on the stars appearing in the films illustrates the highly politicized nature of ordinary life in Germany at this period and the success of Nazi propaganda. With regard to films with an anti-British theme, they tended to become rather more crude as Hitler's hopes of a peace settlement with Britain receded. Between 1940 and 1943, eight feature films were released. Interestingly enough, after the failure of *Die Rothschilds*, Britain was no longer portrayed on racialist grounds as the 'Jews among the Aryans' but as a brutal imperialistic oppressor of smaller nations.

Das Herz der Königin (*The Heart of the Queen*, 1940), was directed by Carl Froelich for Ufa and dealt with the life of Mary, Queen of Scots, from her accession to the Scottish throne until her final betrayal and execution by Elizabeth of England. Giving their reasons for banning the film after the war, SHAEF commented: 'Again the hackneyed and questionable expressions "What England wishes is always right" and "Whoever permits themselves to be helped by England perish" are given prominence in a dialogue banal as it is malicious.' Max W. Kimmich directed two films, *Der Fuchs von Glenarvon* (*The Fox of Glenarvon*, 1940) and *Mein Leben für Irland* (*My Life for Ireland*, 1941), which portrayed the Irish struggle for freedom and independence against the British. In the former the British villain, a treacherous English judge (Ferdinand Marian), is lured into a misty Irish bog to meet a horrible death. The sentiment of the film can be gauged from the opening sequence, a secret meeting of Irish patriots:

ASSEMBLY. We must build new roads.
LEADER. With what shall we build new roads?
ASSEMBLY. With the bones of our enemy!

[69] BA, *R58/155*, 10 October 1940.

LEADER. And who is our enemy?
ASSEMBLY. England!

In Herbert Selpin's *Carl Peters* (1941) and another Kimmich production, *Germanin* (1943), the British record and conduct in Africa is attacked. The two films constitute a superficial argument over the relative merits of England and Germany for ultimate colonial hegemony. In *Carl Peters*, British imperialism is seen as the main threat to Germany's colonial ambitions in the last quarter of the nineteenth century. Although the German colonialist's demands for territorial expansion are rejected by a weak parliamentary Germany, the film makes the point that history has proved Peters (played by Hans Albers) right. The film ends with a disconsolate Peters exclaiming: 'Poor Germany, you are your own worst enemy . . . but my ideas will be taken up one day, they will never destroy them!'

The last anti-British film to be released in Germany was *Titanic* (1943), which purported to show that the capitalist intrigues of the British upper classes were the cause of the ill-fated voyage of the *Titanic*. However, having decided to release the film, Goebbels had it almost immediately withdrawn from circulation. Because the audience knew the fate of the ship in advance they could not but respond in a sympathetic way towards the doomed British passengers. *Titanic* was originally approved after the war by the *Freiwillige Selbstkontrolle*, but banned after objections were raised in 1950 by the British. Two further edited versions were turned down by the British High Commission as it was considered that no amount of cutting could remove the anti-British tendency of the film.[70]

All these film warrant further analysis, but regrettably must be excluded from this book.[71] Instead, I have chosen to discuss *Ohm Krüger* (*Uncle Kruger*, 1941), perhaps the most impressive propaganda film made during the Third Reich. It certainly was the only feature film that came close to fulfilling Goebbels's dream of a Nazi equivalent to Eisenstein's *Battleship Potemkin*.

[70] *Catalogue of Forbidden Films*, p. 38. For a description of the film see *Illustrierte Film-Kurier*, no. 3336.
[71] The one other film not mentioned is *Anschlag auf Baku* (*Attack on Baku*, 1942). Brief, but inaccurate synopses of the films mentioned above can be found in the *Catalogue of Forbidden Films*, pp. 35–8.

Ohm Krüger (Uncle Kruger, 1941)

Directed by Hans Steinhoff with assistance from Herbert Maisch and Karl Anton, *Ohm Krüger* was the first film to receive the honorary title 'Film of the Nation', the highest accolade awarded in the *Filmwelt.* It was passed by the Censor on 2 April 1941 and received its première on 4 April 1941. For his performance as Paul Krüger, President of Transvaal Free State, Emil Jannings was presented by Goebbels with the 'Ring of Honour of the German Cinema'.[72] Krüger is the perfect hero figure for a Nazi film. A suitably authoritative 'uncle' to his people, leading a model nation which draws its strength from the land. Honest, courageous, direct, a family man, but above all a statesman who fought a heroic war against Germany's arch-enemy Britain. Such a scenario allowed the script-writer, Harald Bratt, to rewrite the history of Great Britain to conform to the charge that the English character expressed itself in violence, murder, and the exploitation of enslaved peoples. On the pretext that it is showing historical truth, the film exploits these characteristics with a certain skill, showing the decadence of the British system and the devious machinations of Cecil Rhodes (Ferdinand Marian) and Joseph Chamberlain (Gustaf Gründgens) coupled with malicious characterizations of Queen Victoria and the Prince of Wales. Particularly interesting is the portrait of the young Winston Churchill as a commandant of one of Kitchener's 'concentration camps', kind enough to his bulldog but responsible for the massacre of women inmates.[73] SHAEF commented:

A song of hatred against Britain, elaborately produced, well directed, and with the best cast and technical personnel available to the German film industry. Nothing was omitted that could fail to give the impression that Britain always tried to bully smaller nations – of how ruthless the British methods have always been to gain power, how cynically the Crown, the Government, the Statesmen and how the English people have pursued their greedy aims.[74]

The following plot summary is taken from the illustrated film brochure that was sold at the première of *Ohm Krüger:*

Gold is discovered in the land of the Boers, the Transvaal, and Orange

---

[72] *VB,* 6 April 1941.
[73] Churchill was, of course, a war correspondent at the time.
[74] SHAEF, p. 219.

Free State. The English decide they must acquire this land; Cecil Rhodes and Joe Chamberlain try to provoke them into war; Paul Krüger, the leader of the Boers, goes to England and signs a treaty which provides the English with many advantages but retains the Boers' independence. Returning home, however, Krüger starts to prepare for what he knows is an inevitable conflict. The English start the war, but the Boers repel them, London changes its tactics and appoints Kitchener Supreme Commander. He decides not to engage the Boer Army, but the helpless civilian population. Their homes are burnt, their herds are destroyed, their wells are poisoned, the Negroes are armed, and women and children are forced into concentration camps where they are brutally treated, starved, and infected with diseases in an attempt to break down the morale of the Boer men still fighting. Thousands of men and women are killed in this way whilst Krüger travels around the capitals of Europe imploring for help. English diplomacy assures his failure and while the Boers are finally forced to sacrifice their independence and become part of the British Empire, a broken Krüger finds asylum in Switzerland.[75]

Ohm Krüger must be seen particularly in the wider context of anti-British propaganda in the second year of the war. It was intended to prepare German audiences for the forthcoming invasion of Britain which both Goebbels and the population as a whole believed was imminent. When the the script-writer and the director had started to construct the first outline in September 1940, 'Operation Sea-Lion' had been under way for two months. Hitler eventually postponed the execution of the plans indefinitely, but even so rumours about the coming invasion continued to circulate, a situation that Goebbels encouraged well into 1941.

In the mean time, RAF bombing raids, although not on a large scale, were having a disturbing effect on German morale.[76] Goebbels chose to counter the propaganda effects of the English raids by claiming that the English spirit of inhumanity drove them to bomb cultural and civilian targets, thus murdering helpless women and children and destroying some of Western civilization's most sacred shrines.[77]

By cynically reinterpreting the events of the Boer War for the purpose of war propaganda, *Ohm Krüger* plays upon the feelings of hatred prevalent in Germany at the time. Indeed, the illustrated booklet that accompanied the film mentions

[75] *Ohm Krüger, Aktuelle Filmbucher* (Berlin, 1941).
[76] SD Report, 14 May 1940 in Boberach, pp. 64–5.
[77] See Goebbels's press conference, 7 August 1940, in Boelcke, p. 448.

not only the reasons for producing it but also its significance for a contemporary Germany, involved in another war 'started by the British'. Both the film and the accompanying material therefore corresponded to the wider propaganda aims of Goebbels's anti-British propaganda. In such a way the British, for example, could be shown in the film to have invented concentration camps.

That Goebbels set great importance on *Ohm Krüger* can be gauged not only from the awards he bestowed but also the extremely high costs of the film; more than RM 5½ million.[78] Only one month after shooting had begun on the film he declared the work *reichswichtig* (important for the State),[79] this at a time when he was desperately trying to keep production costs down by encouraging film-makers to be less extravagant. In his speech to the *Reichsfilmkammer* in February 1941 he rationalized the expense by stating that the propaganda and artistic importance of *Ohm Krüger* warranted such a large-scale production. However, he warned the *Filmwelt* not to regard such expenditure as the norm.[80]

The story of *Ohm Krüger* is told by means of flashback. The overriding importance of the film according to the critic from the *Filmwoche* was that it portrayed the 'heroic struggle of the brave little Boers and revealed to the entire world of culture that England is the brutal enemy of order and civilisation'.[81] The tone is set in the first scene where in a Geneva hotel a blind Krüger is besieged by journalists from all over the world, eager to record his reactions to the news of the British victory in South Africa. The isolation of the ailing Krüger and his defencelessness against such intrusions is reinforced when the representative of the London *Times* forces his way in and succeeds in taking a photograph in the surrounding darkness. Afterwards Krüger asks his nurse to read *The Times*'s account of the defeats. She is moved to ask why the Boers had not negotiated with the British and is told by Krüger that 'if one repeats a lie often enough it is believed . . . it is never possible to negotiate with the English.'

[78] BA, *R2/4829/30*.
[79] BA, *Sammlung Sänger, Zsg. 102/62*, 20 September 1940.
[80] Speech of 15 February 1941, reproduced in Albrecht, pp. 465–79.
[81] *Filmwoche*, no. 16, 16 April 1941.

The purpose of the film from this point onwards is to construct a series of principles that Goebbels could apply to the contemporary war in Europe. This is achieved by the contrasting use of archetype in which simple black and white images of the enemy are manipulated to elicit the desired response from cinema audiences. Krüger emerges as a Führer figure to a patriotic Volk to whom he mystically symbolizes the Fatherland. In contrast the British are savagely parodied: a drunken Queen Victoria is shown presiding over a corrupt and ruthless plutocracy. The Boer War is depicted as the struggle of a united free people against a tyrannical imperialist aggressor which cruelly imprisons women and children in concentration camps. A few sequences from the film will serve to illustrate how the stereotype image of the enemy can be used for these purposes.

In the opening scene in Geneva the dying Krüger reminisces, telling his nurse how it all began. Images of the 'Great Trek' inland by the Boers fill the screen as he recalls how two hundred years of peace and prosperity were ended by the coming of 'der Englander'. Krüger continues:

KRÜGER. We had only one aim, peace and liberty. In such a way our children grew into adulthood . . . Transvaal, our Fatherland; our blood; our toil . . . then came the English . . .

As these words trail away, the film cuts to Cecil Rhodes, who, surrounded by slaves and decadent luxury, is gloating over a map of Africa. He is set on securing the rights of the vast gold deposits in the region by 'tricking the Boers out of their rich heritage'. He dispatches Dr Jameson to create fresh border disturbances and sends an associate to Chamberlain in London to secure his co-operation. In the scene that follows, the British missionaries are presented as tools of the imperialists, distributing bibles to the natives with one hand and guns with the other while piously singing the national anthem with the Union Jack draped over the altar!

The scene moves to London. At Buckingham Palace Queen Victoria, attended by John Brown, is giving an audience to Chamberlain (complete with his eyeglass). The news of the border trouble has reached them but Queen Victoria is unwilling to take action:

CHAMBERLAIN. Providence has called on England to educate small and backward nations. It is our duty to take over the Boer lands.

VICTORIA. But the Boers have too many friends; the Dutch, the Germans, Italians, etc. We British have no friends — they all think we are robbers!

CHAMBERLAIN. That may be so, but no nation is as pious as we are.

The thought of an isolated Britain irritates her cough and Brown is instructed to bring her 'medicine' which he pours out of a whisky bottle. Chamberlain then tries another approach and informs her of the gold. She retorts:

VICTORIA. If there's gold to be found, then of course it's our country. We British are the only ones capable of carrying the burdens of wealth without becoming ungodly.

But she insists that they try to get it by peaceful means first, despite Chamberlain's insistence that one 'cannot negotiate with Krüger', and suggests that the President visit Britain:

VICTORIA. It must be easy to trick the old fool [Krüger], after all treaties are cheaper than wars. Instruct him to come.

Krüger visits London and signs a treaty of friendship with Britain. Chamberlain, who conducts the negotiations, remarks: 'The important thing in such a treaty is to abide by it.'

The film cuts immediately to Rhodes complaining about the price that must be paid to the Boers. He decides to visit Krüger personally and offers him a blank cheque. Krüger realizes that the treaty was merely a hypocritical cover for Britain's true motive, greed. He throws Rhodes out exploding: 'Do you think you can bribe Paul Krüger? We are going to fight.'

The war begins with a victory for the Boers who are shown marching to war, arm in arm, singing and carrying anti-British banners. In London Lord Kitchener assumes responsibility for the war and immediately abandons all humanitarian principles. In a speech to the British War Council he explains the concept of total war which is shown to be a British invention:

KITCHENER. My predecessor made the error in respecting certain military conventions which may be applicable in certain circumstances but are misplaced in Africa. What this means is an end to humanitarianism; we must hit the Boers where they are vulnerable. We must burn their farms, separate wives and children from their menfolk, and place them in concentration camps. From today all Boers, without exception, are outlaws. No distinction is to be made between soldiers and civilians.

A concentration camp provides the setting for the climax of the film which is modelled on Eisenstein's Odessa Steps massacre in *Battleship Potemkin*. The commandant of the camp, a caricature of Churchill, gorges himself and feeds rashers of meat to his bulldog while the starving women protest at the rotten food they are given. The commandant and the medical orderly swear to the prisoners that the food is edible (echoes again of *Potemkin*) and to stave off a women's revolt, the commandant (Otto Wernicke) shoots in cold blood the woman who first complained.

Shortly afterwards, Krüger's son Jan, who had been educated at Oxford and was initially pro-British, approaches the camp to find his wife. They are both caught and Jan Krüger (Werner Hinz) is taken up to the dead tree overlooking the camp where his wife is forced to watch him being hanged. As Jan is hoisted up the tree he lets out a violent curse on Britain crying: 'I die for the Fatherland.' The allusion to Golgotha created by Jan's dead body etched against the skyline releases a new hatred for the British as the women storm up the hill towards the troops. A bullet from the commandant kills Jan Krüger's wife and signals the beginning of the massacre which leaves the black figures of the dead women scattered on the white hillside. As the camera draws back to reveal the carnage, an abandoned child can be heard sobbing, and the scene dissolves into a composition of graves and crosses.

The flashback ends with the exiled Krüger awaiting death in his hotel room in Switzerland. Before he dies he has a vision of the future, a prophecy that was aimed specifically at German audiences predisposed to hatred of the British after Hitler's failure at rapprochement with Britain in 1941:

KRÜGER. That is how the British overran and degraded my people. We were a small people, but one day a greater nation will rise to crush Britain. They will crush England; only then will the world be a better place to live in.

By the end of the film Krüger has become the Great Leader, an idealized character whose strength and wisdom and sense of isolation is emphasized by means of heavily modelled photography with low-key lighting and tracking camera close-ups of his face whenever he has a speech to deliver. He forms part of a long tradition of historical figures which appear in Nazi films and legitimize National Socialism and the coming of Hitler as some kind of divine providence. *Filmwoche* noted:

Uncle Krüger dies in Europe, bitterness in his heart but with the certain knowledge that so much noble, bold blood cannot flow for nothing. His last prophetic words reveal a vision of the future as he talks of the eventual coming of the hour of judgement. . . .[82]

Even before *Ohm Krüger* was released, Emil Jannings explained to the film press his reasons for playing Krüger and the historical significance of such a figure for contemporary Germany:

President Krüger was the first conscious champion against England, he is an example for us Germans who are now leading the fight against British imperialism. I played him because he has been chosen to start a struggle which shall be concluded in our lifetime.[83]

Goebbels's propaganda machine was only too willing to exploit the parallel between the leader of the Transvaal and the Führer. According to a *Zeitschriftendienst* (press directive) issued on the morning of the film's première, the essence of *Ohm Krüger* was: 'what it means to be a popular national leader in an historically difficult hour'.[84] The press were instructed to hail the release of the film as a 'special event': an edition of *Simplizissimus* was dedicated to the film and a sixty-page booklet was printed, explaining detailed artistic and political events. However, a week before the film was due to be released a Bavarian newspaper inadvertently referred to the film as 'politically orientated'. This prompted the RMVP to issue the following directive on how *Ohm Krüger* was to be reported:

When discussing the film you are requested to note in particular the artistic qualities in the usual number of lines. Should it be referred to as a 'great politically orientated film' as it was a few days ago? Of course, you should not ignore the political significance of the film – but this should not form the main part of your appraisal. It is important that this film is presented to the public as a work of art and that the political aspect is inserted in this artistic framework.[85]

[82] Loc. cit.
[83] *Filmwelt*, no. 50, 13 December 1940. Cf. Janning's radio speech on the making of *Ohm Krüger* and his views on the role of film as a propaganda medium. Quoted in *Nationalsozialistiche Monatshefte*, vol. 147, June 1942, Berlin, pp. 342-3.
[84] ZD, 101, no. 4317, 4 April 1941.
[85] BA, *Zsg. 102/63*, 4 April 1941.

What emerges from this directive is that Goebbels was as concerned with the artistic appreciation of the film as with the political message. By investing so heavily in *Ohm Krüger* he was attempting to prove that the Nazi film industry could make a distinctive contribution to film art, particularly at such a crucial stage in the war. A month after its première a special SD Report was commissioned on the effect of the film. It came to the conclusion that overall it had been a resounding success:

All reports from the various areas of the Reich confirm that this film has far exceeded the great expectations aroused in all sections of the community by the extensive press campaign. *The film is considered the outstanding achievement of the current year in the cinema*, and particular mention is made of its excellent blending of political message, artistic construction and first class performances. . . .[86]

As far as anti-British propaganda was concerned, it was noted that attitudes towards Britain had hardened and that it captured the present mood of the German people towards England. However, the SD also mentions certain muted criticisms of the film, particularly among the more educated sections of the community:

Critical opinions are comparatively few, but they tend to raise some fundamental points. Firstly, some scenes are 'too heavily loaded'; for example, the English missionaries' distribution of arms and prayer books. The danger of such propaganda exaggerations is to reduce the plausibility of historical episodes in film drama. . . . Furthermore, the question was raised by people with first-hand experience, and by experts on Africa, whether it was opportune to idealize the Boers in this, since along with their good elements as a race they also display some pronounced negative factors. . . . The character of the mixed race is ambivalent, and in view of Greater Germany's colonial tasks after the final victory, it cannot be presented as a picture of the Germanic ideal.

Despite such criticism, Goebbels could be well pleased with the reception given to *Ohm Krüger*. Its success was due not only to the expense lavished on the film but more importantly to the way in which the anti-British propaganda elements were skilfully and effectively handled. The simplicity of the message and the expert manner in which it was employed meant that *Ohm Krüger* remained a potent propaganda weapon until the

[86] BA, *R58/160*, 12 May 1941.

end of the war.[87] In particular the message of heroic resistance in the face of overwhelming odds was seen by Goebbels to be apposite to German's situation after Stalingrad and the military reverses and eventual occupation that followed. Thus in 1944 Goebbels instructed that *Ohm Krüger* be re-released in the hope that it would inspire the *Volkssturm* to similar efforts.[88]

The films discussed in this section reveal that after Britain declared war on Germany she became a distinctive enemy and object of hatred in the Nazi cinema. But on balance these films also demonstrate the same hesitancy and ambivalence that characterized anti-Bolshevik film propaganda and the way in which diplomatic considerations impinged upon film-making during the Third Reich.

Hitler's love–hate relationship towards Britain clearly affected the film industry and explains to a certain extent the admiration and respect that one finds in these films before 1940. Once it became obvious that Britain would not capitulate or come to some sort of agreement, distinctive stereotypes begin to emerge on the cinema screens. Suddenly the British are capitalists and imperialists; they are seen posing both a racial and a military threat. They àre responsible for the outbreak of war (*Gentlemen*); they enslave heroic little nations (*Der Fuchs von Glenarvon, Mein Leben für Irland, Ohm Krüger*); they inhibit scientific and medical progress (*Germanin*) and they impede German colonization in Africa (*Carl Peters*). Furthermore, the English are portrayed as spreading disease (*Die englische Krankheit*) and are racially 'the Jews among the Aryans' (*Die Rothschilds*).

Seven *Staatsauftragsfilme* were produced between 1940 and 1943, when the last anti-British film (*Titanic*) was released. Once again, despite the success of *Ohm Krüger*, it should be noted that Goebbels decided against making such expensive political films about the enemy in the last two years of the war. In comparison with those films having anti-Bolshevik leitmotivs, the films in this section are undoubtedly more impressive stylistically. No doubt this was due to the fact that

---

[87] It remained a favourite with German youth. A. U. Sander's 1944 survey discovered that it was their sixth most popular film. Sander, p. 118.
[88] ZD, 156, no. 833, 3 November 1944.

in general they cost more, making possible elaborate productions and talented artists to be engaged. However as propaganda vehicles of hatred they still lacked (with the notable
exception of *Ohm Krüger*) the conviction, the emotional
appeal, and the consistency that marked the most powerful image of the enemy to be portrayed in the Nazi cinema—the Jew.

THE IMAGE OF THE JEW

> I cannot understand it. If somebody had told me earlier that
> my father's generation tortured human beings to death merely
> because they were Jews, I would have slapped his face.[89]

According to George Mosse, 'a myth is the strongest belief held
by the group, and its adherents feel themselves to be an army
of truth fighting an army of evil.'[90] Myth was at the centre of
National Socialism. During the first year of the war Goebbels
informed his staff at the RMVP that 'propaganda does not have
anything to do with the truth! We serve truth by serving a German
victory.'[91] Thus, as Jay Baird noted, 'the authoritarian power
network and the mass communication and propaganda machinery all served a higher ideal, the National Socialist world view
based on myth and the irrational.'[92]

One of the purposes of this book has been to analyse the
way in which Nazi film propaganda reflects National Socialist
ideology. This ideology embraced a veritable plethora of mythical themes ranging from *Blut und Boden*, the heroic warrior,
to the Bolshevik *Untermensch*, the British 'plutocrats', and the
mystical concept of the *Führerprinzip*. But perhaps the most
important element in the Nazi world view was the myth of
the 'international Jewish conspiracy'. Karl Dietrich Bracher
observed that 'National Socialist control and victory over Jews
and "inferior peoples", the *Völkisch*-racial revolution, remained the single genuine core in Hitler's *Weltanschauung*.'[93]
As with most aspects of Nazi ideology, Goebbels's exploitation of anti-Semitism offered little that was new. Instead he
adopted the *Völkisch* tradition of the primacy of the people

---

[89] Quoted in H. Vogt, *The Burden of Guilt* (London, 1965), preface.
[90] Mosse, *Nazi Culture*, p. xxiii.
[91] Von Oven, p. 32.   [92] Baird, p. 4.
[93] K. D. Bracher, *Die deutsche Diktatur* (Berlin, 1969), p. 198.

and abhorrence of the Jew which had embedded itself firmly into German life and thought for over a century.[94] Furthermore, this contempt for the Jews was legitimized in a number of so-called scientific investigations by writers like Gobineau and Houston Stewart Chamberlain. Ernst Nolte has argued that their racism was 'first and foremost an instrument of defense of a leading class which was threatened or had already lost its power, but yet which still remained influential, and self-conscious.'[95] Whatever the reasons, such racism undoubtedly appealed to the needs of modern man and became an integral part of that cultural pessimism and basic insecurity that found expression in the works of de Lagard, Langbehn, and Moeller van den Bruck.[96]

Goebbels maintained that the purpose of propaganda was to persuade the audience to believe in the viewpoint expressed by the propagandist. But if propaganda is to be effective it must, in a sense, always preach to those who are already partially converted. Aldous Huxley once stated:

Propaganda gives force and direction to the successive movements of popular feeling and desire; but it does not do much to create these movements. The Propagandist is a man who canalises an already existing stream. In a land where there is no water, he digs in vain.[97]

The Nazi attitude to the Jews is an excellent example of this facet of propaganda. It cannot be argued rationally that anti-Semitism was a result of National Socialism or that Goebbels's propaganda made Germans anti-Semitic,[98] but the fact remains that the Third Reich was responsible for an attempt at genocide of unparalleled scope and brutality. This

[94] See P. Pulzer, The Rise of Political Anti-Semitism in Germany and Austria, (London, 1964), and R. Levy, The Downfall of the Anti-Semitic Political Parties in Imperial Germany (Yale, 1975).

[95] E. Nolte, Der Fascismus in seiner Epoch (Munich, 1963), p. 364. Cf. this with Franz Neumann who contends that such racism was a substitute for the class struggle. Neumann, p. 125.

[96] For a discussion of these writers, see F. Stern, pp. 61-3, 89-92. Peter Gay came to the conclusion that anti-Semitism was an irrational protest against the modern world. Freud, Jews and Other Germans (Oxford, 1978).

[97] A. Huxley, 'Notes on Propaganda', Harper's Magazine, vol. 174, December 1936, pp. 32-41.

[98] After the First World War, for example, the impact of the 'Protocols of Zion' was, for a while, greater in Britain than in Germany and the idea of a Jewish world conspiracy influenced even Churchill. W. Laqueur, Out of the Ruins of Europe (London, 1972), p. 419.

situation may be attributed partly to the effects of propaganda itself and partly also to the closed political environment within which that propaganda was necessarily working. Thus when Hitler came to power he needed the Jews as a permanent scapegoat on which those in the movement could work off their resentment; the Jew was manipulated to fulfil a psychological need for Germany. Nazi propaganda simply used the historical predisposition of the audience towards an anti-Semitic explanation for Germany's cultural, economic, and political grievances.

This historical hatred of the Jews was increased by the credence given inside the Party to the 'Protocols of the Elders of Zion', according to which an international clique of Jewish conspirators were preparing to assume total domination over all nations of the world.[99] The alleged 'international conspiracy' was an obsession with Goebbels as it was with Hitler, but although the Führer regarded the 'protocols' as 'absolutely genuine',[100] Goebbels was more cautious, admitting that: 'we cannot speak flatly of a conspiracy of the Jewish race against Western man; this conspiracy is more a matter of race than of thought-out intentions. Jews will always act according to their instincts.'[101]

According to Hitler, the war was less a struggle among nations than a racial war to the finish between Aryan and Jew.[102] Goebbels often referred to Hitler's 'prophecy'; thus, although he recognized a united international Jewish front as good propaganda he also saw it as real threat:

The Jewish race has prepared the war; it is the spiritual originator of the whole misfortune that has overtaken humanity. Jewry must pay for its crime just as our Führer prophesied in his speech in the Reichstag when he said that the Jewish race would be wiped out in Europe and possibly throughout the entire world.[103]

The slogan of the Jewish conspiracy was meant to prepare the people for the successive steps towards the 'final solution' of the Jewish problem. To this end a number of films were

[99] See N. Cohn, *Warrant for Genocide: The Myth of the Jewish World Conspiracy and the Protocols of Zion* (London, 1967).
[100] Lochner, p. 296.
[101] IfZ, *Goebbels Tagebuch*, entry for 13 May 1943.
[102] Cf. speech of 30 January 1939, reprinted in Baynes, p. 741.
[103] Lochner, p. 183. See also, diary entry of 20 March 1942, p. 94.

prepared in co-ordination with a full-scale propaganda campaign waged in the other media in order to make German people aware of the dangers posed by Jewry and also to rationalize the measures that would have to be taken for the genocide that was to follow.

Anti-Jewish characters and themes recur throughout the cinema of the Third Reich. In the early *Kampfzeit* films, the Jews are shown to have deliberately fragmented German society by creating a rift between worker and government. It is the Jews who prompt the Poles to commit atrocities against German minorities (*Heimkehr*); and it is a Jew who attempts to assassinate the Iron Chancellor (*Bismarck*). However the first two anti-Jewish films, *Robert und Bertram* and *Leinen aus Irland* (both 1939), caricature the subhuman Jew within the framework of comedy.[104] In the same year Goebbels forbade the use of the term 'anti-Semitic' and replaced it by 'defence against the Jews' or 'opposition to Jews'.[105] In both *Robert und Bertram* und *Leinen aus Irland* Jews are stereotyped: despite being distinguishable by their repellent physical features, they also represent an economic and sexual threat to Western civilization because of their ability to assimilate themselves in different societies.[106]

These two relatively innocuous films were only the precursors to a number of films that were increasingly anti-Semitic. The course taken by Goebbels was similar to the course he chose in 1933: a series of three films, shown consecutively at short intervals, each one dealing with different aspects of international Jewry. In 1940, three major anti-Semitic films, *Die Rothschilds*, *Jud Süss* (*Jew Suss*), and *Der ewige Jude* (*The Eternal/Wandering Jew*), were released in this manner and represent the RMVP's cinematic efforts to prepare the German public for the full-scale extermination. Deportation of the Jews from Austria and Czechoslovakia to Poland began on 12 October 1939 and by February 1940 Jews were being deported

---

[104] For a detailed, but exaggerated account of the anti-Semitic tendencies in *Robert und Bertram* see Hollstein, pp. 48–52. However, this work contains an excellent analysis of *Leinen aus Irland*, pp. 53–7.

[105] ZD, Issue 6, no. 222, 13 June 1939.

[106] The SD reported an 'extremely favourable reception' for *Leinen aus Irland*: 'spectators called out things like "dirty Jew" and "exploiter".' BA, R58/150/2, 19 April 1940.

from Germany to the East. In May of the same year Goebbels informed all film-makers and critics:

Films in which Jews appear are not to be labelled as anti-Jewish. We want it to be made perfectly clear that such films are not determined by any tendentious considerations, but reflect historical facts as they are.[107]

By Goebbels's own definition of historical objectivity, the films exhibited showed 'Jewry as it is' and could not be accused of any particular bias. *Die Rothschilds*, the first film to be released, has already been discussed in some detail. The following analysis will take *Jud Süss* and particularly *Der ewige Jude*, and look at how these 'historical facts' were disseminated.

Jud Süss (*Jew Suss*, 1940)

Directed by Veit Harlan, *Jud Süss* was produced by Terra from a pseudo-historical dramatization of the Jewish question by Ludwig Metzger, Eberhard Möller, and Harlan. In line with Goebbels's directives, it gave the impression of being a faithful historical presentation. Even before the film was released the German public were being informed that the script was the result of 'an exhaustive study of the Württemberg state archives'. In fact the film was a radical distortion of Leon Feuchtwanger's original novel of the same name in which the Jews are portrayed as the eternal scapegoat. The historical Joseph Süss-Oppenheimer was born in Heidelberg in 1692 and eventually became acquainted with Prince Karl Alexander of Württemberg who, in 1733, became Duke of Württemberg. Süss-Oppenheimer was made his financial adviser and charged with the task of obtaining enough money to pay off the financial debt. Despite making a huge profit, the Württemberg Diet opposed the financial measures and plotted against the Jew. Süss-Oppenheimer was eventually arrested and condemned to death by hanging. The court upheld the sentence but deliberately omitted the only evidence that would have warranted the death penalty, namely, that the accused had engaged in sexual relations with Christian women. However as this would have meant a similar fate for the ladies of the Württemberg court, such evidence was conveniently forgotten

[107] BA, *Zsg. 102/62*, 3 May 1940. *ZD*, Issue 56, no. 2390, 17 May 1940.

and Süss-Oppenheimer was hanged in 1738 on a charge of Christian treachery and hypocrisy.[108] In the following plot summary of the film it can be seen that Veit Harlan deliberately distorted the story of the historical Süss-Openheimer to serve the wider propaganda aims of the Third Reich:

Süss-Oppenheimer of Frankfurt arrives at the Duchy of Württemberg in 1733 which is celebrating the coronation of Karl Alexander (Heinrich George) as Grand Duke of Württemberg. The Duke is characterized as a weak leader whose sensualism leads him into the hands of the Jews. Süss makes large loans of money to the Duke to finance such projects as a new ballet and opera. Süss (Ferdinand Marian) is appointed Finance Minister and he institutes a penal system of taxes, duties, and tolls, causing great suffering among the people of the Duchy. Süss increasingly extends his power, obtains more and more privileges and eventually persuades the Duke to throw the city open to the Jews who arrive in their thousands to the disgust of the German inhabitants. Against the advice of the elderly Rabbi Loew Süss (Werner Krauss), Süss declares his intention of creating the 'Promised Land' in Württemberg. With the help of his secretary Levy (Krauss) he abducts the beautiful Dorothea Sturm (Kristina Söderbaum), daughter of the chief minister Sturm (Eugen Klöpfer) and brutally rapes her while her fiancé (Malte Jaeger), who is planning a revolt against Süss, is tortured in a cellar. Distracted with shame and grief, Dorothea escapes and drowns herself. The finding of her body is the sign for a general revolt, the Duke dies of a heart attack, and Süss's only protection is gone. He is arrested and condemned to death, and then placed in an iron cage and hauled to the top of the scaffold before being executed in the presence of the people. Sturm announces that the Jews must leave the city and hopes that 'this lesson will never be forgotten'.

Before shooting began on the film Veit Harlan visited the Lublin ghetto in Poland and brought back 120 Jews for various parts in the film—although this was forbidden to be mentioned in the press.[109] In a revealing interview with *Der Film* before *Jud Süss* was released, Harlan 'touches' on one of these 'lessons' by drawing a contemporary parallel with events surrounding the historical Süss-Oppenheimer:

Even in the final court scene, the film keeps strictly to historical fact. As is known, the decision to hang Süss was not without its difficulties, as Oppenheimer was a lawyer and used all his business interests, which had brought the people to ruin, in such a skilful way that at first there

---

[108] Details taken from Hollstein, pp. 108–9, and Leiser, p. 81. See also C. Elwenspoek, *Jud Süss Oppenheimer* (Stuttgart, 1926).

[109] ZD, 40, 26 January 1940. Quoted in Wulf, p. 398.

was no lawful case against him. Finally he was brought to justice on the basis of an ancient law which stated: 'should a Jew have relations with a Christian woman he is liable to be put to death'. Here we see an interesting parallel with the Nuremberg Laws.[110]

Harlan's reference to the Nuremberg race laws, which finally named the Jews *persona non grata* in the Reich, reveals once again the aim of the script-writers to dramatize National Socialist ideology by means of historical parallels. Harlan's film attempted to present the historical Süss as the prototype criminal Jew who was currently being dealt with by the Nazi regime. This was achieved by contrasting Aryan and Jewish stereotypes and by emphasizing the specific threat posed by Jews. The final scene in the film is a rationalization both of the measures already taken by the Nazis and the genocide that was to follow. These points can be illustrated by analysing the film dialogue from some of the relevant scenes. The first point to be raised in the film is the inherent rootlessness of the Jew and his ability to assimilate himself in whichever society he chooses. This might be termed the Jew in disguise.

Süss personifies the Jew in disguise; in the opening scene he has shed his distinctive Jewish garb and beard, and attempts to enter Stuttgart where Jews are forbidden. Dressed as an elegant lawyer he succeeds in passing through the city's checkpoint with his fellow traveller Dorothea Sturm. The following discussion highlights not only the abhorred internationalism of the Jew, but also the contaminating sexual threat to the Nordic race posed by the Jews, which ends in the brutal rape of Dorothea by Süss:

DOROTHEA. Oh but I would love to travel — throughout the whole world preferably! You must have travelled a great deal, mustn't you? Have you been to Paris?
SÜSS. Yes.
DOROTHEA. To Versailles?
SÜSS [*nods*]. Yes.
DOROTHEA [*overwhelmed*]. Oh. I envy you! Where else have you been?
SÜSS. Oh — London, Vienna, Rome, Madrid . . .
DOROTHEA [*sighs*]. Oh . . .
SÜSS. . . . Lisbon . . .
DOROTHEA. Heavens — that's nearly the whole world. Where was it best? I mean, where did you feel most at home?

[110] *Der Film*, no. 3, 20 January 1940. For an interesting account of *Jud Süss*, see Hollstein, pp. 76–107.

SÜSS [*smiling*]. At home? Everywhere!
DOROTHEA [*amazed*]. Everywhere? Have you no home then?
SÜSS. Oh yes — the world!
DOROTHEA. But surely you must have felt happiest somewhere?
SÜSS. I think that I've never felt so happy in my whole life, ravishing
lady, as here in Stuttgart near you.

It was important as far as Nazi propaganda was concerned
to point out not only the Jew in disguise but also the archetypal 'subhuman' Jew that was depicted in *Der Stürmer* and
Rosenberg's scurrilous anti-Jewish newspaper the *Völkischer
Beobachter*. This aspect of international Jewry was presented
in even more detail in *Der ewige Jude*, but was also portrayed in
Jud Süss. It was achieved by contrasting the elegant Süss with
the elderly Rabbi Loew. In an interview with a film magazine,
Harlan elaborated on the reasons behind this juxtaposition:

It is meant to show how all these different temperaments and characters
— the pious Patriarch, the wily swindler, the penny-pinching merchant,
and so on — are ultimately derived from the same roots. . . . Around the
middle of the film we show the Purim festival, a victory festival which
the Jews celebrate as a festival of revenge on the Goyim, the Christians.
Here I am depicting authentic Jewry as it was then and as it now continues unchecked in Poland. In contrast to this original Jewry we are
presented with Süss, the elegant financial adviser to the Court, the clever
politician, in short, the Jew in disguise.[111]

In the following scene, Rabbi Loew represents authentic
Jewry and Süss the Jew in disguise. Their exchange, in which
Loew warns Süss against flaunting his power and influence in
such an ostentatious manner, reveals that not only do they
come from the same roots but they also have similar motives
—world domination by Jews and the exploitation of Germany:

[*Süss receives Rabbi Loew in his palace: he is a white-bearded old
man, wearing a long robe with his prayer shawl hanging over it, and
he coughs wheezily.*]
SÜSS. The stars in ascendancy are favourable Rabbi — because they have
to be.
LOEW [*in a Jewish dialect*]. Can you determine the way of the stars as
one wishes?
SÜSS. You can't determine the ways of stars, but you can determine
men's ways, if you decide for them the ways of the stars.
LOEW [*in dialect*]. My son Joseph, the Lord is looking at you and sees
that you have become vain and haughty as a peacock. The Lord's
punishment is harsh when Jews forget who they are.

[111] *Der Film*, loc. cit.

SÜSS [*visibly contrite*]. What shall I do, Rabbi?
LOEW. Haven't you got a palace like Solomon [*he peeps through an open door*]. Hm — don't you sleep in a golden bed [*they walk into the library*]. Haven't you walls full of books, that you shouldn't read? [*He taps the shelves with his stick. His glance falls on the curtains, he feels the material*]. Didn't the damask cost twelve thaler?
SÜSS [*gently reproaching*]. But my dear Rabbuni!
LOEW. The Lord wants his people to serve in sackcloth and ashes to be scattered. Hidden, in this way, they reign over peoples of the earth.
SÜSS. How can I rule if I don't show myself to people?
LOEW. If you want to rule over Gentiles, take control of their money — but keep away from the Prince's squabbles.
SÜSS. If I control the Prince, I control the people!
LOEW. The Prince might be pardoned but the Jew is hanged!
SÜSS. God's will would not wish to prevent me making the promised land of Israel in Württemberg. It's already here before us — I just need to grasp it with my hands. And over there I can already see milk and honey flowing — for Israel! Am I not allowed over the Jordan through God's will? Can that be God's will?
LOEW. You set out God's words to suit yourself.
SÜSS. One should interpret God's words to suit Israel, that's God's will, my dear Rabbi!
LOEW. What should I do? Should I lie?
SÜSS. You don't need to lie — tell them the second truth — tell them *our* sort of truth.
LOEW. What does that mean?
SÜSS. He who dares!

Four days before *Jud Süss* was to be given its première in Berlin, a *Zeitschriftendienst* instructed the press on how they were to interpret such scenes. The point to be noted was that once Jews like Süss gained responsible positions, they 'exploited power, not for the good of the community, but for their own racial ends'. This argument led logically to the international Jewish conspiracy, which challenged the very foundations and values of German civilization. The press were encouraged to stress these dangers by means of the film and to incorporate other examples in their reviews:

It is the duty of all newspapers to point out this typically Jewish trait and to take the opportunity of the film's première to impress on our people, with perhaps other examples as well, the message that every Jew has only his well-being and that of his racial brothers in mind, even when he pretends generous motives.[112]

By concentrating on the *criminal* elements believed to be

[112] ZD, 74, no. 3216, 20 September 1940.

part of Jewish characteristics, their amorality, their lack of
conscience and scruples, *Jud Süss* provided the historical
example for the Nazis' answer to the Jewish menace. Thus the
last scene where Süss-Oppenheimer is hanged provides the
justification for the evacuation of the Jews from Germany in
1940. With the exception of Süss, the Jews are dirty, fat, hook-
nosed, and physically repellent. In contrast are the true Nordic
prototypes: Dorothea the classic German maiden, her father,
the incorruptible Sturm, and Christian Faber her ascetic fiancé.
However in the final court-room scene where Süss is tried and
hanged, he has shed his 'mask' and resembles the original Jew
as portrayed by Loew and Levy. Even his speech is altered; instead of the courtly tones used until now he speaks in the
Yiddish dialect:

JUDGE. There he sits — the unholy Jew. For months he has been issuing
nothing but lies, lies, and more lies!
SÜSS. What you accuse me of I only did according to the wishes of my
Duke. [*Public laughs scornfully*] ... In the charter it is written [*shouting*] ... you only need to read it. I was only an obedient servant of
my master! [*Boos from the courtroom.*]
STURM. Do you really expect us to believe that this slip of paper that
you have swindled from the Duke can absolve the record of your evil
deeds?
[*The court withdraws and eventually returns with the verdict.*]
CHAIRMAN. After a trial lasting a month we have found you guilty of
the crimes you have been accused of: blackmail, profiteering, sexual
indecency, procuring, and high treason. But the Jew's guilt seems to
me far greater when one considers the shame and suffering our people
have been subjected too. And so I think it appropriate that the one
who has suffered most should speak.
STURM. Gentlemen, not retribution, only what is right!
JUDGE. Speak freely, Sturm, you have experienced the greatest suffering. . . .
STURM. Sorrow does not speak of justice; an eye for an eye, a tooth for
a tooth — that is not our way. Just refer to the old criminal court of
the Reich, there it is written for eternity: 'So then a Jew with a Christian woman' . . . [*Sturm hands the book to the Chairman who reads
it out aloud*] . . .
CHAIRMAN. 'Should a Jew make a union of the flesh with a Christian
then he will be put to death by the rope.'

The words of the Chairman merge into the hangman's voice
announcing the judgement at the market-place: 'Should a Jew
make a union of the flesh with a Christian then he will be put

to death by the rope.' Süss is led to the scaffold, the drum beats, and he is hoisted up in a cage in front of the silent gathering.

SÜSS [*screaming*]. I was only a loyal servant of my master! What can I do if your Duke was a traitor! I'll make up for everything — I swear it. Take my property, my money, but spare my life. I want to live, to . . .

The hangman gives a sign and the Jew's voice is abruptly stilled. The cage floor opens and the dead man's feet fall limply out, swinging to and fro, then stop.

STURM [*addressing the people*]. The State Council announces the wish of the Württemberg people that all Jews should leave within the next three days. Given in Stuttgart February 1738. May our descendants hold on to this law so that they may be spared the suffering and harm to their lives and property and to the blood of their children and their children's children.

The last scene depicting Jud Süss dangling from the hangman's noose conveyed Goebbels's message to the German people. The parallel between Württemberg in 1738 and Germany in 1940 could not have been missed by film audiences. Newspapers referred to a 'phantom that was caught in time'.[113] The *Völkischer Beobachter* saw it as a fight to the end between 'the polluting Jewish spirit and a healthy German national core'. It went on to praise the film for 'its complete avoidance of bias, and its clear demonstration of how Jewry in the past has conspired to dominate the globe'.[114]

Jud Süss was shown first in Venice on 5 September 1940, where, according to the German critics, it was an 'unqualified success'.[115] The Berlin première on 24 September 1940 was attended by Goebbels and numerous leading officials of the Party as well as many German film-makers. The following day the press hailed it as 'the decisive breakthrough in creating cinematic art out of our National Socialist ideology'.[116] Himmler was so impressed with the production that he ordered every SS man to see it.[117] The film was subsequently awarded

[113] *Deutsche Allgemeine Zeitung*, no. 461/2, 26 September 1940. Quoted in Hollstein, p. 85.
[114] *VB*, 3 August 1940.
[115] *Deutsche Allgemeine Zeitung*, loc. cit. Cf. Wulf, p. 402.
[116] *VB*, 26 September 1940.
[117] Reproduced in Wulf, p. 405. Goebbels later wrote in his diary: 'Himmler is at the moment carrying out the transportation of Jews from German towns to

the *Prädikate* 'politically and artistically especially valuable' and 'valuable for youth'.

According to the SD Report of 28 November 1940, *'Jud Süss* continues to receive an extraordinarily favourable response':

The total effect of the film can be gauged from such spontaneous expressions of opinion as 'One feels like washing one's hands afterwards' . . . Among the scenes especially singled out by the public — apart from the rape scene — is the entry of the Jews and all their belongings into Stuttgart. In fact this scene has repeatedly prompted *demonstrations against Jews*. In Berlin, for example, there were shouts of 'Drive the Jews from the Kurfürstendamm!' and 'Throw the last of the Jews out of Germany!'[118]

One reason for the popularity of the film was the extremely high quality of the production and particularly the superb acting performances. The SD noted:

It is uniformly reported that in this film, contrary to the majority of other current feature films, it is the acting performances which are being praised above all. A report from Nuremberg, for instance, calls it 'frighteningly real' as far as the portrayal of the Jew is concerned. In this respect, the film is much more impressive and convincing than *Die Rothschilds*.[119]

In fact Werner Krauss, who played the cunning secretary Levy and the grasping Rabbi Loew, was so convincing that he asked Goebbels to announce publicly that he was not Jewish but a loyal Aryan merely playing a part as an actor in the service of the State.[120] Without question *Jud Süss* contributed to the radical anti-Semitism already prevalent in Germany and facilitated the way for the evacuation of the Jews.[121] Not only

ghettoes in the East. I've ordered that extensive film documentation be made of this. We'll use this material to great effect in the subsequent education of our people.' IfZ, *Goebbels Tagebuch*, 27 April 1942.

[118] BA, *R58/156*, 28 November 1940. It emerged from this report that both parents and teachers were against showing the film to children because of the 'extremely powerful psychological after-effects'. The RMVP overruled these objections because parents were still complaining in 1941 of the 'unrestricted' showings of the film to young people in the Youth Film Hours. BA, *R58/159*, 3 April 1941.

[119] BA, *R58/156*, 28 November 1940.

[120] Directive of 25 September 1940, in Boelcke, p. 526.

[121] At the Auschwitz trial, former SS Rottenführer Stefan Baretzki confessed that the effect of showing the film was to instigate maltreatment of prisoners. Quoted in Leiser, p. 85. The film was also shown to 'Aryan' populations in Eastern Europe where concentration camps were being established, to elicit hatred against evacuated Jews and in order to prevent any sympathy shown to them. *Jud Süss* was always shown in these territories when a new deportation was imminent; Wulf, *Theater und Film*, pp. 405-6.

did the film succeed in bringing together themes and archetypes that created the desired antipathy towards Jews, but it
did so under the guise of entertainment that resulted in a great
box-office success.

Der ewige Jude (The Eternal/Wandering Jew, 1940)

Der ewige Jude received its première in Berlin two months after
Jud Süss on 29 November 1940. It was subtitled 'A cinematic
contribution to the problem of world Jewry'. Produced by
Deutsche Film-Herstellungs und Verwertungs GmbH, a eu-
phemism for the Reich Propaganda Department, this documentary film was directed by Fritz Hippler from an idea and
with a commentary by Dr Eberhard Taubert.

The concept of the 'eternal or wandering Jew' was older than
National Socialism; it derived from the Christian legend of
Ahasver, a Jew who prevented Jesus from resting while he was
carrying the cross. Since then, according to the legend, as
punishment he has had to travel the world without the release
of death. Nazi propaganda saw in this proof that other races
had already persecuted the Jews. In 1937 they set up an exhibition in Munich of 'degenerate art' under the heading of the
'Eternal Jew'. The point of resurrecting and amplifying this
old legend was to demonstrate that Jews had no feelings or
civilized qualities.

These accusations are repeated in *Der ewige Jude*; by appealing to primitive, medieval conceptions of a wandering Jew
bearing great epidemics of the plague in an effort to desecrate
other races, the film attempts to strengthen existing prejudices
and to create new ones. Because it was believed that the Jew
never revealed his true face, the facts could be distorted and
presented as revelations. In order that the full extent of this
vehemence should be made clear, I have quoted in full the plot
summary from the *Illustrierte Film-Kurier*, the film programme
which accompanied *Der ewige Jude*:

The film begins with an impressive expedition through the Jewish
ghettoes in Poland. We are shown Jewish living quarters, which in our
view cannot be called houses. In these dirty rooms lives and prays a race,
which earns its living not by work but by haggling and swindling. From
the little urchin to the old man, they stand in the streets, trading and
bargaining. Using trick photography, we are shown how the Jewish racial

mixture in Asia Minor developed and flooded the entire world. We see a parallel to this in the itinerant routes of rats, which are the parasites and bacillus-carriers among animals, just as the Jews occupy the same position among mankind. The Jew has always known how to assimiliate his external appearance to that of his host. Contrasted are the same Jewish types, first the Eastern Jew with his kaftan, beard, and sideburns, and then the clean-shaven, Western European Jew. This strikingly demonstrates how he has deceived the Aryan people. Under this mask he increased his influence more and more in Aryan nations and climbed to higher-ranking positions. But he could not change his inner being.

After the banishment of the Jews from Europe was lifted, following the age of Enlightenment, the Jew succeeded within the course of several decades in dominating the world economy, before the various host nations realized — and this despite the fact that they made up only 1 per cent of the world population. An excerpt from an American film about the 'Rothschilds', made by Jews, reveals to us the cunning foundations of their banking empire. Then we see how Jews, working for their international finance, drive the German people into the November Revolution. They then shed their anonymity and step out openly on to the stage of political and cultural life. Thus the men who were responsible for the disgraceful debasement of the German people are paraded before us. Incontestable examples are shown of how they robbed the country and the people of immense sums. As well as gaining financial supremacy they were able to dominate cultural life. The repulsive pictures of so-called Jewish 'art' reveal the complete decline of cultural life at that time. Using original sequences from contemporary films, the degrading and destructive tendency of Jewish power is exposed. For hundreds of years German artists have glorified figures from the Old Testament, knowing full well the real face of Jewry. How the Jew actually looks is shown in scenes shot by Jews themselves in a 'culture film' of a Purim festival, which is still celebrated today to commemorate the slaughter of 75,000 anti-Semitic Persians, and the doctrine with which future Rabbis in Jewish schools are educated to be political pedagogues. We look into a Jewish 'Talmud' class and experience the oriental tone of the ceremony in a Jewish synagogue, where Jews conduct business deals among themselves during the holy services.

However, the cruel face of Judaism is most brutally displayed in the final scenes, in which original shots of a kosher butchering are revealed. These film documents of the inhuman slaughter of cattle and sheep without anaesthesia provide conclusive evidence of a brutality which is simply inconceivable to all Aryan people. In shining contrast, the film closes with pictures of German people and German order which fill the viewer with a feeling of deep gratification for belonging to a race whose Führer is fundamentally solving the Jewish problem.[122]

The plot summary shows that the film runs through the whole gamut of Nazi allegations against the Jews and these can

---

[122] *Illustrierte Film-Kurier*, no. 3152. Also quoted in Hollstein, p. 108.

be seen as a five-pronged attack. Like most effective propaganda films in documentary format, *Der ewige Jude* moves from the general to the specific. The first section of the film establishes the repellent nature of the Jewish stereotype in his natural environment—the ghetto. Scenes of the Warsaw ghetto are accompanied by a commentary claiming that the Jews have always lived like this:[123]

The civilized Jew that we know in Germany only gives us half the picture of their racial character. This film shows genuine shots of the Polish ghettoes. . . . We recognize that here there lies a plague spot which threatens the health of the Aryan people. Richard Wagner once said: 'The Jew is the evil force behind the decay of man!' And these pictures confirm the accuracy of his statement.

The camera then pans a 'typical' Jewish home. There is a close-up of a mass of flies on a wall; the room is filthy: 'The home life of the Jews shows a marked lack of creative ability. To put it plainly, the Jewish houses are dirty and neglected.' The cinema audience was to find underlined in the juxtaposition of image and commentary the judgement that 'typical' Jews did not wash, merely preferring to live in a state of filth, and interested only in trading. Jews are characterized as materialists, they are not creative but imitative:

Rarely will you find a Jew engaged in useful work. . . . The uninitiated will at first feel inclined to view these haggling children as a sign of great poverty. But to the experienced observer it soon becomes clear that they are proud of behaving like their parents. These children see no ideals before them like our own youth. . . . For the Jews, business is a kind of holy transaction. How he earns his living is a matter of complete indifference to him. . . . Those things that are valued by the creative Aryan have been reduced by the Jew to the level of a mere piece of merchandise, which he buys and sells but cannot produce himself. . . . The Jews are a race without farmers and without manual workers — a race of parasites!

The film then moves on to examine the spread and assimilation of the Jews. The ability of Jews to assimilate themselves in alien societies was a particular feature of both *Die Rothschilds* and *Jud Süss*. In an interview with *Der Film*, Fritz

[123] In fact these scenes were shot in Warsaw and Lodz, where the Nazis had herded together almost half a million Jews, sometimes thirteen to a room *en route* for Auschwitz. For a moving description of how material was shot for the film see B. Goldstein, *Die Sterne sind Zeugen. Der Untergang der polnischen Juden* (Munich, 1965), pp. 56–8.

Hippler outlined the reasons why this theme was so important in all anti-Semitic films:

Today one takes for granted people with whom one comes in contact. A citizen today may well find that the Jew who has lived for decades in a European city makes a perfectly civilized and normal impression. But how different it would be if one were to be shown pictures of Jews before and during their migrations. I have made it my special task in this film to show these contrasts.[124]

Animated maps show how the Jews, starting from Palestine ('the spiritual centre for international Jewry'), have diffused the world, which, particularly in the nineteenth century 'with it vague ideas of human equality and freedom, gave the Jew a powerful impetus'. This expansion is illustrated as a dense network over the map which looks like festering sores. Then follows an analogy between Jews and rats which Hitler had first used in *Mein Kampf*.[125] Hippler cuts to a sequence of rats devouring grain and scurrying in packs to fill the screen. The commentary continues:

Comparable with the Jewish wanderings through history are the mass migrations of an equally restless animal, the rat. . . . Wherever rats appear they bring ruin, they ravage human property and foodstuffs. In this way they spread disease: plague, leprosy, typhoid, cholera, dysentery, etc. They are cunning, cowardly, and cruel and are found mostly in packs. In the animal world they represent the element of craftiness and subterranean destruction — no different from the Jews among mankind!

Hippler could be sure that such images would nauseate and possibly even antagonize many spectators. He therefore used this strong psychological position to overwhelm the audience with an abundance of 'hard' statistical 'facts' to prove that such parasites were also involved in almost every aspect of international crime:

The Jewish race of parasites perpetuates a large part of international crime. Thus in 1932 the part played by Jews, who represent only a small percentage of the world population, in the entire drug trade of the world was 34 per cent, in robberies 47 per cent, in gambling 47 per cent, in international crime organizations 82 per cent, and in prostitution 98 per cent.

As these figures are being announced, a succession of Jewish 'criminal faces' are shown in an attempt to convince the audience by linking the stereotype with the statistics and thus

[124] *Der Film*, no. 48, 30 November 1940.   [125] Hitler, p. 253.

allowing them no time for critical reflection. By comparing the unshaven 'original' Jew with the sophisticated 'assimilated' Jew, the only possible conclusion was that 'these physiognomies refute categorically the liberalistic theories of the equality of all those who bear a human face.' The purpose of this crude masquerade was to make a visual connection between Jews of the Eastern ghettoes and those living in German towns. Hippler therefore induced the fear that descendants of assimilated Jews would not be distinguishable from Aryans.[126]

The third section demonstrates the financial power of the Jews, beginning with an extract from Alfred Werker's American comedy *The House of Rothschilds* (1934) which is made to appear as a searing indictment of Jewish financial practices. It was introduced to German audiences as follows:

Here we show an excerpt from the film which depicts the history of the House of Rothschilds. American Jews produced it.... They honour their hero in typical Jewish fashion and take delight in the way old Meier Amschel defrauds the state which made him welcome and feigns poverty in order to avoid paying taxes.

Once again, the film is following closely Hitler's discourses in *Mein Kampf* when he outlined the rise of the Jews from pedlars to bankers.[127] The spread of the Rothschilds is representative of the whole of the Jews. Such anti-Semitism can be traced to a defensive reaction in late nineteenth-century Germany by the lower middle classes, artisans, and shopkeepers to the advent of full-scale capitalism. We have already seen that intellectually the anti-Semitism of this period was a reaction to features of modernity such as enlightened self-interest. It was also fed by an economic aspect in which Jews were perceived as agents of change, promoting such things as free trade and instalment payments. Amschel says to his sons: 'Union is strength, our five banking houses will rule Europe ... One firm one family. When this power comes, think of the ghetto.' The expansion of the Rothschild family over Europe is then traced on an animated map. It is noted that the course taken by the Jewish race is the same as that taken by plague-carrying vermin. This serves as an introduction to the next sequence which

---

[126] According to the SD Report these scenes made a deep impression on many viewers. BA, *R58/157*, 20 January 1940.
[127] Hitler, pp. 258–64.

looks at the increasing power of Jewish capitalism over international banking, politics, and over Germany in the 1920s:

Today New York is the centre of Jewish power, and the New York stock exchange, the financial centre of the world, is ruled by Jewish banking houses — Kahn, Loew, Warburg, Hanauer, Wertheim, Stern, etc.

The selection of individuals chosen for attack is then linked with a particular hatred for international Marxism and for the cultural movements of the 1920s. A title informs the audience that it is 1918, a documentary film of Jewish politicians in Weimar is shown, and the narrator continues:

1918. Let us remember those vile days, when Germans lay defenceless. It was then that the Jews seized their chance. Other Jews, who represented the radical line, proclaimed against every form of public order, and incited the people to revolt against everything that existed . . . Karl Marx, son of the Rabbi and lawyer Margochei in Trèves. The founder and organizer of the SDP was the Jew Ferdinand Lasalle-Wolfson. The Jewess Rosa Luxemburg — whose real name was Emma Goldmann, one of the most notorious Communist agitators.

It is interesting to note that at a time when America was still neutral and Germany had a pact with the USSR there is no hesitation about expressing views which for different reasons could have been offensive to both Americans and Russians.

Jews also dominate the fields of culture and religion, where, we are told, they are at their most dangerous:

Jews are most dangerous when allowed to meddle in other people's culture, religion, and art, and to give their presumptuous judgements on it. The Nordic concept of beauty is by nature completely incomprehensible to the Jew and will always remain so. The rootless Jew has no feeling for the purity and discipline of the German idea of art.

A montage of the Aryan cultural heritage ranging from Greek temples to Renaissance paintings is contrasted with the Jewish movements of artistic expression—cubism, surrealism, expressionism, and jazz—which are held to be the cause of moral degeneracy:

What he calls art must titillate his degenerate nerves. A smell of fungus and disease must pervade it; it must be unnaturally grotesque, perverted or pathological. These pictures, fevered fantasies of incurably sick minds, were once foisted upon the German public by Jewish art theorists as the highest artistic manifestation. . . .

Their infiltration of the German entertainment industry is also
revealed by a succession of film clips of Jewish artists, culminating in an extract from Fritz Lang's *M* (1932), in which
the child murderer, played by Peter Lorre, is made out to be
Jewish.

The final section of the film attacks Jewish religious practices. Christianity has conveyed a deceptive image of the Jews:

> In the mean time we have learnt to use our eyes and now we know that
> the Hebrews of biblical history could not have looked like this. We must
> correct our historical picture. This is what genuine Hebrews look like.
> The following scenes show a Jewish Purim festival, taken by the Warsaw
> Jews themselves for their own use as a cultural film.

Trading is carried out in the synagogue during services while
praying figures rock back and forth. The film then proceeds to
take a close look at the moral laws and teachings of the Jewish
race. The religious schools are seen as institutions of political
indoctrination. 'What does the ancient law of the Talmud
teach? Let us hear a few passages from it:'

> 'Always be cunning in fear, answer gently and soothe even the anger of
> the stranger, so that you will be beloved above and found pleasing here
> below. Join yourself to him on whom fate smiles. Five things did Canaan
> recommend to his sons: love each other, love pillage, love excess, hate
> your master, and never speak the truth!' . . .
> This is no religion and no religious service, it is a conspiracy against
> all non-Jews, of a cunning, unhealthy, contaminated race, against the
> health of the Aryan peoples and against their moral laws.

The culminating theme of this section is the Jewish slaughter
of animals for kosher meat. After a title warning all 'sensitive
Volksgenossen' not to look at the following pictures, we are
shown some 'original film' of Jewish ritual slaughter. The
emotional effect of its presentation quite overshadows the
scenes of violence and the final execution in *Jud Süss*. The
slaughter scenes are introduced by the following narrative:

> The following pictures are genuine. They are among the most horrifying
> that a camera has ever recorded. We are showing them even though we
> anticipate objections on the grounds of taste. Because more important
> than all objections is the fact that our people should know the truth
> about Judaism.

Press cuttings from the 'Jewish controlled press' show how,
before 1933, the National Socialists' campaign against ritual

slaughter was hindered by liberal and socialist newspapers who defended such dubious practices:

The Jewish press were able to defend kosher butchering because scarcely any German had witnessed such scenes. It would have been inconceivable, considering the well-known German love of animals, that the Jews would be able to perpetuate their cruel tortures on innocent and defenceless animals. These pictures are unequivocal evidence of the cruelty of this form of slaughter. At the same time they reveal the character of a race which conceals its crude brutality under the cloak of pious religious practices.

The commentary continues to relate, above pictures of leering Jewish butchers, that when the Führer assumed power in 1933 he prohibited this form of slaughter (shot of an animal writhing in agony after having its throat slit), and directed that all warm-blooded animals should be given an anaesthetic: 'And just as it dealt with this cruel slaughter, so will the Germany of National Socialism deal with the whole race of Jewry.'

The solution to kosher slaughter is shown as a rationalization for the Nuremberg Race Laws which are read out in some detail, followed by Hitler's speech to the Reichstag on 30 January 1939. The film ends with an idealized sequence of blond Nordic stereotypes against a background of sky, Nazi salutes, and close-ups of flags and banners with a final warning that the Aryan race will only triumph if racial purity is preserved: 'The eternal law of nature, to keep the race pure, is the legacy which the National Socialist movement bequeaths to the German people in perpetuity. It is in this spirit that the nation of German people march into the future.'

Der deutsche Film commented that the final contrast between Aryan and Jew provided a valuable safety-valve after the horrors they had witnessed in the previous hour:

The end is like a return to the light. German people and German life surround us once more. It is as if we have travelled to distant parts and we feel the difference that separates us from the Jew with a horrifying shudder![128]

In their analysis of *Der ewige Jude* after the war, the Allied Commission concluded that it was: 'One of the most striking examples of direct Nazi anti-Semitic propaganda, probably the

[128] *Der deutsche Film*, 6 December 1940. Cf. also *VB*, 30 November 1940.

vilest and subtlest of its kind ever made for popular consumption by the masses.'[129]

By means of 'documentary proof', *Der ewige Jude* was intended as definite evidence which underlined not only racialist theories expressed in films such as *Die Rothschilds* and *Jud Süss*, but also the more vehement anti-Semitism found in magazines such as *Der Sturmer*. By contrasting Jewish individualism and 'self-seeking' with the National Socialist ideal of *Volksgemeinschaft* and by showing that Jews were only motivated by money, it was possible to demonstrate that Judaism was the total antithesis of the cherished values of the German cultural tradition as interpreted by Nazi ideology. But more importantly, the constant analogy made with rats and parasites suggested that not only did the Jew differ from the Aryan in body, but more significantly in soul, for the Jew had no soul. The implication was that here was a menace which had to be 'resisted'. Thus the conclusion to be drawn from watching the film was that the killing of Jews was not a crime but a necessity; Jews after all were not human beings but pests which had to be exterminated. *Der ewige Jude* represents a form of National Socialist 'realism' depicting not so much what was, but what ought to have been, in accordance with the preconceived notions of Nazi ideology.

Goebbels's Ministry was not entirely convinced that the German public was ready for such a film. Hippler felt it necessary to publicize the film in a report entitled 'How the Eternal Jew Came About' in the weekly paper *Der Film*. His argument was that unlike feature films which could only dramatize the Jewish problem, the documentary format allowed 'reality' to be shown as it really was: 'In the film Jews are not impersonated or dramatized in any way, rather they reveal themselves as they really are—not a single image is reconstructed and no Jew was forced into a particular deed or situation.'[130] However, there was still the problem of whether German people wished to see Nazi 'reality' on their cinema screens, given that they would also have to witness a *Kulturfilm* and a newsreel in the same programme. Reports sent back to Goebbels from the SD in January 1941 suggested that despite an intense publicity

[129] *Catalogue of Forbidden Films*, p. 33.
[130] *Der Film*, no. 48, 30 November 1940.

campaign, the public were rather tired of anti-Semitism. The message was quite clear: *Jud Süss* had been an effective propaganda exercise, but it had also been enough:

> Reports . . . all agree that it is often only the politically active sections of the population who have seen the film while the typical film audience has largely avoided it. . . . The film was repeatedly described as being an exceptional 'strain on the nerves'. Comments like 'We have seen *Jud Süss* and we've had enough of this Jewish filth' were made. . . .[131]

Undoubtedly the film appealed primarily to that section of the population who were ardent Party members and therefore receptive to such extreme anti-Semitic propaganda. But *Der ewige Jude* can also be seen as an attempt by the RMVP to introduce to as wide an audience as possible the racial teachings of writers such as Houston Stewart Chamberlain and Alfred Rosenberg, and thus to prepare the nation for the 'final solution' that was to follow the film's release. Hippler had anticipated the response noted in the SD Reports and his argument to counteract such criticism reveals both the intent of the film-makers and the brutal message they were disseminating:

> I can envisage that film audiences may feel that they have had enough of this subject. I can even hear the comments: 'Not another film about the Jewish problem!' But I must reply to this, and it is the intention of the film to stress the fact that the Jewish problem only ceases to be topical when the last Jew has left the *Völkisch* fabric of all nations.[132]

The appeal of *Völkisch* thought was very much linked to its projection of stereotypes—of its own image and the image it created of those who opposed its doctrine. The importance of the image of the Jew was defined in antithesis to *Völkisch* ideology. The Jewish stereotype thus provided the focal point for the feeling of aggression inherent in the ideology. It is interesting to note that films which were explicitly anti-Semitic scarcely existed before the war. Anti-Semitism was propagated chiefly by means of the educational system and the press. It was only after the 'final solution' to the Jewish problem had been decided—to Goebbels's satisfaction at least—that the Propaganda Minister instructed film-makers to produce anti-Semitic works. Furthermore it was no coincidence that this should coincide with the onset of war. For conditions like war

---

[131] BA, *R58/157*, 20 January 1940.
[132] *Der Film*, loc. cit.

or a national crisis provide an excellent example of the power of the 'herd instinct' to unify a diffuse mass into believing with an overwhelming passion in the justice of their own cause. Goebbels appreciated the possibilities that war offered to his propaganda campaigns. Compare the following extract from his diary written in 1942:

It's a life and death struggle between the Aryan race and the Jewish bacillus. No other government and no other regime would have the strength for such a global solution as this. Here, once again, the Führer is the undismayed champion of a radical solution, which is made necessary by existing conditions and is therefore inexorable. Fortunately a whole series of possibilities presents itself to us in wartime which would be denied us in peace. We shall have to profit by this.[133]

The method chosen in 1940 was an intense film campaign backed by extensive coverage in the press and radio to 'educate' the population about the need for such a radical solution at a time when psychologically and emotionally they were most susceptible to such an appeal and less likely therefore critically to appraise the message that was being propagated. All that was required as far as Goebbels was concerned was an initial, even tacit acceptance of the planned solution; once the programme was under way no further discussion was desirable. To the extent that Goebbels thought it unnecessary to repeat such an exercise, the trilogy of anti-Semitic films released in 1940 achieved their purpose.

It has been widely held that propaganda implies nothing less than the art of persuasion, for influencing opinions and changing attitudes. Even Goebbels saw propaganda basically in these terms. However, recent studies have shown that the mass media are not the exploiters of unlimited emotions they were once thought to be. I stated earlier that a successful propagandist must 'canalize an already existing stream'. This is important to bear in mind because not only does it highlight man's resistance to attitudes which conflict with his own, but it also reminds us that we should talk more often about edification than about conversion, and stress pyschological defence rather than psychological attack.[134] The Nazi attitude to the Jew provides a striking example of this.

[133] Lochner, p. 103.

[134] Cf. Furhammar and Isaksson, pp. 218–31, and J. A. C. Brown, *Techniques of Persuasion* (London, 1972), p. 147.

When the National Socialists came to power they had to look for reasons which they could use to attack the political and moral degeneracy associated with the Weimar Republic. Anti-Semitism was not the only ideological tenet of National Socialism; indeed the hatred of Jews is likely to have involved many Germans in a crisis of conscience. Those who could not find any rational argument for Jew-baiting must have been disturbed, and many of them must have felt a need for some form of emotional argument to justify the anti-Semitism that German society demanded.[135] Films such as *Jud Süss* and *Der ewige Jude* were intended to inflame and justify such a situation. They achieved their purpose by the grotesque distortion of Jewish characteristics while bluntly declaring themselves to be 'merely factual reportage' and by no means intended as propaganda. The sentiment behind such films was encapsulated in a speech Goebbels made in 1943:

The complete elimination of the Jews from Europe is not a question of ethics, but a question of State security . . . Like the Colorado beetle which destroys, indeed must destroy the potato crops, so the Jew destroys nations. There is only one cure, namely a radical elimination of the danger.[136]

The whole purpose of anti-Semitic film propaganda was to reinforce such beliefs and to unify the people into the desired thought and action. The Jew provided an escape valve from serious social and political problems. The 'image' of the Jew as portrayed in the mass media was outside the range of serious intellectual analysis, and that was its strength. In this way it was able to rationalize any doubts that may have existed, and at the same time provided the emotional basis for a totalitarian solution to these problems. Thus while *Die Rothschilds*, *Jud Süss*, and *Der ewige Jude* may repel a contemporary audience,[137] in Nazi Germany Jews were being used as scapegoats to divert public attention from genuine social and political problems. George Mosse has written that 'there must have been many who, like Hitler, when faced with real problems, first

135 Furhammar and Isaksson, p. 218.
136 'Überwundene Wirtschaftskrise', address in Berlin Sport Palast, 5 June 1943, quoted in Bramsted, p. 399.
137 Although since the end of the last war, *Jud Süss* and *Der Ewige Jude* have been shown in the Middle East as anti-Israeli propaganda and *Ohm Krüger* was shown in Greece as anti-British propaganda.

awakened to the stereotype of the Jew and then built their ideology around it.'[138] Without anti-Semitism, National Socialism would have been inconceivable, both as an ideology and as a catalyst of the emotions which Goebbels's propaganda could readily prey upon.

The so-called Nazi Revolution was essentially a cultural one built on the foundations of the 'new man' in which highly abstract ideas were made concrete by propaganda. As head of this carefully constructed propaganda machine Goebbels lent a new currency to Le Bon's most telling dictum that 'the improbable does not exist for the crowd'. His propaganda embraced a host of mythical themes which all have their roots and antecedents in *Völkisch* thought. From these ideas, stereotypes emerged of the Aryan and the enemy, the Jew, the Anglo-Saxon, and the Bolshevik. 'Stereotyping' was essential to the transformation of the ideology into a 'fighting movement', for it made the abstract concrete for the purposes of mass suggestion. Hitler wrote in *Mein Kampf* that the art of leadership consisted of 'consolidating the attention of the people against a single adversary and taking care that nothing will split up that attention. . . . The leader of genius must have the ability to make different opponents appear as if they belonged to one category.'[139]

Hitler's argument was that first you find your enemy and then concentrate the people's hatred against one single opponent. But in providing an identikit picture of the enemy, successful propaganda of this kind must be of stylized simplicity; if the stereotype is to be effective it has to be constant. It is surprising to discover, therefore, that the image of the enemy in Nazi film propaganda did not always correspond to these dictums. Anti-Bolshevik propaganda constantly changed its image according to the fluctuating diplomatic situation. Only after Britain declared war on Germany in 1939 did she become an object of hatred in the Nazi cinema; until then British stereotypes were portrayed with a certain admiration and envy. The image of the Jew, however, remained constant

---

[138] G. Mosse, *Germans and Jews* (London, 1971), p. 76.
[139] Hitler, p. 110.

despite changing political circumstances and as a result created the most intense and committed hatred of Judaism.

That such distorted and often contradictory stereotypes were created unchecked was due partly to the affects of propaganda and partly to the isolation of German film audiences. As cinema attendances continued to increase, the appeal of films in general was not only based on the public's desire for aggression and diversion (depending on the military situation) —they appealed because there was simply no opportunity, particularly during the war, to compare them with foreign films. Pictures of foreign film stars had been banned from the film press as early as 1937, and by 1940 Nazi Germany was virtually dominating the European film market.[140] Although up until the war American films were allowed into Germany in surprising numbers,[141] these figures are misleading because the films were invariably prevented from being shown for fear of disturbances in the cinemas.[142] Moreover, the *Gaupropagandaleiter* tended to be more extreme Party members and were continually calling for the withdrawal of American films. Finally, in April 1940 Goebbels banned all American films.[143] It would appear that Goebbels was genuinely concerned about the dangers that Hollywood *Unkultur* posed to the true culture of Europe. In December 1941, after Hitler had declared war on the USA, Goebbels outlined to his subordinates the propaganda campaign that was to be waged against America, pointing out that American films were particularly worthy of attack.[144] Although few anti-American feature films were produced, in the same month as Goebbels issued his directive, a documentary film entitled *Rund um die Freiheitsstatue* (*Around the Statue of Liberty*) was released and the narrative alone is as

---

[140] By the end of 1939, for example, over 8,200 cinemas were at the disposal of German distributors.

[141] Sixty-four films were distributed in Germany in 1933: by 1938, this figure had been reduced to 36. *Jahrbuch des Reichsfilmkammer* (Berlin, 1939), p. 199.

[142] Cf. SD Report, 'On the Showing of American films during the War', BA, *R58/184*, 23 May 1940.

[143] W. Boelcke, *Secret Conferences of Dr. Goebbels: The Nazi Propaganda War, 1939-45* (New York, 1970), p. 31, entry of 10 April 1940. In fact American films were not finally banned until the beginning of 1941, ibid., entry 28 February 1941, pp. 123-4.

[144] Boelcke, *Wollt Ihr den totalen Krieg?*, pp. 259-60.

concise a statement of anti-American propaganda as can be found in any single document.[145]

It can be seen from the films discussed in this chapter that, regardless of their success or failure, no more were produced after 1942/3. One reason was the insurmountable problem of making expensive political propaganda films at a time when studios were badly damaged by Allied bombs and nitrate was in short supply. The other reason, as I have noted elsewhere, is that by this time Goebbels had decided that feature films should help the population to escape from the harsh realities of war. The few propaganda films he did choose to produce— *Kolberg*, for example—were directed not at the enemy but aimed at the German people in an attempt to lift morale and give them something to believe in. By their very nature, films which attacked an opponent had to be agitational and aggressive. After Stalingrad, however, the military situation no longer permitted Goebbels to utilize the image of the enemy in this fashion. The need for a barbarically exaggerated image of the enemy is perhaps common to all totalitarian propaganda. Not only does this harness aggression within such a restricted society, but it also channels the positive energies into an equally exaggerated and unquestioning idealization of its own leader figures. In the Third Reich this was confined almost exclusively to the projection of the *Führerprinzip*.

[145] For a synopsis of this film, see Imperial War Museum's information sheet which comes with the hire of the film. Cf. also, *Catalogue of Forbidden Films*, p. 110.

CONCLUSION

Let the world learn to look upon our films as a herald of the
German way of life and a messenger of our ideology. There
can be no art but that which has firm roots in our ideology.

Hans Steinbach, Press Chief in the Reichsfilmkammer[1]

IN 1949 and 1950 Veit Harlan, one of the leading film directors during the Third Reich, was twice accused of 'crimes
against humanity' for his involvement in the anti-Semitic film
Jud Süss. However, the prosecution failed to establish the
exact effectiveness of the film, and Harlan was subsequently
acquitted owing to lack of sufficient evidence.[2] The failure of
the Allied authorities to convict Harlan (who was seen as a
test case), highlights the difficulty of attempting to calculate
the effects that films have on cinema audiences. Such problems are even more pronounced when one is analysing these
films thirty years later, especially as we are looking for evidence
of influence and are therefore perhaps likely to exaggerate
what influence we might find. For those who saw National
Socialist films are now under psychological pressures that prevent them from giving objective accounts of their impressions.
This is particularly the case with film-makers who are still
alive, who must have consciously followed the effects of their
films. They are either reluctant to discuss their work or have
found it necessary to make excuses for their involvement.[3]

[1] Quoted in *VB*, 19 March 1937.
[2] The first trial lasted between 3 March and 29 April 1949, after which Harlan
was set free. As a result of an appeal a second trial took place on 30 March 1950.
For an account of the first trial see H. Pardo and S. Schiffner (eds.), *'Jud Süss'.
Historisches und juristisches Material zum Fall Veit Harlan* (Hamburg, 1949). The
second trial is reported in considerable detail in the *Suddeutsche Zeitung*, no. 100,
2 May 1950.
[3] Cf. V. Harlan, *Im Schatten meiner Zeitung* (Gütersloh, 1966), and A. Maria
Rabenalt, *Film im Zwielicht* (Munich, 1958).

Furthermore, it is impossible to say whether such films could convert an unbeliever to National Socialism or could change public opinion from, for example, an indifferent attitude towards Jews to a marked anti-Semitism. It should be noted, however, that almost every film discussed in this investigation was banned by the Allied Control Mission after the war as politically objectionable.

It has already been indicated that no reliable information exists with which to measure the success or failure of Nazi film propaganda, but the historian can look at the means of control and the content and style of the films themselves to gain some idea of the policy of indoctrination employed by Goebbels during the twelve years that the Third Reich existed. It must be remembered when discussing the effectiveness of film propaganda that the cinema has to be seen in the wider context of mass communications within which it was operating. Film was only one factor in creating an uncritical audience, but it was an important function in the sense that, when people read newspapers or listened to the radio they were more conscious of the propaganda content. The cinema, on the other hand, was associated with relaxation and entertainment and was therefore all the more dangerous, particularly as the *Gleichschaltung* of the German cinema had been carried out behind the scenes, by a process of which the ordinary citizen was largely unaware. It is clear that when the Nazis assumed power they thought highly of film as a propaganda weapon. The need for conformity in a totalitarian state meant that the film industry had to be reorganized according to the ideas of the NSDAP. Like all forms of mass communication, film had to correspond with the political *Weltanschauung* and the propaganda principles of the Party. Therefore the communications media—the press, radio, and film—had a circular interrelationship in that they supplied each other with themes in the manner prescribed by the State, and supported each other in their effect by a simultaneous and graduated release of information, which was circulated, controlled, and modulated by the State.

Thus the required appreciation of films was carefully directed; to a certain extent the reaction of the public was prepared in advance by concerted publicity campaigns that preceded all films deemed important to the National Socialist cause. Using slogans based on the principle that propaganda for the masses had to be simple and had to be repeated many times, the press introduced the public to the films, explained them in terms of Nazi ideology, and linked the events in the film to the actual political situation existing at the time the film was being shown. The directives of the RMVP guided the formation of definitions and the use of language, which enabled the whole press to present a common approach to its film reviews. Furthermore, in 1936 Goebbels forbade 'art criticism' (*Kunstkritik*) in favour of 'observation of art' (*Kunstbetrachtung*). The 'critic' was now only permitted to evaluate new films 'by means of description and praise'. Objectivity and opinion were therefore eliminated and replaced by a definition of truth as defined by the Nazi regime.

Conformity of opinion and action were also secured within the *Filmwelt* itself. In order that film should reflect the ideological precepts of National Socialism, it was imperative that the film-makers themselves should be sympathetic towards the aims and ideals of the new regime. Accordingly, a 'cleansing' process of *Entjudung* eliminated Jews and other political undesirables from working in the German film industry. The result was that some of the most distinguished artists were driven from the country to be replaced by a well-trained but generally uninspired company of directors and actors who could be relied upon to produce the type of films demanded by the State. Because the skills involved in film-making are so intricate, this corpus of film-makers remained constant throughout the Third Reich and was never replaced. It is interesting to note in the *Filmography* the recurrence of the same directors and casts. Quite obviously, Goebbels felt that these were the only artists willing to or capable of presenting the regime's more prestigious political films.

I stated in the introduction that Goebbels and the Party believed in the 'power' of the cinema to influence people's thoughts and beliefs. I also argued that to understand more precisely the way in which the Nazis attempted to exert such covert and psychological influences by means of film propaganda, one had to be familiar with that tradition of *Völkisch* political and cultural thought that found expression in

Germany in the eighteenth and nineteenth centuries. National Socialism was characterized by charismatic leadership, nationalism, racism, emphasis on the Volk, anti-Semitism, stress on violence and force, and an appeal to national unity. It is precisely these themes that recur in Nazi film propaganda.

The need for reassurance also helped to dictate the content of the films. The middle classes in particular associated the ideology of *Völkism* and the film propaganda with a world of order and traditions, as opposed to the chaos and alienation of modern society. Such traditions were created by means of myths and symbols which would appeal to their longing for security and action, and to their prejudices. Goebbels wanted the National Socialist film to be understood as a 'People's Culture' which would 'capture the heart of the people' and artistically represent 'those joys and sorrows that shaped the nation's destiny'. This should not, however, imply that he wanted film propaganda to reflect public opinion. On the contrary, he believed that as long as people were in the cinemas of their own free will then skilfully produced film propaganda could 'educate' public taste according to the dictates of the Party. In this respect, films not only reassured people but also had an educational function in that they presented the nation in a positive light. From the way themes and messages were presented, the spectator learnt how to behave as a good citizen of the National Socialist State. Such a process assumed the public's desire for conformity. Both intrinsic enjoyment of the film together with its educational role would have been nullified had the public resisted this basis of communication. Moreover, as the public was fully aware that these films contained only valid National Socialist opinions, any lack of agreement on the part of the individual with the ideas that were being propagated must have constituted an unpleasant identity crisis. Goebbels and his company of film-makers sought to avoid this conflict by encouraging the spectator to conform by assuming 'correct' conduct, at the same time warning him about the consequences of any lack of conformity. With a critical audience this crude form of manipulation may not have succeeded; its success in Germany was due partly to the effects of propaganda and partly to the increasing isolation of German film audiences who were prevented from making comparisons. Even so Goebbels regularly received extraordinarily detailed reports from the Security Police about the mood of the people in case of discontent. To assure themselves of continued popular support was an unwavering and important concern of the Nazi leaders, and of Goebbels in particular.

Thus the themes that recur in the Nazi cinema are central to the Nazi *Weltanschauung*. Until 1943 and the retreat from Russia, these ideas were repeated at carefully chosen intervals. Goebbels chose to keep prestigious film propaganda at its maximum effectiveness by spacing out the films concerned— except, that is, for the *Deutsche Wochenschauen* (newsreels), which depended on their ability to capture the immediacy of events. The full-length documentaries were all the more effective for their comparative rarity. Given the all-embracing organization of the German film industry under the control of the RMVP, it is surprising to discover that this is the only pattern of film propaganda that emerges. It is true that a trilogy of films eulogized the *Kampfzeit* and glorified the Movement and its martyrs. Similarly, in 1940, three films were produced which helped to prepare the way for the final solution to the 'Jewish problem'. Equally 1941 marked the highest concentration of *Staatsauftragsfilme* commissioned by the RMVP. But Goebbels' main concern was to keep the most important themes of the Party's ideology constantly before the public by releasing an optimum number of State-commissioned propaganda films which were given a disproportionate amount of financial assistance and publicity.

This strategy illustrates his desire to mix entertainment with propaganda. For, unlike Hitler, Goebbels believed that propaganda was most effective when it was insidious, when its message was concealed within the framework of popular entertainment. Therefore, although the *Staatsauftragsfilme* consisted of only one-sixth of all film production in the Third Reich, their importance far outweighed purely numerical considerations in that they served to promote the official 'world view' of things and reinforced the existing social and economic order as well as establishing the themes, the style, and the standards for the film industry in general.

Nazi film propaganda embraced a host of mythical themes,

all of which had their roots in *Völkisch* thought and which dramatized the Nazi *Weltanschauung* in fictionalized form. By commissioning a steady output of *Völkisch* themes, Goebbels believed he could create an ideologically committed cinema that was essentially German in character. Goebbels was considerably influenced by the Soviet example. He demanded that film-makers strive to produce a *Battleship Potemkin*. He even ordered film education to be extended to schools and youth organizations in an effort to make German youth more conscious of the cinema. But the failure of the Third Reich to produce a revolutionary 'People's Culture' was due partly to the inherent contradictions of National Socialism, where romantic conservatism and revolutionary ideas formed a precarious alliance, and partly to Goebbels' own personality. The Propaganda Minister would constantly change his opinions about the overall objectives and methods of artistic creativity according to his judgement of the political situation at a given time. Moreover he chose to staff his Ministry with loyal Party servants who knew little about the process of film-making yet who were arrogant enough to dictate to the professionals in the industry. In practical terms this meant that decisions regarding policy and content came downwards from the top instead of being worked out by discussion and choice among the artists themselves. It is revealing that my reading of contemporary documents has revealed no serious ideological debate about the role of film art within the *Filmwelt* comparable to the polemics that accompanied Soviet Realism in Russian film circles. All these factors contributed to an environment that was not conducive to creativity and outstanding artistic achievement.

The real test of both National Socialism and Goebbels' film policy came with defeat at Stalingrad. And yet after 1943 Goebbels largely abandoned his desire for an ideologically orientated cinema and instead concentrated on a policy of escapist entertainment that would divert people's attention from the war. The results of Goebbels' *Filmpolitik* were a monopolistic system of control and organization which maintained profits, increased attendances, produced an extremely high standard of technical proficiency, yet, in the final analysis, contributed little stylistically to the history of the cinema.

After the grandiose edifice of the Third Reich was laid bare in 1945, the legacy left by the Minister for Popular Enlightenment and Propaganda was a deep distrust throughout the world of the medium of film and a new awareness of how easily the mass media could be manipulated to serve the opportunist purposes of their masters. Instead of building a German cinema that would conquer the world as the vanguard of the Nazi troops, Goebbels died leaving a demoralized and declining film industry that would take almost thirty years to rediscover itself.

APPENDIX

SELECTED FILM PRODUCTION IN THE THIRD REICH:
ESTIMATED COSTS, PROFITS, LOSSES*

Year	Production costs (in thousands RM)	Estimated Revenue (Gross)	Estimated Profit	Loss
1933				
Hitlerjunge Quex	225	—	—	—
Flüchtlinge	814	—	—	—
1934				
Ein Mann will nach Deutschland	400	—	—	—
1936				
Verräter	465	—	—	—
1937				
Urlaub auf Ehrenwort	598	2,650	1,596	
1938				
Pour le mérite	1,076	3,700	1,937	
1939				
D III 88	1,268	3,500	1,666	
Leinen aus Irland	744	1,350	178	
Robert und Bertram	1,219	1,400		—120
1940				
Bismarck	1,794	4,400	1,989	
Die Rothschilds	951	2,500	1,093	
Friedrich Schiller	1,935	2,600	238	
Jud Süss	2,081	6,200	3,172	
Wunschkonzert	905	7,200	4,239	

Year	Production costs (in thousands RM)	Estimated Revenue (Gross)	Estimated Profit	Loss
1941				
Carl Peters	3,190	3,300		−453
Heimkehr	4,020	4,900		−423
Ich klage an	960	5,400	3,641	
Ohm Krüger	5,477	5,500		−801
Stukas	1,961	3,500	956	
1942				
Der grosse König	4,799	6,000	343	
Die Entlassung	3,600	6,500	2,081	
GPU	1,849	3,500	1,161	
1943				
Paracelsus	2,709	3,500	1,161	
1944				
Junge Adler	1,886	4,000	1,637	
1945				
Kolberg	8,800	7,000		−3,350

* All figures quoted are for the domestic German market only. The figures are taken mainly from two sources: BA, *R1091/1028c, 1029b, 1032b, 1031b*. This folder gives the estimated production costs of the films cited between 1933–6. All other figures are taken from BA, *R2/4829-30*. These are based on four financial reports by the Kautio Treuhand GmbH (17 June 1939, 26 February 1941, 27 January 1942, and 30 April 1943).

FILMOGRAPHY

The following list contains the films cited in the text (including documentaries and short films) and wherever possible the date they were passed by the *Zensur* (Z) and the subsequent date they were released for distribution (U: *Uraufführung*). All films commissioned by the Film Section of the Propaganda Ministry are indicated by an S. (*Staatsauftragsfilm*).

Abbreviations:

d: Director	p: Producer	sc: Screenplay
LP: Leading players	P: Prädikat	

Abbreviations for Prädikate:

aw:	*anerkennenswert* (from 1 September 1942)
bw:	*besonders wertvoll* (7 June 1933–5 November 1934)
FN:	*Film der Nation* (honorary *Prädikat* from 1939)
Jf:	*Jugendfrei* (allowed to be shown to children over the age of 6)
Jw:	*Jugendwert* (honorary *Prädikat* from 21 November 1938)
kbw:	*künstlerisch besonders wertvoll* (from 1 April 1933)
küw:	*künstlerisch wertvoll* (from 1933)
kuw:	*kulturell wertvoll* (from 1933)
Lf:	*Lehrfilm* (from 1920)
sbw:	*staatspolitisch besonders wertvoll* (from 1 May 1933)
skbw:	*staatspolitisch und künstlerisch besonders wertvoll* (5 November 1933–1 September 1942)
ST:	Staatspreisfilm (honorary Prädikat from 1933)
sw:	*staatspolitisch wertvoll* (from 7 June 1933)
vb:	*volksbildend* (from 1924)
vw:	*volkstümlich wertvoll* (from 1 April 1939)

A. FEATURE FILMS

1933

S *Der Choral von Leuthen* (*The Hymn of Leuthen*)
 (Z: 30 January; U: 3 February) p: Carl Froelich Film GmbH; d: Carl Froelich; sc: Dr Johannes Brandt and Isle Spath-Barom (from an idea by Friedrich Pflughaupt based on themes in the novel *Fridericus* by Walter von Mole); LP: Otto Gebühr, Olga Tschechowa, Elga Brink.
 P: vb.

S *Flüchtlinge (Refugees)*
(Z: 1 December; U: 8 December) p: Ufa; d: Gustav Ucicky;
sc: Gerhard Menzel (from his own novel); LP: Hans Albers, Käthe
von Nagy, Eugen Klopfer, Andrews Engelmann.
P: ST, kbw.

S *Hans Westmar (Ein deutsches Schicksal aus dem Jahre 1929)*
(Z: 23 November; U: 13 December) p: Volksdeutsche Film GmbH;
d: Franz Wenzler; sc: Hans Heinz Ewers (from his own book *Horst
Wessel*) LP: Emil Lohkamp, Paul Wegener, Carla Bartheel.

S *Hitlerjunge Quex (Hitler Youth Quex)*
(Z: 7 September; U: 19 September) p: Ufa; d: Hans Steinhoff;
sc: K. A. Schenzinger and B. E. Lüthge (from Schenzinger's novel);
LP: Heinrich George, Bertha Drews, Claus Clausen.
P: kbw.

Morgenrot (Dawn)
(Z: 26 January; U: 31 January) p: Ufa; d: Gustav Ucicky; sc:
Gerhard Menzel (from an idea by R. Freiherr von Spiegel); LP:
Rudolf Forster, Adele Sandrock, Fritz Geuschow.
P: küw.

S *SA-Mann Brand*
(Z: 9 June; U: 14 June) p: Bavaria d: Franz Seitz; sc: Joseph
Dalman and Joe Stöckel; LP: Heinz Klingenberg, Otto Wernicke,
Elise Aulinger.
P: kbw, vb.

1934
S *Das alte Recht (The Old Right)*
(Z: 23 January; U: 27 January) p: Andersen Film; d: Igo Martin
Andersen; sc: Igo Martin Andersen and Armin Petersen; LP: Edit
Linn, Bernard Cötzke, Hans Kettler.

Der Schimmelreiter (Phantom Rider)
(Z: 3 January; U: 12 January) p: Tobis (Europa) d: Curt Örtel and
Hans Deppe; sc: Curt Örtel, H. Deppe from the novel by Theodor
Storm; LP: Marianne Hoppe, Mathias Wiemann, Hans Deppe.
P: kbw

S *Die Reiter von Deutsch — Ostafrika (The Riders of German East-
Africa)*
(Z: 17 October; U: 19 October) p: Terra; d: Herbert Selpin; sc:
Marie-Luise Droop (from the novel *Kwa heri*); LP: Ilse Stobrawa,
sepp Rist, Peter Voss.
P: vb

S *Ein Mann will nach Deutschland (A Man Must Return to Germany)*
(Z: 24 July; U: 26 July) p: Ufa; d: Paul Wegener; sc: Philipp
Lothar Mayring and Fred Andreas (from the novel by Andreas);
LP: Karl Ludwig Diehl, Brigitte Hornsey, Siegfried Schürenberg.

S *Ich für Dich —Du für mich* (*I for You — You for Me*)
(Z: 19 November; U: 30 November) p: Carl Froelich Film; d: Carl Froelich; sc: Hans G. Kernmayr; LP: Maria Wanck, Inge Kick, Ruth Eweler.
P: sbw, küw.

S *Stosstrupp 1917* (*Shock Troop 1917*)
(Z: 13 February; U: 20 February) p: Arya Film; d: Hans Zöberlein and Ludwig Schmid-Wildy; sc: Franz Adam, Marian Kolb, Hans Zöberlein (based on Zöberlein's book Der Glaube an Deutschland); LP: Ludwig Schmid-Wildy, Albert Penzkofer, Beppo Brem.
P: sw, küw.

1935

S *Der alte und der junge König* (*The Old and the Young King*)
(Z: 29 January; U: 29 January) p: Deka; d: Hans Steinhoff; sc: Thea von Harbou and Rolf Lauckner; LP: Emil Jannings, Werner Hinz, Claus Clausen.
P: skbw, vb.

S *Der höhere Befehl* (*The Higher Order*)
(Z: 13 December; U: 30 December) p: Ufa; d: Gerhard Lamprecht sc: Philipp Lothar Mayring, Kurt Kluge, Karl Lerbs; LP: Karl Ludwig Diehl, Lil Dagover, Karl Dannemann.
P: skbw.

S *Friesennot* (*Frisians in Peril*)
(Z: 15 November; U: 19 November) p.: Delta; d: Peter Hagen; sc: Werner Kortwich; LP: Friedrich Kayssler, Inkijinoff, Helen Fehdmer.
P: skbw.

S *Das Mädchen vom Moorhof* (*The Girl From the Marshland Farm*)
(Z: 4 October; U: 30 October) p: Ufa; d: Detlef Sierck; sc: Lothar Mayring from the novel by Selma Lagerlöf; LP: Friedrich Kayssler, Theodor Loos, Tina Carsteus, Dorothea Thiess.

Viktoria
(Z: 14 November; U: 27 November) p: Tobis (Europa); d: Carl Hoffmann; sc: Robert A. Stemmle from the novel by Knut Hansun; LP: Mathias Wiemann, Theodor Loos, Alfred Abel, Maria Sedler.

1936

S *Fährmann Maria* (Ferryman Maria)
(Z: 2 January; U: 7 January) p: Pallas-Film (Terra); d: Frank Wysbar; sc: Hans Jürgen Nierentz, F. Sysbarf; LP: Aribert Mog, Sybille Schmitz, Pete Voss, Gerhart Bienert.

S *Fridericus*
(Z: 11 December; U: 8 February 1937) p: Diana Film; d: Johannes Meyer; sc: Erich Kröhnke, Walter von Molo (from his novel); LP: Otto Gebühr, Hilde Körber, Kil Dagover.
P: sw.

S *Standschütze Bruggler* (*Home Guardsman Bruggler*)
(Z: 21 August; U: 28 August) p: Tonlicht; d: Werner Klingler;
sc: Joseph Dalmen; LP: Ludwig Kerschner, Franziska Kinz, Beppo
Brem.

S *Verräter* (*Traitors*)
(Z. 19 August; U: 9 September) p: Ufa; d: Karl Ritter; sc: Leonard
Fürst (from an idea by Walter Herzlieb and Hans Wagner); LP: Lida
Baarova, Willy Birgel, Theodor Loos, Rudolf Fernau.
P: skbw, vb.

S *Weisse Sklaven* (*White Slaves*)
(Z: 16 December; U: 5 January 1937) p: Lloyd Film; d: Karl Anton,
Felix von Eckhardt and Arthur Pohl; LP: Theodor Loos, Camilla
Horn, Agnes Straub, Werner Hinz.

1937

S *Der Herrscher* (*The Ruler*)
(Z: 15 March; U: 17 March) p: Tobis; d: Veit Harlan; sc: Thea von
Harbou and Curt J. Braun (from the play *Vor Sonnenuntergang* by
Gerhart Hauptmann); LP: Emil Jannings, Marianne Hoppe, Theodor
Loos, Paul Wagner, Herbert Hübner.
P: ST, skbw.

Mein Sohn, der Herr Minister (*My Son, the Minister*)
(Z: 28 June; U: 6 July) p: Ufa; d: Veit Harlan; sc: H. G. Külb,
Edgar Kahn (from the play *Fiston* by André Birabeau); LP: Hans
Moser, Paul Dahlke, Hilde Körber, Hans Brausewetter.
P: küw.

S *Menschen ohne Vaterland* (*Men without a Fatherland*)
(Z: 10 February; U: 6 March) p: Ufa; d: Herbert Maisch; sc: Walter
Wasserman, C. H. Diller, Ernst von Salomon and Herbert Maisch
(from a novel by Gertrud von Brockdorff); LP: Willy Fritsch, Willy
Birgel, Maria von Tasnady.

S *Patrioten* (*Patriots*)
(Z: 14 May; U: 24 September) p: Ufa; d: Karl Ritter; sc: Philipp
Lothar Mayring, Felix Lützkendorf & Karl Ritter (from an idea by
Ritter); LP: Lida Baarova, Mathias Wiemann, Bruno Hübner, Hilde
Körber.
P: skbw.

Petermann ist dagegen (*Petermann is Against It*)
(Z: 19 November; U: 14 January 1938) p: Neucophan-Tonfilm;
d: Frank Wysbar; sc: Otto Bernhard Wendler, Frank Wysbar;
LP: Ernst Waldow, Fita Beulchoff, Johannes Bathel, Berthold
Ebbecke.

S *Unternehmen Michael* (*Operation Michael*)
   (Z: 3 September; U: 7 September) p: Ufa; d: Karl Ritter; sc: Karl
   Ritter, Mathias Wiemann and Fred Hildenbrand (from the play by
   Hans Fritz von Zwehl); LP: Heinrich George, Mathias Wiemann,
   Paul Otto, Willy Birgel, Otto Graf.
   P: skw.

S *Urlaub auf Ehrenwort* (*Leave on Word of Honour*)
   (Z: 31 December; U: 11 January 1938) p: Ufa; d: Karl Ritter
   sc: Charles Klein, Felix Lützkendorf (from ideas by Lilian Koll,
   Walter Bloem, and Charles Klein); LP: Rolf Moebias, Fritz Kampers,
   Rene Deltgen, Otto Graf.
   P: skbw.

   Ein Volksfeind (*An Enemy of the People*)
   (Z: 11 October; U: 26 October) p: Terra; d: Hans Steinhoff;
   sc: Erich Ebermager, H. Steinhoff, from a story by Henrik Ibsen;
   LP: Heinrich George, Herbert Hübner, Carsta Löck, Hans Richter,
   Albert Florath, Edward Wenck.

1938

S *Dreizehn Mann und eine Kanone* (*13 Men and a Canon*)
   p and d: Johannes Meyer; sc: Fred Andreas, George Hurdalek
   and Peter Francke (from an idea by Pizarro Forzano); LP: Otto
   Wernicke, Herbert Hübner, Friedrich Kayssler, Paul Wagner.

   Heimat (*Homeland*)
   (Z: 31 May; U: 25 June) p: Ufa; d: Carl Froelich; sc: Harald Braun
   (from a story of Hermann Sudermann); LP: Zarah Leander, Heinrich
   George, Lina Caistens, Ruth Hellberg, Paul Hörbiger.
   P: skbw, Nationale Filmpreis 1939.

S *Kameraden auf See* (*Comrades at Sea*)
   (Z: 7 March; U: 12 March) p: Terra; d: Heinz Paul; sc: Peter Franke,
   J. A. Zerbe (from an idea by Toni Huppertz and J. A. Zerbe);
   LP: Paul Wagner, Theodor Loos, Fred Döderlain, Carola Hühn.
   P: sw.

   Jugend (*Youth*)
   (Z: 21 March; U: 12 April) p: Tobis; d: Veit Harlan; sc: Thea von
   Harbou (from the play by Max Halbe); LP: Kristina Söderbaum,
   Eugen Klöpfer, Werner Hinz, Hermann Braun.
   P: küw.

S *Pour le Mérite*
   (Z: 7 December; U: 22 December) p: Ufa; d: Karl Ritter; sc: Fred
   Hildenbrand and Karl Ritter; LP: Paul Hartmann, Paul Otto, Albert
   Hehn, Fritz Kampers.
   P: skbw, jw.

1939
S *D 111 88*
(Z: 4 October; U: 26 October) p: Tobis; d: Herbert Maisch; sc:
Hans Bertram, Wolf Neumeister; LP: Heinz Welzel, Otto Wernicke,
Christian Kayssler, Carsta Löck.
P: sbw, jw.

S *Das Gewehr über (Shoulder Arms)*
(Z: 24 November; U: 7 December) p: Germania; d: Jürgen von
Alten; sc: Kurt Walter (based on the novel by Wolfgang Marken);
LP: Carsta Löck, Rolf Möbins, Ruddi Codden.

S *Leinen aus Irland (Irish Linen)*
(Z: 22 September; U: 16 October) p: Styria Film for Wien Film;
d: Heinz Helbig; sc: Harald Bratt (from the play by Stefan von
Kamare); LP: Irene von Meyendorff, Siegfried Breuer, Rolf Wanka.
P: sw, küw.

Mutterliebe (Mother Love)
(Z: 24 October; U: 19 December) p: Ufa; d: Gustav Ucicky;
sc: Gerhard Menzel; LP: Paul Hörbiger, Käthe Dorsch, Hans Hotter,
Fritz Imhoff.

Robert und Bertram (Robert and Bertram)
(Z: 20 June; U: 7 July) p: Tobis; d: Hans Heinz Zerlett; sc: Hans
Heinz Zerlett (from a sketch by Gustav Raeder); LP: Rudi Godden,
Kurt Seifert, Herbert Hübner, Fritz Kampers.

Sensationsprozess Casilla (Sensational Trial of Casilla)
(Z: 29 July; U: 8 August) p: Ufa; d: Eduard von Borsody; sc: Ernst
Salomon, Eduard von Borsody; LP: Heinrich George, Albert Hehn,
Erich Fiedler, Jutta Freybe, Dagny Servaes.

1940
S *Bismarck*
(Z: 19 November; U: 6 December) p: Tobis; d: Wolfgang Liebeneiner
sc: Rolf Lauckner and Wolfgang Liebeneiner; LP: Paul Hartmann,
Friedrich Kayssler, Werner Hinz, Walter Franck, Lil Dagover.
P: skbw, jw.

Das Herz der Königin (The Heart of the Queen)
(Z: 29 October; U: 1 November) p: Ufa; d: Carl Froelich; sc: Harald
Braun, Jacob Geis, Rolf Beissmann; LP: Zarah Leander, Willy
Birgel, Hubert v. Meyerinck, Erich Ponto, Herbert Hübner.
P: küw, kuw.

S *Der Fuchs von Glenarvon (The Fox of Glenarvon)*
(Z: 22 April; U: 24 April) p: Tobis; d: Max W. Kimmich; sc: Wolf
Neumeister, Hans Bertram (from the novel by Nicola Rohn);
LP: Olga Tschechowa, Ferdinand Marian, Karl Ludwig Diehl.
P: küw.

S *Die Rothschilds* (*The Rothschilds*)
(Z: 16 July; U: 17 July) p: Ufa; d: Erich Waschneck; sc: C. M. Köln, Gerhard T. Buchholz (from an idea by Mirko Jelusich); LP: Carl Kuhlmann, Hilde Weissner, Herbert Hübner, Albert Florath, Erich Ponto.

S *Feinde* (*Enemies*)
(Z: 11 November; U: 13 November) p: Bavaria; d: Viktor Tourjansky; sc: Emil Burri, Arthur Luethy, and V. Tourjansky; LP: Brigitte Horney, Willy Birgel, Hedwig Wangel, Ludwig Schmid-Wildy.
P: sw, küw, jw.

Ein Robinson
(Z: 23 April; U: 25 April) p: Bavaria; d: Arnold Franck; sc: A. Franck, Rolf Meyer; LP: Herbert A. E. Böhme, Claus Clausen, Malte Jaeger, Wolf Dietrich, Ludwig Schmid-Wildy.
P: kuw.

Friedrich Schiller (*Der Triumph eines Genies: The Triumph of Genius*)
(Z: 11 November; U: 13 November) p: Tobis; d: Herbert Maisch; sc: Walter Wassermann, C. H. Diller, from an idea by Paul Josef Cremers; LP: Horst Casper, Heinrich George, Lil Dagover, Hans Nielsen, Friedrich Kayssler, Herbert Hübner, Albert Florath.
P: sw, küw, jw.

S *Jud Süss* (*Jew Süss*)
(Z: 6 September; U: 24 September) p: Terra; d: Veit Harlan; sc: Veit Harlan, Eberhard Wolfgang Möller, Ludwig Metzger; LP: Ferdinand Marian, Heinrich George, Werner Krauss, Kristina Söderbaum, Eugen Klöpfer, Malte Jaeger, Albert Florath, Theodor Loos.
P: skbw, jw.

S *Wunschkonzert* (*Request Concert*)
(Z: 21 December; U: 30 December) p: Cine-Allianz; d: Eduard von Borsody; sc: Felix Lutzkendorf, E. von Borsody; LP: Ilse Werner, Malte Jaeger, Carl Raddatz, Albert Florath, Heinz Gödecke.
P: sw, küw, vw, jw.

1941
S *Carl Peters*
(Z: 20 March; U: 21 March) p: Bavaria; d: Herbert Selpin; sc: Ernst von Salomon, Walter Zerlett-Olfenius, H. Selpin; LP: Hans Albers, Friedrich Otto, Karl Dannemann, Fritz Odemar, Herbert Hübner.
P: skw, kuw, vb, jw.

S *Heimkehr* (*Homecoming*)
(Z: 26 August; U: 10 October) p: Wien; d: Gustav Ucicky; sc: Gerhard Menzel; LP: Paula Wessely, Carl Raddatz, Peter Petersen, Otto Wernicke, Attila Hörboger.
P: FN, skbw, jw

S *Ich Klage an (I Accuse)*
(Z: 15 August; U: 29 August) p: Tobis; d: Wolfgang Liebeneiner; sc: Eberhard Frowein, Harald Bratt (from an idea by Bratt and the novel *Sending und Gewissen* by Hellmuth Unger); LP: Paul Hartmann, Mathias Wiemann, Heidemarie Hatheyer, Albert Florath.
P: kbw, vb.

S *Kadetten (Cadets)*
(Z: 12 November; U: 2 December) p: Ufa; d: Karl Ritter; sc: Felix Lützkendorf, K. Ritter, from an idea by Alfons Menne; LP: Mathias Wiemann, Andrews Englemann, Carsta Löck, Klaus Detlef Sierck.

S *Kampfgeschwader Lützow (Battle Squadron Lützow)*
(Z: 20 February; U: 28 February) p: Tobis; d: Hans Bertram; sc: H. Bertram, Wolf Neumeister, Heinz Orlovius; LP: Christian Kayssler, Heinz Welzel, Peter Voss, Adolf Fischer, Hermann Braun.
P: skbw, vw, jw.

S *Kopf Hoch, Johannes! (Chin up, John!)*
(Z. 5 February; U: 11 March) p: Majestic; d: Viktor de Kowa; sc: Toni Huppertz, Wilhelm Krug, Felix von Eckhardt (from an idea by Huppertz); LP: Albrecht Schoenhals, Klaus Detlef Sierck, Otto Gebühr.

S *Mein Leben für Irland (My Life for Ireland)*
(Z: 12 February; U: 17 February) p: Tobis; d: Max W. Kimmich; sc: M. W. Kimmich, Toni Huppertz; LP: Werner Hinz, Eugen Klöpfer, Paul Wegener, Claus Clausen, Anna Dammann.
P: sw, küw, jw.

S *Ohm Krüger (Uncle Krüger)*
(Z: 2 April; U: 4 April) p: Tobis; d: Hans Steinhoff; sc: Harald Bratt, Kurt Henser, (from themes in the novel *Mann ohne Volk* by Arnold Krieger); LP: Emil Jannings, Gustaf Gründgens, Otto Wernicke, Ferdinand Marian.
P: FN, skbw, kuw, vw, vb, jw.

... reitet für Deutschland (Riding for Germany)
(Z: 4 April; U: 11 April) p: Ufa; d: Arthur Maria Rabenalt; sc: Fritz Recke Malleczewen, Richard Riedel, Josef Maria Frank; LP: Willy Birgel, Herbert A. E. Böhme, Walter Werner, Herbert Hübner.
P: sw, jw.

S *Stukas*
(Z: 25 June; U: 27 June) p: Ufa; d: Karl Ritter; sc: K. Ritter, Felix Lützkendorf; LP: Carl Raddatz, Adolf Fischer, Albert Hehn.
P: sw, küw, vw, jw.

S *U-Boote westwärts (U-Boat Westwards)*
(Z: 7 May; U: 9 September) p: Ufa; d: Günther Rittau; sc: Georg Zoch; LP: Ilse Werner, Joachim Brennecke, Carsta Löck.
P: sw, küw, vb.

S *Über alles in der Welt (Above All in the World)*
(Z: 14 March; U: 19 March) p: Ufa; d: Karl Ritter; sc: Karl Ritter,
Felix Lützkendorf; LP: Carl Raddatz, Fritz Kampers, Paul Hartmann,
Carsta Löck.
P: sw, jw

1942

Andreas Schluter
(Z: 11 September; U: 19 November) p: Tobis; d: Herbert Maisch
sc: Helmut Brandis, H. Maisch, (from the novel *Der Münzturm* by
Alfons von Zibulka); LP: Heinrich George, Theodor Loos, Mila
Kopp.

S *Der grosse König (The Great King)*
(Z: 28 February; U: 3 March) p: Tobis; d: Veit Harlan; sc: Veit
Harlan; LP: Otto Gebühr, Kristina Söderbaum, Gustav Fröhlich,
Paul Wegener, Claus Clausen, Klans Detlef Seirck, Herbert Hübner.
P: FN, skbw, kuw, vw, vb, jw.

S *Die Entlassung (The Dismissal)*
(Z: 28 August; U: 6 October) p: Tobis; d: Wolfgang Liebeneiner;
sc: Curt Johannes Braun, Felix von Eckardt; LP: Emil Jannings,
Theodor Loos, Werner Krauss, Werner Hinz, Herbert Hübner,
Christian Kayssler.
P: FN, skbw, kuw, vw, aw, vb, jw.

S *Die grosse Liebe (The Great Love)*
(Z: 6 June; U: 12 June) p: Ufa; d: Rolf Hansen; sc: R. Hansen,
Peter Groll (from an idea by Alexander Lernet-Holenia); LP: Zarah
Leander, Paul Hörbiger, Viktor Staal, Hans Schwartz.
P: skw, vw.

S *Geheimakte WBI (Secret Paper WNI)*
(Z: 23 January; U: 26 January) p: Bavaria; d: Herbert Selpin;
sc: H. Selpin, Walter Zerlett-Olfenius (from the novel 'Der eiserne
Seehund' by Hans Arthur Thies); LP: Herbert Hübner, Richard
Hanssler, Willi Rose
P: skw, jw.

S *G.P.U.*
(Z: 17 July; U: 14 August) p: Ufa; d: Karl Ritter; sc: Karl Ritter,
Felix Lützkendorf, Andrews Engelmann (from an idea by Engel-
mann); LP; Andrews Engelmann, Laura Solari, Will Quadflieg.

S *Himmelhunde (Sky Hounds)*
(Z: 29 January; U: 20 February) p: Terra; d: Roger von Norman;
sc: Philipp Lothar Mayring; LP: Malte Jaeger, Lutz Götz, Albert
Florath.

S *Wien 1910 (Vienna 1910)*
(Z: 21 August; U: 26 August 1943) p: Wien; d: E. W. Emo; sc:
Gerhard Menzel; LP: Heinrich George, Lil Dagover, Herbert Hübner,
Rudolf Forster.
P: skw.

1943

S *Der unendliche Weg* (*The Unending Road*)
(Z: 8 April; U: 24 August) p: Bavaria; d: Hans Schweikart; sc: Walter von Molo, Ernst von Salomon (from the novel *Einer Deutsche ohne Deutschland* by von Molo); LP: Eugen Klöpfer, Herbert Hübner, Lisa Hellwig, Eva Immerman.
P: skbw, jw, LF.

S *Germanin*
(Z: 11 May; U: 15 May) p: Ufa; d: Max W. Kimmich; sc: M. Kimmich, Hans Wolfgang Hillers (from the novel by Hellmuth Unger); LP: Peter Petersen, Luis Trenker, Ernst Stimmel, Lotte Koch.
P: skw.

Immensee
(Z: 28 September; U: 17 December) p: Ufa; d: Veit Harlan; sc: Alfred Braun, V. Harlan from an idea by Theodor Storm; LP: Kristina Söderbaum, Carl Raddatz, Otto Gebühr, Malte Jäger, Albert Florath.
P: küw, kuw, vw.

Paracelsus
(Z: 4 March; U: 12 March) p: Bavaria; d: G. W. Pabst; sc: Kurt Heuser; LP: Werner Krauss, Mathias Wiemann, Harald Kreutzberg.
P: skw.

Titanic
(Z; 30 April; — Banned) p: Tobis; d: Herbert Selpin and Werner Klinger; sc: Walter Zerlett-Olfenius from an idea by Harald Bratt; LP: Otto Wernicke, Theodor Loos, Sybille Schmitz.

1944

S *Die Degenhardts* (*The Degenhardts*)
(Z: 28 June; U: 6 July) p: Tobis; d: Werner Klinger; sc: Wilhelm Krug, Georg Zoch (from an idea by Hans Gustl Kernmayr); LP: Heinrich George, Erich Ziegel, Wolfgang Lukschy.
P: sw, küw.

S *Junge Adler* (*Young Eagles*)
Z: 16 May; U: 24 May) p: Ufa; d: Alfred Weidenmann; sc: Herbert Reinecker, Alfred Weidenmann; LP: Willy Fritsch, Herbert Hübner, Albert Florath, Aribert Wascher, Paul Henckels, Josef Sieber.
P: sw, küw, jw.

1945

S *Kolberg*
(Z: 26 January; U: 30 January) p: Ufa; d: Veit Harlan; sc: Veit Harlan, Alfred Braun; LP: Heinrich George, Kristina Söderbaum, Paul Wegener, Otto Wernicke, Irene von Meyendorff, Claus Clausen, Horst Caspar, Gustav Diessl.
P: FN, skbw, kuw, vw, aw, vb, jw.

B. DOCUMENTARIES AND SHORT FILMS

1931

Kampf um Berlin (Battle for Berlin)
(Z: 2 May) For showing at Party functions only.

Das neue Italien (New Italy)
No credits available.

Hitlers braune Soldaten kommen (Hitler's Brown Soldiers are Coming)
No credits available.

1932

Deutsche Wehr, deutsche Ehr (German Arms, German Honour)
(Z: 6 July) p: NSDAP—Reichsleitung, Munich.

Kirche und Staat (Church and State)
(Z: 28 July) p: NSDAP—Reichsleitung, Munich.

Hitler über Deutschland (Hitler over Germany)
(Z: 19 October) p: NSDAP—Reichsleitung, Munich.

Blutendes Deutschland (Bleeding Germany)
(Z: 31 December) For showing at Party functions only.

1933

Deutschland erwacht (Germany Awake)
(Z: 19 April) p: Reichspropagandaleitung, Hauptabteilung. bzw.
Amsteitung Film (RPL), Berlin.

Wir marschieren (We are Marching)
(Z: 23 September) No further credits.

Terror oder Aufbau (Terror or Rebuilding)
(Z: 2 November) p: RPL.

*Blut und Boden (Grundlage zum neuen Reich) (Blood and Soil:
Foundation of the new Germany)*
(Z: 20 November) p: Propagandistische Darstellung des deutschen
Bauerntums.

1935

Triumph des Willens (Triumph of the Will)
(Z: 26 March; U: 29 March) p: NSDAP—Reichspropaganda Abteilung; d: Leni Riefenstahl; music: Herbert Windt; photographic
supervision: Sepp Allgeier.

Abseits vom Wege (By the Wayside)
(Z: 5 October) p: Rassenpolitische Amteilung.

1936

Erbkrank (Congenitally Ill)
(Z: 20 February) p: Rassenpolitische Amteilung.

Jugend der Welt (Youth of the World)
(Z: 3 July) p: RPL (1936 Olympic Games).

Der ewige Wald (The Eternal Forest)
(Z. 20 August) p: NS-Kulturgemeinde; d: Hans Springer.

1937
Opfer der Vergangenheit (Victims of the Past)
(Z: 20 March) p: RPL; d: Dr Gernot Bock-Stieber.

1938
Wort und Tat (Word and Deed)
(Z: 9 April) p: RPL.

Olympiade
(Z: 14 April; U: 20 April) p: Olympia Film GmbH; d: Leni Riefenstahl; music: Herbert Windt; prologue: Willy Zielke.

1939
Feldzug in Polen (Campaign in Poland)
(Z: 5 October) p: Deutsche Filmherstellungs- und Verwertungs GmbH (DFG).

1940
Glaube und Schönheit (Faith and Beauty)
(Z: 2 February) p: DFG.

Feuertaufe (Baptism of Fire)
(Z: 3 April) p: Tobis (for the Luftwaffe); d: Hans Bertram; sc: H. Bertram; commentator: Herbert Gernot, Gerhard Jeschke; music: Norbert Schultze.

Der ewige Jude (The Eternal/Wandering Jew)
(Z: 4 November; U: 28 November) p: DFG; d: Fritz Hippler; sc: Eberhard Taubert.

1941
Sieg im Westen (Victory in the West)
(Z: 2 February) p: DFG; d: Svend Noldan; sc: S. Noldan, Fritz Bruscha.

Gentlemen
(Z: ? December) p: Deutsche Wochenschau GmbH.

Rund um die Freiheitsstatue (Around the Statue of Liberty)
(Z: 30 December) p: Deutsche Wochenschau GmbH.

SELECT BIBLIOGRAPHY

UNPUBLISHED SOURCE MATERIAL

Bundesarchiv, Koblenz
Akten des Reichsfinanzministerium (R2)
Akten des Reichsministeriums für Volksaufklärung und Propaganda (R55)
Akten der Reichsfilmkammer (R56)
Akten des Reichssicherheitshauptamtes (R58)
Akten der Ufa-Film GmbH (R1091)
Akten der Reichspropagandaleitung der NSDAP/Gruppe Filmwesen (NS 18)
Sammlung Brammer 1933–36
Sammlung Sänger (Aus der Kulturpolitischen Presskonferenz, Zsg. 102)

Deutsches Institut für Filmkunde, Wiesbaden
Miscellaneous unpublished material

Institut für Zeitgeschichte, Munich
Goebbels Tagebuch (unpublished sections)
Zeitschriften Dienst

Staatliches Filmarchiv der DDR, East Berlin
Miscellaneous unpublished material

Wiener Library, London
NSDAP 'Hauptarchiv'

Imperial War Museum, London
Miscellaneous unpublished material

NAZI PUBLISHED WORKS

Belling, C., *Der Film im Dienste der Partei* (Berlin, 1937).
— *Der Film in Staat und Partei* (Berlin 1936).
Belling, C., and Schütze, A., *Der Film in der Hitlerjugend* (Berlin, 1937).
Böhmer, H. von, and Reitz, H., *Der Film in Wirtschaft und Recht* (Berlin, 1933).
Brohmer, P., *Biologieunterricht und völkische Erziehung* (Frankfurt, 1933).

Bub, G., *Der deutsche Film im Weltkrieg und seiner publizistischer Einsatz* (Quackenbrück, 1938).

Dietrich, O., *Auf den Strassen des Sieges* (Munich, 1940).

Dreyer, E. A. (ed.), *Deutsche Kultur im neuen Reich. Wesen. Aufgabe und Ziel der Reichskulturkammer* (Berlin, 1934).

Eckert, G., 'Filmintendenz und Tendenzfilm', *Wille und Macht, Führerorgan der nationalsozialistischen Jugend*, vol. 4, 15 November 1938, pp. 19-25.

Ehrlich, E., *Die Auslandsorganisation der NSDAP* (Berlin, 1937).

Funk, A., *Film und Jugend. Eine Untersuchung über die psychischen Wirkungen des Films im Leben der Jugendlichen* (Munich, 1934).

Giese, H. J., *Die Film-Wochenschau im Dienste der Politik*, Diss. (Leipzig, 1941).

Goebbels, J., *Michael. Ein deutsches Schicksal in Tagebuchblättern* (Munich, 1929).

— *Das eherne Herz. Reden und Aufsätz aus den Jahren 1941/42* (Munich 1943).

— *Vom Kaiserhof zur Reichskanzlei, Eine historische Darstellung in Tagebuchblättern* (Munich, 1934).

— *Der Kampf um Berlin. Der Anfang* (Munich, 1932).

— *Die Zeit ohne Beispiel. Reden und Aufsätze aus den Jahren 1939-41* (Munich, 1943).

Gunther, H., *Kleine Rassenkinde des deutschen Volkes* (Munich, 1933).

Günther, W., *Hans Westmar. Einer von vielen. Staatspolitische Filme* (Munich, 1933).

— *Der Film als politisches Führungsmittel. Die anderen gegen Deutschland* (Leipzig, 1934).

Hadamovsky, E., *Propaganda und nationale Macht. Die Organisation der öffentlichen Meinung für die nationale Politik* (Oldenburg, 1933).

Heyde, L., *Presse, Rundfunk und Film im Dienste der Volksführung* (Dresden, 1943).

Hippler, F., 'Beruf und Berufung. Angebot und Nachfrage im deutschen Filmschaffen', *Der deutsche Film* (December, 1936), pp. 161-5.

— *Betrachtungen zum Filmschaffen* (Berlin, 1942).

— 'Das Neuste und Aktuellste. Von der Arbeit und Wirkung der Wochenschau', *Der deutsche Film* (August, 1937), pp. 50-3.

Hitler, A., *Mein Kampf* (London, 1939).

Jahrbuch der Reichsfilmkammer, Jahrgang 1-3 (Berlin, 1937-9).

Jason, A., *Das Filmschaffen in Deutschland 1935-9*, 2 vols. (Berlin, 1940).

Kalbus, O., *Vom Werden deutscher Filmkunst. Teil 2: Der Tonfilm* (Altona-Bahrenfeld, 1935).

Klär, K. (ed.), *Der deutsche Film 1942/3. Übersicht uber die Filmproduktion. Struktur des Filmschaffens in Deutschland* (Berlin, 1943).

Koch, H., and Braune, H., *Von deutsche Filmkunst. Gehalt und Gestalt* (Berlin, 1943).

Kolb, R., and Siekmeier, H., *Rundfunk und Film im Dienste nationaler Kultur* (Düsseldorf, 1933).

Kriegk, O., *Der deutsche Film in Spiegel der Ufa. 25 Jahre Kampf und Vollendung* (Berlin, 1943).

Maraun, F., 'Der Held: die Gemeinschaft', *Der deutsche Film* (August, 1939), pp. 49–52.

Messter, O., *Mein Weg mit dem Film* (Berlin, 1936).

Neumann, C., Belling, C., and Betz, H., *Film-Kunst, Film-Kohn, Film-Korruption. Ein Streifzug durch vier Jahrzehnte* (Berlin, 1937).

NSDAP, *Der Kongress zu Nürnberg vom 5. bis 10 September 1934. Offizieller Bericht über den Verlauf des Reichsparteitages mit sämtlichen Reden* (Munich, 1934).

— *Ohm Krüger. Zur festlichen Aufführung des Emil Jannings Films der Tobis* (Berlin, 1941).

Plugge, W., 'Wesen und Aufgaben des Films und der Reichsfilmkammer', *Deutsche Kultur im neuen Reich. Wesen, Aufgabe und Ziel der Reichskulturkammer*, Drayer, E. A. (ed.) (Berlin, 1934), pp. 114–29.

Riefenstahl, L., *Hinter den Kulissen des Reichsparteitagfilms* (Munich, 1935).

Röber, G., 'Warum-Wochenschaugesetz?', *Der deutsche Film* (December, 1936), pp. 86–9.

Rumlow, R., '*Herbert Norkus?–Hier!' Opfer und Sieg der Hitler Jugend* (Berlin, 1933).

Sander, A. U., *Jugend und Film* (Berlin, 1944).

Schirach, B. von., *Revolution der Erziehung. Reden aus den Jahren des Aufbaus* (Munich, 1938).

Stephan, W., *Bismarck: Aktuelle Filmbücher* (Berlin, 1940).

Tackmann, H., *Filmhandbuch als ergänzbare Sammlung herausgegeben von der Reichsfilmkammer* (Berlin, 1938).

Traub, H., *Der Film als politisches Machtmittel* (Munich, 1933).

— *Die Ufa. Ein Beitrag zur Entwicklungsgeschichte des deutschen Filmschaffens* (Berlin, 1943).

Wolf, K., *Entwicklung und Neugestaltung der deutschen Filmwirtschaft seit 1933* (Heidelberg, 1938).

Ziegler, M., 'Blut und Boden. Ein Film von den Grundlagen deutscher Zukunft', *Völkischer Beobachter*, 25 November 1933.

Zimmereimer, K., *Die Filmzensur* (Breslau, 1934).

NON-NAZI WORKS

Albrecht, G., 'Korrektur zum Nazifilm', *Film* (Hanover, October 1963), p. 46f.

— *Nationalsozialistische Filmpolitik. Eine soziologische Untersuchung über die Spielfilme des Dritten Reichs* (Stuttgart, 1969).

Altmann, J., 'Movies' Role in Hitler's Conquest of German Youth', in *Hollywood Quarterly*, vol. 111, no. 4.

Baird, J. W., *The Mythical World of Nazi War Propaganda, 1939–45* (Minneapolis, 1974).

Balfour, M., *Propaganda in War, 1939–45: organisations, policies and publics in Britain and Germany* (London, 1979).

Barkhausen, H., 'Die NSDAP als Filmproduzentin. Mit Kurzübersicht: Filme der NSDAP 1927-45', *Zeitgeschichte im Film- und Tondokument*, Moltmann, G., and Reimers, K. F., eds. (Göttingen, 1970), pp. 145-76.

Barsam, R. M., *Filmguide to 'Triumph of the Will'* (Indiana, 1975).

Bateson, G., 'An analysis of the Nazi film Hitlerjunge Quex', *The Study of Culture at a Distance*, Mead, M., Metraux, R. (eds.) (Chicago, 1953), pp. 302-14.

Bauer, A., *Deutsche Spielfilm-Almanach, 1929-1950* (Berlin, 1950).

Baynes, N. H. (ed.), *The Speeches of Adolf Hitler*, 2 vols. (Oxford, 1942).

Becker, W., *Film und Herrschaft* (Berlin, 1973).

Bischoff, R., *Nazi Conquest Through German Culture* (London, 1942).

Bleuel, H. P., *Strength Through Joy* (London, 1973).

Blobner, H., and Holba, H., 'Jackboot Cinema. Political Propaganda in the Third Reich', *Film and Filming*, vol. 8, no. 3 (December 1962), pp. 14-18.

Boberach, H., *Meldungen aus dem Reich. Auswahl geheimen Lageberichten des Sicherheitsdienstes der SS 1939-44* (Berlin and Neuwied, 1965).

Boelcke, W. A., *Kriegspropaganda 1939-41. Geheime Ministerkonferenzen im Reichspropagandaministerium* (Stuttgart, 1966).

— *'Wollt Ihr den totalen Krieg?' Die geheimen Goebbels-Konferenzen 1939-43* (Stuttgart 1967).

Bracher, K. D., *Die deutsche Diktatur* (Berlin, 1969).

Bramsted, E. K., *Goebbels and National Socialist Propaganda 1925-45* (Michigan, 1965).

Brautigam, O., *Überblick über die besetzen Ostgebiete wahrend des 2 Weltkrieges* (Tübingen, 1954).

Bredow, W. von, and Zurek, R. (eds.), *Film und Gesellschaft in Deutschland. Dokumente und Materialien* (Hamburg, 1975).

British Film Institute, German Clipping Files.

Brown, J. A. C., *Techniques of Persuasion. From Propaganda to Brainwashing* (London, 1972).

Bucher, F. (ed.), *Germany* (Screen Series) (London, 1970).

Buller, E. A., *Darkness Over Germany* (London, 1943).

Bullock, A., *Hitler. A Study in Tyranny* (London, 1962).

Burden, H. T., *The Nuremberg Party Rallies 1932-39* (London, 1967).

Carroll, B., *Design for Total War* (The Hague, 1968).

Carsten, F. L., *The Reichswehr and Politics: 1918-33* (Oxford, 1966).

— *The Rise of Fascism* London, 1976).

Catalogue of Forbidden German Feature and Short Film Productions held in the Zonal Film Archives of the Film Section. Information Services Division, Control Commission for Germany (BE) (Hamburg, 1951).

Cecil, R., *Myth of the Master Race. A. Rosenberg and the Nazi Ideology* (London, 1974).

Chamberlain, H. S., *Foundations of the Nineteenth Century*, trans. Rees, J., (New York, 1912).

Childers, T., 'The Social Bases of the National Socialist Vote', *Journal of Contemporary History* (1976, no. 11), pp. 17–24.

Cohn, N., *Warrant for Genocide: The Myth of the Jewish World Conspiracy and the Protocols of Zion* (London, 1967).

Courtade, F., and Cadars, P., *Histoire du cinéma nazi* (Paris, 1972).

Dallin, A., *German Rule in Russia. A Study of Occupation Policies* (London, 1957).

Delahaye, M., 'Leni et le loup. Entretien avec Leni Riefenstahl', *Cahiers du Cinéma* (September, 1965), pp. 42–51.

Domarus, M. (ed.), *Hitler: Reden und Proklamation 1932–45*, 4 vols. (Munich, 1965).

Doob, L., 'Goebbels' Principles of Propaganda', *Public Opinion Quarterly* (Fall 1950), pp. 419–42.

Eilers, R., *Die nationalsozialistische Schulpolitik* (Köln, 1963).

Eisner, L., *Fritz Lang* (London 1976).

— *The Haunted Screen* (London, 1973).

Ellul, J., *Propaganda. The Formation of Men's Attitudes* (New York, 1973).

Elton, A., 'The Film as Source Material for History', *Aslib Proceedings*, vol. 7, no. 4 (1955), pp. 207–39.

Elwenspoek, C., *Jud Suss Oppenheimer* (Stuttgart, 1926).

Farquharson, J. E., *The Plough and the Swastika. The NSDAP and Agriculture in Germany 1928–45* (London, 1976).

Ferro, M., *Cinéma et histoire. Le cinéma, agent et source de l'histoire* (Paris, 1977).

Fest, J., *The Face of the Third Reich* (London, 1972).

— *Hitler* (London, 1974).

Flannery, H. W., *Assignment to Berlin* (London, 1942).

Ford, C., *Emil Jannings* (Paris, 1969).

Fraser, L., *Propaganda* (London, 1957).

Fredborg, A., *Behind the Steel Wall* (New York, 1944).

Freeden, H., *Jüdisches Theater in Nazi Deutschland* (Tübingen, 1964).

Furhammar, L., and Isaksson, F., *Politics and Film* (London, 1971).

Gay, P., *Freud, Jews and Other Germans* (Oxford, 1978).

Gillet, J., 'Germany: A Lost Decade', *Sight and Sound*, vol. 41, no. 4 (Autumn 1974), pp. 224–6.

Glaser, H., *The Cultural Roots of National Socialism* London, 1978).

Goldstein, B., *Die Sterne sind Zeugen. Der Untergang der polnischen Juden* (Munich, 1965).

Grebing, H., *Der Nationalsozialismus. Ursprung und Wesen* (Munich, 1959).

Grenville, J. A. S. *Film as History: The Nature of Film Evidence* (Birmingham, 1971).

Grunberger, R., *A Social History of the Third Reich* (London, 1974).

Hale, O. J., *The Captive Press in the Third Reich* (Princeton, 1964).

Hanfstaengl, E., *Hitler: The Missing Years* (London, 1957).

Hardy, H. F. (ed.), *Grierson on Documentary* (London, 1946).

Harlan, V., *Im Schatten meiner Filme. Selbstbiographie* (Gütersloh,

1966), translated into French as *Souvenirs ou Le Cinéma allemand selon Goebbels* (Paris, 1974).

Hassel, U. von, *The von Hassel Diaries 1938-44* (London, 1948).

Hauner, M., 'Did Hitler Want a World Dominion?', *Journal of Contemporary History*, vol. 13, no. 1 (January 1978), pp. 15-32.

Heiber, H., *Joseph Goebbels* (Berlin, 1962).

Henderson, N., *Failure of a Mission* (London, 1940).

Herma, H., 'Goebbels' Conception of Propaganda', *Social Research*, vol. 10, no. 2 (May 1943), pp. 200-18.

Herzstein, R. E., 'Goebbels et le Mythe Historique par le Film', in *Revue d'Histoire de la Deuxième Guerre* (Paris, January 1976), no. 101, pp. 41-62.

Hesse, F., *Hitler and the English* (London, 1954).

Hiden, J., 'The Weimar Republic and the Problem of the Auslandsdeutsche', *Journal of Contemporary History*, vol. 12, no. 2 (1977), pp. 273-89.

Hilderbrand, K., *Foreign Policy in the Third Reich* (London, 1973).

Hitler's Table Talk 1941-44, introduced and with a new Preface by H. Trevor Roper (London, 1973).

Hoffman, H., *Hitler was my Friend* (London, 1955).

Holba, H., *Illustrierter Film-Kurier 1924-44* (Wiesbaden, 1972).

Hollstein, D., *Antisemitische Filmpropaganda. Die Darstellung des Juden im nationalsozialistischen Spielfilme* (Munich, 1971).

Hubatsch, W., *Weserübung* (Göttingen, 1960).

Hull, D. S., *Film in the Third Reich* (Berkeley and Los Angeles, 1969).

Huxley, A., 'Notes on Propaganda', *Harper's Monthly Magazine*, vol. 174 (December 1936), pp. 32-41.

Jacobsen, H. A., *Nationalsozialistische Aussenpolitik 1933-38* (Frankfurt-am-Main, 1968).

Jannings, E., *Theater- Film- Das Leben und ich* (Berchtesgaden, 1951).

Kelman, K., 'Propaganda as Vision – Triumph of the Will', *Film Culture* (Spring, 1973), pp. 162-7.

Klemperer, V., *Lingua Tertii Imperii* (Munich, 1949).

Kliesch, H. J., 'Die Film- und Theaterkritik in NS-Staat' (unpublished doctoral thesis, Free University, West Berlin, 1957).

Klimsch, G. W., *Die Entwicklung des national-sozialistischen Film-Monopols 1933-40* (Munich, 1954).

Kochenrath, H. P. (ed.), *Der Film im Dritten Reich* (Cologne, 1963).

Konlecher, P. M., and Kubelka, P. (eds.), *Propaganda und Gegenpropaganda im Film 1933-45* (Vienna, 1972).

Kracauer, S., *From Caligari to Hitler. A Psychological History of the German Film* (Princeton, 1947 and 1973).

Krauss, W., *Das Schauspiel meines Lebens, einem Freund erzählt* (Stuttgart, 1958).

Kreimeier, K., 'Das Kino als Ideologiefabrik', *Kinemathek*, no. 45 (Berlin, November 1971).

Kris, E., and Speier, H., *German Radio Propaganda. Report on Home Broadcasts during the War* (London, 1944).

Laqueur, W., *Out of the Ruins of Europe* (London, 1972).
Lasswell, H. D., 'Propaganda' entry in *Encyclopedia of the Social Sciences*.
Leiser, E., *Nazi Cinema* (London, 1974).
Levy, R., *The Downfall of the Anti-Semitic Political Parties in Imperial Germany* (Yale, 1975).
Lewy, Günther., *The Catholic Church and Nazi Germany* (London, 1964).
Leyda, J., *Films Beget Films* (London, 1964).
Lippmann, W., *Public Opinion* (New York, 1945).
Lochner, L. P. (ed.), *The Goebbels Diaries* (London, 1948).
Lüdecke. W., *Der Film in Agitation und Propaganda der revolutionären deutschen Arbeiterbewegung 1919-33* (Berlin, 1973).
Mckee, I., *Tomorrow the World* (London, 1960).
Mackenzie, A. J., *Propaganda Boom* (London, 1938).
Mandell, R., *The Nazi Olympics* (London, 1972).
Manz, H. P., *Ufa und der frühe deutsche Film* (Zurich, 1963).
Marcorelles, L., 'The Nazi Cinema', *Sight and Sound*, vol. 25, no. 4 (Autumn 1955), pp. 65-9.
Martin, K., *Propaganda's Harvest* (London, 1941).
Meisner, O., *Magda Goebbels* (London, 1979).
Mayer, M., *They Thought They Were Free* (Chicago, 1966).
Meyer, M., 'The Nazi Musicologist as Myth Maker in the Third Reich', *Journal of Contemporary History*, vol. 10, no. 4 (October 1975), pp. 649-65.
Milward, A. S., *The German Economy at War* (London, 1965).
Mosse, G., *Nazi Culture: Intellectual, Cultural and Social Life in the Third Reich* (London, 1966).
— *Germans and Jews* (London, 1971).
— *The Crisis of German Ideology: Intellectual Origins of the Third Reich* (London, 1964).
Neumann, F., *Behemoth. The Structure and Practice of National Socialism* (London, 1942).
Neumann, P., *Other Men's Graves* (London, 1958).
Nolte, E., *Der Fascismus in seiner Epoche* (Munich, 1963).
Orlow, D., *The History of the Nazi Party 1919-33*, 2 vols. (London, 1971).
Oven., W. von, *Mit Goebbels bis zum Ende*, 2 vols. (Buenos Aires, 1949/50).
Pardo, H., and Schiffner, S. (eds.), *Jud Süss. Historisches und juristisches Material zum Fall Veit Harlan* (Hamburg), 1949).
Petley, J., *Capital and Culture. German Cinema 1933-45* (London, 1979).
Phillips, B., *Swastika. Cinema of Oppression* (London, 1976).
Phillips, D. M., *Hitler and the Rise of the Nazis* (London, 1975).
Phillips, M. S., 'The German Film Industry and the Third Reich' (unpublished doctoral thesis, University of East Anglia, 1974).
— 'The German film industry and the New Order', in Stachura, P. D. (ed.), *The Shaping of the Nazi State* (London, 1978), pp. 257-81.

— 'The Nazi Control of the German Film Industry', *Journal of European Studies*, vol. 1 (March 1971), pp. 37–68.

Pudovkin, V., *Film Technique and Film Acting* (New York, 1958).

Pulzer, P., *The Rise of Political Anti-Semitism in Germany and Austria* (London, 1964).

Qualter, T., *Propaganda and Psychological Warfare* (New York, 1962).

Rabenalt, A. M., *Film im Zwielicht. Über den unpolitischen Film des Dritten Reiches und die Begrenzung des totalitären Anspruches* (Munich, 1958).

Raleigh, J. M., *Behind the Nazi Front* (London, 1941).

Reitlinger, G., *The Final Solution* (London, 1953).

Richards, J., *Visions of Yesterday* (London, 1973).

Roberts, S., *The House that Hitler Built* (London, 1937).

Scheffler, K. N., 'Die Verstaatlichung der deutschen Filmwirtschaft 1937 bis 1942 und die Bildung der "Ufa Film GmbH" ('Ufi')', *Deutsche Filmkunst*, vol. 9 no. 1 (January 1961), pp. 20–3.

Shirer, W., *Berlin Diary 1934–41* (London, 1972).

Schleunes, K., *The Twisted Road to Auschwitz* (Chicago, 1970).

Schoenbaum, D., *Hitler's Social Revolution. Class and Status in Nazi Germany 1933–39* (London, 1967).

Schulberg, B., 'Nazi pin-up girl', *Saturday Evening Post*, 30 March 1936.

Semmler, R., *Goebbels. The Man Next to Hitler* (London, 1947).

Sington, D., and Weidenfeld, A., *The Goebbels Experiment. A Study of the Nazi Propaganda Machine* (London, 1942).

Smith, B. L., 'Propaganda' entry in *International Encyclopedia of the Social Sciences*.

Smith, H. K., *Last Train From Berlin* (London, 1943).

Smith, P. (ed.), *The Historian and Film* (Cambridge, 1976).

Speer, A., *Inside the Third Reich* (London, 1971).

Spiker, J., *Film und Kapital* (Berlin, 1975).

Stephenson, J., *Women in Nazi Society* (London, 1975).

— *The Nazi Organisation of Women* (London, 1980).

Stern, F., *The Politics of Cultural Despair: A Study in the Rise of the Germanic Ideology* (Berkeley, 1961).

Stern, J. P., *Hitler. The Führer and the People* (London, 1975).

Supreme Headquarters Allied Expeditionary Force. SHAEF, Psychological Warfare Division. Viewed and graded by Major F. L. Evans and H. J. Lefebre. List of impounded films with comments. Deposited with the British Film Institute.

Taylor, R., *Architecture and National Socialism* (California, 1974).

Taylor, R., *Film Propaganda* (London, 1979).

Terveen, F., *Die Entwicklung der Wochenschau in Deutschland: Ufa–Tonwoche Nr 451/1939. Hitlers 50. Geburtstag* (Göttingen, 1960).

— 'Das Filmdokument der Nazis und sein Wahrheitsgehalt. Wochenschauen aus der Hitlerzeit erforden kritische Beobachter', *Das Parlament*, 25 May 1955.

— 'Historischer Film und historisches Filmdokument', *Geschichte in Wissenschaft und Unterricht*, vol. 7 (1956), pp. 750–2.

Trevor-Roper, H. (ed.), *The Goebbels Diaries. The Last Days* (London, 1978).
— *The Last Days of Hitler* (London, 1962).
— *Hitler's Table Talk* (London, 1973)
Vas, R., 'Sourcerers or Apprentices. Some Aspects of Propaganda Films', *Sight and Sound* (Autumn 1963), pp. 199-204.
Vogt, H., *The Burden of Guilt: A Short History of Germany 1914-45* (London, 1965).
Waite, R., *Vanguard of Nazism. The Free Corps Movement* (Harvard, 1952).
Welch, D., 'The Proletarian Cinema and the Weimar Republic', in *Historical Journal of Film, Radio and Television*, vol. 1, no. 1 (March 1981), pp. 3-18.
Wipperman, K. W., *Die Entwicklung der Wochenschau in Deutschland: Ufa-Tonwoche no 410/1938* (Göttingen, 1970).
— *Die Entwicklung der Wochenschau in Deutschland: 'Die Deutsche Wochenschau' Nr 10/651. Februar 1943* (Göttingen, 1970).
Witte, K. (ed.), *Theorie des Kinos. Ideologiekritik der Traumfabrik* (Frankfurt-am-Main, 1972).
Wollenberg, H. H., *Fifty Years of German Film* (London, 1948).
Wulf, J., *Die Bildenden Künste im Dritten Reich. Eine Dokumentation* (Gütersloh, 1963).
— *Theater und Film im Dritten Reich. Eine Dokumentation* (Gütersloh, 1964)'
Zarek, O., *German Odyssey* (London, 1941).
Zeman, Z. A. B., *Nazi Propaganda* (London, 1973).
Zglinicki, F. von, *Der Weg des Films. Die Geschichte der Kinematographie und ihrer Vorläufer* (Berlin, 1956).

GLOSSARY

Blut und Boden	Blood and Soil
Bund	tightly knit all-male community
Deutsche Arbeitsfront	German Labour Front
entartete Künstler	degenerate artist
Entjudung	the removal of Jews
Filmkontingentstelle	the office responsible for the implementation of the 'Quota' law which stipulated that films had to be made by Germans
Filmprufstelle	Film Censorship Office
Filmwelt	not simply the film industry but a term used to convey what it was like to live and work in the film world
Führerprinzip	the leadership principle
Gaufilmstellen	Party Film Centres
Gauleiter	Regional Party Leader
Gleichschaltung	the obligatory assimilation within the Nazi State of all political, economic, and cultural activities
Heimatfilme	films dealing with oppressed German communities living abroad
Herrenvolk	Master Race
Jugendfilmstunden	Youth Film Hours
Kampfzeit	time of struggle
Landesbildstellen	Regional Picture Centres
Landesfilmstellen	Regional Film Centres
Lebensraum	living space
Neuordnung	the New Order
Prädikat	distinction mark
Reichsfilmdramaturg	Reich Film Director
Reichsfilmintendant	Reich Film Intendant—responsible for film 'art'
Reichsfilmkammer	Reich Film Chamber
Reichslichtspielgesetz	Reich Film Law
Staatsauftragsfilm	film commissioned by the State
Stadtbildstellen	Urban Picture Centres
Staatsschauspieler	State Actor—the highest accolade given to an actor
Tendenzfilme	films advocating themes and archetypes commonly associated with National Socialism

Völkisch	Originally a Germanization of 'nationalist', it acquired racialist and mystical overtones which an English translation of 'folkish' fails to convey
Volksdeutscher	German nationals abroad
Volksgemeinschaft	Community of the People
Volkssturm	People's Storm—the armed civilian militia
Volkstum	the nation as an ethnic unity—national characteristics
Zeitfilm	militarist feature films set in a contemporary context
Zeitschriftendienst	press directive

INDEX